ACCOUNTING FOR VIOLENCE

The Cultures and Practice of Violence Series

The study of violence has often focused on the political and economic conditions under which violence is generated, the suffering of victims, and the psychology of its interpersonal dynamics. Less familiar are the role of perpetrators, their motivations, and the social conditions under which they are able to operate. In the context of postcolonial state building and more latterly the collapse and implosion of society, community violence, state repression, and the phenomena of judicial inquiries in the aftermath of civil conflict, there is a need to better comprehend the role of those who actually do the work of violence — torturers, assassins, and terrorists — as much as the role of those who suffer its consequences.

When atrocity and murder take place, they feed the world of the iconic imagination that transcends reality and its rational articulation; but in doing so imagination can bring further violent realities into being. This series encourages authors who build on traditional disciplines and break out of their constraints and boundaries, incorporating media and performance studies and literary and cultural studies as much as anthropology, sociology, and history.

ACCOUNTING FOR VIOLENCE

Marketing Memory in Latin America

KSENIJA BILBIJA AND LEIGH A. PAYNE, EDS.

DUKE UNIVERSITY PRESS | DURHAM AND LONDON 2011

Printed in the United States of America on acid-free paper ∞
Designed by April Leidig-Higgins
Typeset in Minion Pro by Copperline Book Services, Inc.

Library of Congress Cataloging-in-Publication Data appear
on the last printed page of this book.

From the middle of the story of our lives
we dedicate this book to our friendship

Contents

Foreword: On Memory and Memorials

LUISA VALENZUELA

TRANSLATED BY CATHERINE JAGOE

One of the problems facing us in these times, defined by Zygmunt Bauman as Liquid Modernity, is that everything becomes diluted, in a constant, disconcerting flux. Even words, I believe. They either flow or they stagnate, losing their true nature. The word "memory," for example, runs the risk of becoming a mere label or an empty signifier into which everything fits, so nothing has value. True value, not mere exchange value.

I have consulted many texts to write these few words, for a good book always elicits further reflection and investigation. It will never tell us what or how to think, but instead broadens our horizons of thought and illuminates obscure areas of topics so familiar we tend to pass over them.

This volume, edited by Ksenija Bilbija and Leigh A. Payne, is one such catalyst. Both editors have been analyzing the issue for a long time, as shown by their scholarly work on the legacies of authoritarianism and the anthology entitled *The Art of Truth-Telling about Authoritarian Rule*. *Accounting for Violence: Marketing Memory in Latin America* represents a change of direction. It is not about remembering or avoiding the past, but about how to keep remembrance alive without losing respect. The various essays point to the razor's edge we are treading, and to the chasms yawning on either side into which it is very easy to slip. There is a strong pull from those in favor of oblivion at all costs, those who accept the two Argentine laws known as "Due Obedience" and "Full Stop" as well as the pardons. They say we need to clean the slate and start over (*borrón y cuenta nueva*). According to them, nothing happened here; you cannot live in the past. They demand we turn the page.

But when you turn that page the other tendency appears, the chasm on the opposite side: those who seek to profit in one way or another from others' pain and the morbid curiosity of some audiences. They degrade the word "memory," misusing it to the point where it loses its meaning.

We would not be able to concentrate on the razor's edge if we did not point to these two extremes and give examples of them. At that edge, the recuperation of memory is working to obliterate a word that was imposed on us by state terrorism: *desaparecidos* (the disappeared). First coined in Argentina, the term spread to other countries with authoritarian regimes, and was used to cover the criminals' tracks and make their victims invisible. From the very first marches of the Madres de Plaza de Mayo to the tireless efforts of present-day human rights organizations in Argentina, the goal has always been to restore the victims' identities and their presence in collective memory, and to pursue punishment for the perpetrators, which is essential to the health of society. The Space for Memory Institute (known as IEM in Argentina) leads the recuperation effort today: recuperation of the children of the disappeared, and also of the clandestine spaces where the horror took place.

There has been rigorous debate on the issue, debate that speaks to various tragic circumstances around the world. What to do, for example, with Ground Zero, which is in fact an enormous cemetery? The question echoes one that arose in this southern latitude during the first months of the Kirchner administration: should ESMA, the Navy School of Mechanics, where so many were tortured, be made into a museum? A disturbing question, given the ever latent danger of banalizing evil. The controversy surfaced more recently in Argentina when March 24th, the anniversary of the start of the last, and most ferocious, military dictatorship, in 1976, was declared a national holiday. The decision caused widespread unease: should families be going out for picnics on such a day of mourning? I personally am in favor of the holiday; it is important to pause, to mark the day. That is what it is about, after all: marks, wounds that have turned into scars that recall the military coup. There will always be people who attempt to profit from those wounds, and so it is important to reflect on the paradoxes presented in this book. One of them is still ongoing in my country these days. It was reignited during the inauguration of the Rodolfo Walsh Space at ESMA. Walsh was one of the most emblematic victims of the repression, the author who wrote the Open Letter to the Armed Forces. His daughter Patricia, a Socialist Party congresswoman, was deeply opposed to the inauguration. A place such as ESMA, she said, should only be used for silence and recollection and not for the sound and fury of cultural events. She had expressed her indignation even before it was announced by Hebe de Bonafini that she intended to open a cooking school for low-income women in another part of the complex, dedicated to the Universidad de las Madres.

On the pro-museum side, the recuperation of marks is an important issue. On 28 August 2008, to mention just one case, the newspaper *Página/12* published the story of a man who only recently came to learn the facts about his detention thirty years ago. A team from the IEM, engaged in a meticulous cleaning of the basement of the officers' quarters at ESMA, a place infamously known as the Capuchita (little hood), came across a faint inscription engraved on a water tank. "De Marco-PC," it read. They managed to find the Communist Party member who had written the inscription. Ernesto de Marco, now a taxi driver, had been kidnapped in 1978, and he always thought he had been held at a police station. Only when he recognized his own inscription did he find out the truth about the place where he had been left, naked and tortured, until one day they gave him back his clothes. Not knowing whether he would leave the building alive, he had scratched his name with his belt buckle as a last message that has now returned to him from the past.

This is how we are constructing the ambivalent narrative of memory, or rather the scaffolding to hold it up, which the essays that follow analyze in depth. For my part, if I want to play devil's advocate, I concentrate on one of Jean Baudrillard's latest books, *The Intelligence of Evil or the Lucidity Pact*, in which he speaks yet again of representation and simulacra. But simulacra no longer exist, he says, because nowadays the distance between the real and the imaginary has disappeared. Everything hinges on an Integral Reality (Baudrillard's term), which rests on "the deregulation of the very reality principle." Virtual reality has superseded ordinary reality and we have lost our grip on experience in the process: "Once all transcendence is conjured away, things are no longer anything but what they are and, such as they are, they are unbearable. All illusion is gone from them and they have become immediately and totally real, with no shadow and no commentary." In which case, all memory, all references to the past, become useless, merely one more commodity permitting the freedom of exchange proposed by Adorno.

But if I wish to defend the structure of the bastions of memory (museums, monuments, parks, books, teachings), I turn to Marc Augé and his book *Le temps en ruines* (*Time in Ruins*), in which he proposes returning in various ways to a time when there was "a need to identify at the very least with [one's] own past—even if that meant, as it often has, completely reinventing it." According to Augé we are now in a time of Supermodernity. "Humanity is not in ruins, it is under construction. It still belongs to history. A history that is frequently tragic, always unequal, but unavoidably shared." In that case, it is better to keep the memory of the past alive in order, as is often said, not to repeat it.

And so: Liquid Modernity, Integral Reality, Supermodernity. Each of these models is horrifying in a different way. We can only protect ourselves by drawing our own conclusions. That is, by reading books like the one you have in your hands, which are open to controversy and paradox and not closed to dialogue.

Acknowledgments

In the narrowest and most technical sense that the concept of truth implies, we could say that this book grew out of the panel on Truth-Telling in the Aftermath of Atrocity at the Latin American Studies Association meeting in Montreal. Drawing on the marketing notion, the book should also be thought of as a product, a product of a particular convergence of thinking that emerged while reflecting on the price and the cost of memory and memorializing trauma in Latin America. Rather than staying up into the early hours of the morning at the *gran baile,* we instead outlined the book in the hotel hallway from notes that we scribbled during dinner onto a notepad with the words "Let It Go." And we did.

LASA and its unique ability to create intellectual space for interdisciplinary dialogue, therefore, deserve acknowledgment. The Latin American, Caribbean, and Iberian Studies Program at the University of Wisconsin–Madison organized a follow-up conference and workshop, which allowed the authors to present their work and receive critical feedback on it. As a show of appreciation for that support, all proceeds from this book will go to one of its funds supporting research on Latin America. A number of other organizations shared in the funding of the conference, including several University of Wisconsin–Madison sources, such as the Anonymous Fund, the Mellon Foundation Workshops in the Humanities, the Trauma Tourism Research Circle, and the Cyril W. Nave Endowment. The Université de Montréal and George Mason University provided additional support for the Memory Market conference.

We are indebted to numerous scholars who participated in various phases of the project. Among those who presented their work and comments at the University of Wisconsin–Madison, we particularly thank Severino Albuquerque, Glen Close, Geneviève Dorais, Paola Hernández, Alexandra Huneeus, Yeri López, Nicolás Lynch, Sarli Mercado, Elisa Shoenberger, Kristina Stanek, Steve Stern, and Djurdja Trajković. Additional participants at LASA and beyond who inspired and creatively shaped this project include Kate Doyle, Anne Pérotin-Dumon, Victoria Sanford, David Sheinin, and Alex Wilde. Our colleagues at the University of Wisconsin–Madison who provided both intellectual and administrative guidance include Jo Ellen Fair, Sara Guyer, Deborah Jenson, Guido Podestá, and Neil Whitehead. The staff at the Latin American, Caribbean, and Iberian Studies Program contributed their time and assistance cheerfully and generously, particularly Angela Buongiorno, Alice Cassidy, Valeria Galetto, Darcy Little, Sarah Ripp, and Alberto Vargas.

Many scholars who shaped our thinking about the project did not carry out specific roles, and yet should not go unidentified. In particular, we thank Hugo Achugar, Idelber Avelar, Louis Bickford, Branko Andjić, Hiber Conteris, Jason Doroga, Robert Folger, Courtney Kay Lanz, Ana María Shua, and Nora Strejilevich.

From the very beginning of this project to the very end, we drew on Andrew Reiter to help us manage the production of a book written in various countries of the world by extremely busy individuals. We particularly thank him for his patience, efficiency, and good humor. Elisabeth Becker, Alice Nelson, and Kathleen Pertzborn provided invaluable editing of some chapters, for which we are extremely grateful. Steve Meili and Brad and Carol Ricker helped at various stages of the project. We would also like to acknowledge our editors, Valerie Millholland, Miriam Angress, Gisela Fosado, and Neal McTighe at Duke University Press, the anonymous reviewers for the Press, and our copyeditor, Ruth Steinberg, and indexer, Carol Roberts.

From the middle of the story of our lives, we dedicate this book to our friendship. We met early in our professional careers and have grown up together. We have learned from each other in ways that go far beyond what language can capture. Through some difficult times and many celebrations, our friendship has endured. We have enjoyed the process of learning each other's ways of seeing, not only through different disciplinary prisms but also through our varied experiences and cultural journeys.

THE EDITORS' ROYALTIES from the sale of this book will be directed to the Latin American, Caribbean and Iberian Studies Program at the University of Wisconsin–Madison, to support subsequent research and writing on topics related to memory, human rights, and political violence.

ACCOUNTING FOR VIOLENCE

INTRODUCTION

KSENIJA BILBIJA AND
LEIGH A. PAYNE

Time is Money

The Memory Market in Latin America

The familiar maxim "Time is money" and its Spanish version "Tiempo es oro" (Time is gold) reflect two economic notions in contention. For example, a person can profit from time; time itself has value. Yet if one does not use that time wisely, it is wasted. In the latter sense, time itself does not have value; it is, rather, how one uses time that has value.

Both notions provide insight into the memory market in Latin America. The time since the recent dictatorships (that began roughly with the 1960s and ended in the late 1980s) has value in itself. That time has meant relative freedom from the kind of state violence that defined the repressive authoritarian regimes of the region. The repressive regimes exist as memory. That time, and the memory it created, have value. Failing to use that time and memory could waste it. What gives the time value is the struggle to remember, to not repeat. The cry "Never Again" engages the value and constructive use of time and memory. The memory market, in this sense, explores the ways in which time and memory are used to produce value and values—to profit, or benefit, from remembering the repressive past, to not repeat it.

While individuals and groups in Latin America engage in valuable memory-making, global marketing strategies are penetrating the region. The so-called Washington Consensus of the 1990s promoted the reduction of trade barriers, increased exports, privatization, deregulation, and shrinking the role of the state in the economy.[1] Global business practices also shifted, from an emphasis on product promotion to one on "branding." Adopting a term resonant with Latin America, Jay Conrad Levinson promoted the idea of "guerrilla marketing," which called on businesses to invest time, energy, and imagination in creating "buzz" about their products so that they would then spread "virally." According to Levinson, "It means not using the brute force of a giant budget, but that of a giant idea."[2] The global business model generated its own counter "giant ideas." The "no logo" movement took off. Anti-globalization movements spread throughout the world, from the Carnival against Capitalism in London and elsewhere, to the Battle in Seattle, to protests against the "global dictatorship of the rich" in Santiago, Chile.[3]

In this context, in which the market is emphasized favorably, critically, and imaginatively, the "giant idea" of remembering, to deter future political violence, also emerges. The present volume examines the memory market in the same way. It values the memory market and its products in some cases, criticizes it in others, and explores the imaginative uses of such a market. In this volume the essayists study the memory market in-depth in six countries that have emerged from authoritarian state repression in the 1980s and 1990s, specifically, Argentina, Brazil, Chile, Mexico, Peru, and Uruguay. Those memory markets offer a variety of sometimes competing products. Bookstores, cinemas, theaters, and the music industry trade in testimonial and fictional accounts of the authoritarian past. Television shows about the authoritarian past, complete with advertisements, receive high ratings, demonstrating that memory sells, and that it also sells products. The tourist industry has added trauma sites and memory museums to its itineraries. Memory studies has emerged as a field of academic scholarship, with its own journals, conferences, book series, websites, blogs, and courses.[4] A new label, *desaparecidología* (disappearedology), or the study of the disappeared, recognizes this emerging academic market.[5] One might even dare to declare that the memory market has developed a "brand," or a "Never Again" logo.[6]

Just as anti-globalization and no-logo movements have responded to the spread of neoliberalism and branding, anti-marketing forces exist within the memory field. Some reject a market for memory as morally or ethically suspect. Some discount the notion of a memory market altogether, especially when a primary element of any market—investment for profit—appears to be absent.

This book argues that its memory-market focus both describes and analyzes a phenomenon. The market exists. Marketing is a transaction between sellers of goods and services and buyers who offer something in exchange for those goods and services. The memory market includes those elements. Memory-makers supply the memory goods. Memory promoters target the goods and the buyers. Those consumers, or memory patrons, not only "buy" memory goods, they also promote the cause of human rights.[7] A transaction takes place between memory patrons and memory-makers. This transaction does not always involve money or financial profit. What individuals and groups may expect, in terms of a return on their mnemonic investment, includes the moral, psychological, social, and political payoffs of remembering. On the memory market, therefore, profit should be thought of in terms of its Latin etymology: *profectus* implies progress. Profiting from memory means progress toward human rights goals, acknowledgment of events in the past, justice, and deterrence.

In addition to a heuristic descriptive device, the memory market also provides an analytical framework for examining transactions over memory. The business term "accounting" forms an integral part of the memory project. Accounts of the past are exchanged by victims, survivors, and even perpetrators. Victims and survivors also hold states and security forces accountable for past violence. The Latin root of the term "accountability" suggests calculation *(computare)*, which, in turn, emerges from *putare* ("reckon"). Memory of past atrocities, therefore, involves a calculation of loss and an effort to reconcile, or balance, accounts. The memory market, when successful, creates profit (or progress) through accountability for the past. No monopoly (single seller) or monopsony (single buyer) exists in the memory market. Instead, competition exists among memory patrons, memory-makers, memory goods, and the expected benefits or profits from the memory enterprise. In short, a market analysis allows the contributors to this volume to explore such questions as: Who is producing memory (memory-makers)? What kinds of products (memory goods) are produced? How are they promoted? Who is targeted (memory patrons) and toward what end (profit)? What kind of competition exists among memory-makers, promoters, patrons, and goods on the memory market? Are there winners and losers in the memory market?

A memory market analysis is provocative, but appropriate given what has transpired in terms of business, the economy, and the politics of memory since the end of the dictatorships in the countries included in this volume. Our project does not promote such a market; it describes and analyzes it. We explore when commercialization cheapens memory goods and derails progress toward building a human rights culture. We do not assume, however, that the memory market is inherently immoral or savage. The promotion of memory beyond borders potentially creates a global memory market that condemns political violence and calls for "Never Again" everywhere.

The expression "Time is money," therefore, captures the notion of the value inherent in the time of political transition and the utility of that time to develop a human rights culture through the promotion of memory. A certain paradox prevails during this time. Just as the monetary currencies in the region lost value in the global economic market beginning in the 1980s, memory became a currency whose value steadily increased in the global promotion of human rights and democracy. In the remainder of this introduction, we first examine the development of the Latin American memory market and its anticipated value for human rights, and then we explore the forces competing in that market which potentially impede progress on human rights.

The Market Concept

Scholars have previously referred to a memory market. Huyssen, for example, explores and rejects the notion that "commodification [of memory] equals forgetting" and that "the marketing of memory generates nothing but amnesia."[8] He suggests instead "a slow but palpable transformation of temporality in our lives, brought on by complex intersections of technological change, mass media, and new patterns of consumption, work, and global mobility" that produce "the desire for the past in the first place," and that "make us respond so favorably to the memory markets."[9] For Huyssen, the desire for memory is a displaced fear of the future and is related to our present anxiety regarding "the speed of change and the ever-shrinking horizons of time and space."[10] There is a perceptual and informational overload that our psyche cannot handle. "The faster we are pushed into global future that does not inspire confidence, the stronger we feel desire to slow down, the more we turn to memory for comfort."[11] According to Huyssen, memory goods should produce a sense of comfort.

The work presented in this volume challenges Huyssen's notion. The memory of atrocity is hardly comforting. The discomfort of memory keeps it valuable, edgy. The unsettling nature of these memories, moreover, might render greater profit—in terms of catalyzing human rights action—than comforting memories. Perhaps Huyssen has a point, however, in thinking about the comfort that certain individuals and groups derive from a shared experience and identity in the past. When applied to past human rights violation, this shared experience and identity might catalyze a movement to prevent future atrocity. What is marketed, therefore, might not be memory itself, but the action that memory inspires. The possibility of acknowledgment, action, and change might bring comfort to those traumatized by the past. As in any market, however, goods, buyers, producers, and promoters compete. They do not share the same goals from participating in the marketplace.

Memory Goods

Memory goods are products created out of the memory of terror. The term "goods" connotes the positive value of remembering and representing the past. It is good to remember; it is important to remember to avoid repeating the past. This is not only an activist perspective. Discussing the normative approach in memory scholarship, Avelar states, "There is, for sure, a tacit assumption, amongst Latin American studies scholars, anyway, that the labor of memory is something one is necessarily supposed to defend, that it is something worth fighting for; that memory, in other words, is something always and necessarily good."[12] Robert Folger links that academic emphasis on memory "good" to the marketplace: "Memory is a commodity of sorts for those who study it. Academia is more than ever a marketplace, increasingly absorbed by the ideology of efficiency and 'practical' use. Memory sells in academia—that is, memory studies are easily understood by the utilitarian outside of academia as being useful. . . . An emphasis on this field of research reaffirms the utilitarian market logic."[13]

The memory activist and the academic community therefore concur with the notion of a memory "good." Yet we use the plural form of the term, to recognize the existence of multiple, and sometimes competing, "goods." More than one memory of the past exists, despite efforts to contain it. Different types of memory goods, moreover, account for this past—specifically, memory accounts, memoryscapes (sites of memory), and memorabilia.

MEMORY ACCOUNTS. Accounting for the past takes different forms, which, as time progresses, necessarily go beyond recording the debit, to reckoning and computing the balance sheet of trauma. This complex accounting system can be said to begin with the first-person testimonials of survivors. They speak out despite, or because of, their personal trauma. In Latin America, the accounts of exiled survivors emerged even before the end of the dictatorships. Other accounts followed shortly after their demise, creating something of a genre of Latin American testimonials. Perpetrators also produced their own accounts of the past, often made through journalists, in self-published books, or in news interviews. Albeit scarce, these accounts disrupted a particular—victim—perspective on the past. Fictional accounts in short stories, plays, poetry, songs, and film attempted to fill in gaps of representation and meaning. Fiction can often elucidate what lies beyond the possibility of language, what is inaccessible or inexpressible by those coping with the trauma of memory. Rather than producing a uniform narrative on the past, these different genres challenge that notion. With democratization, moreover, efforts to silence certain kinds of accounts have failed, sometimes heightening tension—not comfort—over memory and its representation.

Only a few of these accounts appeal to a mass audience. Apart from the reports from Argentina's, Uruguay's, and Brazil's commissions of inquiry, there are no best sellers in the group. Still, it is impossible to imagine Rigoberta Menchú's Nobel Peace Prize without recognizing the importance of her testimonial account of state terrorism against the Guatemalan indigenous people.[14] The demand for Jacobo Timerman's account of the anti-Semitic treatment he received in Argentina's clandestine torture centers has generated numerous editions and translations.[15] And the film *The Official Story* won an Oscar for best foreign film. These accounts have had broad and lasting appeal.

Recently, video games seem to have arrived in the memory market, adapting modern technologies of representation to a new political realm. Video games provide an opportunity for those interested in the memory of atrocity, and even those who are not, to relive, and even alter, the past. Gamers adopt particular political roles or identities, usually based on simplified dichotomies of good and evil. By providing simple and violent solutions to past atrocity, these games may simultaneously reach a wider market and provide the comfort of eliminating emotion.

In contrast, advertisements, a key component of marketing, may advance discomforting, rather than comforting, accounts of the past. Ads confront their viewers to make them act. Sometimes they deliberately call for action as part of a political project. At other times commercial ads that use images of torture in a country that has suffered repression do not comfort victims but, on the contrary, mobilize them against the imagery. Ads, in other words, can catalyze thought and action.

Accounts might also take the form of action, or performance. In Argentina, the political performances known as *escraches* provide an example. These performances call attention to the impunity of those responsible for the atrocities of the dictatorship—basically the pardoned criminals of human rights abuses. The group H.I.J.O.S. (Sons and Daughters for Identity and Justice against Forgetting and Silence) organized the first event in 1996, to correspond with the twentieth anniversary of the military coup. The carnivalesque atmosphere of the escraches draws young people who were not directly victimized by state terror into a festive popular-justice project complete with music, art, singing, and parading.

Academics, journalists, and activists have analyzed these different forms of memory accounts. Their work shows that more than one memory has emerged from state terrorism. The range of perspective creates some competition and conflict. Memory, therefore, is not always, or even often, comfortable. Indeed, at times memory has proven to be intentionally uncomfortable, to catalyze action.

MEMORYSCAPES. Sites of memory also play an important role in the memory market. Rather than contracting, these may expand with time. A glut of sites may create competition among them, as each attempts to attract visitors by utilizing a range of marketing techniques. For now, the marketing of such sites remains fairly underdeveloped. Some of them have appeared, however, in major international tour guides, and others have developed their own websites. International non-governmental organizations provide links to both physical and Internet memory sites in various Latin American countries. Scholars have also studied these sites. The scholarship on Latin American memoryscapes thus joins the earlier trend of examining Second World War battle sites, concentration camps, and museums.[16]

One might expect these sites of memory to provide comfort. They offer, after all, a physical space and an opportunity for mourning, grieving, and reflecting on the losses from state terrorism. Museums and monuments, moreover, acknowledge past crimes, which can bring a certain degree of comfort.

The existence of memoryscapes, however, does not eradicate disagreements over how to remember the past. Those disagreements create conflict and discomfort. These conflicts emerge as a result of efforts by the perpetrators of past violence and their supporters to represent that violent past as one of national salvation and glory. Conflict also emerges within the community of those who were directly affected by the violence, since they may disagree over the design of the sites, or their sponsorship, accessibility, or marketing. Some of the sites, moreover, are intentionally distressing rather than comforting. They seek to represent the openness of the wounds—the enduring sense of loss, fear, and distrust—so as to catalyze action and to ward against comfort and complacency. The marketing of these sites—which must attract visitors to places of discomfort rather than solace—therefore can be quite challenging.

MEMORABILIA. True to its Latin etymology (*memorable*), memorabilia triggers memory. This term differs somewhat from the French term "souvenir," which implies an object "for memory," or for remembering where one has been. "Memorabilia," on the other hand, constitutes an object that recreates in memory a place, person, or event. While we might not collect a souvenir from a place in which we have had a difficult experience, we might possess memorabilia that recall that place and time and the emotions associated with it. Similarly, individuals keep the clothing or letters of a deceased loved one *not* to recreate the bad feelings of loss but to remember the good times with that person. Memorabilia may also hold a future-oriented purpose: one may retain a talisman, or good luck charm, from the past because of the promise it holds for the future.

Some people, particularly victims, may not consider either souvenirs or memorabilia appropriate to the remembrance of atrocity. Carrying off a piece of the Berlin Wall does not have a Latin American equivalent. The triumphalism associated with the end of communism in Europe does not resonate with the end of the dictatorships in Latin America. Memory in Latin America focuses on survival and endurance, on maintaining those symbols of state terrorism that can catalyze action. This difference might be exemplified by victims and survivors who fight to preserve torture centers intact, versus efforts by government and the private sector to destroy or disguise them.

Triggers to memory, moreover, still exist. Victims and survivors with post-traumatic stress disorder no doubt desire fewer, not more, reminders of past atrocity than they already have. What they might hope to take away, or give away as a memento, is hope for a better future. To date, however, such memorabilia are underdeveloped, as marketing efforts have not yet penetrated into the production of memorabilia. Instead, most of the mementos available at memory sites are given away rather than sold. Of those that are sold, not all of them represent the dictatorships in a negative light.

Thus, competition has emerged, even though the market for memorabilia of the past dictatorships is still underdeveloped.

Memory Patrons

A market needs buyers. A traditional marketing study would examine four characteristics of potential consumers: demographics (age, gender, income, ethnic or racial background, education, occupation, and generation); psychographics (social and psychological characteristics, including values and attitudes); geographics (local, state, national, regional, and global location); and trends. In terms of geographics, the memory market targets various categories of customers: victims and survivors of a particular atrocity at a specific site; all victims and survivors in a country; all citizens of a country; the global human rights community. These patrons have some overlapping needs and desires, but conflicts also emerge when those needs and desires do not match.

The location of customers may reveal less about memory-marketing techniques than about trends, demographics, and psychographics. Trends, often oriented toward global consumption patterns, influence the creation of memory products for local patrons. Local patrons, moreover, include both bystanders and the victims and survivors who were directly affected by the violence of the authoritarian state, as well as new generations. Despite their shared national identity, new generations of patrons, without firsthand knowledge of the experiences of twenty or thirty years ago, may not resemble those who were directly affected. As memory consumers, they may have more in common with their international counterparts. Yet international patrons sometimes also include individuals who were directly affected, and who are now part of the exile or diaspora communities that remain involved in developing, promoting, and distributing memory goods. Patrons of memory thus defy neat categorization by location. Instead, taking into account the direct experiences, and the corresponding psychographic, demographic, geographic, and trend characteristics that accompany those experiences, allows for greater understanding of the memory market.

The memory market targets at least three types of groups: the directly affected generation of victims and survivors; bystanders and new generations who are learning about the past; and regime supporters who defend the past. Our assumption is that memory marketing is aimed at one or more of these groups, but rarely at all three. Each group is sensitive to geography, demographics, psychographics, and current trends.

What appears to differentiate these markets is demand and supply. The memory market for regime supporters is small and local. The demand for memory goods that endorse the authoritarian regime hardly exists and faces condemnation from victims and survivors of that regime. Few entrepreneurs would emerge to market products with such low demand, although this is not to say that it never happens.

Indeed, rather than a "mass market," the memory market may resemble "niche markets." In such a market, goods do not necessarily compete with each other. Instead, they fill a particular need or niche. Memory patrons, therefore, are not looking indiscriminately for all memory goods, but for ones that respond to their particular needs. In a sense, then, memory patrons may resemble collectors. They are not selecting among goods by their value, but rather each good has value because it is part of a set. The goods in that set do not compete with each other, since the patron wants them all. Collectors value each piece. Each piece has a distinct role or function as part of the complete set. What is new about each piece is not how different it is from the other pieces, but that it contributes to forming a complete set. Without one of the pieces, the set is incomplete. Collectors, thus, keep adding each memory good as they discover it. They seek a complete collection, even if this is an impossible goal. Borges has taught us, through the parable of *Funes the Memorious*, that complete and absolute memory is impossible.[17] Memory studies, on the other hand, have taught us that memory is a composite of many different versions of an event that offer unique paths toward the truth.

Memory-Makers and Promoters

One might expect that the memory marketplace would involve only entrepreneurs who were directly affected by state terrorism. They might be the only individuals with the credibility and with sufficient understanding of the market to produce and distribute memory goods. They might be the only individuals willing to invest in such an enterprise. Yet time and location reenter our analysis here. In the early years of the transition from authoritarian rule, memory-makers consisted largely of victims and survivors. With time, however, and with the expansion of memory beyond the local market and into a global one, new memory-makers have emerged. These new memory producers do not always share the traumatic experiences from the past. They also produce for a wider, and previously untargeted, population.

Elizabeth Jelin refers to the concept of "memory entrepreneurship," an adaptation of "moral entrepreneurship," coined by the U.S. sociologist Howard Becker. Memory entrepreneurs are those who express themselves and seek to define the field of struggle over memory. Jelin further expresses a preference for the Spanish term *emprendedor* over *empresario*. A memory emprendedor develops a memory enterprise or venture that could be a public and social project. In contrast, the memory empresario would tend to create a memory business (*empresa*) for financial profit.[18]

Capitalizing on the image of the authoritarian regime is not new to the post-dictatorship period. Scholars have analyzed the role that public relations firms have played in promoting, or cleaning up, the image of authoritarian regimes.[19] Little research exists, however, to show how supporters of the authoritarian regime have attempted to sell a positive image of the past in the post-dictatorship era. Instead, the assumption prevails that those promoting memory are the same ones who reject the authoritarian regime. The commercialization of the memory of atrocity, however, opens up the possibility for the promotion of memory goods without a political message. Memory, in other words, can become business. That business may create a space for a variety of memory products, including those that "sell" the image of the past regime as heroic, and the victims and survivors as subversives. Rather than depoliticization, market competition may increase political tensions and polarization in society.

Jelin's concept of memory entrepreneurship, however, suggests that the memory market resembles a "moral economy." Producers and consumers are often the same individuals or communities. They do not necessarily seek financial gain. Nor are they motivated by rational cost-benefit calculations. Instead, they hope to profit from (or progress to) greater security, greater emotional and physical well-being, and justice.[20]

Victims and survivors, for example, simultaneously produce memory goods, promote them, and acquire them. The tourist industry may promote particular memoryscapes, but in describing them it imbues them with a particular meaning. The tourist industry thus becomes a memory-maker and promoter. Non-governmental organizations may become the sponsors of particular memory goods and help promote them. In the process, they may be memory-makers and patrons in influencing certain types of designs and in acquiring more sites or members to build a network.

These roles often overlap, but they also create tensions. Tensions emerge over the goals of particular memory-makers, promoters, and patrons. For some, commercialization cheapens and undermines the goal of building a human rights culture. In addition, they see certain individuals profiting for their own personal gain, without attending to the collective enterprise. For others, marketing becomes essential to expanding knowledge and acknowledgment of past atrocity in order to promote a global movement to prevent its repetition. Additional problems arise over the way groups wish to remember the past. These tensions further fragment the community and the notion of a shared memory or memory project.

Profiting from Memory

Conflict over the profit-making enterprise associated with the memory market can be illustrated with the contrasting notion of a "sellout." A sellout event, for example, suggests value in the product and enhanced profit or gain. Someone who "sells out," in contrast, has devalued the product, enhancing only his or her own individual gain. In memory market terms, "sellout" memory goods or events mean they have widespread appeal, heightening the possibility of progress toward a human rights culture. In this sense, profiting on the memory market would seem positive. In contrast, those who "sell out" discount the value of a human rights culture in order to maximize their own personal payoff. Profit is not inherently positive or negative in the memory market; the kind of profit is what matters, particularly if it comes at victims' expense.

In speaking of a memory "market," profit is assumed. Profit, however, need not involve monetary gain. That gain, when achieved, could provide a side benefit to the ultimate goal of building a human rights culture. But any progress toward that goal, even if it did not turn out to be financially lucrative, would have value on the memory market. The intention, or the kind of profit desired, is what distinguishes the positive form of sellout events from the negative notion of sellout producers.

The memory market intentionally downplays the importance of financial profit. Several examples are illustrative of efforts to provide memory goods for free, without cost, and at a loss. The guides at the Museo de la Memoria in Montevideo, Uruguay, emphasize their volunteer status, lest visitors consider them to be profiting from the enterprise. Books related to human rights abuses that took place at ESMA (the Navy School of Mechanics, in Argentina) are given away to visitors at no charge. In addition, in an advertisement for a book and a compact disc containing the testimony of political prisoners, the Argentine anti-dictatorship daily newspaper

Página/12 wrote: "The book and set are free. The CD, in which La Pandilla del Punto Muerto and guest musicians play themes based on poems of the disappeared, costs only five pesos. The CD is called, simply, '30,000 cries.'" The emphasis placed on the "free" (*gratuitos*) set and on "hardly any money" (*apenas*) for the CD makes it clear that no one is profiting from these memory goods.[21]

Failing to generate monetary profit, or individual gain, from memory, however, may undermine certain goals of the memory market. The failure to generate funds, for example, may force memory-makers to depend on public—that is, government—support. Many memory groups reject sponsorship by the government. Changing leadership within the government can also make groups dependent on a stream of support that can disappear. Other problems also emerge with state sponsorship. The Madres de Plaza de Mayo in Argentina refused a state-sponsored memorial for the disappeared because it would have represented a closure of the crimes of the state and, consequently, would have released the state from its responsibility to hold individuals accountable for past violations. They, as well as other human rights groups, need state funds yet reject them because of the limited scope of action, and the implicit compromise and stigma, the acceptance of such funds would imply.

The politics of reparations further illustrates the conflict over profiting from memory and the role of the state. Reparations have meant that individuals who identify themselves as victims or survivors of atrocity receive financial support from the government to "repair" the damage caused by the former regime. How victims and survivors see this financial support varies widely within the memory market.

The etymology of the word "reparation" would appear to have nothing to do with profiting from loss. Instead, it denotes "recovery and repair," or "restoring something to its previous condition." Human life cannot be calculated as a monetary transaction; no money or support can restore the lost dreams, innocence, profession, livelihood, health, security, and well-being that have been taken from victims and survivors of atrocity. At best, reparations provide some compensation, but they can never repair or restore survivors. Perhaps because of the limited value of reparations, and the high degree of need, survivors question their value and their distribution. Defensiveness emerges among some survivors who have decided to accept reparations: "The compensation owed to political prisoners from governments where state terrorism occurred is essentially fair; I don't count myself among the most economically needy, but a great majority of ex-prisoners suffer great economic privation, and the money that they are receiving is only a band-aid. . . . I don't have any problem expressing my opinion regarding the reparations that a left-wing government, after all, approved for ex-political prisoners, nor in saying what I will do with this money."[22]

As the statement above suggests, some victims of state violence do not see reparations as a personal payoff, but rather as a legitimate payment of a debt owed to them. It becomes a form of accounting, or a public acknowledgment of wrongdoing through the only currency possible: money.

The courts have also provided certain benefits to victims and survivors. Individuals who bring civil lawsuits against torturers or murderers, therefore, could be seen as profiting from their loss. There have been famous cases, like that of Tarnopolsky in Argentina or Filártiga in Honduras, in which multimillion-dollar judgments have been rendered.[23] To avoid any possible criticism for seeking an individual payoff, the Teles family in Brazil did not demand financial compensation for the torture they experienced. Instead, they demanded the public recognition—an acknowledgment—of torture as their "payoff." They argued that no price could be put on the pain and suffering they had experienced.

The ultimate payoff, or profit, from the memory market may never be realized, or at least not in the lifetime of the survivors of recent atrocities. Expectation of the big payoff, however, may cause one to fail to recognize the smaller payoffs, in terms of progress. Evidence of progress does exist. It comes in the form of outrage when commercialization attempts to sell products by using the imagery of torture (Bilbija). Commercialization can also produce counter-mementos that tarnish the image of the perpetrators of past violence (Oquendo-Villar). The memory marketplace generates competition over past events, providing a space for victims and survivors to contest the past (Burt). This occurs, for example, when television stations feature past atrocities and condemn them (Atencio; Kaiser). It also emerges when victims and survivors finally establish sites to condemn past violence (Ruisánchez Serra; Collins; Gates-Madsen; Draper). Progress is also evident when local and foreign tourists visit such sites, which provide exposure to past atrocities in an effort to condemn them (Clark and Payne; Milton and Ulfe). Globalization poses challenges to the memory market (Nelson). Mobilization, however, has allowed victims, survivors, and the human rights community to benefit from the events of the past, rather than the events' succumbing to memory loss or erasure. Each of the chapters here explores these complexities of the memory market.

Avelar has reflected that "it is not always clear 'who' benefits from the memory market, or what 'benefiting' in this context might mean." He suggests that post-dictatorial societies need restoration and comprehension of the horrors of the recent past. He quotes Marx as claiming that the past rests "as a nightmare upon the brains of the living."[24] The profit of the memory market, therefore, is the notion of "Never Again." It is not the belief that the memory will necessarily fade or disappear, but rather that it should be remembered to prevent future atrocities. Memory, therefore, has a purpose.

The Memory Brand

"Never Again" has become the slogan for the purposeful action of remembering past atrocity. In terms of marketing, slogans always accompany sale campaigns, and their function is to increase profits. Slogans are convincing, evocative, and short. Importantly, they reveal collective identity and contain a promise of satisfying a need for something desired and appealing. The Gaelic etymology of the term "slogan" is "battle cry." Such origins connect marketing to a call to arms. In memory terms, the "Never Again" battle cry urges against complacency, as well as glorifying and forgetting the violent past.

"Never Again" is not the only battle cry emerging from the dictatorships. In Argentina, the expression "Ni Olvido, Ni Perdón" (Never Forgive, Never Forget) reflects a promise that contrasts sharply with the push for reconciliation around the world. The expression "Never Again" could be interpreted as satisfying the notion of reconciliation by focusing on the future rather than the past. The saying "Never Forgive, Never Forget" holds perpetrators accountable: there is no exchange; perpetrators will pay for their acts.

Sloganeering is not a new method of mobilization in Latin America. During the dictatorship in Argentina, supporters of the authoritarian regime used the slogan "Los argentinos somos derechos y humanos" (We Argentines are human and right). The play on words provided a clever way for regime supporters to defend themselves against the international outcry against the deaths and disappearances in the country. During the dictatorship and beyond, Argentines widely believed that their smartly crafted slogan was a spontaneous and homegrown expression. Many still remain unaware of the fact that it was the public relations firm of Burson-Marsteller, one of the largest in the world, that actually created the slogan for the Argentine government, to defuse condemnation of the regime's human rights record.[25]

While catchy, the slogan did not survive the dictatorship. "Never Again," in contrast, has not only spread throughout the country, but around the world. The two words still appear everywhere. They are chanted at rallies and printed on posters. They are the titles of reports that have investigated atrocities in the region. These two words have begun to symbolize a way, or brand, of remembering. One does not remember passively. Instead, one engages in the act of remembering in order to mobilize against past abuses and to remain vigilant against future ones. One could even say that a "Never Again" enterprise has emerged as a catalyst to human rights action. But this enterprise is not without its competition.

Market Competition

Memories tend to compete. Individuals are often shocked at how very differently they experience, or remember, the same set of events. Market analysis enables us to think about the competing memories of dictatorships, and, specifically, about which ones "sell," which ones do not, and why.

The competitive marketplace for memory-makers and promoters, memory patrons, and memory goods creates various levels of competition. With regard to memory-makers and promoters, competition emerges over whether to remember at all. The forces promoting silence and forgetting compete with the forces in favor of remembering. Memory-makers and promoters also disagree over the sort of market that should exist for memory—whether it should be regulated or unfettered. Market strategy also raises questions of whether to compete for mass consumption of memory goods, or whether memory goods should be targeted to a niche market. Related to that question is the question of competition for memory patrons and whether they should be primarily local or international. Competition also exists over the type of memory goods produced, with some claiming authenticity for their own goods while charging others as being mere counterfeits. All of these tensions have implications for the type of profit, or progress, that the memory good is likely to generate.

Memory versus Forgetting

The recently deceased Uruguayan writer Mario Benedetti once famously declared: "El olvido está lleno de memoria" (Forgetting is full of memory).[26] A primary threat to memory, therefore, is the effort to obliterate it, to purposely forget or silence the expression of memory of past atrocity. In post-dictatorship societies, memory competes with forgetting and efforts to silence debate over the past.

The obvious proponents of forgetting, or silencing the past, are the perpetrators of violence. Even when amnesty laws protect them from prosecution for human rights violations, perpetrators are still likely to choose a protective silence over speaking out about the past. By speaking out, they can potentially damage their reputation within their families, among their friends, or in their communities. They might also further violate official or informal codes of silence within the security apparatus. And they risk reprisals from victims or survivors who might take justice into their own hands. Only a few perpetrators have spoken out in Latin America; most have opted to remain silent. When perpetrators do speak out, they often promote a different kind of memory or forgetting: the memory of a heroic war against subversion, and the forgetting of the crimes committed.[27]

Perpetrators thus operate on a different logic. Rather than the "Time is money" maxim that mobilizes victims and survivors to promote memory in the post-dictatorship era, perpetrators tend to operate under the "Silence is golden" axiom. In their calculation, silence incurs fewer costs and renders greater potential profit than speaking out. Speaking out, given the high risk and limited expected return, would appear to be a poor investment. Choosing not to speak out is not a rejection of the memory market but a response to it that offers a competing good: silence. For perpetrators, the longer the time and the longer the silence, the greater the profit.

Perpetrators may be the most obvious, but they are not necessarily the most threatening forces promoting silence, or forgetting, to compete with memory. The democratic governments that replaced the dictatorships sometimes have proven to be more forceful than perpetrators in imposing the "Silence is golden" rule. Concerned about opening up deep ideological conflict, returning the country to violence or authoritarian rule, or governing across deep memory schisms, democratic governments may attempt to suppress traumatic memory, usually to no avail. These governments tend to react against memory only after it is already available for public consumption. Argentine president Carlos Menem, for example, used particular speech laws to repress perpetrators' confessions of past violence, and referred to their speaking out about the past as "pouring salt into the wounds."[28]

Scholars have critiqued certain memory projects adopted by democratic governments as imposing silence over the past. As Robert Folger states: "Certain kinds of memory goods may be viewed as erasing the past, or putting the past into distant history rather than keeping it alive to promote the 'Never Again' project." Museums may play the role of allowing governments to simultaneously acknowledge the past and put it at a safe distance from the present, to "transform vivid memory into distant history."[29]

Indeed, government efforts at silencing debate about the past may emerge when perpetrators desire to speak out and participate in that "vivid memory," refusing to relegate their role in the security forces to "distant history." When they do speak out, they present a version of the past that competes with the versions of victims and survivors. Rather than condemn past violence, they justify it. They use just-war analogies to defend their actions as having been necessary to save the nation from the violence perpetrated by so-called "subversives." They attempt to undermine the "atrocity" memory good by promoting an alternative "salvation" memory good.[30] As the titles of their books suggest—*Breaking the Silence*; *The Historic Truth*; *The Other Side of Never Again*—perpetrators believe it is their memories, and not those of their victims and survivors, that provide the full accounting of the past.[31] These perpetrators attempt to overpower victims' and survivors' memories with their own. Their heroic interpretations of the past directly compete with "silence" and "atrocity" memory goods.

These heroic memory goods do not compete very well, however. Only in rare cases do they attract more than a fringe, or niche market, of memory patrons who accept, or "buy," their version. This was not always the case. In Latin America, the public celebrations of former coups that had toppled previous democracies and installed authoritarian regimes at one time involved much fanfare. Such celebrations have now become closed, private events. These anniversaries have not slipped into oblivion, but they are more likely to be acknowledged in infamy than in glory.[32] As is the case for the market for Nazi paraphernalia, in Latin American memorabilia from previous authoritarian regimes has also appeared for sale, primarily on the Internet. It is a limited market, however. Although one can buy trinkets from the Pinochet era, no other Latin American dictator appears to have garnered much interest in the sale of such souvenirs.

Similarly, few of the volumes written by the perpetrators themselves have sold well.[33] Some exceptions exist. The journalist Horacio Verbitsky's interviews with an Argentine naval officer who admitted to throwing bodies from a plane appeared in Argentina as *El Vuelo*, and were subsequently published in English under the same title, *The Flight*. A new version of the book has come out under the title *Confessions of an Argentine Dirty Warrior*.[34] The change of title appears to be a marketing technique designed to increase sales among readers less familiar with Argentina's recent repressive past.[35] According to rumors, Adolfo Scilingo's decision to tell his death flight story was strictly business: he was negotiating a multimillion-dollar Hollywood deal for the movie rights. Believing this rumor, other perpetrators also began to speak out and peddle their confessional wares. Marguerite Feitlowitz refers to the proliferation of perpetrator confessions in Argentina as the "Scilingo Effect." These perpetrators made an impressive media splash, but none of them—not even Scilingo—seems to have made any money from their sale of memory goods. The only high number in Scilingo's account is the number of years he will spend in prison: 1,084! Perpetrators' accounts have also failed to overwhelm the memory market; victims' and survivors' accounts continue to hold sway. While the Brazilian torturer Carlos Alberto Brilhante Ustra probably intended his memoir to resurrect the heroic version of the past, it instead ended up serving as evidence for civil charges of torture brought against him by the Teles family.[36]

Luz Arce's testimonial *El Infierno*, describing her path from a Socialist Party leader in the Allende era to a member of Pinochet's secret police, is so widely read and valued that it has become standard reading for students of Latin American culture. It was translated into English in 2004 as *The Inferno*. Arce's account emphasizes her criticism of the regime. Rather than glorify or excuse Pinochet's secret police, she condemns specific acts and asks pardon for her role in them. Her account, in other words, did enjoy some success on the memory market. It shared the enterprise of "Never Again," however, and not the silence or heroism enterprise promoted by other perpetrators.

Perpetrators' accounts do not compete effectively with the blockbuster sales of books by victims and survivors. Consider the top selling *Prisoner without a Name, Cell without a Number*, by Jacobo Timerman. Some authoritative accounts on the authoritarian past, like *Brasil Nunca Mais*, and *Nunca Más* in Argentina and Uruguay, respectively, have become "instant best sellers" in their countries.[37] These reports appeared early in the transition to democratic rule and revealed information that had been suppressed by the countries' military regimes. In the Brazilian case, the volume became a best seller within two weeks of its publication, and remained on the bestseller list for ninety-one consecutive weeks. More than 100,000 copies were sold within ten weeks, when the usual press run for a work of nonfiction in Brazil is between 3,000 and 5,000 issues.[38] The timing of the release of the Argentine report made it the reading of choice in the summer of 1984–85 for a certain segment of society. And Louis Bickford reports that *Uruguay Nunca Más* became an "enormous bestseller."[39] The human rights community has applauded such commercial successes.

In short, competition exists, but the victims and survivors of the violence have so far appeared to do better than perpetrators in promoting memory. The pressure for silence and forgetting has simply failed to compete with the vocal and visible condemnation of past violence. The promotion of transitional justice, particularly truth commissions, around the world has given a competitive edge to memory produced by victims, survivors, and the human rights community.

Free or Fettered Markets of Memory

With their competitive edge over perpetrators' versions of the past, one might expect the memory-makers among the victims and survivors to be interested in promoting a free, and unfettered, market of memory goods. Instead, they seem to be deeply divided over whether to control the promotion of memory or not, and over how much control is appropriate.

In sharp contrast to Argentine President Menem's silencing of memory and debate, Chilean President Patricio Aylwin seemed to promote it. He held his inauguration ceremony in the infamous National Soccer Stadium and invited women from the Association of Family Members of the Disappeared-Detainees to dance a traditional couples' dance (the *cueca*) alone, to symbolize the human losses that had been caused by the authoritarian regime. Perhaps consistent with only allowing certain memory goods, the Chilean state television channel has controlled the distribution of one perpetrator's account. In this case, the Miami-based Univision broadcasting firm had produced a *Primer Impacto* program featuring the Chilean perpetrator Osvaldo Romo discussing his use of torture. While shown throughout the Spanish-speaking world, the program only finally appeared on Chilean television after it had provoked outrage elsewhere. Even then, the state television channel edited out the most depraved segments of Romo's confession. But Chilean audiences still demanded that its showing be censored.[40] In contrast, Claudia Feld's research on televised confessions in Argentina shows that perpetrators' accounts get high ratings there from local audiences.[41]

Internationally, fewer controls have prevailed. Video games provide one example. A game called *Just Cause* allows participants to reenact the role of the United States government in ousting Panamanian dictator Manuel Noriega. Another somewhat futuristic but not necessarily un-prophetic example is the video game *Mercenaries 2: World in Flames*, which depicts the virtual invasion and destruction of Venezuela, the overthrow of Hugo Chávez's government, and the takeover of the oil industry. Neither the producer nor the financial backers of this game (Pandemic Studio and Elevation Partners, who invested $300 million) have issued any statements, despite the widespread controversy surrounding it.

The argument in favor of a free market of memory is that when these kinds of memory goods emerge on the market they can be contested. Certain groups remain poised to challenge perpetrators' versions of the past. The Argentine group GAC (Grupo de Arte Callejero, or Street Art Group), established in 1997, has used street art projects to identify violators of human rights and demand justice. They produced a poster in 1998 that appeared on the streets of Buenos Aires, persuading citizens to spit on Alfredo Astiz, the former navy captain and a perpetrator of authoritarian state violence. They have also transformed ordinary traffic signs into markers for where perpetrators live. GAC promoted its own freedom to market a "Never Again" memory project, while successfully constraining one business's marketing campaign to sell jeans by eroticizing torture.

The notion of "free" in the free market for memory raises important questions. Memory-makers may see the promotion of memory along the lines of the maxim, "The truth will set you free." By providing the truth about the past on the open market, memory-makers and promoters contribute to the "Never Again" enterprise. Competition from perpetrators' versions of the past, on the other hand, casts doubts on whether market freedom advances the goal of "Never Again." By allowing that competition, memory may not "free" individuals, but trap them in a perpetrators' version of the world.

Some memory scholars further question whether memory is the liberating force that it appears to be in expressions like "The truth will set you free." As Idelber Avelar states: "If there's one notion that is in crisis in the most sophisticated contemporary Argentine fiction, it is that of memory as a necessarily liberating activity. Scholarship should follow those art forms carefully and learn from them, as there is much that is being grasped with unprecedented complexity in fiction and from film."[42] The fear of competition from silence and from heroic memories may drive memory-makers and promoters to demand control over the free market of memory. They may hope to limit memory production to certified memory-makers, informed memory patrons, and quality memory goods. That control, they believe, will advance a human rights culture, or at least fail to undermine it the way that a free market in memory goods might. Controlling the memory market seems counterintuitive. One would expect that the more memory and the more memory contestation that exists, the deeper the human rights progress. Such an assumption creates another market tension around mass versus niche or anti-marketing.

Memory for the Masses?

Despite the potential benefit of a mass market for the "Never Again" enterprise and its corresponding memory goods, not all memory-makers, promoters, and patrons share enthusiasm for such a market. Those who hope to promote memory widely compete with those who oppose any kind of marketing because of its "cheapening" effect. Still others prefer a niche market, in which memory goods reach only those who were directly affected by state terrorism or those who are actively engaged in the human rights community.

Those who distrust mass marketing suspect that it will erode the unique experience of victims and survivors, thereby trivializing it. They believe the negative "bandwagon" effect outweighs the positive effect of generating mass condemnation of human rights violations. The negative side of that effect is that anyone who condemns the violent past forms part of a solidarity movement, regardless of their personal circumstances. Everyone, in some sense, becomes a victim of state repression, since all of us are members of a global community that shuns political violence. Creating a wider network of victims and survivors, on one hand, elevates that status. On the other hand, if everyone is a victim and survivor of state violence, then the specific experience of those who were directly affected is minimized. In the process of building solidarity around "Never Again," the mass market capitalizes on, yet diminishes, the tragic experiences of certain individuals. The dignity that victims and survivors acquired from knowledge and acknowledgment of the past—that someone committed a crime against them—is lost when the identity of victim and survivor is shared widely. In addition, the restorative process serves to transform the victim and survivor from a "subversive," in the regime's lexicon, to a citizen deserving respect and equal treatment under the law. Creating a global identity and a global political struggle for "Never Again" potentially robs victims and survivors of that unique historical role. Victims' and survivors' identity is thus "hijacked" by the larger global project. Rather than expanding knowledge about the past, in other words, mass marketing potentially trivializes it.

Suspicion of mass marketing does not necessarily mean an anti-market perspective, however. Instead, memory-makers, promoters, and patrons compete in a different—niche—market. Particular memory goods are promoted to a targeted group of memory patrons. These tend to be the directly affected. They form and create solidarity around their relationship with the past regime. Identity-formation creates a support network. By attempting to control the saturation of the memory market with goods for mass consumption, memory-makers maintain the high value of memory. If they were to let go of that control, the commercialization of memory could cheapen it and create a trend toward politically neutral memory goods. Competition emerges among victims and survivors over the mass-memory market, with some seeking a "sellout" audience and sometimes facing charges for having "sold out" for personal profit.

Distrust of the mass market also takes the form of competition with those who have no personal connection to the repressive era. Once the repressive past becomes a marketing tool, distortions may result. Individuals or organizations may seek financial profits at any cost; they may not see profit as progress toward a human rights culture. Such distrust is not unwarranted. Mass marketing and free marketing opens up the possibility of using memory in ways that overstep ethical or moral boundaries. Commercial use of memory goods may trespass existing frontiers of taste, aesthetics, and morality. Ksenija Bilbija writes about that boundary in her chapter on Diesel and Ripley ads, depicting torture scenes to sell jeans in Argentina and Chile. She quotes Sergio Laurenti of Amnesty International, who asks, "How far [are firms] willing to go with the effort to sell and support a message with an object that is likely to cause distress?"[43] In her chapter, Susana Draper shows how the market and the dictatorial past have embraced each other in the architectural space of Montevideo's upscale mall Punta Carretas, former detention center.

The mass marketing of memory, therefore, runs the risk of derailing the "Never Again" enterprise by promoting financial profits over social transformation. Inherent in this critique is the fear of depoliticization that mass marketing promotes. The Diesel ads do so by rendering torture sexy and trendy. In his 1994 novel, *Por favor, rebobinar* (*Please Rewind*), the Chilean author Alberto Fuguet anticipated the depoliticization of memory through commercialization. In the novel, a marketing firm called Right Hemisphere has revamped an old Santiago city hotel. It develops a hotel bar, "73," named after the year of the coup. The "73" bar is adorned with the infamous photograph of Pinochet wearing his dark glasses, but video screens throughout the bar play Patricio Guzmán's *The Battle of Chile*, a documentary film critical of the coup.[44] Fuguet captures the notion of a post-memory era in which the coup, the right-wing dictatorship, and the human rights response become depoliticized, and thus functional as a marketing tool. Memory of the dictatorship "sells"; in this illustration, it sells drinks and atmosphere.

The commercial use of Guzmán's *The Battle of Chile* in Fuguet's novel contrasts sharply with the film's actual promotion. Indeed, the film represents the danger of anti-market, or anti-commercialization, approaches to memory. Not surprisingly, since it depicts the military overthrow of President Salvador Allende in 1973, the film circulated clandestinely during the dictatorship in Chile. Thomas Miller Klubock claims, however, that the film has never achieved commercial success in Chile—not in commercial theaters, nor on television—not even in the decade after the dictatorship ended. State-run television did not show the film, even when the anti-Pinochet Concertación government controlled it. When it did finally appear on television, in 1999 and 2000, the multinational satellite television company SKY promoted it on pay-per-view. Only elite Chileans who owned a satellite dish (and had the funds and desire to purchase the viewing) could benefit from the televised broadcast. A few years later, an international movie theater chain in Santiago presented a week-long retrospective of Guzmán's films to packed (near "sellout") audiences. According to Klubock, Guzmán's films have not been shown in Chile since, although they continue to enjoy success outside the country.[45] Chileans do have access to non-commercial (pirated) copies of Guzmán's films, which are sold at the annual Fiesta de los Abrazos organized by the Communist Party. And, contrary to Klubock's claims, his films are available at online video stores and in retail video stores, including Blockbuster.

Klubock's perspective on *The Battle of Chile* is that its circulation is limited to a niche market. Those already connected with a particular version of the past have access to it. Others would not know enough about the film to find it. To contribute to a human rights culture, Guzmán's films, including *Obstinate Memory* and *The Pinochet Case*, should be watched by those who do not know the stories he tells. The films present nuanced versions of the past that expose audiences to the complexity of the past. Whether deliberate or not, the absence of commercialization of memory goods limits their circulation. They do not always reach those who are most likely to profit from them, thus limiting the construction of a human rights culture.

In his chapter on the Tlatelolco massacre and museum, José Ramón Ruisánchez Serra further identifies the harm that the absence of commercialization poses to the "Never Again" enterprise. Ruisánchez Serra notes that it was only during the initial opening of the Tlatelolco Museum that visitors were attracted to the site. Subsequently, the museum has not appeared on any of the published lists of cultural activities available in Mexico City. As a result, potential memory seekers, or even the uninformed, are prevented from learning more about the massacre and the efforts to preserve its memory as a political project. Individuals who want to visit ESMA, the infamous Buenos Aires torture center, face the same kind of frustration. ESMA does not have regular hours for visitors, which prevents tourists from simply showing up. And tourist agencies do not have enough information to inform visitors on how to arrange a tour. As a result, only a niche market has access to the insider information that is necessary to arrange tours of ESMA or the Tlatelolco Museum.

The absence of memorabilia reflects an anti-market sentiment. It is rare to find mementos for sale at any of the memory sites in Latin America. The Uruguayan Museo de la Memoria is an exception, providing a small case of postcards, T-shirts, magnets, and books for purchase. The memorabilia that one can find for sale tends to be marketed on the Internet. Djurdja Trajković has found that most of these items target a pro-dictatorship, rather than an anti-dictatorship, niche market.[46] A commemorative keychain, for example, depicts Pinochet's military cap and the words "Mission Accomplished. Thank you, my country, I have been your soldier" on one side, while words from the national anthem ("Your names, brave soldiers") appear on the other side. Another keychain has Pinochet's face embossed on one side, and the back reads, "I'm a grateful Chilean." Pinochet T-shirts also exist. Several feature Pinochet's face. Another says, in English, "9/11/73: We won't forget."[47] A beer glass found on eBay features Pinochet's face and his name. Interested shoppers are enticed to purchase a signed photograph of Pinochet, with the starting bid at over $300. Recognizing that the Pinochet paraphernalia might evoke outrage, one vendor pleads with potential consumers: "Please, don't turn this exchange into a political platform. If you do not wish to buy it or you do not support General Pinochet, abstain from commenting."[48] Such a comment provokes wonder over the vendors' perspective on these items: are they apolitical profit-makers or pro-Pinochet memory-makers promoting a different pro-regime memory enterprise? Certain items for sale seem politically ambiguous. For $145, for example, one can buy the original Santiago plaque for "Calle September 11," the street name commemorating the 1973 coup.[49] Is that merely a collector's item, like license plates, or does its political (coup) content determine its value?

Memory goods for a "Never Again" niche market also exist. But very few items are actually for sale in this niche market. The Madres de Plaza de Mayo do not sell their headscarves; they consider such an act tantamount to selling their children, since the headscarves represent the diapers of their disappeared children. The mothers, however, do sometimes give their headscarves away. Those gifts come with a great deal of responsibility, since the mothers warn that they only entrust the headscarves to those individuals whom they believe care about their children's future. They also give away pins that depict the headscarves. And they provide books and calendars for free. Visitors, however, can buy some items, such as an expensive coffee-table book of photographs.

Some examples of a "Never Again" mass market also exist. Trajković found a T-shirt with the words "Nunca Más" on the front, along with a skull, right under the words, adorned with the caption "Repressor." The back of the shirt reads "¿Dónde Están Los Desaparecidos?" (Where are the disappeared?), with a picture of the ESMA building. Other attempts to create a mass-memory or commercial-memory market have created more controversy. Many protested the opening of a café in October 2007 on the Plaza de la Memoria of the Pontificia Universidad Católica del Perú campus in Lima. The Plaza commemorates all the university students victimized by terrorism in Peru. Critics saw the opening of the café as indecent, as failing to show respect for victims by using them to sell coffee. Nancy Gates-Madsen writes in her chapter about a similar clash over commercialization of memory in Buenos Aires, where a restaurant across the street from Memory Park raised a banner with the word "Remember." This was seen as a controversial play on words, since it evoked both the good feelings one might have from eating at the restaurant and a call to remember the state terrorism represented by the park. Selling memory, therefore, is associated with vulgar commercialization, which reduces the value of the good.

In economic logic, value is also reduced with oversupply of a particular product. One criticism of memory mass marketing, therefore, is that the proliferation of memory goods will reduce the value of the "Never Again" enterprise. Mass marketing might create a wider human rights movement, but in the process it might drive down the value of memory goods. David Berliner has analyzed this issue with regard to the academic memory marketplace. He claims that the academic memory market has attracted scholars. But these scholars are simply repackaging old ideas under the new, and trendier, memory label. Individual producers of these academic products gain personally from the visibility they receive, but Berliner contends that their contributions do not enhance our understanding of memory. Berliner seems to suggest that memory studies only became an academic fad because of the perceived newness of that label.[50]

Robert Folger might disagree with Berliner's assumptions. In contrast to the idea of memory as a marketing tool to sell goods (jeans, coffee) or places (restaurants, cafés), Folger claims that "good consumers do not remember—or care." He suggests, therefore, that the capitalist marketplace should tend toward oblivion, away from memory, and that "within today's 'late-capitalist' system, memory with an ethical impact is an obstacle to consumerism."[51] The Diesel Jeans ads do not demand memory of the authoritarian past, but forgetting. One would need to forget that past to accept the notion of torture as chic. The distrust of mass marketing thus emerges not from the impact of oversupply of memory goods alone, but from the loss of meaning that oversupply might entail. Memory-makers, in other words, do not fear the production of too many films, songs, sites, mementos, and books. They fear that the memory patron may not understand the value of those goods. The goods will become mere commodities rather than memory goods with a purpose. The financial profit for these goods thus increases on the mass market, even as progress toward a human rights culture becomes secondary or lost altogether. The kind of "'deep' attention, memory and care" desired by memory activists will thus be replaced by mass, but superficial, understanding of the past.[52] Folger thus shares the skepticism around a commercialization of memory that expands its appeal but diminishes its activist value.

Market competition, however, may have an activist component. Carmen Oquendo Villar's chapter develops the history of Pinochet's marketing strategy through his image. Only Pinochet's image in a business suit could be "sold off" for profit, since the suit lacks powerful political meaning and value, thereby allowing the image to enter the commercial market. Pinochet's military uniforms, his caps and capes, are all charged with political value, and thus cannot be sold, or at least not on the open market. Oquendo Villar's and Cath Collins's chapters in this volume examine the competition over Pinochet's image through the image of Chilean wine, a booming Chilean commodity produced for both local and international consumption. Pinochet supporters promoted an expensive wine to raise funds for his legal defense. His opposition countered with the promotion of a cheap wine, accessible to the masses and designed to be consumed in celebration of Pinochet's criminal conviction or death. The expensive wine was developed for a niche market to heighten Pinochet's image. The cheap wine undermined that image, but also made this devalued image of Pinochet accessible to a mass market. The battle lines drawn by the purchase and consumption of the wine became a metaphor for the political battle lines around the truth of the Pinochet regime.

Memory Counterfeit and the Genuine Article

In the previously mentioned novel, *Please Rewind*, Alberto Fuguet invokes the image of the "still unavailable dark glasses" of General Augusto Pinochet. Those glasses are not yet available for sale or for display. Yet another pair of politically charged glasses has become available for purchase. The Fundación Salvador Allende has produced replicas of Allende's glasses, in the form of a keychain, and these are sold in the art museum bookstore. Allende's glasses reveal his eyes through the lenses. They seem to represent the clear, intellectual vision of the democratic leader, and thus they contrast with Pinochet's dark glasses that attempt to hide the terror he has inflicted on the country.

Allende's keychain glasses, however, are not real. They are a replica that "stands in" for a political past. Some might even consider them to be revolutionary "kitsch," along the lines of the Ernesto "Che" Guevara T-shirts, paper dolls, magnets, mouse pads, finger puppets, and wine. Interviews with young Argentine consumers of the Che image demonstrate that many have no idea what Che represents politically. They ascribe to an image of "coolness" that has become depoliticized. One must assume that the Che image "sells" on the capitalist market only because he no longer poses a

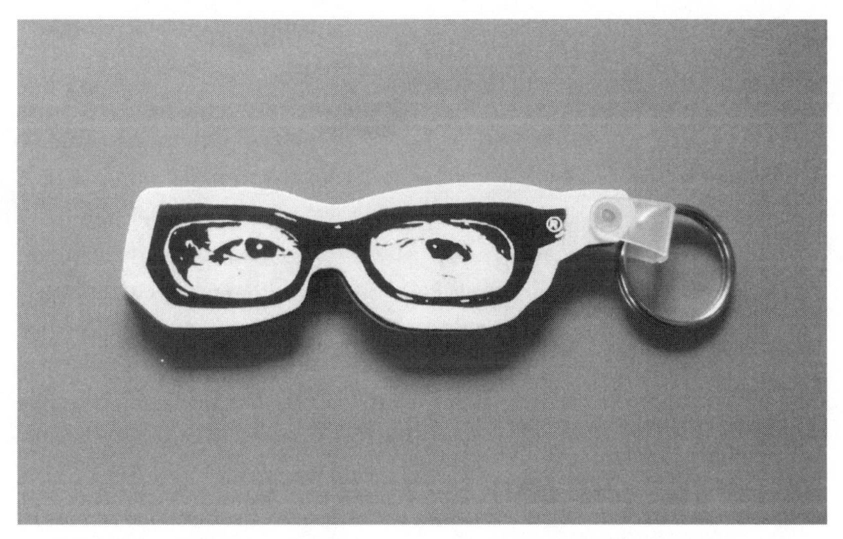

Figure 1. Allende keychain. The Museo de la Solidaridad Salvador Allende sells keychains depicting the former president through his iconic glasses. (Photography by Stephen E. Meili)

(Revolutionary Socialist) threat to that market. Thus, Allende's image may only appear on a keychain when he is no longer perceived as a threat to capitalism or democracy. Creating an Allende replica may ignore the struggle over the authentic version of the past.

Such a struggle plays out in sites of memory. The ruins of certain memory sites, like Villa Grimaldi in Chile or Club Atlético in Argentina, have been restored even when little remains of their former horror. Locating the place of horror seems more important than re-creating the experience of horror. Authenticity is valued over emotion.

Particular memory sites, however, attempt to provide both authenticity and emotion through guided tours. In their chapter, Cynthia E. Milton and María Eugenia Ulfe reflect on the importance placed on training for the guides of the Ayacucho Museo de la Memoria in Peru. The survivors of political violence have begun learning English in order to lead these tours. Laurie Beth Clark and Leigh A. Payne, however, argue in their chapter that such "authentic" experiences often increase tension and competition within the victim and survivor communities, where jealousy or resentment can be targeted at those former prisoners who lead many of these tours. To some in the community, it appears as though the guides are "selling out."

Visitors are sometimes struck by the ritualized and scripted grieving that takes place through these guides. The tour guide's identity as victim gives visitors a sense of authenticity, but ritualistic emotion sometimes strikes them as overly rehearsed, and therefore acted out rather than authentic.[53]

Ana María Shua's novel *La muerte como efecto secundario* (Death as a Side Effect) explores the tension between market demand for authenticity and the complications of supply. The Argentine writer provocatively imagines a future in which too few mothers are alive or well enough to carry out their Thursday afternoon procession around the Plaza de Mayo in Buenos Aires to demand the return of their disappeared children. The procession nonetheless remains an important tourist attraction. To accommodate tourist demand in the face of the diminished supply of authentic mothers, tour agencies press "extras" into service, who pose as mothers of the disappeared. The agencies also add additional days for the processions, in order to accommodate short-term tourists who might otherwise miss the traditional Thursday ritual. Using her narrator's voice, Shua writes: "With time [the mothers] became one more tourist attraction, like Bariloche [ski resort] or the Iguazú Falls. The tour agencies took charge of replacing with extras the mothers who were dying due to old age or illness. The processions became daily, permanent, and they were included in daytime tours and Buenos Aires at Night tours, to accommodate even those tourists who could spend only a little time in the city."[54] Shua's version does not seem too far from reality, since the numbers of mothers have dwindled but tourist enthusiasm to witness the procession remains strong. Shua suggests that tourists can be as fulfilled watching the procession forgery as with the real thing. Indeed, some of them might be happier to be able to fit the mothers' procession into their schedule.

Issues of authenticity emerge over the ownership of particular memories. Jo-Marie Burt's chapter discusses the ways in which different groups have used the memory of María Elena Moyano in Peru for different ends. Moyano's sister appropriated the story—using her authenticity as a relative of the victim—to "spin" support for Alberto Fujimori's political party. Never mind that Moyano herself rejected Fujimori's party and his government. Her sister used María Elena's death to glorify Fujimori's successful counteroffensive against Moyano's killers: the Sendero Luminoso (Shining Path). Never mind that Moyano had condemned human rights violations by both the government and Shining Path. By using her authentic and blood relation with her martyred sister, Marta Moyano employed the legitimacy of family ties to speak her truth about the past. María Elena Moyano's political allies were forced to compete with her sister's version, so as to present a different—and, in their view, more authentic—representation of the martyr's life, death, and political beliefs.

Authenticity may help promote memory goods, but it does not necessarily contribute to a political project. Brett Levinson explores the result of a testimonial by Marcia Merino, also known as Flaca Alejandra, the second-in-command in the MIR guerrilla movement in Chile. Kidnapped and tortured, Merino abandoned the MIR and became an agent of Pinochet's secret police (DINA). Her testimonial, *Mi verdad* (My Truth) attempts to explain her past and to provide information about the DINA from the inside. Chileans bought and discussed this book, and a film was made about Merino's life (*La flaca Alejandra*). Levinson contends, however, that Merino provides no new insights in her testimonial, since all of the information had already appeared in public elsewhere. Levinson's criticism of the book seems to ignore the fact that it is not simply about "exposure" to events, but rather who is exposing those events. Since so few perpetrators, or collaborators, in Merino's case, speak out, their perspective remains novel, even if the information they provide is not. Levinson also ignores the possibility that overexposure may prove less dangerous than its opposite, underexposure, or the suppression of memory and memory goods from those who experienced the past.[55]

The slogan "Never Again" illustrates the danger of overexposure. While created specifically as a way to remember not to repeat the violence of the authoritarian era, it was also used by environmentalists in Galicia in 2006 to call for an end to environmental hazards. The Galician protesters were calling for "solutions and justice." A popular song by the American singer Kelly Clarkson also uses "never again" in its refrain. Certain parts of the song's lyrics might resonate with the memory project: "Never again will I hear you . . . never again will I kiss you." But the song is not about state terror and the disappearance of young lovers. Instead, it is about a young woman convincing herself to let go of a cheating boyfriend: "Never again will I miss you, never again will I fall to you. . . . Never again will I want you, never again will I love you."[56] It is likely that the "never again" slogan was accidental or unconscious for Clarkson, and not a deliberate tribute to memory politics in Latin America. The mass marketing of memory products, in other words, may reduce their value to the specific—authentic—memory goals.

Underexposure to past atrocity, on the other hand, may make commercialization imperative in an effort to revive the "Never Again" enterprise. Susana Kaiser's work in this volume on Televisión X la Identidad, for example, demonstrates how commercial television can work at the service of memory and human rights. The project, honoring the Abuelas (Grandmothers) Plaza de Mayo, received prime-time scheduling. Rebecca J. Atencio's chapter on the Brazilian soap opera *Anos rebeldes* further suggests how audiences relive the past through commercialized versions of it. TV Globo was known for its support of the authoritarian regime, but it nonetheless promoted memory of atrocity through its mass-marketed soap opera. Young audiences took up the theme song for the television show, intended to represent a protest song from the 1960s. During the massive marches behind the impeachment of President Fernando Collor, protesters sang the *Anos rebeldes* theme song.[57] An art installation created by Marcelo Brodsky, titled *El pañol* (The Storeroom), re-created the stockroom in which the military regime stored items stolen from the houses of the disappeared. The artist had to reassure viewers that the items were not the actual items, only replicas. Yet the re-created stockroom captured the essence of the destruction of daily life by the Argentine military. In this case, replicas made sense; one would hope that if Brodsky had actually found the stolen objects that he would have returned them to their rightful owners and not stored them in an art piece. The replicas, moreover, without re-creating the actual storeroom, provided the meaning behind the installation. Similarly, the pop singers Sting and Bono never directly experienced state terrorism, and yet their songs "They Dance Alone" and "Mothers of the Disappeared" created a global understanding of Latin American atrocity. In contrast, when the Argentine popular singer Carlos "La Mona" Jiménez promoted a love song about a disappeared girlfriend, his music created controversy. As Jelin and Susana G. Kaufman write: "The author was criticized because of the style of his music (it is music to dance [*sic*], too festive, too 'popular'). He was also criticized on the grounds that he has not told such a story before, so the truthfulness of his account is questionable." Jiménez did not have the authentic experience. Instead of a memory good, Jiménez's music was seen by memory-makers, promoters, and patrons as a memory "knockoff." He had transgressed the hazy boundary between authenticity and aesthetics.[58]

The desire to identify with the "Never Again" enterprise draws in the uninitiated, who will sometimes transgress the boundaries of acceptable behavior. Those with political interests, however, will sometimes overlook these trespasses. In 2008 in Argentina, for example, President Cristina

Fernández de Kirchner failed to appear at ESMA on the anniversary of the coup of 25 March 1976, explaining that she did not want to capitalize politically on the memory of the Argentines. Yet she appeared to do so in a speech just a few days later, on 1 April. With Leon Gieco's song "La memoria" filling the Plaza de Mayo and reaching her 200,000 supporters, Kirchner led a "memory exercise." She attributed attacks on her presidency to her decision to "choose the path of the people, of human rights, and of a fair and equitable society," and she likened the farmers' protests in 2008 against her government to the military coup of 1976. Her speech won her the prized white headscarf from Asociación Madres de Plaza de Mayo leader Hebe de Bonafini. Kirchner identified herself as an authentic victim of repressive forces in Argentine society and capitalized on that identity to appeal to her supporters and condemn her opponents.[59]

Similarly, the headscarf has become an authentic emblem of the Madres de Plaza de Mayo, even though its use developed from the symbolic reproduction of the diapers their disappeared children once wore. The words written on those scarves—Aparición con vida (We want them alive)—became an authentic demand. Even when it was clear, after the end of the dictatorship, that their children would not appear alive again, the mothers continued their struggle. But issues over "payoffs" divided the group. One group of mothers considered the reparations that the democratic government offered to pay out to surviving family members a form of "blood money," as a way of paying them off without returning their children. Although they knew intellectually that they would never see their children alive again and should take the funds as some minor compensation for their loss, they could not give up the struggle, embroidered on their headscarves, that had become their mission.

Authenticity in the "Never Again" activist enterprise focuses on exposing the truth of past atrocity. Memory studies thus puts academics in conflict with activists by its effort to distinguish memory from truth and historical fact. As Folger states, "Memory is a construct, both on an individual and on a collective level, implying the inaccessibility or non-existence of 'authentic' memories." Activists, on the other hand, consider memory as the evidentiary basis of the "Never Again" memory project.[60]

Global versus Local Marketing

Implicit in the discussion about authentic and counterfeit memory goods and mass marketing versus niche marketing is the role of global and local memory-makers, promoters, and patrons. Our previous references to the music of Sting and U2 demonstrate that a highly commercialized global memory market exists. Tensions regarding La Mona Jiménez's music suggest that local memory-makers attempt to protect against commercialization and distortions by attempting to bar entrance to inauthentic representatives of human rights abuses. Competition emerges, thus, between those who promote the "Never Again" enterprise as a global human rights market, and those memory-makers and promoters who wish to keep the project focused on local issues.

Renato Ortiz describes an "international popular culture" of "collective memory made from fragments of different nations."[61] Milton and Ulfe contend in their chapter that organizers of local memory projects are building upon the tourist industry's promotion of Peru to attract international tourists to their memory sites. Following Ortiz, these tourists come from a range of different countries. Local memory entrepreneurs have responded by learning English, often before or in place of mastering Spanish, to guide tours. They have taken a development course run by Germans. And they sell the souvenirs missing from most other memory sites in the region.

Clark and Payne acknowledge the influx of international tourists to memory sites but challenge the assumption that local memory-makers always embrace their arrival. In contrast to Milton's and Ulfe's study of Peru, Clark and Payne find that local memory-makers only reluctantly, if at all, value international tourism as part of the "Never Again" memory project. The sites they studied rarely appear in commercial tour guides and often prove difficult to locate or interpret without the help of local guides. With the Chilean Villa Grimaldi and Peruvian exceptions, little effort has been made so far to accommodate non-Spanish-speaking visitors.

Moreover, some of the most innovative aspects of the memory market in Latin America are purely local and not oriented around the global market at all. The escraches and *funas* in Argentina and Chile, respectively, in attempting to "out" perpetrators by remembering their past actions, attract large numbers of the new and old generations. These could be considered a homegrown, or cottage, industry, marketed through flyers and announced in the newspapers. International visitors can participate in these activities if they happen to be in Argentina or Chile, but the events themselves are semi-spontaneous (not regularly programmed). They are sometimes available to watch on YouTube. Only Spanish speakers will understand them, however, since they do not exist in translation.[62]

Global and local "Never Again" memory enterprises may actually compete, and not just exist on parallel planes. The transitional justice industry has promoted "truth and reconciliation" commissions around the world.[63] The promotion of truth and reconciliation over justice has not resonated as well in Latin America as it did in South Africa. In the region, reconciliation is viewed as a possible outcome *after* justice is achieved, and not in place of it. At the international level, therefore, victims and survivors have participated most actively in promoting justice through the International Criminal Court, the Spanish courts, and the Inter-American Court of Human Rights.

The recipient of the Nobel Prize for Literature in 2010, Mario Vargas Llosa, has explored the transformative process of market globalization. As he states, "One of the ideals of our youth is being realized today—the disappearance of borders, the integration of the world's countries into a single system of exchange that benefits everyone, especially those who urgently need to leave underdevelopment behind." He goes on to write that disappearing borders have resulted not from socialist revolution but through capitalism and the market. He refers to this phenomenon as "the most beautiful advance in modern history because it lays the foundations for a new civilization on a global scale."[64] In addition to Latin Americans being memory-makers and promoters within their own region, if we apply Vargas Llosa's celebratory and uncritical enthusiasm regarding globalization to the memory market, we would expect one part of the global patrons of memory goods to be comprised of Latin Americans as well. No doubt, privileged Latin Americans who travel internationally might visit the Vietnam War Memorial in Washington, D.C., or Ground Zero in New York, or the Holocaust Memorial in Berlin. Indeed, following Vargas Llosa, they might be more likely to visit these sites than their own local sites of past atrocity. Their quest to think beyond borders, their search for new global identities and citizenship, the desire for cosmopolitanism and to shed underdevelopment, therefore works against expansion of the local memory market. The Diesel ad promoters seemed to adopt this level of criticism, charging Argentines with viewing the ads only through the prism of their local culture and failing to think outside their own borders to decipher a global message.

Competition between global and local markets need not necessarily exist. Some scholars contend that access to justice for past atrocities depends on linkages between local and international human rights organizations. International courts respond to local advocates for justice who have international exposure. Local advocates without those linkages are unlikely to succeed at promoting international justice, and perhaps not even local justice.[65] Generating international interest in local memory goods, therefore, increases the chances of progressing toward a human rights culture.

Closing the Deal

The notion that "time is money" complicates a conclusion to a study of the memory market. The most significant profit to be made from the memory market is illusive. It is unknowable whether human rights violations will "Never Again" occur. Not even time will tell.

By considering the roots of the term "profit" as "progress," and not an end result, we can examine what has happened to the memory market over time and as a result of changes in the economy and business climate in Latin America. Time, and the free market ideology that has spread throughout the region, have produced less than sanguine results for the memory market. The forces in favor of silence and forgetting continue to prevail, despite the time since the dictatorship. Those who have historically fought for memory against silence and forgetting are aging and dying. It is not clear what groups or individuals will continue to make and promote memory once the iconic leaders of the past are gone. Those who share a past as victims of the authoritarian regime have not always agreed on how to guide the memory enterprise. There is no consensus on how much control is necessary to protect memory goods and promote the "Never Again" goal. Disagreements arise over market strategy. Distrust of commercialization imposes limits on the expansion of the memory market to the masses at the global level. But signs that such an expansion cheapens memory goods, and alienates local patrons, reinforce that distrust. Despite these tensions, the studies in this book reveal that a memory market has successfully emerged throughout the region. A range of memory goods exist, from television shows and memorabilia (Atencio, Kaiser), to images and stories (Oquendo-Villar, Burt), to advertising and shopping malls (Bilbija, Draper), to sites for trauma tourists (Payne and Clark) in Argentina (Gates-Madsen), Chile (Collins), Mexico (Ruisánchez Serra), and Peru (Milton and Ulfe). This introductory chapter has provided the analysis of the memory-market forces that the empirical chapters develop. Alice Nelson's concluding chapter returns to the economic and political forces that have shaped that market.

NOTES

1. Williamson, "What Washington Means by Policy Reform."
2. Levinson, *Guerrilla Marketing.*
3. This refers to the November 2004 protests against President George W. Bush and the Asia-Pacific Economic Conference.
4. For a sample of this scholarly enterprise in and about Latin America, see the journal *History & Memory: Studies in Representation of the Past* (published by Indiana University Press; edited at the Eva and Marc Besen Institute for the Study of Historical Consciousness, Tel Aviv University), and Colección Memorias de la Represión, volumes 1–12 (published by the Social Science Research Council and Siglo XXI in Spain and Argentina). The Hemispheric Institute of Performance and Politics' "Encuentro" and the Latin American Studies Association conferences include memory, trauma, and post-dictatorship panels at each of their meetings. Memory events surround particular dates and places of repression, as discussed in Jelin, *Las conmemoraciones* and in Jelin and Langland, *Monumentos, memoriales y marcas territoriales*. For blogs, see http://en.wordpress.com/tag/desaparecidos. In Buenos Aires, IDES (Instituto de Desarrollo Económico y Social) includes a Núcleo de Estudios de Memoria that runs conferences and seminars with an emphasis on memory in the Southern Cone of Latin America, as well as presenting guest speakers on that subject.
5. Interview with Ana María Shua, 18 May 2008.
6. Marguerite Feitlowitz locates the origin of the phrase "Never again!" in a "Warsaw Ghetto cry," later used by the Argentine military regime, before it was reappropriated by the Argentine National Commission on the Disappeared (CONADEP) (see Feitlowitz, *A Lexicon of Terror*, 90, 269n4).
7. The English definition of "patron" includes the term "customer." In addition, the Latin etymology of *patronus* encompasses "defender, protector, and advocate" and "one who advances the cause."
8. Huyssen, *Present Pasts*, 21.
9. Ibid.
10. Ibid., 23.
11. Ibid., 25.
12. Interview with Idelber Avelar, 26 May 2008.
13. Interview with Robert Folger, 31 May 2008.
14. Menchú, *I, Rigoberta Menchú.*
15. Timerman, *Prisoner without a Name, Cell without a Number.* In 1981, Knopf translated the first edition and portions appeared in the *New Yorker.* The book was published, by El Cid, in Buenos Aires for the first time in 1982 . Stacey Alba Skar refers to the book as "one of the most widely read and translated Argentine testimonial narratives from the Dirty War" (Skar, "Jacobo Timerman's *Preso sin nombre, celda sin numero* and the Reconstructing 'I' " [paper presented at the Middle Atlantic Council of Latin American Studies: Latin American Essays, 1 April 2000]).
16. See Jelin and Langland, *Monumentos, memoriales y marcas territoriales.*

17. Borges, *Ficciones.*
18. Jelin, *Los trabajos de la memoria,* 48–49.
19. Feitlowitz, *A Lexicon of Terror,* 41–43.
20. Scott, *The Moral Economy of the Peasant.*
21. Esteban Pintos, "Todos los formatos de la memoria," *Página/12,* 23 March 2001, 24–25 (translation ours).
22. Interview with Hiber Conteris, Uruguayan novelist and former political prisoner (1976–85), 10 January 2008.
23. Noga Tarnopolsky, "The Family That Disappeared," *New Yorker,* 15 November 1999, 48–55; Stephens, "Filártiga v. Peña-Irala."
24. Interview with Idelber Avelar, 26 May 2008.
25. María Seoane, "Somos derechos y humanos: Cómo se armó la campaña," *Clarín,* 23 March 2006.
26. Benedetti, *El olvido está lleno de memoria.*
27. Payne, *Unsettling Accounts.*
28. Leigh A. Payne, "The Politics of Speech and Memory in Argentina and Chile," paper presented at the XXVII International Congress of the Latin American Studies Association, Montreal, Canada, 5–8 September 2007.
29. Interview with Robert Folger, 31 May 2008.
30. Payne, *Unsettling Accounts*; Stern, *Remembering Pinochet's Chile.*
31. Ustra, *Rompendo o silencio*; Contreras Sepúlveda, *La verdad histórica*; Contreras Sepúlveda, *La verdad histórica II*; Etchecolatz, *La otra campana del Nunca Más.*
32. Carvalho and da Silva Catela, "31 de marzo de 1964 en Brasil."
33. Contreras Sepúlveda, *La verdad histórica*; Contreras Sepúlveda, *La verdad histórica II*; Etchecolatz, *La otra campana del Nunca Más.*
34. Verbitsky, *The Flight*; Verbitsky, *Confessions of an Argentine Dirty Warrior.*
35. By doing this, the publisher is also giving an incorrect representation of the historical situation, since the term "dirty war" was coined by the dictatorship and referred to the organized Left.
36. Ustra, *Rompendo o silencio.*
37. The Argentine *Nunca Más* report sold 300,000 copies. According to Diana Taylor, thirteen editions of the report were published between November 1984 and May 1986. Taylor writes that not only did the report become an instant best seller, but that "copies of *Nunca Más* dotted the beaches as summer vacationers in swimwear read the dreadful testimonies" (Taylor, *Disappearing Acts,* 12). *Publishers' Weekly* also refers to *Uruguay Nunca Más* as a "remarkable book, a bestseller in Uruguay" (www.temple.edu). See also *Brasil: Nunca Mais* (São Paulo: Archdiocese of São Paulo, 1985); *Nunca Más: The Report of the Argentine National Commission on the Disappeared* (New York: Farrar Straus Giroux, 1986); and Servicio Paz y Justicia–Uruguay, *Uruguay Nunca Más,* trans. Elizabeth Hampsten (Philadelphia: Temple University Press, 1993). And see Weschler (*A Miracle, A Universe,* 72) for a discussion of *Brasil: Nunca Mais* and its no. 1 position for twenty-five weeks on the best-seller list, followed by nearly two years at a lower position on the same list.

38. Archdiocese of São Paulo, Jaime Wright, and Joan Dassin, *Torture in Brazil*, xiv; Ginway, "Literature under the Dictatorship," 253.
39. Bickford, "Unofficial Truth Projects," 1009.
40. Payne, *Unsettling Accounts*; Guzmán, *Romo*.
41. Feld highlights the particularly high rating for the documentary *ESMA: El día del juicio*, broadcast by Canal 13 on 24 August 1998 (Feld, *Del estrado a la pantalla*, 4).
42. Interview with Idelber Avelar, 26 May 2008. In addition, Avelar, *The Untimely Present*, discusses the writing of the five novelists: Ricardo Piglia and Tununa Mercado from Argentina, Silviano Santiago and João Gilberto Noll from Brazil, and the Chilean Diamela Eltit.
43. Interview with Kristina Stanek, 19 June 2007.
44. Fuguet, *Por favor, rebobinar*, 235.
45. Miller Klubock, "History and Memory in Neoliberal Chile."
46. Trajković, "Memorabilia and Video Games of the Post-dictatorship Period in Latin America."
47. Zazzle.com, www.zazzle.com/pd/find?qs=Pinochet.
48. "Por favor, no haga de este remate una tribuna política. Si no desea comprarlo o no simpatiza con General Pinochet, absténgase de comentar" (http://oferta.deremate.cl/id=17759677_llavero-pinochet-chileno-agradecido#).
49. http://oferta.deremate.cl/id=18808462_cartel-enlozado-11-setiembre-pinochet.
50. Berliner, "The Abuses of Memory."
51. Interview with Robert Folger, 31 May 2008.
52. Ibid.
53. Taylor, "Trauma as Durational Performance."
54. Shua, *La muerte como efecto secundario*, 102.
55. Levinson, "Dictatorship and Overexposure."
56. Kelly Clarkson, "Never Again," *My December* (album; RCA, 2007).
57. *Montecristo*, an Argentine soap opera that premiered on 25 April 2006 on the Telefe channel, enjoyed the highest ratings during its run. The story takes place in 1995, and one of the main characters, Marcos Lombardo, is an executive who was previously involved with clandestine torture centers that operated during the dictatorship.
58. Elizabeth Jelin and Susana G. Kaufman, "Layers of Memories: Twenty Years after in Argentina" (paper presented at the "Legacies of Authoritarianism: Cultural Production, Collective Trauma, and Global Justice" conference, Madison, Wisc., 3–5 April 1998).
59. President Kirchner stated, "No one should interpret the personal action of the highest state authorities as an effort to politically capitalize on the memory of all Argentines" ("El reclamo por mayor celeridad en los juicios a genocidas marcó el tono del Día de la Memoria," *Buenos Aires Económico*, 25 March 2008, 6). She is also quoted as saying, "We have chosen the path of the people, human rights, and a just and egalitarian society" ("Están acá también en defensa propia," *Página/12*, 2 April 2008, 3).

60. Interview with Robert Folger, 31 May 2008.
61. Renato Ortiz quoted in García Canclini, *Consumers and Citizens*, 44.
62. For a funa, see www.youtube.com/watch?v=nwqTWP5AXiE. For an escrache, see www.youtube.com/watch?v=yv-plu4_smo&feature=related.
63. "Mission and History," International Center for Transitional Justice, www.ictj.org/en/about/mission/.
64. Mario Vargas Llosa, "Cher Régis, tu sais aussi bien que moi . . . *Libération*," 2 December 1993, quoted in Finkielkraut, *In the Name of Humanity*, 104.
65. Sikkink and Walling, "The Impact of Human Rights Trials in Latin America."

REBECCA J. ATENCIO

A Prime Time to Remember

Memory Merchandising in Globo's *Anos Rebeldes*

On the evening of 14 July 1992, an unprecedented event took place on Brazilian television: the premiere of the first serial drama ever to portray the political violence and repression that took place under the military regime. Airing on the Globo television network, the miniseries *Anos Rebeldes* (Rebel Years) transported an estimated thirty million viewers back to the authoritarian period through the fictional story of a group of high school friends who come of age during the most repressive phase of the dictatorship and whose fates become enmeshed with the political and cultural upheavals of the era.[1] The plot revolved around two star-crossed lovers: João, a student activist whose youthful idealism eventually leads him to join the armed struggle, and Maria Lúcia, an individualist with little patience for political crusades. Not only did the drama feature a member of the resistance as its romantic lead, it also explored subjects rarely discussed before on the small screen, particularly torture and censorship.

Anos Rebeldes is one of a growing number of Brazilian *telenovelas*, miniseries, and other entertainment programs that have revisited the turbulent period of the authoritarian regime.[2] As Latin America's dictatorships recede further into the past, stories about them are increasingly becoming fodder for "must-see TV," and not just in Brazil, although the trend is most evident there.[3] Brazilian telenovelas (or *novelas*, as they are commonly referred to) and miniseries are particularly well-suited as vehicles for marketing memory because of their characteristic realism and long tradition of discussing and interpreting controversial political and social issues.[4] They serve not only as "an echo chamber . . . for public debate"[5] but also as "a central forum for the construction of the idea of nation."[6] Furthermore, by incorporating perspectives and social actors normally ignored by newscasts and other programming, novelas and miniseries have helped democratize Brazilian television, and even national culture.[7]

Even as far back as the dictatorship period, Brazilian scriptwriters—many of whom came from the political theater—found ways to explore subjects banned by government and internal censors, often by creating microcosms that served as allegories for the nation.[8] This tradition of engaged programming has only strengthened since the transition to democracy. It has also been commodified with the advent, in the early 1990s, of what the Brazilian television industry calls "social merchandising," the institutionalized practice of using telenovelas and miniseries to raise awareness about pressing social problems and issues related to public health and safety (such as domestic abuse, gun control, drug addiction, organ donation, and missing children) while boosting the broadcasting network's profile as a socially responsible corporate citizen.[9] Social merchandising applies the marketing principle of product placement (known as "merchandising" in Brazil), in which the conspicuous display or mention of a specific commercial good is deliberately woven into the plot of a telenovela or miniseries in exchange for a negotiated fee. The difference in the case of social merchandising is that the "product" being promoted is a message, issue, or behavior rather than a consumer item, and no monetary transaction takes place.

In lieu of direct financial gain, networks profit indirectly from social merchandising by boosting their public image, which translates into larger audiences and more advertising revenue. The technique thus exemplifies media scholar Jesús Martín-Barbero's assertion that Latin American telenovelas have a tendency to turn social demands into motives of profit.[10] While promoting worthy causes is certainly a noble goal, it also serves as an effective strategy for connecting with viewers as consumers.[11]

Social merchandising not only explores social problems, it also presents strategies for resolving them that can be emulated in daily life. It works by integrating a given issue into the plot or subplot of the novela or miniseries in question, thereby turning the fictional characters into credible "public-opinion-forming agents" with whom viewers can easily identify or empathize.[12] The way social merchandising is developed varies depending on whether it is to be inserted into a telenovela or a miniseries. Novelas, which typically have 180 to 200 episodes and last an average of eight months or longer, are considered relatively "open" works: only the first twenty chapters, or episodes, are taped in advance, whereas the others are written and produced while the program is on the air. As it progresses, the script of a telenovela constantly incorporates audience feedback and current events into the plot. Social merchandising in novelas must therefore remain open-ended as well, "continu[ing] as the story unfolds, perfectly integrated with the central plot and parallel threads that are developed."[13] A miniseries, although similar in basic structure, is more compact—averaging 25 installments and a run of four to six weeks—and the script for the entire program is usually written in advance, meaning that any social merchandising must be determined prior to airing. Moreover, miniseries are traditionally shown in a later time slot and target a more sophisticated audience than novelas, thus permitting "scenes of greater realism and impact."[14]

Social merchandising has proven to be an effective means of promoting public awareness about a variety of contemporary issues. In 1995, the Globo novela *Explode Coração* (Bursting Heart) launched a campaign to help real-life parents find their missing children. The parents made appearances on the program to ask the fictional characters (and viewers) for help locating their sons and daughters. By the end of the novela's run, more than seventy-five children had been successfully located.[15] When, in 2001, another Globo production, *Laços de Família* (Family Ties), chronicled the saga of Camila, a young leukemia patient in desperate need of a bone-marrow transplant, Brazil's National Cancer Institute registered a fifteen-fold increase in bone-marrow donations, a phenomenon that became known as the "Camila effect."[16] Social merchandising has even been credited with helping pass legislation. The 2003 novela *Mulheres Apaixonadas* (Women in Love), which included a subplot that dramatized the plight of older Brazilians, was praised by one senator for pressuring the congress to pass in six months a bill protecting the elderly that had previously been stalled for five years.[17] The same novela also became known for its success in raising public awareness about the national debate over gun control.

Although social merchandising is a potent tool, one must be careful not to overstate its influence on the Brazilian public: people are not just passive receptors of ideas, and television portrayals are more complex than they appear, often conveying multiple and contradictory messages that people respond to in different ways depending on what they bring to their viewing. Nonetheless, the concept provides a useful framework for analyzing the transmission or mediation of memory in Brazilian telenovelas and miniseries like *Anos Rebeldes* by illuminating how social and political messages are conveyed on commercial Brazilian television. Indeed, Globo's 1992 miniseries engaged in a kind of merchandising—a merchandising of memory—by advocating the need to remember the authoritarian past and repudiate the crimes committed by the military regime. "Memory merchandising," as defined here, is the marketing of a corrective version of a contested past in a serial television drama by using characters who act as memory agents, as well as historical or documentary elements (such as video footage and photographs, newspaper articles, music, etc.), and other devices that educate the viewer about "what really happened," or otherwise authenticate the story being told. Far from imposing a single meaning or interpretation on its "host" (the serial drama into which it is inserted), memory merchandising promotes one set of messages among the many others that are transmitted in a given novela or miniseries.

The notion of "memory merchandising" raises questions about entertainment television's suitability as a vehicle for transmitting memory: What limitations do commercial, aesthetic, and political agendas impose on how telenovelas and miniseries engage with the past? Who profits—and how—when stories of repression and violence are transformed into media spectacles for mass consumption? This chapter explores how the memory of the dictatorship was packaged in key scenes of *Anos Rebeldes*, and how the miniseries itself was marketed to the Brazilian public. The case of *Anos Rebeldes* helps shed light on how the Globo television network, known for its historic ties to the military dictatorship, has made over its image from authoritarian ally to champion of democracy and model corporate citizen.

Globo's Extreme Makeover

Globo pioneered social merchandising in Brazil, as it likes to remind its audience periodically through frequent public relations campaigns. In 2003, for instance, the network broadcast a series of self-promotional advertisements touting its role as a socially responsible corporate citizen and highlighting the success of its social merchandising under the slogan "Globo's novelas have greatly contributed to the recovery of citizenship." According to network spokesman Luís Erlanger, the purpose of the commercials was "to portray what Globo has stood for over the years," adding that "if anyone has the historical legitimacy to talk about social responsibility . . . it's Globo."[18]

Like the commercials to which he was referring, Erlanger glossed over a significant chunk of his employer's history: for the first twenty years of its existence, Globo enthusiastically supported a military regime that brutally repressed civil society with violence, censorship, and fear—a record that can hardly be construed as "socially responsible." Under its founder, the late Roberto Marinho, the network regularly extolled the regime and its projects while censoring information about the torture, murder, and political disappearance of the government's opponents.[19] Marinho justified keeping the public in the dark by declaring that censorship was "a good thing when it comes to [fighting] terrorism."[20]

Globo's complicity with the dictatorship has been well documented;[21] however, it is also important to stress that the network is not—nor has it ever been—a monolith, and that its relationship with the military governments was far more complex and dynamic than is generally acknowledged.[22] Despite its close ties to the generals, throughout much of the dictatorship period Globo hired novela writers who were known critics of the regime (many of whom came out of political theater, as previously noted) and granted them at least some degree of autonomy to express their political views using allegory. Moreover, even Marinho sometimes found himself at odds with the regime, resulting, on one occasion, in the explosion of a bomb at his private residence.[23] Still, on the whole, Globo showed a marked tendency to support, rather than to challenge or contest, the dictatorship and its abuse of power.

The military governments repaid Globo's loyalty by tacitly permitting, at least for a time, an illegal joint business venture with the Time-Life Corporation, from which the Brazilian network derived tremendous financial and technical advantages over its competitors.[24] They also granted Marinho preferential treatment in the distribution of licenses and state-funded advertising contracts.[25] By the time the military relinquished control of the government in 1985, Globo had established a virtual monopoly over the national television industry; more than twenty years later, it remains Brazil's leader in terms of audience ratings and advertising revenue, although rival networks, particularly Record, have become increasingly competitive in the past decade. Like its counterparts elsewhere in Latin America, the Globo conglomerate has been consolidated upon the popularity of its prime-time telenovelas and miniseries.[26]

The characteristic that most distinguishes the post-transition Globo from its former incarnation under the military regime is its self-appointed role as a champion of democracy and of the average Brazilian citizen. The network's transition from authoritarian ally to democratic watchdog has been gradual, taking place over a period of several years. Many Brazilian media analysts identify a 1984 scandal involving the network as a turning point in this process.[27] At the time, a nationwide campaign for direct presidential elections, known as the "Diretas Já" movement, was rapidly gaining momentum. In a period of three months, as many as ten million Brazilians participated in rallies throughout the country.[28] Despite this outpouring of public support for the movement, the administration of General João Figueiredo opposed calls for an immediate return to civilian rule. Once again, Globo sided with the government by deliberately neglecting to report on the historic protest marches in its national newscasts, even after rival networks and the print media started giving the movement broad coverage. Public support for direct elections was so overwhelming, however, that Marinho's network soon found itself mired in a major public relations disaster: viewers signaled their discontent by changing the channel, and key commercial sponsors threatened to pull their ads unless Globo reversed its policy.[29] The network subsequently shifted its support to the civilian opposition, and eventually became "a major factor in legitimating the new [democratic] regime."[30]

In its own way, *Anos Rebeldes* also constitutes a landmark in Globo's stunning transformation from authoritarian mouthpiece to advocate of democracy. By becoming the first Brazilian television network to criticize the military dictatorship openly on prime-time television in its 1992 miniseries, Globo signaled its investment in the new democratic order. It also came off as hip and global. Through *Anos Rebeldes*, Globo marketed more than just an alternative version of the past: it marketed itself.

The Merchandising of Memory in *Anos Rebeldes*

According to Gilberto Braga, creator and head scriptwriter of *Anos Rebeldes*, the miniseries was originally conceived as a vehicle for promoting the memory of the authoritarian period so as not to repeat it.[31] Although he has never explicitly referred to this intention in marketing terms, a kind of memory merchandising is evident in the development of certain characters as memory agents, and in the frequent insertion of historical and documentary elements between scenes.

The drama's passionately idealistic hero, João, is an agent of memory by virtue of the fact that he embodies the perspective of the left-wing opposition to the military dictatorship, a point of view long excluded from Brazilian television. This fictional character is modeled loosely on Alfredo Sirkis, a real-life militant and author of a memoir of youthful rebellion, *Os Carbonários,* on which the plot of *Anos Rebeldes* is also partially based.[32] Published shortly after the 1979 amnesty law, Sirkis's memoir became an instant best seller, due in part to the enthusiasm of young readers who regarded it as a bible on how to become a revolutionary. *Anos Rebeldes* capitalized on the popularity of *Os Carbonários,* but ultimately liquidated the book's cult appeal by turning it into mainstream fare. João's role as memory agent is only partial: he represents the viewpoint and experiences of the leftist militancy, but does not explicitly serve as a mouthpiece advocating the need to remember. That function is left to the other major characters in the miniseries.

The character who most fully embodies the cause of memory in *Anos Rebeldes* is Heloísa, a friend of João and Maria Lúcia who is arrested and tortured for her involvement in the armed struggle; she also happens to be the daughter of Fábio Andrade Brito, a wealthy businessperson and loyal supporter of the military regime. In one of the drama's most powerful scenes, Heloísa confronts her father with the grim reality of her detainment in a military prison. When the ever arrogant Fábio dismisses the idea that a daughter of his could have been mistreated by the government, Heloísa unbuttons her blouse and reveals the signs of torture on her breasts. Her back is turned to the camera the entire time her wounds are exposed, a strategy that maximizes the dramatic charge of the scene by leaving the extent of her injuries to the imagination of the viewer, who sees only the look of shock and horror on the father's face.[33]

From a merchandising perspective, Heloísa is an ideal memory agent: although not the romantic lead in the story, she quickly became a favorite with the audience, especially younger Brazilians, who admired the spoiled rich girl turned militant.[34] Yet her role in the merchandising of memory is also problematic. Heloísa is not just a mouthpiece for a pro–human rights message, she is also the only character who is tortured, and therefore in a sense comes to represent all torture victims. This gendering of the torture

Figure 1. Fábio (José Wilker) stares in shock at the marks of sexual torture on the body of his daughter Heloísa (Cláudia Abreu) in *Anos Rebeldes*.

victim has disturbing implications because Heloísa is also an obvious sex symbol and the only female character in the miniseries that appears in a nude love scene. By casting her as the token torture victim, *Anos Rebeldes* implicitly eroticizes torture. Moreover, Heloísa is also the most sexually liberated character in the story: she is the first to lose her virginity, has a child out of wedlock, and participates in what is portrayed as a man's war. By contrast, her male comrades in the armed struggle who take similar risks but who adhere more closely to conventional morality invariably escape harm, as if to imply that torture is justified when people step too far outside their prescribed social roles.

A less problematic memory agent is Avelar, the popular history teacher at the high school attended by the main characters. Upon learning of Heloísa's ordeal, he resolves to write a clandestine report denouncing the human rights violations committed at the behest of the military regime. As a teacher of history and someone who is universally respected within the microcosm of the miniseries, Avelar is a credible seller of the "Never Again" message. His integrity and courage are emphasized in a number of scenes in which other characters attempt to dissuade him from sending his torture exposé to a foreign journalist. These foils are portrayed as well-intentioned, but misguided: unlike Avelar, they would rather not find out what is going on in the military prisons, either because they are apathetic or because they fear the consequences of knowing too much. Avelar manages to convince them, and presumably the viewer, that "everyone needs to know . . . otherwise we'll keep on covering it up forever."[35]

Paradoxically, it is the apolitical heroine, Maria Lúcia, who delivers the most provocative line regarding torture and the government agents who made it possible; in the final chapter of the miniseries, she declares: "As far as I can recall, none of those scoundrels ever got what was coming to him."[36] This statement is the closest that *Anos Rebeldes* comes to questioning the 1979 blanket amnesty that unconditionally pardoned state perpetrators. With these words, Maria Lúcia comes to stand for the argument that even people with no interest in politics have a moral obligation to take a stand on the issue of human rights crimes. Whereas younger viewers admired Heloísa, many seemed to identify even more closely with Maria Lúcia and her aloofness from politics,[37] making the romantic heroine a particularly credible and effective memory agent.

Anos Rebeldes repudiated not only torture, but also censorship. The character who serves as the memory agent in this regard is one of João's friends, the television writer Galeno. In a scene based on one of Braga's own experiences as scriptwriter for Globo's 1976 novela *A Escrava Isaura* (The Slave Girl Isaura),[38] Galeno is summoned to Brasília to defend his latest project, also a serial drama about slavery. In the miniseries, the fictional censor, Dona Marileia, insists that the subject matter of the novela is too inflammatory for a mass audience and threatens to cancel it unless the author promises to omit the word "slave" from the remaining one hundred chapters. For Marileia, the term conjures up painful memories that most Brazilians would prefer to forget: "The very word *slave*: why put these ideas into people's heads? Why bother to remember?" When Galeno points out that all Brazilian children learn about slavery in elementary school, she retorts that it is "a page that should be ripped from the history books."[39]

Once again, *Anos Rebeldes* advocates the need to remember the mistakes of the past, this time by ridiculing those who, like Marileia, would rather forget. Yet the scene is constructed in such a way that the novela writer comes to represent commercial television (and specifically Globo, through the allusion to *A Escrava Isaura*) pitted against the authoritarian regime.

In the process, Globo's history of complicity with the dictatorship is erased and the network is deceptively portrayed as having always been on the side of memory and justice.[40] Meanwhile, other groups are not spared exposure, particularly the economic elite and the corporations that helped finance the repression, represented by the wealthy entrepreneur Fábio, who, as the plot unfolds, is revealed to be corrupt and amoral.

Memory merchandising is also evident in the insertion of historical and documentary elements such as video footage, photographs, newspaper headlines, and music into the story. These vestiges of the past presumably help educate the uninformed viewer about the authoritarian period, in addition to authenticating the corrective version of it presented in the miniseries. The documentary sequences, which show key events during the dictatorship as well as instances of everyday political violence in Brazilian streets, had a powerful impact, especially since much of the footage had never before been broadcast on national television, due to government and internal censorship. The exhibition of these images in *Anos Rebeldes* was therefore a truly historic event.

These video montages were inserted at the end of key scenes in the miniseries. In most cases, an abrupt change from color to black-and-white images clearly signals the shift between fictive and historical frames. In other instances, however, the distinction between fiction and reality is deliberately blurred by the filming of certain scenes in black and white and the doctoring of some historical footage to create the illusion that the fictional characters participated in important historical events. In one scene, for instance, the actors playing João and Maria Lúcia are shown at the front of an actual protest march from the 1960s. Although this strategy encouraged empathy with real-life student activists and militants and made memory more palatable and entertaining for a mass audience, it also undermined the function of providing hard evidence to substantiate the version of the past presented in *Anos Rebeldes*. Moreover, even the purely historical montages consist primarily of a barrage of images with little meaningful contextualization, an effect reminiscent of the "fragmented visual discourse of advertising."[41] In the most famous historical sequence, set to the upbeat theme song of the miniseries, political violence is turned into a source of titillation as disturbing images of police brutality alternate with a prolonged backside view of a woman dancing samba in a miniskirt. The sequence may very well have been intended as a nostalgic invocation of the 1960s counterculture movement known as Tropicália, which, as Christopher Dunn explains, "purposefully invoked stereotypical images of Brazil as a tropical paradise only to subvert them with pointed references to political violence and social misery."[42] But it is also likely that spectators unfamiliar with Tropicalist aesthetics, especially those from younger generations, missed the allusion. In any case, the footage and its accompanying soundtrack are so enthralling that the viewer is "suspended between shock, ecstasy, and fascination, without ever having the opportunity to think and reflect."[43]

Although *Anos Rebeldes* was the first serial drama to discuss the authoritarian period by explicitly portraying political violence and repression on prime-time television, it was not the first to engage in memory merchandising pertaining to the military dictatorship. That distinction belongs to another Globo production, the 1986 novela *Roda de Fogo* (Wheel of Fire), which presented a negative portrayal of Brazilian society during the democratic transition by featuring a cast of villains that included a former torturer, a retired general, and a pack of unscrupulous businesspersons with lingering loyalties to the ancien régime. The marketing of memory was most evident in a subplot involving the suspenseful buildup to a confrontation between Maura, a former political prisoner, and Jacinto, the man who had tortured her several years earlier.

As novelas often do, *Roda de Fogo* incorporated into its plot a significant current event hovering at the forefront of its viewers' minds at the time: not long before the drama went on the air, the public's curiosity about the authoritarian period was piqued by the publication of *Brasil Nunca Mais* (Brazil Never Again), an unauthorized report on the practice of torture under the military dictatorship, based on evidence secretly compiled under the auspices of the Archdiocese of São Paulo.[44] This explosive exposé, which became an instant best seller, definitively proved the existence of widespread, systematic torture in the country's political prisons. In several scenes, Maura appears with a copy of the volume conspicuously tucked under her arm, promoting not so much the tangible product (the bestselling book), as the cause it had come to symbolize. Many Brazilians first learned that torture had existed under the military dictatorship from watching *Roda de Fogo*,[45] demonstrating the potential of novelas to help disseminate and validate alternative versions of the past.

Repression "Lite"

As a commercial television network, Globo is motivated "above all to generate maximum revenue by attracting and selling to the broadest possible audience."[46] Indeed, all of Globo's telenovela and miniseries scripts have to be approved by the network's marketing department prior to production to ensure the marketability of the final product.[47] Commercial interests are therefore bound to impose constraints on how controversial subjects, such as the military dictatorship, are handled in its entertainment programming. Braga has acknowledged the existence of these constraints, telling a foreign journalist: "I am aware of the fact that when I sign a contract with TV Globo I am, in effect, as a person on the left, accepting limitations. . . . Within the limits of the system, I do what is possible to work for . . . change with my chosen vocation."[48]

In the case of *Anos Rebeldes*, commercial interests dictated the need to approach the authoritarian period in a way that would be perceived as neither threatening to the military nor alienating to those viewers tuning in purely for entertainment purposes. These interests, moreover, necessitated the delicate treatment of certain themes held to be politically sensitive, especially the central role played by military personnel in the political violence. The result is a diluted portrayal of the repression: repression "lite."[49] By softening harsh realities, the miniseries perpetuated the widespread conviction that the Brazilian military dictatorship was relatively benign and the repression mild, a message diametrically opposed to the one promoted through the memory merchandising just described.

The view of Brazil's military dictatorship as "lite" authoritarianism was—and still is—prevalent in mainstream culture, an extreme example being Jorge Durán's 1986 film *A Cor do Seu Destino* (The Color of Destiny). Set in Rio de Janeiro in the 1980s, the film tells the fictional story of Paulo, a teenager tormented by flashbacks of soldiers arresting and executing his older brother. Paulo's repressed traumatic memories come flooding back at the precise moment when Brazil is emerging from authoritarian rule, yet these nightmares pertain not to the Brazilian repression, but rather to the protagonist's childhood in Chile before he and his parents fled as exiles. Marketed at a Brazilian audience during the politically sensitive moment of that society's democratic transition, *A Cor do Seu Destino* vividly evokes the trauma and suffering inflicted on the Chilean people under Pinochet while completely ignoring Brazil's own authoritarian past, implying that unlike their Chilean counterparts, Brazilians can afford to forget the past because the repression they endured was relatively mild.

The myth of "repression lite" persists even today, albeit not unchallenged. In February 2009 (during the writing of this chapter), a major controversy erupted over this very issue when another of Brazil's most powerful media outlets, the *Folha de São Paulo* newspaper, referred in passing to the Brazilian military dictatorship as an example of *ditabranda* (or soft dictatorship, as opposed to a *ditadura*, or hard dictatorship) in an editorial criticizing Venezuelan president Hugo Chávez.[50] A number of prominent Brazilian scholars and activists publicly denounced the use of the term in letters to the editor, petitions, and blog postings. The newspaper's unapologetic and even hostile response to its detractors,[51] coupled with its refusal to acknowledge its own history of collaboration with the military governments, only served to fan the flames of public outrage. The controversy culminated in a protest rally in front of *Folha*'s downtown headquarters, drawing approximately two hundred former political prisoners, social activists, and students from local high schools and universities. Demonstrators gave speeches denouncing the offending term and brandished photos of the tortured, dead, and disappeared. The ditabranda controversy demonstrates that while the notion of "repression lite" still has some currency (at least in the mainstream media), it is nonetheless very much contested by both the older and younger generations.

Like Durán's film, when *Anos Rebeldes* dramatizes or makes reference to political violence, it tends to tone down harsh realities and distort established historical facts, thereby mitigating its denunciation of the repression. While the miniseries does show scenes in which the regime uses force against its enemies, it tends to understate the degree of brutality employed. In such scenes, the repression is invariably personified by the fictional character Detective Camargo, who—unarmed, in civilian clothes, and accompanied by only one or two henchmen—relentlessly pursues João and his comrades. Sirkis (the former militant on whose memoir the drama was partly based) complained that these scenes trivialized real-life repressive operations: "[Detective Camargo] in a suit, looking like a secret agent . . . it wasn't really like that. [The national security forces] acted in groups of 30 or 40 people, all well-armed, against two or three militants. An indescribable violence that Globo didn't want to show on television."[52] In other cases, the miniseries tempered its portrayal of the repression by altering established historical facts, as when it adjusted downward the number of arrests in a notorious government raid from one thousand to three hundred.[53]

The military, for its part, is all but absent from *Anos Rebeldes*, and escapes relatively unscathed from the critique of the dictatorship.[54] Sirkis notes that in depicting political violence the miniseries only shows "regular cops when in fact the operations were conducted by the military."[55] The role of repressor falls solely to the civilian Detective Camargo, whose villainous manner (accentuated by sinister music) and wardrobe (a suit and dark glasses) distinguish him from the few military officers in the miniseries. Indeed, there are only two characters, both minor, who are clearly identifiable as members of the armed forces. One is referred to only by his rank, Comandante, which is the only clue to his military identity. The Comandante wears a suit and tie, sits innocuously behind a desk, and has a kindly, almost paternal air in the lone scene in which he makes an appearance to help Fábio rescue Heloísa from prison (although the silent glare Heloísa directs at the Comandante upon leaving captivity, and her visibly deteriorated physical condition, provide an eloquent denunciation of his true character). The only other military figure in the miniseries is Capitão Rangel, who dresses in uniform but appears mostly in scenes set inside the home he shares with his wife and brother-in-law, Galeno. In one such scene, this character tries to persuade Galeno to abandon the counterculture movement out of concern for the youth's safety and future. Capitão Rangel thus further solidifies the drama's depiction of military men as benevolent father figures. Finally, there are no torturers in *Anos Rebeldes*, in spite of numerous references to torture and the moving scene with Heloísa and her father. Instead, it is as if the brutalization of political prisoners somehow occurred without perpetrators. By casting only non-military characters in the role of repressors, portraying military officers as paternal figures, and making torturers invisible, *Anos Rebeldes* carefully hewed to the commercial interests of its broadcasting network while sacrificing truth and contradicting the very message it was meant to communicate through the merchandising of memory.

Aesthetic considerations also impose significant constraints on the development of social and political themes in telenovelas and miniseries, as various television scholars have shown. Ana M. López, for one, observes that Latin American television serials tend to explore and contain national problems by recasting them as personal or familial dramas.[56] Often their plots revolve around a romantic pair or a love triangle. In period dramas, especially those like *Anos Rebeldes* that revisit a particularly discomfiting chapter of the past, the love story is usually foregrounded and the historical context is relegated to the background. Martín-Barbero notes that although telenovelas have the merit of incorporating social actors otherwise ignored by television, these characters rarely participate in the development of the plot.[57] Instead, by including them, novelas give the impression of discussing sensitive topics without actually doing so, demonstrating how purporting to talk about something can sometimes be a potent means of silencing.

The classic example of this silencing tendency is the Brazilian slavery novela of the 1970s and 1980s, which usually featured a pair of white lovers and only showed Afro-Brazilians in secondary or supporting roles. Many of these dramas reinforced the official version of history by telling the story of a white hero who single-handedly brings about abolition and by concluding with a touching scene of interracial brotherhood.[58] Slavery novelas proved to be immensely popular not only in Brazil, but also abroad, where they exported the myth of Brazil as a racial democracy. Similarly, *Anos Rebeldes*, despite its merits, perpetuated the officially sanctioned version of a tragic chapter of Brazilian history by relegating the tragedy itself to the background. In doing so, the miniseries soothed the national conscience with the message that the repression that occurred under the dictatorship was "not really that bad."

One Memory Fits All

Anos Rebeldes conveyed at least two contradictory messages about Brazil's authoritarian past: on one hand, the miniseries argued for the need to remember the crimes of the dictatorship and to remain vigilant so as not to repeat them, while on the other, it depicted the repression as relatively "gentle," implying that perhaps Brazilians could afford to forget about this unpleasant chapter of their past after all. This same ambivalence is evident in Globo's early attempts to market *Anos Rebeldes* to the Brazilian public. As will be shown in the discussion that follows, Globo aggressively promoted the drama before, during, and after it was on the air, but its marketing strategy evolved over time and eventually turned into a campaign of blatant self-promotion by the network.

In the weeks leading up to its much-anticipated premiere, *Anos Rebeldes* was featured repeatedly in newspaper and magazine articles that included statements by Braga and other participants involved in making the miniseries. These impromptu spokespeople touted the drama as a unifying narrative that would appeal to all Brazilians, evidence of what producer Denis Carvalho called Globo's "democratic spirit."[59] In an interview granted to the popular magazine *Isto É*, Braga expressed his desire to please both the military and the leftist opposition, explaining: "We used the greatest possible tenderness in portraying the characters on the right. We don't defend any particular point of view. . . . But of course we attack the dictatorship."[60] This baffling series of statements speaks to Braga's faith in the demonstrated ability of Globo's novelas and miniseries to absorb and neutralize divergent social demands;[61] it also encapsulates Globo's initial marketing strategy, the purpose of which was to attract the broadest possible audience for the miniseries.

Indeed, around the time when *Anos Rebeldes* was set to premiere, Braga and others began making overtures to the Left and the Right in an effort to "sell" the miniseries. The military was, predictably, the toughest sell. In a rare interview granted to *Folha de São Paulo*, the network's vice-president of operations, José Bonifácio de Oliveira Sobrinho (known as Boni), whose title conferred upon him conservative credentials and credibility, tried to assuage the military's fear of being demonized, describing *Anos Rebeldes* as "pure fiction, with a few historical facts thrown in to give a feel for the period." He stated categorically that the miniseries would not include any torture scenes, further reassuring this particular constituency that "*Anos Rebeldes* was never meant to document or discuss the dictatorship."[62] Instead, the executive presented the miniseries as a love story, with the authoritarian period serving only as a backdrop. According to Boni, then, the miniseries merely capitalized on the entertainment value of memory.

Left-leaning participants in the miniseries, for their part, also spoke out in an attempt to head off criticism from their end of the political spectrum. These advocates of the miniseries touted their commitment to maximizing the memory value of entertainment. Braga, a self-identified leftist, proclaimed that *Anos Rebeldes* was "against the authoritarianism and intolerance exemplified by the military dictatorship" and echoed the human rights motto "Never Again" by suggesting that the miniseries would help "so that the mistakes of the past are not repeated."[63] Nevertheless, the actor Gianfrancesco Guarnieri, who played the role of the guerrilla fighter Saviano, admonished the Left to keep its expectations realistic: "You can't expect a miniseries to be a documentary. It's a television show [and] its main objective is to reach a mainstream audience."[64] Any blame for the drama's shortcomings in transmitting memory was thereby shifted from the network (and scriptwriters) to the audience, which, Guarnieri implied, was incapable of handling the complexity of the subject matter.

In spite of these attempts to market *Anos Rebeldes* to the broadest possible audience, many viewers on both sides of the political spectrum refused to "buy" the idea of a miniseries about the military dictatorship. Some even publicly declared their intention to boycott the program altogether.[65] The much anticipated premiere elicited an immediate negative response from the armed forces, which issued a press release shortly thereafter, stating that "the present moment calls for conciliation and harmony," and insisting that "the gentle breeze of the amnesty should continue to blow."[66] The military clearly did not see *Anos Rebeldes* as conducive to "conciliation and harmony." An entity made up of retired military officers called the Independent Group denounced the program as "historically false" and threatened to send a letter of protest to various government agencies. One member took the opportunity to dispute the existence of torture under the military regime: "The miniseries says so and so was imprisoned, so and so was tortured. Yes, there were imprisonments back then, but the prisoners were no saints. . . . As for torture, I never saw it. If it did happen, it was an accident."[67]

By contrast, former militants expressed ambivalence about *Anos Rebeldes* in statements made to the press. The majority was pleased to see the authoritarian period portrayed from a perspective other than that of the military, but many were dissatisfied with how the opposition was portrayed in the drama.[68] Some were understandably suspicious of Globo because of its historic ties to the dictatorship.[69] Curiously, media reports tended to exaggerate the Left's enthusiasm for the miniseries. A headline from the *Folha de São Paulo* newspaper proclaimed that "For Ex-Militants, *Anos Rebeldes* Is Faithful," even though the accompanying article told a somewhat different story. One of those interviewed for the piece was Sirkis, who criticized the program by stating that the most authentic part of the entire miniseries was the opening credits. Another ex-militant quoted in the article praised the realistic portrayal of the 1960s cultural milieu, but failed to mention the depiction of the armed struggle, which was presumably the reason for interviewing her in the first place.[70]

Many television critics lambasted what they viewed as a caricatural portrait of the Left in *Anos Rebeldes*. Eugênio Bucci accused the miniseries of portraying the militants as "imbeciles," and concluded that it "did a disservice to the memory . . . of the Brazilian Left."[71] Luís Antônio Giron concurred that the generation of 1968 was depicted as a "band of gutless pretty boys."[72] These critics also expressed skepticism about Globo's motives for airing the program. Giron mused that *Anos Rebeldes* was less a sign that Globo had really changed than an example of the network's tendency to rewrite the past to suit its own needs.[73] A reviewer for *Isto É* wryly remarked that the network had simply figured out how to turn formerly taboo subjects like censorship, repression, and torture into a formula for high audience ratings.[74] Marcelo Coelho dismissed *Anos Rebeldes* as collective oblivion wrapped in "fancy packaging," and accused Globo of using the miniseries to absolve itself of any blame for what happened under the dictatorship.[75]

In fact, with the surfacing of reports that network executives had ordered changes to the original script, *Anos Rebeldes* had begun generating negative publicity for Globo even during the early stages of production. Several participants involved in the miniseries went on the record to dispel these rumors. Boni acknowledged that certain scenes had been "altered," but blamed commercial considerations by claiming that an excess of political content would alienate a mainstream audience. He concluded that "all of Globo's entertainment programming" was subject to internal cuts, "in accordance with . . . the network's interests."[76] Boni thus attempted to minimize the significance of the network's interference by pointing out that the practice of internal censorship was not the exception but rather the norm in the Brazilian television industry. Braga, for his part, admitted that he and co-writer Sérgio Marquês had been told to rewrite four of the most political chapters, but he insisted unconvincingly that he and Marquês "were in total agreement with the order to make the changes," adding that he was "very satisfied with how the rewritten chapters had turned out."[77]

A few weeks later, the *Jornal do Brasil* newspaper published fresh allegations that Globo executives had censored *Anos Rebeldes* to conceal "crimes against human rights committed by Brazilian military and police officers."[78] This time the accuser was Frei Betto, a respected human rights activist, and the alleged cuts pertained specifically to the documentary sequences. The next day, the same paper published a sharply worded rejoinder from filmmaker Sílvio Tendler (who created the sequences) vehemently denying the charges.[79]

The reports of internal censorship also led to speculation surrounding the possibility of additional cuts to—and even the cancellation of—*Anos*

Rebeldes. As *Isto É* reported: "No one will swear . . . that . . . freedom of expression will remain unaffected once the miniseries hits the air. Everything will depend on whether or not the network comes under pressure."[80] Another magazine, *Veja*, expressed similar doubts: "The test will be to find out whether Globo will actually see through to the end its bold move of putting in front of thirty million viewers questions hitherto limited to textbooks and newspaper articles."[81]

In addition, the allegations of network interference reignited a dormant controversy surrounding *Anos Dourados* (Golden Years), another Globo miniseries set in the gilded 1950s that had partly inspired *Anos Rebeldes* as its sequel. This earlier drama included an epilogue with clips of the main characters accompanied by a voice-over describing the eventual fate of each. Looking back from the "present day" (the mid-1980s), the narrator reveals that one character, the heroine's younger brother, was arrested during a student protest rally against the dictatorship and subsequently disappeared from a military prison. The voice-over also mentions another character, Claudinor, who built a "fine military career" by working for the army's center of intelligence, an agency notorious for its role in the repression.[82]

Globo broadcast the epilogue when the finale of *Anos Dourados* originally aired in 1986; however, when the miniseries was shown as a rerun two years later, the entire epilogue portion was deliberately suppressed. Angry viewers called the network to protest the omission, but the network persisted in censoring the epilogue in a subsequent rerun in 1990. When rumors began circulating in May 1992 that *Anos Rebeldes* had suffered similar cuts, the media pressed Globo to justify the incident involving the earlier miniseries as well. Boni obliged by explaining that in the case of *Anos Dourados* the network had simply omitted a scene that it judged "irrelevant to the plot"; he also insinuated that the epilogue had originally aired by mistake.[83] Globo censored the controversial finale yet again when *Anos Dourados* was shown as a rerun for the third time in 2005, suggesting that the dictatorship remains taboo on Brazilian television even more than twenty years after the return to democracy.

Between the harsh early reviews it received in the press and the rampant rumors of internal censorship, *Anos Rebeldes* generated significant negative publicity for Globo when it first went on the air. Moreover, the strategy of marketing the miniseries as a unifying or conciliatory narrative of Brazil's authoritarian past failed to convince key constituencies on the right and left. Paradoxically, a brewing political crisis presented a golden opportunity for Globo to retool its strategy for marketing *Anos Rebeldes*—and itself—to the Brazilian public.

Anos Rebeldes and Collorgate

Anos Rebeldes happened to air—less by coincidence than by design—at a moment when the fledgling Brazilian democracy was in crisis: two months before its premiere, corruption charges were brought against Fernando Collor de Mello, the nation's first democratically elected president in over thirty years. As so often occurs with Brazilian novelas and miniseries, fiction and reality seemed to merge temporarily: on television, *Anos Rebeldes* showed João and Maria Lúcia participating in demonstrations against the military dictatorship, while a new generation of Brazilian youth, mostly middle-class high school and university students, began taking to the streets in strikingly similar protest marches to demand Collor's impeachment. The 1992 demonstrators, who became known as the *caras-pintadas* because of their colorful face-painting, revived—and were partly inspired by—the tradition of street protest so vividly portrayed in the Globo miniseries.

The premiere of *Anos Rebeldes* was deliberately calculated to capitalize on the unfolding political crisis: its run roughly coincided with a parliamentary investigation into Collor's actions. Network executives at Globo were in such a rush to broadcast the program—after having put the project on hold for a year—that the first chapter aired before most of the remaining ones had even been taped, unheard of for a miniseries.[84] Yet, as shown in the previous section, Globo representatives initially marketed *Anos Rebeldes* as a conciliatory narrative about the authoritarian past; hardly any mention was made of Collorgate (as the crisis came to be known) when the miniseries first went on the air.[85]

In fact, much as it had done with the "Diretas Já" campaign several years earlier, the Globo network all but ignored the parliamentary investigation into the president and the growing pro-impeachment movement during their early stages, even in its national news programs. As in the past, the network was reluctant to jeopardize its alliance with a sitting administration.[86] Moreover, Collor was, in the eyes of many, the product of Globo's political machinations: according to this widely held view, the network not only propelled Collor into the national spotlight by publicizing his early crusades against corrupt state officials (or "maharajas"), it also guaranteed his successful bid for the Brazilian presidency in 1989 through the deliberate manipulation of its campaign coverage, and even certain telenovelas.[87]

As Collorgate evolved, however, so did Globo's strategy for marketing its latest miniseries. Once the investigative parliamentary committee found the president guilty of involvement in the corruption scandal in August, Globo began giving the political crisis comprehensive coverage in its prime-time national newscasts.[88] Initially, footage of the caras-pintadas and *Anos Rebeldes* were juxtaposed by a coincidence in the network's evening programming, since the miniseries was slotted after the nightly news program *Jornal Nacional*.[89] It was not long before Globo began deliberately showing clips of the two media spectacles together in an effort to package *Anos Rebeldes* as an allegory of the contemporary situation, in the process abandoning, once and for all, its failed strategy of marketing the drama as a conciliatory narrative of the authoritarian past.

Anos Rebeldes was neither conceived nor originally marketed as an allegory for Collorgate; however, as it neared the end of its run, Globo nimbly changed tack and repackaged the series in those terms. Moreover, the final episode seems designed to encourage and confirm this allegorical reading. With the jubilant return of the exiles in 1979, João and Maria Lúcia reunite and rekindle their relationship, only to end it soon after upon realizing that their priorities and worldviews are fundamentally incompatible. In the very last scene, the heroine tearfully opens a photo album and gazes nostalgically at pictures of happier times. The heart-rending breakup of the two romantic leads and this nostalgic final scene are a fitting allegory for the national mood in August 1992: a time when Brazilians, stung by the presidential corruption scandal and the seemingly unbridgeable social divisions it exposed, could not help but wistfully look back upon the founding of the New Republic in 1985—a moment so full of promise—and wonder what went wrong, how it could be that the high hopes they had invested in their new democratic order had been so quickly and cruelly dashed.[90] This ending not only captured the prevailing emotional climate in Brazil at the time, it also perfectly complemented the new interpretation of the miniseries that Globo was by now actively attempting to promote. One month after *Anos Rebeldes* went off the air, when Collor's fate was virtually sealed, Globo began airing a 75-second self-promotional advertisement highlighting its role in the pro-impeachment movement. The ad began with a scene from *Anos Rebeldes* and then switched to strikingly similar images of caras-pintadas; it also showed clips from other Globo programs criticizing Collor.[91] With this commercial, the network definitively shifted from marketing *Anos Rebeldes* to using the miniseries to market the network.

In 2003, a Globo subsidiary, Som Livre, released *Anos Rebeldes* on DVD with a bonus feature recounting the story behind the miniseries through interviews with the cast and crew. The bonus feature reinforces the interpretation of the drama as an allegory of Collorgate, describing the connection between the miniseries and the pro-impeachment movement in terms that sound strikingly similar to social merchandising. Actor Marcelo Serrano, who played João's best friend, Edgar, emphasizes the "extremely important political and didactic function" of the miniseries.[92] Malu Mader, who starred as Maria Lúcia, discusses how entertainment can be used to educate the masses and bring about real political change: "Mostly our job is to entertain people . . . but it is wonderful when we feel we're also helping people to reflect, to question the country's political situation, when we feel we're part of something important . . . that can influence the life of the country."[93] Cláudia Abreu, who drew rave reviews for her performance as Heloísa, recounts that many fans expected her to act like her character and take a leading role in the pro-impeachment campaign,[94] implying that Heloísa served as a public-opinion-forming agent not so much for memory as for student activism. The bonus feature concludes with director Denis Carvalho's description of *Anos Rebeldes* as "a work of fiction, with a historical backdrop, that culminated in the impeachment of Collor."[95]

Carvalho's claim that *Anos Rebeldes* "culminated in the impeachment of Collor" is clearly an exaggeration, but one that is not entirely unfounded. There is little doubt that *Anos Rebeldes* influenced how the caras-pintadas marketed their movement. The demonstrators appropriated the theme song of the miniseries as their unofficial anthem and carried banners with allusions to the miniseries.[96] Even their trademark face-painting appears to have been inspired by the program.[97] As a love story that modeled a viable solution (the protest march) to a real-life political crisis (Collorgate), *Anos Rebeldes* had all the makings of a modern-day "foundational fiction" for Brazil's new democracy.[98] But most scholars who have researched the subject dismiss the assumption that the Globo drama directly contributed to Collor's ouster, particularly because the pro-impeachment movement preceded the premiere of the miniseries.[99] Contrary to Globo's self-promotional version of events, then, *Anos Rebeldes* did not "make" the impeachment happen; rather, the caras-pintadas helped make the miniseries into a success after the network's original marketing strategy failed. The network capitalized on the positive publicity generated by the drama's presumed connection to the caras-pintadas to market itself as a champion of democracy and model corporate citizen. As it had done with the "Diretas Já" movement in the early 1980s, Globo once again demonstrated its ability to ride the waves of change and brand them as its own.

In December 1992 Collor was ousted from the presidential office, a historic event that signaled a triumph for democracy, if not ultimately for memory (fourteen years later Collor would win election to the Brazilian senate, the same body that had once voted to impeach him). Today, *Anos Rebeldes* is remembered more for its supposed role in helping bring down a president than for its true achievement: that of being the first serial drama ever to depict the authoritarian period on prime-time Brazilian television.

A Prime Time to Forget?

The media analyst Renato Ortiz has observed that "telenovelas . . . are not made to be remembered."[100] He was referring to the ephemerality of most television programming—at least before the age of YouTube, Tivo, and boxed DVD sets—and the dizzying speed with which one hit novela replaces another. Yet the networks that produce these novelas and miniseries do not necessarily want them to be forgotten. Indeed, Globo has made several attempts to keep *Anos Rebeldes* in the public eye over the years. In addition to the 1992 self-promotional commercial and the 2003 DVD, the Globo media conglomerate has unveiled a line of merchandise that includes an abridged version of the series on VHS, a partial soundtrack on CD and LP, and even a paperback novel that retells the entire story with a literary flourish. Globo has profited from these extremely popular spin-off products both directly (in terms of sales revenues) and indirectly (in terms of the continued publicity they bring to the network and its supposed role in the impeachment crisis).[101]

Yet these products also reveal how little the Globo conglomerate is invested in promoting the notion of "Never Again." The cover design of the CD and LP features a head shot of an elegantly dressed Maria Lúcia, whereas the book cover shows an image of romantic rivals João and Edgar. In both cases, what is promoted is the love story angle of *Anos Rebeldes*, not the memory of the dictatorship. Moreover, this commodification in the form of spin-off products has further diluted the program's human rights message:

the commercial soundtrack does not include the two most explicitly political songs from *Anos Rebeldes*, Elis Regina's "O Bêbado e o Equilibrista" and Geraldo Vandré's "Caminhando," whereas the novel glosses over the most powerful scenes from the drama, including the confrontation between Heloísa and her father. Most tellingly of all, the novel engages in a kind of "memory laundering" by ensuring that the diluted version of memory it does present cannot be traced back to its original source: the story of João, Maria Lúcia, and their friends is presented as the fictional memoir of the apolitical Edgar, completely erasing its actual origins and inspiration in the nonfiction memoir of João's real-life counterpart, the former militant Alfredo Sirkis.

The merchandising of memory, albeit an integral part of the original miniseries, is absent from the soundtrack and novel; all that remains is the portrayal of "repression lite." These spin-off products tell the same story as this chapter: *Anos Rebeldes* is a miniseries to remember, but one that ultimately did little to transmit the memory of the Brazilian military dictatorship.

NOTES

I wish to thank Leigh A. Payne, Nancy Gates-Madsen, Severino Albuquerque, Jerry Dávila, Mauro Porto, and Carmen Oquendo-Villar, all of whom provided valuable feedback on earlier drafts and helped me formulate thoughts on various aspects of this project.

1. An earlier Globo novela, *Roda de Fogo* (Wheel of Fire, 1986), set in the post-dictatorship period and including a former torture victim and her tormentor among its cast of characters, alerted the Brazilian public to past torture. Unlike *Anos Rebeldes, Roda de Fogo*, discussed later in this chapter, did not include actual images and dramatizations of the dictatorship's political violence.
2. On the Globo network as well as the miniseries *Queridos Amigos* (2008) these included the novelas *Roda de Fogo* (1986) and *Senhora do Destino* (2004). Another miniseries *Anos Dourados* (1986) briefly mentioned repression. Other kinds of programming, such as the network's popular historical crime show *Linha Direta Justiça*, have probed the dictatorship on some occasions, including two episodes of that series dedicated to the high-profile murder cases of Zuzu Angel (2003) and Vladimir Herzog (2004). *Globo Repórter*, an investigative journalism program, and *Você Decide*, which uses audience polls to determine how its stories should end, have addressed the unearthing of the remains of *desaparecidos* and the Araguaia massacre, respectively. For a discussion of these last two programs, see Barcellos, "O *Globo Repórter* sobre a Vala de Perus," and Kehl, "'Sangue no Araguaia.'"

3. In Argentina, the Telefe network telenovela *Montecristo* (2006) addressed that country's authoritarian past.
4. López, "Our Welcomed Guests: Telenovelas in Latin America," 261; Porto, "Realism and Politics in Brazilian Telenovelas," 38.
5. Mattelart and Mattelart, *The Carnival of Images*, 79.
6. Porto, "Realism and Politics in Brazilian Telenovelas," 43.
7. Porto, "Political Controversies in Brazilian TV Fiction," 355.
8. Porto, "Mass Media and Politics in Democratic Brazil," 298.
9. Prior to the early 1990s, "the social content of *telenovelas* [was] not planned by broadcast owners, advertisers, or government in a specific way" (see Straubhaar, "The Reflection of the Brazilian Political Opening in the *Telenovela* [Soap Opera], 1974–1985," 71–72).
10. Martín-Barbero, "Memory and Form in the Latin American Soap Opera," 281.
11. Machado-Borges, "Brazilian Telenovelas, Fictionalized Politics, and the Merchandising of Social Issues," 172.
12. Ruiz Schiavo, "Social Merchandising," 258.
13. Ibid., 259–60.
14. Ibid., 260.
15. Márcio Ruiz Schiavo, "Merchandising social: As telenovelas e a construção da cidadania," in Proceedings of the XXV Congresso Brasileiro de Ciências da Comunicação, Salvador, Brazil, 1–5 September 2002.
16. Rêgo, "Novelas, Novelinhas, Novelões."
17. Laura Mattos, "Personalidades aproveitam a vitrine em campanha da Globo," *Folha de São Paulo*, 21 March 2004, www1.folha.uol.com.br/folha/ilustrada/ult90u42605.shtml.
18. Laura Mattos, "Globo diz que objetivo de campanha é mostrar apoio ao social," *Folha de São Paulo*, 21 March 2004, www1.folha.uol.com.br/folha/ilustrada/ult90u42604.shtml. All translations from the Portuguese are the author's unless otherwise noted.
19. For an in-depth discussion of the symbiotic relationship between Globo and the military dictatorship, see Mattelart and Mattelart, *The Carnival of Images*, 19–35. See also Straubhaar, "The Reflection of the Brazilian Political Opening in the *Telenovela* [Soap Opera], 1974–1985," 60–72.
20. Quoted in Gaspari, *A ditadura derrotada*, 234.
21. In 1993, one year after *Anos Rebeldes* went off the air, Channel 4 in the U.K. broadcast a documentary directed by Simon Hartog entitled *Brazil: Beyond Citizen Kane* that investigated Globo's complicitous relationship with the military dictatorship and likened Marinho to the antihero of Orson Welles's classic film *Citizen Kane*. The documentary remains banned in Brazil to this day.
22. Xavier, "Lembrar para esquecer," 249.
23. Gaspari, *A ditadura encurralada*, 276–77.
24. Globo also paid off its outstanding debt to Time-Life using government loans (see Straubhaar and La Pastina, "Television and Hegemony in Brazil," 159).
25. Ibid.

26. López, "Our Welcomed Guests," 256.
27. See, e.g., Straubhaar and La Pastina, "Television and Hegemony in Brazil," 157; De Lima, "The State, Television, and Political Power in Brazil," 114; Porto, "Mass Media and Politics in Democratic Brazil," 292.
28. Porto, "Mass Media and Politics in Democratic Brazil," 292.
29. Straubhaar and La Pastina, "Television and Hegemony in Brazil," 157; Porto, "Mass Media and Politics in Democratic Brazil," 292.
30. Porto, "Mass Media and Politics in Democratic Brazil," 293.
31. Luís Antônio Giron, "Gilberto Braga restaura 'Anos de Chumbo' na Globo," *Folha de São Paulo*, 14 July 1992, sec. 4.
32. Sirkis, *Os carbonários*. Ventura, *1968*, also influenced *Anos Rebeldes*. Globo reportedly paid each author $5,000 for the rights to his book (see Sílvio Giannini, "Romance nos porões," *Veja*, 15 July 1992).
33. This scene, along with Heloísa's death scene, can be viewed on YouTube: www.youtube.com/watch?v=MYpSD1oZvuc&feature=related.
34. Caten, "1968," 59.
35. *Anos Rebeldes* (Som Livre, 2003).
36. Ibid.
37. Mauricio Stycer, "Filhos da rebeldia mostram a cara," *Folha de São Paulo*, 16 August 1992, sec. 4.
38. "Globo não é bobo," *Isto É*, 15 July 1992, 61.
39. *Anos Rebeldes* (Som Livre, 2003).
40. Xavier, *O olhar e a cena*, 160.
41. Martín-Barbero, "Memory and Form in the Latin American Soap Opera," 280.
42. Dunn, *Brutality Garden*, 3.
43. Caten, "1968," 59.
44. See Weschler, *A Miracle, A Universe*.
45. Page, *The Brazilians*, 447.
46. Straubhaar, "The Reflection of the Brazilian Political Opening in the *Telenovela* [Soap Opera], 1974–1985," 59.
47. Ortiz, Borelli, and Ramos, *Telenovela*, 131.
48. Quoted in Guillermoprieto, *The Heart That Bleeds*, 302.
49. I am indebted to Leigh Payne for suggesting the expression "repression 'lite'" for this chapter.
50. The editorial defined *ditabranda* as a label for regimes that were "born out of an institutional rupture and later preserved or instituted controlled forms of political participation and access to justice" (see "Limites a Chávez," *Folha de São Paulo*, 17 February 2009, www1.folha.uol.com.br/fsp/opiniao/fz1702200901.htm).
51. In one case, it printed the dissenting opinions of two well-respected professors from the Universidade de São Paulo, only to characterize them as "cynical and dishonest" (see "Painel do Leitor," *Folha de São Paulo*, 20 February 2009, www1.folha.uol.com.br/fsp/opiniao/fz2002200910.htm).
52. Quoted in Lobo, *Ficção e política*, 304.
53. Caten, "1968," 59.

54. Narciso Lobo notes that "the participation of the Armed Forces in the repression is still taboo in the electronic media," referring particularly to television and cinema. He cites as examples the films *Pra frente Brasil* (1982) and *O que é isso companheiro?* (1997), which dramatize political violence but show only civilian perpetrators (see Lobo, *Ficção e política*, 310–11).
55. Ibid., 304.
56. López, "Our Welcomed Guests," 261.
57. Martín-Barbero, "Memory and Form in the Latin American Soap Opera," 281.
58. Araújo, *A negação do Brasil*, 213.
59. Quoted in Marcelo Migliaccio, "Minissérie ainda está em gravação," *Folha de São Paulo*, 14 July 1992, sec. 4.
60. Quoted in "Globo não é bobo," *Isto É*, 15 July 1992.
61. López, "Our Welcomed Guests," 262.
62. Quoted in Fernando Molica, "Globo faz mudanças em *Anos Rebeldes*," *Folha de São Paulo*, 22 May 1992, sec. 4.
63. Luís Antônio Giron, "Gilberto Braga restaura 'Anos de Chumbo' na Globo," *Folha de São Paulo*, 14 July 1992, sec. 4.
64. Quoted in "Para ex-militantes, *Anos Rebeldes* é fiel," *Folha de São Paulo*, 16 July 1992, sec. 4.
65. Armando Antenore, "Militares discutem *Anos Rebeldes* no Rio," *Folha de São Paulo*, 15 July 1992, sec. 4; Mauricio Stycer, "Filhos da rebeldia mostram a cara," *Folha de São Paulo*, 16 August 1992, sec. 4.
66. "Exército divulga editorial com alusões à série *Anos Rebeldes*," *Folha de São Paulo*, 20 July 1992, sec. 4.
67. Quoted in Armando Antenore, "Militares discutem *Anos Rebeldes* no Rio," *Folha de São Paulo*, 15 July 1992, sec. 4.
68. Bucci, *O peixe morre pela boca*, 150; Lobo, *Ficção e política*, 304; Sirkis, *Os carbonários*, 31; Mauricio Stycer, "Filhos da rebeldia mostram a cara," *Folha de São Paulo*, 16 August 1992, sec. 4.
69. Mauricio Stycer, "Filhos da rebeldia mostram a cara," *Folha de São Paulo*, 16 August 1992, sec. 4.
70. "Para ex-militantes, *Anos Rebeldes* é fiel," *Folha de São Paulo*, 16 July 1992, sec. 4.
71. Eugênio Bucci, "Minissérie imbeciliza militante de esquerda," *TV Folha*, 9 August 1992.
72. Luís Antônio Giron, "Minissérie faz geração 68 parecer bando de mauricinhos desmiolados," *Folha de São Paulo*, 16 July 1992, sec. 4.
73. Ibid.
74. "Globo não é bobo," *Isto É*, 15 July 1992.
75. Marcelo Coelho, "*Anos Rebeldes* é exercício de cinismo global," *Folha de São Paulo*, 17 July 1992, sec. 4.
76. Quoted in Fernando Molica, "Globo faz mudanças em *Anos Rebeldes*," *Folha de São Paulo*, 22 May 1992, sec. 4.
77. Quoted in Luís Antônio Giron, "Gilberto Braga restaura 'Anos de Chumbo' na Globo," *Folha de São Paulo*, 14 July 1992, sec. 4.

78. Quoted in "Globo não é bobo," *Isto É*, 15 July 1992.
79. Ibid.
80. Ibid.
81. Sílvio Giannini, "Romance nos porões," *Veja*, 15 July 1992.
82. *Anos Dourados* (Som Livre, 2004).
83. Quoted in Fernando Molica, "Globo faz mudanças em *Anos Rebeldes*," *Folha de São Paulo*, 22 May 1992, sec. 4.
84. Marcelo Migliaccio, "Minissérie ainda está em gravação," *Folha de São Paulo*, 14 July 1992, sec. 4.
85. A rare exception is an article based on an interview with producer Denis Carvalho that was published the day of the premiere. See ibid.
86. Porto, "Mass Media and Politics in Democratic Brazil," 301–2.
87. See the debates in De Lima, "Brazilian Television in the 1989 Presidential Election"; Straubhaar, Olsen, and Nunes, "The Brazilian Case: Influencing the Voter"; Lins da Silva, "The Brazilian Case: Manipulation by the Media?"; Guillermoprieto, *The Heart That Bleeds*, 305–7; and Porto, "Mass Media and Politics in Democratic Brazil," 296–99.
88. Porto, "Mass Media and Politics in Democratic Brazil," 302.
89. Claúdio Cardoso de Paiva, "Crimes de paixão: Natureza selvagem, cultura e comunicação," in Biblioteca On-Line de Ciências da Comunicação, http://bocc.ubi.pt/pag/cardoso-claudio-crimes-paixao.pdf.
90. Xavier, "Lembrar para esquecer," 254.
91. Fernando Molica, "Globo vincula manifestações a *Anos Rebeldes* em anúncio," *Folha de São Paulo*, 29 September 1992, sec. 1.
92. *Anos Rebeldes* (Som Livre, 2003).
93. Ibid.
94. Ibid.
95. Ibid.
96. Christopher Dunn notes that the demonstrators' choice of protest anthem was ironic, since Veloso's "Alegria, Alegria" narrates the story of a solitary flâneur who is disengaged from political debates (see Dunn, *Brutality Garden*, 206).
97. Guillermoprieto, *The Heart That Bleeds*, 311.
98. Doris Sommer coined the term "foundational fiction" in *Foundational Fictions*. For a discussion of the Latin American telenovela as a modern foundation fiction, see Estill, "The Mexican Telenovela and Its Foundational Fictions," 169–70.
99. See, e.g., Porto, "Mass Media and Politics in Democratic Brazil," 302–3; O'Dougherty, *Consumption Intensified*, 158; Bucci, *O peixe morre*, 152–53.
100. Ortiz et al., *Telenovela*, 121.
101. The video, CD, and LP quickly sold out; the novel is currently in its tenth printing.

JO-MARIE BURT

Accounting for Murder

The Contested Narratives of the Life and Death of María Elena Moyano

On 14 February 1992, in the context of relentless insurgent attacks and car bombings, the Maoist group known as Sendero Luminoso (Shining Path) declared an armed strike in Lima, the capital city of Peru. María Elena Moyano, a prominent Afro-Peruvian community leader, decided that the time had come to openly challenge Sendero. The group had initiated a "prolonged popular war" against the Peruvian state in 1980, and its tactics included attacking leaders of Peru's democratic Left, which it viewed as an obstacle to the revolutionary conquest of power in Peru. Since 1991, Sendero Luminoso had been gaining ground in Villa El Salvador, the popular district on the southern outskirts of Lima where Moyano lived and worked, and where she was serving her first term as deputy mayor.

Moyano was especially concerned about Sendero's advances among the rank-and-file members of the different women's organizations in Villa El Salvador.[1] As co-founder and former president of the Popular Women's Federation of Villa El Salvador (FEPOMUVES), she had worked closely with many of these organizations since the mid-1980s.[2] Moyano was a frequent and vociferous critic of government austerity programs, which she saw as exacerbating poverty and inequality and fueling violence in the country. And she had organized numerous protest marches demanding greater state support for community soup kitchens, the Glass of Milk program, and other social programs. But for Sendero, organizations such as FEPOMUVES offered only palliatives to Peru's urban poor, and represented a dangerous form of revisionism that undermined the revolution.

Moyano was part of a generation of community leaders of Villa El Salvador who believed strongly in an emancipatory project of grassroots participation and local democratic governance. She, like many of her colleagues, was a member of the United Left (IU), a coalition of left-wing parties for whom Villa El Salvador was an important model of community organization and participation. For Sendero, the IU and its model communities were obstacles to the conquest of state power and needed to be eliminated or otherwise neutralized. Moreover, Sendero viewed IU leaders who had been elected into local office, like Moyano, as "agents of the state" and of "imperialism," and they were mercilessly fustigated in Sendero's newspaper, *El Diario*.

On the day of Sendero's armed strike, Moyano organized a march for peace. She sought to mobilize broad support from different political parties and social organizations in the district. By that time, fear had settled over Villa El Salvador, and only about fifty people participated in the march, a small number compared to past mobilizations. The recent history of division of the IU, and the pervasive fear that gripped Lima's residents in the context of the ongoing violence, meant that few people were willing to challenge Sendero in a head-on confrontation such as the one Moyano was proposing.

The day after the armed strike, while she was visiting a community fundraiser in Villa El Salvador with her two children, Moyano was ambushed by a Sendero hit squad. She stood before her would-be assassins, telling her children to turn the other way so that they would not see what she knew was going to be her murder. After the assassins shot her, they placed sticks of dynamite under her body, physically obliterating her in a brutal display of violence.

Subjectivity, Memory, and Politics

This chapter explores the way memory is deployed by different social and political actors to specific political ends. Scholars of memory have noted that in societies that have experienced long periods of internal conflict or state terrorism, competing and conflicting interpretations of the past vie for credibility in the public realm.[3] Memories about the past are highly subjective, and competing memories play a critical role in the constitution

Figure 1. Girl carrying María Elena Moyano's photograph at her funeral, 17 February 1992. (Photograph by Vera Lentz)

of collective understandings of past violence, as well as in the construction of present subjectivities.[4]

Scholars have also noted that memory may be deployed to press claims for truth and justice, as has been the case for victims and survivors of human rights violations and their family members. Memory may also be deployed to justify past and current political projects. The "battles of memory" are intense and contentious, as they often represent distinct conceptualizations of politics and the collective good, and subjective renderings of the meaning of past events.[5] As Steve Stern has argued in the Chilean case, people from different social sectors, with distinct political trajectories and varied personal and collective experiences, have vastly different memories of the same political events.[6]

This chapter reflects on a single individual, María Elena Moyano, and the way in which different political sectors have deployed or appropriated her memory to support quite divergent political projects and ideas. This focus on a single individual is merited for a number of reasons. María Elena Moyano is without a doubt the most well-known victim of Sendero Luminoso. She was widely hailed in the media as a heroic figure who repudiated violence, and her assassination is often cited as a turning point in the war between the Peruvian state and Sendero. At the same time, the state sought to appropriate her memory in its effort to win the hearts and minds of Peruvian citizens in the war against Sendero. President Alberto Fujimori (1990–2000) and his allies often invoked her memory to remind Peruvians of Sendero's brutality and to lend credibility to the state's counterinsurgency policy. In this packaging and marketing of Moyano's memory, her left-wing politics, as well as her outspoken criticism of state violence and of the Fujimori government's neoliberal economic policies, were erased and silenced.

This appropriation of Moyano's memory acquired special intensity in the aftermath of the 5 April 1992 coup d'état (*autogolpe*), in which Fujimori dissolved Congress, suspended the constitution, and took over the judiciary with the backing of the armed forces. Fujimori claimed such measures were necessary to combat corruption and defeat terrorism. The latter goal, in particular, had become one of Fujimori's principal objectives; he had often promised that by 1995 both Sendero and the smaller Tupac Amaru Revolutionary Movement (MRTA) would be dismantled. The autogolpe was carried out just six weeks after Moyano's murder, and she would become an important symbol in the regime's efforts to construct an image of unity between the state, the armed forces, and the *pueblo* (the people), and thereby justify its authoritarian appropriation of power.

Certain progressive groups challenged the unidimensional construction of Moyano's memory early on. Their varied interventions suggested that a deeper examination of her life and social activism revealed a woman deeply committed to progressive causes, one who was outspoken about both state and insurgent violence, as well as on the broader issues of poverty and inequality. The collapse of the Fujimori regime in 2000—after a series of corruption scandals prompted Fujimori to flee to Japan and to resign the presidency by fax—saw renewed efforts to recuperate the memory of the victims of Peru's internal armed conflict. One of the most important elements of this process was the formation, in 2001, of the Truth and Reconciliation Commission, but a multiplicity of initiatives emerged within the social and cultural realms to provide a fuller account of Peru's conflict and to give voice to the victims.[7] In this process of restoring protagonism and subjectivity to the victims of Peru's internal armed conflict, the case of María Elena Moyano was among the most prominent.

This chapter analyzes the different constructions of Moyano's persona and the political significance of her memory. It is not a linear analysis; on the contrary, diverging views of Moyano intersected in the public realm and competed with one another. Sometimes there were surprising crossovers: for example, Moyano's younger sister, Martha Moyano, initially articulated a discourse about María Elena that coincided with the progressive view of her life and death, deploying that image to criticize the Fujimori regime's human rights abuses and economic policies. A few years later, however, Martha Moyano was invited to run for the Lima city council as a member of Fujimori's political party, Cambio 90. Then, in 2000, she was elected to parliament on Fujimori's party ticket, and she is currently serving her second term as a *fujimorista* legislator. As we shall see, Martha Moyano has altered the way she represents her sister, in accordance with her own political realignment. Martha's narrative of María Elena's life now emphasizes her sister's status as a victim of Sendero, and silences her left-wing activism and ideals.

The power of this official appropriation of María Elena Moyano became evident during the judicial proceedings against Fujimori for human rights violations, which began on 10 December 2007, after he was extradited from Chile. During the trial, prominent members of Fujimori's political party (primarily Martha Moyano), members of the armed forces (also on trial for human rights violations), and even Fujimori himself invoked María Elena's memory in an effort to bolster Fujimori's image as the nation's savior. Given the fact that this discourse had been challenged from diverse sectors—political, social, and cultural—in the years since María Elena Moyano's death, it was striking to see it being resurrected to construct and reinforce an image of Fujimori as the president who had defeated terrorism, and to justify the human rights violations for which he was standing trial as merely the inevitable, if lamentable, social cost of war. Murder was justified if it was done in the name of defeating terrorism, and to avenge the deaths of activists like María Elena Moyano.

Constructing Memories I: The Figure of María Elena Moyano in the Context of War

María Elena Moyano became an iconic figure in the weeks following her assassination. Peru's internal conflict was at its height, and the battle over the meaning of her life and death acquired special intensity in the context of Sendero Luminoso's efforts to seduce the urban poor to its cause, and the state's equally intense efforts to win the "hearts and minds" of the urban poor. Both the state and Sendero sought to cast an image of Moyano that best suited their own political purposes. Sendero portrayed her as an enemy of the revolution, and repeated unsubstantiated charges against her in order to discredit her and the political project she represented, and of course to justify her murder. The state highlighted only her principled stance against Sendero Luminoso, silencing her critique of Fujimori's economic and social policies and of state repression. Before analyzing these constructions of Moyano's memory, it is important to examine how her murder impacted Peruvian society on a broader cultural level, since this facilitated the state's ability to produce an image of Moyano almost exclusively as a victim, erasing her political beliefs and affiliations in order to deploy her memory to legitimize the Fujimori regime's authoritarian political project.

The Media and Memory

The murder of María Elena Moyano shocked Peru. She was one of the few grassroots leaders who had gained national recognition, largely because of her outspoken defiance of Sendero Luminoso. She was celebrated by the local press, and was often invited to give interviews on television and in the print media. In one exchange on the late-night Sunday news program *La Revista Dominical*, in September 1991, Moyano sat on a panel with a left-wing politician and a retired army general, debating how state and society could unify their efforts to combat Sendero.[8] (In a country as hierarchically segmented along race and class lines as Peru, it is worth noting how remarkable it was for a working-class Afro-Peruvian woman to be debating head-to-head with a middle-class politician and a general.) Moyano described Sendero's efforts to infiltrate women's organizations in Lima's shantytowns, and denounced its attacks against the leaders of such organizations.[9] The conservative newspaper *Expreso* ran a column the day after the broadcast: "The person who made the greatest impression with her declarations was Ms. Moyano, who described the ongoing struggle in the shantytown—infiltrated by Sendero Luminoso—and among the popular organizations, mainly the women's organizations."[10]

Indeed, the media paid very close attention to Moyano and her efforts. A march she organized in mid-September received front-page billing in the state-owned newspaper, *El Peruano*.[11] The slogan of the march—"Organized Women Reject Hunger and Terror"—reflected Moyano's efforts to stake out a middle ground between state and insurgent violence, and to highlight the neoliberal economic policies she considered to be the underlying cause of social conflict in Peru.[12] She continued these efforts from her post as deputy mayor of Villa El Salvador, co-founding the Commission for Peace and Development, which sought to unite key sectors in the district, including the municipal government, progressive political parties, the Catholic Church, local NGOs, and community organizations, to develop an integral strategy to counter Sendero's growing presence in the district.[13] In November 1991, Moyano was invited to speak at the Annual Conference of Executives (CADE), another remarkable sign of her national transcendence. "We cannot combat terror," she told the executives in the room, "if we do not also combat the people's hunger."[14]

So well known had she become that by the end of 1991 the progressive daily *La República* named her "Person of the Year," and the influential weekly magazine *Caretas* ran a major story about her. Invoking the name of a play by Bertolt Brecht, *Caretas* hailed Moyano as "Mother Courage" for her defense of the poor in the face of hunger and political violence—a moniker that stuck and was used often to refer to her, even after her death. Yet as her friends and colleagues noted after her murder, despite the extensive media coverage, Moyano was very much alone in her determined but quixotic campaign to challenge political violence on the part of both Sendero and the armed forces.[15]

The assassination of María Elena Moyano was widely repudiated domestically and internationally. Media coverage emphasized Moyano's community activism and her courage in the face of Sendero's threats. Progressive media highlighted the failure of the government to protect Moyano adequately, given the intensity of the threats against her. But the primary image was of Moyano as a martyr who gave her life in the struggle against Sendero Luminoso,[16] as evident in the headlines of *La República* the day following her murder: "They shot her, they dynamited her body, but they cannot kill her! María Elena Moyano continues fighting for peace!"[17] Media coverage of Moyano's funeral depicted her as a victim whose murder unified society against terrorism: "Multitude repudiates Sendero Luminoso and demands peace and life: Your death unites us against terrorism."[18] These claims of unity were largely illusory: even as her murder was repudiated by broad sectors of Peruvian society, and by the domestic and international media, its intended effect of instilling fear among grassroots activists had been largely achieved.[19] Moreover, just a few weeks after her murder, Fujimori announced his autogolpe, which was followed by a massive crackdown and the imposition of martial law.

The autogolpe was part of a broader project to reorganize state power, centralize control in the hands of the Executive and the armed forces, and restructure state-society relations.[20] In the discourse developed by Fujimori and his associates to justify this authoritarian reconstitution of the state, it was democracy, political parties, and "traditional" politicians that were vilified, while the (presumed) new unity between the president, the armed forces, and the "pueblo" was portrayed as the only real solution to Peru's economic, political, and social problems. The production of an image of María Elena Moyano as an emblematic victim of Sendero Luminoso would play an important role in the construction of this discourse.

Moyano as Emblematic Victim of Sendero Luminoso

The media's portrayal of Moyano as a heroine and martyr was quickly appropriated by the Fujimori regime, especially after the 5 April autogolpe. As the official discourse took shape, Moyano was portrayed as an exemplary community leader who stood up to Sendero and whose sacrifice was incontrovertible proof that the insurgents were repudiated by the people. As Fujimori noted in his 28 July "Message to the Nation": "Sendero Luminoso is moving away from society, and the people are increasingly rejecting them. The cowardly murder of Mrs. Moyano can be explained only by the terrorists' lack of coherence. Their mistake has generated the organized resistance of the people of Villa El Salvador, the people whom Sendero Luminoso wants to subdue with brutal killings."[21]

Fujimori went on to describe his government's new counterinsurgency strategy. Just as the *rondas campesinas* (peasant defense patrols) were presented as evidence of a new alliance between the state and rural peasants in the battle against Sendero, Moyano now became the stand-in figure for the state's new relationship with the urban poor. Moyano's left-wing activism, her critique of the Fujimori regime's economic and social policies, and her denunciation of state violence were erased in this selective account of her life.

In this same speech, Fujimori announced that he was convoking elections for a new unicameral Congress, which would draft a new constitution. This was in response to sharp international criticism of the autogolpe carried out a few months earlier. New congressional elections were indeed held later that year, and a new Constitution was approved in late 1993. Nevertheless, these institutions remained subordinated to the authoritarian project Fujimori and his associates had set in motion. The regime's discourse sought to link popular rejection of Sendero as coterminous with support for Fujimori and his authoritarian political project. In this vein, Moyano would become more than just a victim: the regime would construct an image of her as a key ally in the war against Sendero. This was exemplified by the words of the commander-in-chief of the Peruvian armed forces, General Nicolás Hermoza Ríos, who asserted that Moyano had been "one of the best generals in the war against subversion."[22]

Sendero's top leader, Abimael Guzmán, was arrested on 12 September 1992. In a message to the nation two days later, Fujimori again invoked Moyano's memory: "This is Abimael the exterminator. . . . We are facing a monster. This is the man who, with truly inhuman coldness, ordered the crime against Mrs. Moyano and the massacre of Tarata Street [a car bomb detonated in Miraflores, a residential middle-class district of Lima, in July 1992, killing twenty-two people and wounding over a hundred more]. This is the man who often ordered suicidal incursions into villages and peasant towns, where men and women were beheaded and mutilated."[23] Fujimori's discourse abides no middle ground. There are only two sides in this conflict—Sendero and the state—a dichotomization that facilitated the repositioning of Moyano as an ally of the state against Sendero.

Fujimori and his allies continued to invoke Moyano's memory to validate the authoritarian project they were seeking to consolidate, as close Fujimori associate and president of the Congress Jaime Yoshiyama did at the opening session of the newly elected Congress on 30 December 1992: "I have learned many important things. . . . One of them is that we cannot forget the examples set by popular leaders such as María Elena Moyano, who could not be intimidated. They could not be intimidated by the violence of the genocide of terrorism [*sic*]."[24] Yoshiyama was deploying Moyano's image to give legitimacy to an institution that was created primarily to assuage international critics of the autogolpe, and that would remain a faithful executor of the regime's authoritarian project for the rest of the decade.

The Fujimori regime sought to appropriate the memory of María Elena Moyano, a potent symbol in the battle for hearts and minds being waged in the context of the war against Sendero Luminoso. The official portrayal of Moyano focused exclusively on her well-publicized rejection of Sendero, with no mention of her equally impassioned repudiation of government violence,[25] or of her critique of the regime's neoliberal economic program, which she viewed as the root cause of violence in Peru.[26] The regime's spin doctors also sought to represent Moyano as having participated in state initiatives to defeat Sendero Luminoso, including civic action programs with the armed forces. This is inconsistent with Moyano's political practice and, based on numerous interviews with Moyano's colleagues, seems to represent the intentions of the state rather than what actually occurred.[27]

Sendero's Spin on Moyano

Sendero Luminoso similarly constructed its own image of María Elena Moyano: it portrayed her as a state collaborator and a member of the revisionist Left, an enemy of the revolution whose betrayal must be paid in blood. *El Diario* frequently published invectives against Moyano and other left-wing community leaders and politicians. Three years before her murder, *El Diario* published an article that accused Moyano and her colleagues in Villa El Salvador of being "opportunists" and "revisionists" whose policies "castrate the combativeness and the revolutionary potential of the masses."[28] In 1991, *El Diario* accused Moyano and other left-wing mayors and deputy mayors of popular districts in Lima of corruption and of "working against the Maoist revolution."[29] Flyers circulated in Villa El Salvador making similar claims.

In mid-1991, a bomb exploded at one of the food warehouses maintained by FEPOMUVES to stock the community soup kitchens, destroying the building and much of the stored provisions. Moyano and others immediately blamed Sendero for the bombing; a year earlier, *El Diario* explicitly attacked Moyano and FEPOMUVES, accusing them of serving as a "buffer" for the existing political and economic system by providing palliatives rather than authentic social change for the masses.[30] Sendero, however, circulated flyers accusing Moyano of having orchestrated the bombing, presumably to cover up acts of corruption within FEPOMUVES. No evidence was provided to support these claims, which seemed contrived to discredit Moyano and to justify her subsequent murder. Moyano countered with a public letter of her own, noting, "I could never destroy what I have built with my own hands."[31]

In the days following Moyano's assassination, Sendero circulated pamphlets in Villa El Salvador claiming authorship of her murder and outlining the reasons why the party had decided to "punish" her. *El Diario* published an extensive article as well, accusing Moyano of corruption and of collaborating with the state and the armed forces: "The people charged Moyano with serious crimes for many years. She has been denounced by local people for misappropriating the funds of the charity programs intended for the relief of the hungry. . . . Was the regime's 'Mother Courage' an honest 'activist' helping self-organization of the masses? No. Moyano was openly working to transform charity and the people's self-help organizations into networks of informants and armed death squads."[32]

The accusation about organizing urban defense patrols played upon local mistrust of the military and sought to discredit Moyano's leadership. In a 1991 interview, Moyano explained that the patrols had a long history in Villa El Salvador—a community with minimal state presence, where neighbors worked together patrolling the streets to prevent theft and other types of crime from overtaking their communities. She also stated that the patrols would be autonomous from the armed forces.[33] Sendero also accused Moyano of silencing her opponents by snitching on them to government authorities, and blamed her for fingering more than a dozen Sendero militants who allegedly had been subsequently arrested.[34]

It is important to point out that Sendero rarely went to such great lengths to justify its practice of "selective assassination." They did so in the case of María Elena Moyano in response to the widespread repudiation of Moyano's murder in the local and international media, and because of the need to present a revolutionary "justification" for the decision to assassinate her. Sendero provided no evidence to support these claims, which Moyano herself had challenged six months before her murder: "[Sendero] accuses me of being allied with the government and with the armed forces. You are witnesses to the fact that, even as a young leader, I always fought against governments that oppressed the people. I also denounced human rights violations (genocide in the prisons, searches, paramilitary groups)."[35]

Constructing Memories II: Reclaiming Moyano's Memory

Progressive activists, intellectuals, and the media challenged the unidimensional images of María Elena Moyano crafted and disseminated by the state and Sendero Luminoso. A series of initiatives sought to reclaim what these sectors viewed to be the true meaning of her identity and her life, especially after the arrest of Sendero's top leaders in late 1992 and its structural implosion by mid-1995. These efforts have been heterogeneous, multiple, uncoordinated, nonlinear, and pluralistic. They emerged on numerous fronts, including in Villa El Salvador, where Moyano lived and worked as a community activist and municipal authority until her death in 1992. The efforts include memorials, the production of written and audio material about her life in print and online, artistic renditions of Moyano's life and political praxis, and other forms of commemoration. After the collapse of the Fujimori regime in late 2000, these efforts took on new meaning, reflecting what one of Moyano's close friends and fellow community activist terms "rescatando la memoria de María Elena."[36]

María Elena Moyano: Progressive Activist, Popular Feminist

Left-wing politicians who were close to María Elena, such as the former mayor of Villa El Salvador, Michel Azcueta, and feminist intellectuals such as Virginia Vargas, were among the first to articulate an image of Moyano that emphasized her left-wing activism, community leadership, women's rights activism, feminism, and maternal role. Each of their portrayals claimed to reflect a true image of her life, while placing emphasis on different aspects of that life. Azcueta, for example, emphasized Moyano's role as a left-wing activist who had worked on behalf of women, but not necessarily her role as a feminist. Feminists, on the other hand, recognized her progressive politics, but their main focus was on Moyano as a "popular feminist."[37]

Feminist activist Diana Miloslavich, a close friend of Moyano's, published an important collection of Moyano's writings, poems, and public interviews that highlighted her feminist ideas but also reflected her political and social struggles as a community leader and as a member of the United Left.[38] Both Vargas and Miloslavich were members of the feminist collective Flora Tristán, which worked closely with women from poor urban communities in Lima and elsewhere. They had struggled to link middle-class, professional feminists and NGOs with women from the popular sector such as Moyano. Her memory provided an opportunity to highlight her life and struggle as the essence of "popular feminism," and to advance the feminist ideas that they had promoted for years among poor Peruvian women.

The Curious Case of Martha Moyano

María Elena's sister, Martha Moyano, became an important early advocate of reclaiming her sister's memory and restoring to it her progressive political ideals and praxis. In 1993 she founded the Fundación María Elena Moyano, an NGO designed to promote progressive alternatives locally and nationally. Martha became president of the Fundación, with her sister's close friends and colleagues on its board of directors. Honorary members of the board included former U.N. general secretary Javier Pérez de Cuellar and indigenous rights activist Rigoberta Menchú.[39]

Martha Moyano appeared to be following in her sister's footsteps, vocally criticizing the Fujimori regime's political, economic, and social policies. During the April 1993 inaugural ceremony of the creation of the Fundación, for example, she admonished the government for its failure to address the "underlying social tensions caused by hunger and unemployment," and asserted that only by doing so could the government truly eliminate terrorism in Peru.[40] Otherwise, she asserted, "there will be no solution, because Sendero Luminoso exploits hunger, misery, the lack of work, to recruit people to its ranks. When there are concrete alternatives, the subversives will have very little space to grow."[41] She also criticized the government's counterinsurgency policies for failing to respect human rights.

Martha Moyano directly asserted that these ideas were in line with those of her sister María Elena: "She and I had our differences, but in the matters that count, I know that we are in agreement."[42] She cited a poem her sister had penned about the meaning of revolution: "Revolution is the affirmation of life, of individual and collective dignity . . . It is the struggle for a life based on justice, dignity, and solidarity." And then added, "We want this legacy to be the source of inspiration for our work."[43]

The Fundación organized a series of discussions among left-wing community activists in Villa El Salvador to rebuild local progressive alternatives and began working with the Women's Federation, FEPOMUVES, on women's issues in the district.[44] Moyano continued her criticism of the Fujimori regime for its clientelistic policies, charging that his government only provided assistance to community soup kitchens affiliated with his political party, Cambio 90.[45] On 15 February 1994, the second anniversary of her sister's murder, Moyano led a pilgrimage to María Elena's gravesite. Local human rights and FEPOMUVES leaders accompanied her. In her public speech, she again laid claim to her sister's example as someone whose commitment to social change could inspire new generations in the struggle for justice: "We must always keep alive María Elena's example."[46]

Moyano also used this opportunity to press for human rights and to criticize the government's counterinsurgency practices. At that time, Peru was riveted by revelations of the forced disappearance, torture, and murder of nine students and a university professor from La Cantuta University by a government death squad. The students and professor had been abducted in July 1992, but it was not until nearly a year later, when the partial remains of their bodies were discovered, that opposition leaders, human rights groups, and relatives of the victims began to pressure the government to investigate and punish those responsible. Moyano allied herself with these efforts, invoking her sister's memory to support her position: "María Elena always raised her voice in protest against those who violated justice. I am certain that she would have already initiated a march to protest about the Cantuta case."[47]

It thus surprised many local and national observers when, in 1995, Moyano agreed to run for the Lima city council as a candidate of Fujimori's party, Cambio 90. In 2000, Martha Moyano was elected to Congress on the Fujimori ticket, and she was elected to a second term in 2006. In this new role, Moyano became one of the most ardent public supporters of Fujimori (who, let us not forget, fled the country in 2000 to avoid corruption and other criminal charges). During her first congressional term, Moyano worked with other legislators to have her sister officially proclaimed a national heroine—the first civilian to receive such an honor, and the *only* victim of Peru's internal armed conflict to be proclaimed a national hero.[48]

In an interview in 2009, Martha Moyano asserted that her motive for joining Fujimori's party was to continue promoting the memory of her sister: "I accepted because it was an opportunity for me . . . to continue speaking about the memory of María Elena. So, I accepted Fujimori's proposal for this reason. . . . It was so that her murder would not remain unpunished. It was so the world would know that Sendero Luminoso was a band of criminal terrorists, and not guerrillas, as people call them now."[49]

Moyano acknowledges the central role of her sister's image in her political career, but she asserts that her decision to join Fujimori's party was based on her desire to promote her sister's memory. She did achieve this objective by advocating to have her sister named a national heroine, and by having her story included in primary school textbooks alongside the stories of other national heroes. Yet it is clear that in many ways Martha Moyano owes her political career to her willingness to recraft her own narrative about her sister's life and death. Her alliance with Fujimori required a shift in her discourse about the meaning of her sister's life, one that silenced María Elena's left-wing activism and ideas, and highlighted her victimization. One could say Martha Moyano rebranded her sister's image in order to market herself as a politician. We will return to this complicated relationship below in the discussion of the Fujimori trial, when Martha Moyano deployed her sister's memory to defend Fujimori and discredit the judicial proceedings against him.

Popular Culture and Memory

The meaning of María Elena Moyano's life has been extensively explored at the level of popular culture, particularly since the end of the Fujimori regime. An early initiative was the film produced in 1998 by filmmaker Alberto Durand entitled *Coraje* (Courage), a direct reference to the "Mother Courage" image of Moyano that had circulated since before her murder. *Courage* is a feature-length film that dramatizes María Elena Moyano's life and death through a linear narrative, beginning with her early social work in Villa El Salvador, continuing with her emergence as a community leader (in particular, her work with women in the important community kitchen movement in Lima) and her efforts to stop Sendero Luminoso's advance in Villa, and ending with her murder. While the film attempts to convey the complexity of Moyano's life—including an impassioned sex scene—no mention is made of her political affiliation or of the fact that when she was killed she was deputy mayor of Villa El Salvador.

Courage was screened at the Human Rights Watch Film Festival in New York City in 1999. During a question-and-answer session with the director following the screening, I asked Durand why the film does not mention Moyano's militancy in the IU, or the fact that she was not just a community leader but deputy mayor of Villa El Salvador at the time of her death. His answer, interestingly, was that the film had to leave out "certain truths" so that the "real truth" could be revealed. Her political activism was deemed, somehow, unimportant, or perhaps too controversial, to be included in the biopic of her life. The result is a sanitized version of Moyano's life that purposely depoliticizes her history because it complicates the narrative of her status as victim. Moreover, although the film makes reference to Moyano's criticism of state violence, this is mentioned only in passing, the primary emphasis being on her opposition to Sendero Luminoso. The film thus reproduces and reinforces a unidimensional image of María Elena Moyano as an emblematic victim of Sendero, erasing her leftist politics and her pointed critique of state violence and neoliberalism—which is, ironically, the very image of her that the state has promoted.

Truth-Telling and Memory

After the collapse of the Fujimori regime, a transitional government led by opposition legislator Valentín Paniagua took power. In June 2001, Paniagua created the Truth and Reconciliation Commission (CVR), an official state

Figure 2. "I too am a victim," Congresswoman Martha Moyano tells the press on the first day of the Fujimori trial. Behind her is an image of her sister, María Elena Moyano, killed by Shining Path in 1992. (Photograph courtesy Canal N)

body tasked with investigating the causes and consequences of political violence in Peru, and with developing recommendations so that such atrocities will never again recur. The CVR dedicated a chapter of its *Final Report* to Moyano and another female community leader, Pascuala Rosado, also assassinated by Sendero (in 1996).[50] During its investigations, the CVR organized a series of public hearings, one of which was dedicated to María Elena Moyano. Ester Flores, the president of the FEPOMUVES at the time of Moyano's murder, gave a powerful statement about Moyano's life, the context in which she was killed, and the effects of her murder on the community.[51] The CVR also included an important memorial to Moyano in its photography exhibit about the political violence, titled "Yuyanapaq," which was displayed temporarily at the Rivera Agüero mansion in Chorrillos and is currently on view at the Museum of the Nation.

The original exhibit organized and curated by the CVR dedicated an entire room to María Elena Moyano, a deeply emotional experience that emphasizes Moyano's humanity. The exhibit featured several photographs of Moyano, including a larger-than-life image of her nursing her young son. The exhibit also featured looped audio recordings of Moyano speaking about her work and life. While there are images of Moyano's political activism (including the iconic image of Moyano at a public protest march speaking through a bullhorn), and the audio recordings make reference to her political work and convictions, the overall focus is on her status as a woman, mother, and victim.

María Elena Moyano has been widely commemorated in Villa El Salvador, where she lived and worked. The municipal government has named streets, plazas, and schools after her, and a statue was erected to honor her memory just a few years after her murder. Yearly commemorations are held in Villa on the anniversary of her death, to remember her life and example; these include nightly vigils on the eve of the anniversary of her murder, followed by a walk to her gravesite, and a mass the following day.[52] These commemorations provide an opportunity for Moyano's colleagues to challenge the image of her as a victim, and to remember her as a community activist who was deeply committed to social change, an active member of the legal Left that aspired to construct in Villa and other places an alternative society. As Villa's former mayor, Michel Azcueta, said at the fifteenth anniversary commemoration of her murder: "By killing María Elena Moyano, Sendero wanted to destroy the experience of order and organization that existed here [in Villa El Salvador], a popular experience that was distinct from the order that the military and Fujimori [wanted to impose]."[53] Moyano's colleagues, aided by solidarity communities in Spain and Italy, have also developed a website about Villa El Salvador that features Moyano prominently and seeks to reclaim her identity as a progressive grassroots activist and leader.[54]

Such efforts to remember and reclaim Moyano's memory as a figure of the progressive Left and as an activist for peace and social justice challenge the memories of Moyano spun by the state and by Sendero Luminoso. As Jelin has noted, memory is often deployed to construct meaning and understanding, and this process of signification and interpretation takes place at the symbolic and subjective levels.[55] In this sense, the initiatives spearheaded by colleagues and friends of Moyano in Villa El Salvador, in the Left, and in feminist organizations—and even at the level of the state and popular culture—represent an effort to reclaim the meaning of her life by pointing to her social and political activism, her praxis of nonviolent social change, and her rejection of state *and* insurgent violence. Together they constitute an effort to construct new meanings and identities based on the progressive ideals Moyano held in favor of peace and social justice.

Contested Memories: María Elena Moyano and Fujimori's Trial

Memory is contested and contentious. The construction and deployment of memory is never a linear process, and quite different memories of specific historical figures may acquire special significance for a variety of reasons. This became very clear in the context of renewed efforts to achieve truth and justice for past human rights violations in Peru, which has led to dozens of trials against state agents accused of violating human rights during Peru's internal armed conflict. In the most prominent of these—the trial of former president Fujimori—the memory of María Elena Moyano has resurfaced in surprising ways.

The Trial of Alberto Fujimori

Fujimori fled Peru in November 2000 amid a series of corruption scandals, bringing to an inglorious end his ten-year rule. He was granted citizenship in Japan, and Tokyo ignored the Peruvian government's requests to extradite him. Fujimori left his safe haven in September 2005 for Chile, presumably to launch his political comeback in Peru's presidential elections the following year. Instead, he was arrested and, two years later, extradited to Peru. His first trial began on 10 December 2007.

In this trial, Fujimori was charged with aggravated murder, assault, and kidnapping in four cases: the Barrios Altos massacre of 1991, in which fifteen people were killed and four gravely wounded; the disappearance and later killing of nine students and a professor from La Cantuta University in 1992; and the kidnapping of journalist Gustavo Gorriti and businessman Samuel Dyer in the aftermath of the April 1992 autogolpe. After sixteen months of public sessions, the Special Criminal Court of the Peruvian Supreme Court found Fujimori guilty of all counts and sentenced him to twenty-five years in prison.[56] The verdict and sentence were upheld on appeal. Fujimori has also been found guilty of several counts of corruption and abuse of authority.[57]

The trial scrutinized the Fujimori regime, reigniting dormant debates about national security, counterinsurgency, and human rights. As the trial unfolded, the figure of María Elena Moyano was newly deployed by Fujimori and his allies in an effort to remind Peruvians of Sendero's brutality, as well as to bolster Fujimori's image as the savior of Peru and to discredit the proceedings against him. Moyano's image was again being deployed not merely to construct meaning (though this is part of it), but primarily to justify an authoritarian project and to exculpate state authorities, including former president Fujimori, from wrongdoing in the context of Peru's internal conflict. In this sense, the memory of María Elena Moyano is being woven into a narrative that has a very specific political objective: the exoneration of Fujimori and the political survival of his party. Most paradoxically, it is María Elena's sister, Martha Moyano, who is one of the leading voices in this effort to reconstitute the image of Moyano as a victim of Sendero in the service of *fujimorismo*.

Family Members and Victimhood

On the first day of the Fujimori trial, a large tour bus carried the human rights lawyers and activists, survivors and family members of victims, and international observers to the special forces police base in the dusty, working-class district of Ate-Vitarte where Fujimori was imprisoned and where the proceedings against him were being held. At the entrance to the base, a small but strident group of Fujimori supporters had gathered, their faces painted orange to symbolize their solidarity with the former president. Martha Moyano was directing the protesters. As noted earlier, Martha Moyano has become a prominent face of the Fujimori movement in Peru today, which remains influential. The protesters carried signs saying "Fujimori is innocent!" and shouted slogans of support in favor of the ex-president.

Also present at the trial were the family members of the victims of the La Cantuta and Barrios Altos massacres. The *familiares* in these two cases have become the face of the victims' rights movement in Peru, and they have become critical actors on behalf of justice and accountability for human rights violations in Peru. While most victims in Peru's conflict were rural, Quechua-speaking peasants,[58] the Cantuta and Barrios Altos victims lived in Lima (though many were originally from the provinces). Most of the familiares speak Spanish, are educated, and were thus able to articulate their demands in the public sphere. Gisela Ortiz, whose brother Luis Enrique was one of the Cantuta victims, and who was herself a university student at the time of her brother's disappearance, became the primary spokesperson of the familiares movement in Peru. Indeed, La Cantuta and Barrios Altos—largely through the persistent claims for truth and justice on the part of the survivors and family members of victims—have become iconic cases of state violence against unarmed civilians, and it is no coincidence that these are the principal cases for which Fujimori was extradited and put on trial.[59]

The opening day of the Fujimori trial was extensively covered on the nightly news. The protest of Fujimori's supporters was featured prominently on several news programs. Martha Moyano could be seen carrying a poster of her sister María Elena—the same image that was used in María Elena's funeral procession. Martha was accompanied by others who were also victims of Sendero Luminoso, including a soldier who had lost the use of his legs in an insurgent assault. However, Martha Moyano was the only one among the group who was widely recognized by Peruvians. When asked by a reporter why she was carrying a picture of her sister, Moyano said, "I am also a victim." She then held up the poster featuring her sister's image and reminded viewers that María Elena had been assassinated by Sendero Luminoso.[60] Moyano said that she wanted to remind the people that Fujimori's government had eradicated terrorism in Peru.[61] "The legacy of Alberto Fujimori in the Peru of today is peace, which was constructed with a strategy of community development, using a concept of new democracy in which the state has to be present in those places where the people need it," she said.[62] When a reporter asked Moyano if her sister would support Fujimori if she were alive today, Martha Moyano responded that she could not answer the question, since each person has his or her own ideas.

Martha Moyano would not go so far as to suggest that her sister would have supported her position in defense of Fujimori. But she did deploy her sister's image skillfully, recalling the image of María Elena that was constructed by the state and the media after her murder as an emblematic victim of Sendero Luminoso, and reasserting the link between her sister's murder and Fujimori's success in defeating terrorism. In effect, Martha Moyano was marketing the memory of her sister, not for economic gain, but for political purposes. Moyano was asserting her right to defend Fujimori not merely on the basis of her political convictions, or of a rational analysis of his government's policies, but rather based on her status as a family member of a victim of Sendero violence. Indeed, by invoking her sister's image, her status as María Elena's sister and therefore as a victim of political violence, she deployed a potent symbolic image to influence public opinion in relation to the ongoing trial of Alberto Fujimori: that of the familiares of victims of political violence.

Martha Moyano deployed her sister's image, and asserted her rights as a victim, to give credibility to her own voice as a familiar of a victim of political violence and to sustain her defense of Fujimori and his government. Moyano's assertion of her rights as a victim and, implicitly, as a familiar, was particularly important symbolically. Typically, in Latin America, the term "familiares" refers to the family members of victims of state terror—the Madres de Plaza de Mayo in Argentina being the iconic familiares movement—and their role as defenders of human rights, truth, and justice has been widely celebrated. In effect, Moyano was adopting the language of the human rights community, but deploying it in defense of Fujimori. This raises vexing questions about the positionality of a family member speaking in the name of or in representation of a loved one who was killed or disappeared (in this case by Sendero Luminoso) as a way to legitimate specific political projects. Jelin has noted the complex politics of the familiares movement, and the charged issue of how to define who has the right to speak out in the name of the victims.[63] Those who "suffered in their own flesh" often purport to have greater legitimacy in their political claims than those who did not. But in the Peruvian case, how does one determine which victims have a right to speak? Who is empowered to make such a determination? This is one of the Gordian knots of Peru's human rights movement, and reflects the complicated politics of reconciliation.

María Elena Moyano, Foot Soldier in the War against Subversion?

The memory of María Elena Moyano was invoked again in February 2008, at another critical point in the Fujimori trial. The operative head of the Colina Group death squad, retired Army Major Santiago Martin Rivas, had been called to testify.[64] Though several lower-ranking members of the Colina Group have acknowledged the unit's existence, its participation in several massacres, including the Barrios Altos and La Cantuta massacres, and the deliberate covering up of its activities by officials at the highest levels of government, in his testimony Martin Rivas denied the group's existence and any participation in human rights violations.[65]

During his testimony, Martin Rivas sought to buttress the argument put forth by Fujimori's defense lawyers that the counterinsurgency plan Fujimori's government had put in place was based on intelligence gathering, surveillance, and new government policies, such as the "soldier-friend" program, that presumably sought to develop close ties between the armed forces and the urban and rural poor. The defense argued, disingenuously, that a counterinsurgency strategy that permitted human rights violations would have put this policy at risk. Human rights activists and scholars of Peru's internal conflict have long noted that the shift toward intelligence and surveillance, while crucial to capturing Sendero's top leaders, and hence to the defeat of the insurgency, had not meant an end to human rights violations. Instead, there was a shift in the pattern of human rights violations. Large-scale massacres, such as those that occurred with frequency during the 1980s, were less common, but other types of abuses, particularly forced disappearance, targeted extrajudicial executions, torture, and arbitrary detention, had continued apace.[66]

In his testimony, Martin Rivas said that his job had been to analyze the situation and suggest policies to reverse Sendero's growing influence. He highlighted the importance of developing alliances between the armed forces and the civilian population. In the countryside, the army's key civilian allies were the rondas campesinas; in Lima, particularly in the urban barriadas where Sendero had developed a significant presence, the army's allies were community leaders like María Elena Moyano. In his testimony, Rivas mentioned Moyano by name: "We decided to support . . . the *rondas campesinas* so that the population itself could . . . participate socially in the counterinsurgency war. We also organized the population in the urban areas, so that they too could confront [Sendero] socially. This occurred, as evidenced years later by the massive social protests in different parts of the country, which gave rise to leaders such as María Elena Moyano. . . . In different parts of the country, the people, side by side with their authorities, began to come out and engage in massive protests, and this . . . [led to] the victory against terrorism."[67]

Martin Rivas referred to María Elena Moyano (and the rondas) to sustain his claim that it was this new alliance between the armed forces and the rural and urban population that was central to the defeat of Sendero Luminoso. His discourse sought to construct (or reconstruct) an image of the heroic armed forces in alliance with the pueblo, which revisits the triumphalist discourse deployed by the Fujimori regime throughout the 1990s. It was also meant to legitimize the regime's counterinsurgency policy, and to downplay human rights violations as "excesses" committed by a few. Martin Rivas spun the image of María Elena Moyano to justify the actions of the Fujimori government, exculpate himself, and deny human rights violations.

In Martin Rivas's playbook, the armed forces provided a new structure for the urban and rural poor to challenge Sendero Luminoso. While this was partly true in the countryside with the rondas campesinas,[68] many of which emerged on their own to expel Sendero from their communities, the situation was much more complex in urban areas. The case of María Elena Moyano is illustrative. My interviews with informed observers in Villa El Salvador revealed that military officials sought out Moyano—who was deputy mayor of Villa El Salvador but who was also viewed as someone with significant social capital due to her history of grassroots activism—to convince her to participate in the civic-action programs they were planning to carry out in the district's newer urban settlements, where Sendero Luminoso had established an important foothold. Such efforts were intended to dislodge Sendero from local communities while also legitimizing the military and social operations of the armed forces. While in some cases community leaders did agree to participate in these operations, my informants uniformly affirm that Moyano refused to do so.[69] Because of her political convictions in favor of human rights, she viewed such a relationship as undesirable, given the military's dismal human-rights record. Furthermore, she understood the suspicion within the communities in which she worked regarding the military. Moyano thus consistently made public statements in interviews on TV and radio denouncing not only Sendero's violence but also human rights abuses committed by the military.

At the trial's end, Fujimori was allowed to make his own closing argument to the court. He presented a vigorous defense of his government, echoing many of the themes outlined above. He asserted that his government had saved Peru from terrorism and economic chaos. The trial, he claimed, was the handiwork of his enemies, whose objective was to destroy him and his party. To bring home his point, he asked why other presidents were not also being prosecuted for human rights violations that were committed during their regimes.[70] He reiterated that his government had worked closely with community and grassroots leaders in the city and in the countryside to combat terrorism and rebuild the country. Once again, the memory of Moyano was invoked by Fujimori:

> We rescued Villa El Salvador from the terror in which it had lived during the 1980s. When residents could not leave their homes or walk in the streets after 6 p.m. because they were afraid of the continuous explosions, shootouts, blackouts, and the assassinations of their neighbors and leaders by Sendero Luminoso, my government rescued them. . . . We developed the Industrial Park, institutes, schools, police stations, roads and avenues, as well as programs to bring electricity, water and sewerage, always with the help and participation of the organized community of Villa El Salvador and its valiant leaders, leaders such as María Elena Moyano, a popular leader, a woman of great courage who bravely pointed the way to reject Sendero Luminoso. . . . She did not stop in the face of their impositions or blackmail. The terrorists believed that by blowing up her body they could also destroy her ideals, but she has left

> us this example of dignity that has made her immortal. Permit me to make this caveat to express with this symbolic case my homage to all the leaders, all the men and women, as well as all the anonymous Peruvians, who delineated, with their example, the path to never accept the ruse of terrorism.[71]

The Final Spin?

We might refer to Moyano as an "emblematic victim" of Peru's internal conflict. A grassroots community leader, she rejected the violence of the state and of Sendero Luminoso, and her bold defiance put her in the national spotlight. Her outspokenness prompted Sendero to target her for assassination. The brutality of her murder made it all the more significant symbolically: it crystallized popular fears about Sendero's willingness to deploy violence against anyone—even civilians, even women—who it perceived as an obstacle to its revolutionary conquest of power. The state exploited this collective fear in its frequent references to Moyano's murder, but more importantly, it set out to construct an image of Moyano as a faithful ally in the battle against terrorism, ignoring and erasing her political affiliations and praxis.

At the same time, there has been a broad, if uncoordinated and heterogeneous, effort at the level of civil society and within the cultural sphere to reclaim the memory of María Elena Moyano. In the press, film, blogs, artistic representations, and through commemorations and memory sites in honor of her life, the appropriation of the memory of María Elena Moyano by Fujimori and his allies is being contested by a wide variety of people and organizations who seek to present a fuller and more complete understanding of her life and praxis as a progressive activist who championed peace, grassroots democracy and participation, and social justice. Indeed, the unidimensional image of María Elena Moyano deployed in the context of the Fujimori trial is now very much contested, as a result of this process of truth-telling and memorializing of Moyano that has taken place at the level of popular culture and other social spheres.[72]

Underlying these competing and contested constructions of the life of María Elena Moyano is a larger battle of memory that continues to rage on in Peru: a battle over how to understand Peru's internal conflict; the role of Fujimori and his regime in ending terrorism; and whether there is necessarily a tradeoff between security and human rights.

In the discourse deployed by Fujimori and his associates, political violence in Peru is the sole responsibility of Sendero Luminoso; whatever violations were committed by the armed forces were isolated acts, "excesses" committed by low-ranking personnel, or lamentable casualties of war. Fujimori and his regime are the architects of the defeat of Sendero Luminoso. Although civil society participation is mentioned—especially the role of the rondas campesinas and of grassroots leaders such as María Elena Moyano—it is always in a role subordinate to the state and the armed forces. And on the issue of security and human rights, following classical conceptualizations of national security doctrine, national security is always placed ahead of individual human rights, which are expendable when the former is perceived to be at risk.

The alternative view, articulated by the Peruvian Truth and Reconciliation Commission, by progressive intellectuals, journalists and activists, and others, is that Peru's violence can only be understood by examining the historical roots of discrimination and exclusion that led so many Peruvians to believe that violence was the only response to a system unwilling to address the basic needs and human rights of the majority of its citizens. While the CVR determined that Sendero was responsible for the majority of violent deaths (54 percent), it noted that state security forces and their allies (such as rondas) were responsible for about a third of all violent deaths. The CVR squarely condemned Sendero Luminoso for initiating the conflict and for its dogmatism and massive use of violence, but it also rebuked the Peruvian armed forces for engaging in—at some places and moments in the conflict—the "generalized and/or systematic practices of human rights violations that constitute crimes against humanity."[73]

These alternative accounts also challenge the assertion of Fujimori and his associates that it was his regime's hard-line policies that led to the defeat of Sendero Luminoso. This view emphasizes, on the one hand, the careful police work of a small group of intelligence officials within a specialized police unit, the Dincote, who were responsible for the capture and arrest of Guzmán, which involved no bloodshed and which proved to be a decisive blow to the structure and operational capacity of Sendero Luminoso—and on the other hand, the rejection by the majority of Peruvians of Sendero's violent methods.[74] Finally, this account challenges the core premise of the national security model, arguing that all individuals have inalienable rights and that the ends—in this case, the defeat of terrorism—can never justify the means—murder, torture, and forced disappearances.

On 7 April 2009, Fujimori was found guilty on all four counts of human rights violations. His conviction marked a significant shift in the terms of the debate over memory in Peru.[75] And yet, as of this writing, Fujimori's daughter Keiko—who was elected to Congress in 2006 with the highest number of votes of any legislator—is a leading contender for president in the 2011 elections. There are credible fears that Fujimori could be granted a presidential pardon. All of which reveals that the discourse articulated by Fujimori and his associates remains very much alive in the collective imagination. It is stoked frequently by the print and electronic media that remain staunch allies of Fujimori and his associates, by economic elites who benefited from Fujimori's economic policies and who fear a turn to populist policies that might endanger their power and privilege, and by the small contingent of fujimorista legislators who continue to extol the virtues of the former president and who characterize the efforts to prosecute him as acts of political persecution rather than impartial judicial proceedings. As efforts to achieve truth and justice move forward, it is certain that the battles over memory—and over the meaning of the memory of key figures such as María Elena Moyano—will continue to rage on in Peru.

NOTES

I wish to thank the participants of the Marketing Memory in Latin America Workshop, held at the University of Wisconsin, Madison, 11–12 April 2008, for their comments and critiques of an earlier version of this paper, especially Leigh Payne, Ksenija Bilbija, Steve Stern, and Nicolás Lynch. Thanks also to Narda Henríquez, Patricia Ruiz Bravo, and Rolando Ames for their insight and friendship, and to the many others who shared their ideas about the meaning of María Elena Moyano's life.

1. This history is recounted in Burt, "Sendero Luminoso and the 'Decisive Battle' in Lima's *Barriadas*." See also my report on Villa El Salvador for the Final Report of Peruvian Truth and Reconciliation Commission (Burt, "La batalla por las barriadas de Lima"). For a general history of Villa El Salvador, see Zapata, *Sociedad y poder local.*
2. For a history of women's organizations in Villa El Salvador, see Blondet, *Muchas vidas construyendo una identidad.*
3. Jelin, *State Repression and the Labors of Memory*; Passerini, *Memory and Totalitarianism*; Boyarin, *Remapping Memory.*
4. Jelin and Kaufman, *Subjetividad y figuras de la memoria.*
5. Jelin, *State Repression and the Labors of Memory.*
6. Stern, *Remembering Pinochet's Chile.*

7. See Milton, "At the Edge of the Peruvian Truth Commission."
8. María Tellería Solari, "Terror y crisis política," *Expreso* (Lima), 19 September 1991.
9. On 31 August 1991, Sendero Luminoso assassinated Juana López León, from Callao, who was a community leader for the Glass of Milk program.
10. *Expreso* (Lima), 13 September 1991, A15.
11. *El Peruano* (Lima), 13 September 1991, 1.
12. See Tupac, *The Autobiography of María Elena Moyano.*
13. *El Peruano* (Lima), 17 September 1991, B9.
14. *Oiga* (Lima), 24 February 1992, 14.
15. Interviews conducted in Villa El Salvador in 1994 and in 2002 by the author (see Burt, "Sendero Luminoso and the 'Decisive Battle' in Lima's *Barriadas*"; and Burt, "La batalla por las barriadas de Lima").
16. On the media's role in constructing an image of Moyano as a heroine, see McEvoy, "The Construction of the Heroic Image through Journalistic Discourse."
17. *La República* (Lima), 16 February 1992, 1.
18. *La República* (Lima), 18 February 1992, 1.
19. For international condemnations of her murder, see Robin Kirk, "Murder in a Shantytown: Sendero Luminoso's War on Hope," *The Nation*, 30 March 1992, 412–13; and Virginia Vargas, "Chronicle of a Death Foretold," *The Guardian*, 19 April 1992, 37. For an analysis of the impact of Moyano's murder at the local level, see Burt, "Sendero Luminoso and the 'Decisive Battle' in Lima's *Barriadas*."
20. For an analysis of the Fujimori regime, see Conaghan, *Fujimori's Peru*; and Burt, *Silencing Civil Society.*
21. "Mensaje a la nación," *El Comercio*, 29 July 1992.
22. "La historia verdadera de la Madre Coraje," *El Diario*, February 1992. Also published in English at www.blythe.org/peru-pcp/rights/mother.htm.
23. Address to the Nation by President Alberto Fujimori, Lima, 14 September 1992, *BBC Summary of World Broadcasts*, 15 September 1992.
24. Speech by Democratic Constituent Congress (CCD) president Jaime Yoshiyama at the opening session of the CCD, Televisión Panamericana, Lima, 30 December 1992, *BBC Summary of World Broadcasts*, 1 January 1993. The *sic* refers to the misnomer "genocide of terrorism."
25. In a letter denouncing Sendero Luminoso's accusations against her, Moyano also sharply criticized the state security forces: "The people don't have any confidence in the police force of this country. The police practice violence and often murder people. They would have to do much to gain the confidence of the people. Let them bring about justice with the disappeared, tortured, imprisoned, and assassinated. Then we could have faith in their desire for order" ("The Terror of the Shining Path," in Tupac, *The Autobiography of María Elena Moyano*, 63).
26. See, especially, "The Economic Crisis," in Tupac, *The Autobiography of María Elena Moyano.*
27. Interviews conducted in Villa El Salvador in 2002.
28. *El Diario* 551, 7 June 1989.

29. *El Diario* 613, 1991.
30. "The Terror of the Shining Path," in Tupac, *The Autobiography of María Elena Moyano*, 61.
31. "Letter of reply to Sendero Luminoso from María Elena Moyano," in Tupac, *The Autobiography of María Elena Moyano*, 65.
32. "La historia verdadera de la Madre Coraje," in Tupac, *The Autobiography of María Elena Moyano.*
33. "The Terror of the Shining Path," in Tupac, *The Autobiography of María Elena Moyano.*
34. "La historia verdadera de la Madre Coraje," in Tupac, *The Autobiography of María Elena Moyano.*
35. Open letter from María Elena Moyano published in various media outlets in September 1991, in Tupac, *The Autobiography of María Elena Moyano*, 64.
36. Interview with author, 12 December 2002.
37. Virginia Vargas, "Chronicle of a Death Foretold," *The Guardian*, 19 April 1992, 37.
38. Tupac, *The Autobiography of María Elena Moyano.* Originally published in Spanish as *María Elena Moyano: En busca de una esperanza* (Lima: Ediciones Flora Tristán, 1993).
39. *La República* (Lima), 25 April 1993, 7.
40. *Expreso* (Lima), 24 April 1993, A7.
41. *La República* (Lima), 25 April 1993, 7.
42. Ibid.
43. Ibid.
44. The author was a participant-observer to two such meetings in 1993.
45. *La República* (Lima), 25 July 1993, 4.
46. *La República* (Lima), 15 February 1994, 4.
47. Ibid.
48. The initiative was launched by progressive congresswoman Anel Townsend, who had worked closely with Moyano. Moyano was named a national heroine in 2002.
49. Interview conducted by Tamara Feinstein, Ph.D. candidate at the University of Wisconsin–Madison, with Martha Moyano, Lima, 14 May 2009. I thank Tamara Feinstein for sharing her interview transcript for this essay.
50. On women and gender issues in Peru's conflict, see Henríquez, *Cuestiones de género y poder en el conflicto armado en el Perú* .
51. Author interview, Ester Flores, Villa El Salvador, December 2002. For a transcript of Flores's testimony to the CVR, see Audiencias Públicas en Lima, Cuarta Sesión, 22 junio 2002, CASO 22, Esther Flores, www.cverdad.org.pe/apublicas/audiencias/trans_lima04b.php.
52. Ana Nuñez, "Y no pudieron matarla . . . el ejemplo de María Elena Moyano sigue presente," *La República*, 16 February 2007, 8.
53. Ibid.
54. The website "Amigos de Villa" can be viewed at www.amigosdevilla.it/.
55. Jelin, *State Repression and the Labors of Memory.*
56. See Jo-Marie Burt, "Guilty as Charged."

57. Jo-Marie Burt and Coletta Youngers, "Fujimori Faces Justice," Foreign Policy in Focus (29 January 2010) at www.fpif.org/articles/fujimori_faces_justice.
58. Comisión de la Verdad y Reconciliación, *Informe Final* (Lima, 2003).
59. Both massacres were carried out by the Colina Group death squad, a unit of military officers and soldiers that operated out of the Army Intelligence Service (SIE), and that was overseen by Vladimiro Montesinos, de facto head of the National Intelligence Service (SIN), who Fujimori empowered to direct counterinsurgency policy.
60. "Fujimoristas tuvieron deslucida actuación frente a la DIROES durante primera audiencia de juicio," *La Ventana Indiscreta,* Lima, Canal 4 (10 December 2007), www.agenciaperu.tv/ventana/?q=node/120.
61. "Minuto a Minuto: Juicio contra Alberto Fujimori," *El Comercio,* 10 December 2007, www.elcomercioperu.com.pe/ediciononline/HTML/2007-12-10/minuto-minuto-juicio-contra-alberto-fujimori.html.
62. *BBC Mundo,* Lima, 10 December 2007, http://news.bbc~co.uk/hi/spanish/latin_ameryca/newsid_7135000/7135782.stm.
63. Jelin, "The Politics of Memory."
64. I observed these sessions as an international observer of the Fujimori trial for the Washington Office on Latin America (WOLA).
65. However, in declarations to journalist Umberto Jara when he was a fugitive in 2001, Martin Rivas recognized the existence of the Colina Group and described in gruesome detail its operations, including the Barrios Altos and Cantuta massacres (see Jara, *Ojo por ojo*).
66. Carlos Iván Degregori and Carlos Rivera, *Fuerzas armadas, subversion y democracia: 1980–1993,* Documento de Trabajo 53 (Lima: Instituto de Estudios Peruanos, 1993). See also Comisión de la Verdad y Reconciliación, *Informe Final* (Lima, 2003), and Burt, *Silencing Civil Society.*
67. Author's field notes, Fujimori trial, 27 February 2008.
68. See, e.g., Degregori et al., *Las rondas campesinas y la derrota de Sendero Luminoso.*
69. Based on interviews for the CVR with community leaders and municipal authorities in Villa El Salvador, December 2002. Pascuala Rosado, a community leader from the Huaycán district who was assassinated by Sendero Luminoso in 1996, collaborated closely with the Fujimori government.
70. He was clearly referring to the incumbent president, Alan García. The CVR documented severe violations of human rights during García's first presidential term (1985–90).
71. Alberto Fujimori's Closing Remarks, Official Transcript of Fujimori Trial (Lima), 1 April 2009, AV. 19–2001 (Acumulado al Av. No. 45–2003).
72. This is explored further in Burt, "Los ugosy abusos de la memoria de María Elena Moyano."
73. Comisión de la Verdad y Reconciliación, *Informe Final* (Lima, 2003), 324.
74. See, e.g., the comments by journalist José Alejandro Godoy, "María Elena Moyano y la derrota de Sendero Luminoso," *Desde el Tercer Piso,* 17 February 2008, www.desdeeltercerpiso.com/2008/02/maria-elena-moyano-y-la-derrota-de-sendero-luminoso.
75. See Jo-Marie Burt, "Las 'verdades jurídicas' del juicio a Fujimori," *Revista Memoria* (IDEHPUCP) (April 2009).

LAURIE BETH CLARK AND
LEIGH A. PAYNE

Trauma Tourism in Latin America

In a section called "Some Social Dos and Don'ts," the *Lonely Planet* tour guide for Argentina warns tourists that the recent dictatorship is among the "sensitive subjects to avoid in conversation with Argentines (at least until you know them better)."[1] The entry presents the authoritarian repression in Latin America's recent past as contested terrain locally and a tourist taboo. It also recognizes the curiosity of international tourists about that past and their desire to explore it in their journeys in the region.

The guidebooks published by *Lonely Planet*, *Rough Guide*, *Moon*, *Frommer's*, and *Fodor's* have responded to that demand by offering descriptions of some of the sites of atrocity in Latin America.[2] In some cases, it is the sites themselves that provide overviews, tour information, and relate visitors' experiences, on official websites and in print publications. Visitors' travel blogs provide further exposure for such sites and the experiences they offer to tourists. So despite the taboo on tourism to them, the sites of authoritarian regime repression and of the resistance to repression nevertheless form part of the tourist experience in Latin America.

Laurie Beth Clark's term "trauma tourism" describes this practice of visits to sites of past political atrocity by those who have been directly affected and by others.[3] Our analysis of trauma tourism in Latin America exposes a set of overlapping tensions in the memory market—tensions between local needs and the international demand for and consumption of sites; over the profits generated by representing the past in a particular way; and over the design and location of these sites and their value for visitors. Underlying these tensions is a central paradox: sites of memory raise awareness of the traumatic past but risk commercializing, trivializing, or depoliticizing that past through tourism.

The Latin American Experience

A variety of terms have recently emerged to identify sites of atrocity. Memory studies scholars employ "*lieux de mémoire*," "traumascapes," or "memoryscapes" to name the specific places where the past is represented, and the political meaning that representation evokes.[4] These terms emphasize social and individual meaning at these sites without engaging tourist practices. "Thanatourism," for example, derives from the Greek *thanatos*, meaning the personification of death, and the term is used to focus on tourist engagement at a range of death sites: watching death (e.g., lynching, the electric chair); reenacting death (e.g., Civil War battles); or the visiting of sites that represent death (e.g., memorials or museums of state terrorism or genocide).[5] "Dark tourism" describes visits to places of sensationalized tragedies, including natural disasters (e.g., earthquakes and hurricanes) and crimes (e.g., bank robberies or kidnapping), as well as politically oriented sites of genocide and state terrorism.[6] The terms "grief tourism" and "tragedy tourism" similarly describe excursions to sites of natural or human-made disasters.[7] "Fatal attraction" captures the nature of these sites as simultaneously abhorrent and beguiling, as arousing prurient or voyeuristic interest.[8] These terms do not emphasize the social responsibility placed on tourists at sites of political atrocity. While "voluntourism" and "impact tourism" engage visitors in a deliberate project of social, active, and purposeful work during their vacations, they do not tend to include memory sites in Latin America.[9]

"Trauma tourism" combines elements of existing studies of tourism at sites of memory, while also defining a unique practice. The term juxtaposes leisure (tourism) with horror (trauma), highlighting the inherent contradictions in its practice. It also invokes the notion that "leisure should be productive."[10] We do not assume that tourists desire only "superficial experiences with other peoples and places"; trauma tourism reflects instead Dean MacCannell's claim that "tourists desire . . . deeper involvement with society and culture to some degree . . . a basic component of their motivation to travel."[11] Rather than highlighting "shock value" or voyeurism on the part of the tourist, the term "trauma tourism" emphasizes the social responsibility that the site and the history it recalls impose on the tourist. Trauma tourism thus involves representation of a past trauma, engagement by visitors at a traumatic memory site, and a sense of social responsibility invoked by the place onto the visitor.

Trauma tourism in Latin America emerged in the wake of more established practices in other regions. Since the Second World War, tourists have visited concentration camps in Europe and atomic bomb sites at Hiroshima and Nagasaki, all of which have been constructed as part of an international call for "Never Again." Post–World War II trauma tourism expanded to include sites of atrocity that predated the war, such as the former slave forts in Ghana and Senegal that now attract tourists.[12] These sites do not exist exclusively for the project of "Never Again." Rather, the "practice" of "Never Again" co-exists with heritage and return tourism. It is not uncommon for tourists to travel to slave forts or concentration camps specifically because of past trauma. On the other hand, in Latin America, as in Rwanda, Vietnam, Cambodia, and South Africa, trauma tourism is rarely the primary purpose of travel. It is, nonetheless, a fairly common practice among tourists visiting these countries for other reasons to include trauma sites in their itineraries.

In comparison with other regions, Latin America's trauma tourism industry remains underdeveloped. The sites of memory there are neither well-marked nor well-marketed. On the surface, this relative lack of development appears surprising. The dictatorships in Latin America occurred at nearly the same historical moment as the genocide in Cambodia (1970–80). The international attention to atrocities in Germany, Poland, and Rwanda also prevails in Latin America, where the U.S. government bears responsibility for the coups that toppled democratic regimes and imposed notoriously abusive dictatorships in the region. In addition, a global human rights movement, international governmental organizations, and President Jimmy Carter's human rights policy heightened international attention to the region's atrocities.

Several characteristics of the region and the past repression may explain the relative underdevelopment of trauma tourism in Latin America. The greatest challenge that Latin American countries face in marketing trauma tourism at sites of atrocity is the lack of consensus over the past within the country or the world. The near universal condemnation of the Holocaust, apartheid, the genocides in Rwanda and Cambodia, and even the Vietnam War facilitates the project of "Never Again." Such a consensus does not exist in Latin America, where strong local and international forces continue to see the wars against subversion, if not the violence they engendered, as crucial to the region's current capitalist economies. The taboo mentioned at the beginning of this chapter reflects the disagreement over whether the leaders of the recent authoritarian regimes in Argentina, Brazil, Chile, El Salvador, Guatemala, Peru, and Uruguay should be prosecuted or praised. A tourist industry motivated to sell guidebooks and trips may avoid the controversy altogether. Those tensions, after all, do not exist only within the region, but also internationally, since many businesses and groups around the world promoted and benefited from the regimes and their actions.

The Trauma Tourism Paradox

Tourism to particular sites of violence in Latin America thus poses a dilemma. Some believe that access to trauma sites should be restricted to those directly affected (e.g., to victims and survivors and their families) and those previously aware of and committed to the project of "Never Again." As such, the sites remain sacred spaces to reflect on the past, to mourn and grieve, or to remember to not repeat. A socially responsible practice of trauma tourism, in this sense, would preserve the memory of atrocity at the site without cultivating wider visibility. Such an orientation limits the sites' potential to advance the broader social project of "Never Again" that extends the local experience to a universal condemnation of political violence. The political mission of the sites, therefore, depends on some kind of marketing to attract those unaware of the violent past and to promote an international "Never Again" project.

These two dynamics of trauma tourism—marketing and social justice—exemplify its inherent tensions. Critics of marketing sites of memory consider the commercialization of memory anathema to the sites' emotional significance to victims' and survivors' recovery. They believe that mass tourism devalues these sites for those directly affected. Commercialization further removes the politics of the site, rendering it merely a routine stop on the tourist circuit. Commercialization trivializes these sites, eroding rather than promoting their value and social function. Here the paradox emerges: by heightening awareness of past events, marketing threatens to empty the site of its emotional and social value. In response, others contend that the failure to attract visitors to these sites threatens the "Never Again" project by hiding the past and missing the opportunity to raise awareness and commitment to human rights from an otherwise uninformed population. The paradox of trauma tourism in Latin America raises three questions: Memory for whom? What memory of the past? And, why remember?

Glocalization

Latin American sites represent both the ideals and the limitations of global trauma tourism. The former clandestine torture center Villa Grimaldi in Santiago, Chile, which has been transformed into a Peace Park, offers an example of an internationally marketed, known, and visited site. As a leading member of the International Coalition of Historic Sites of Conscience, it consciously advances social responsibility through the memory site.[13] The coalition's mission is "to change the role of historic sites in civil life from places of passive learning to centers for active citizen engagement . . . to build a lasting culture of human rights." The coalition further recognizes that "the power of historic sites is not inherent; it must be harnessed as a self-conscious tactic in the service of human rights and civic engagement. Sites of Conscience play this critical role." The coalition thus unites sites that promote a transformative—human rights—experience in various parts of the world, including Latin America.[14]

The coalition describes Villa Grimaldi Peace Park as "dedicated to remembering victims of human rights violations; to disseminating information on the history of state terrorism in Chile; and to promoting a culture of human rights."[15] It highlights the park's commitment to locating human rights violations in a specific place and time while simultaneously contributing to a broad human rights agenda.

The park owes its existence to mobilization by Villa Grimaldi's victims and survivors. They claimed the site after it had been sold to a private investor and demolished for condominium development. They salvaged parts of the original villa, notably the floor tiles that survivors had seen beneath their blindfolds. They reconstructed other significant sections of the torture center, specifically the torture tower and the rose garden. They also brought in railroad ties to represent the ones that had been attached to prisoners to disappear them in the ocean. Markers on the ground (as if seen only under a blindfold) recount what occurred on the site. The park also includes a wall of 226 names of Villa Grimaldi victims, an artificial stream, and a fountain. The decision to leave the estate mostly deconstructed makes the park more evocative than representative. As the *Lonely Planet* guidebook states: "It's a powerful testament, you need only read the descriptions and see the names of the dead and disappeared to imagine what happened here."[16]

The park's design extends beyond visitors' imaginations to address the needs of torture survivors who relive the horror through traumatic memory. The Villa Grimaldi website claims, "The Wall evokes deep emotions and is a ceremonial place for family members of the victims." To avoid trapping victims, survivors, and other visitors in the past, the park consciously builds hope. Its website, for example, describes the stream that leads visitors from the Wall of Names to the Wished Patio as "a place to play, live, cry, think. A place to be more humane." Villa Grimaldi also calls for active vigilance to protect against future human rights atrocities. As the website states: "Although the park cannot be seen from Arrieta Avenue until one actually enters, as soon as one does, one enters a space full of poetry—a feeling that is created by two axes that intersect to form an 'X' or a cross. These axes are two big circular paths that take one all around the grounds. In the future they will be lit by 8-meter high lampposts that will shed a misty light symbolizing a permanent vigil."[17]

At the park, a wide array of visitors commingles. Neighboring residents stroll, sunbathe, or admire the roses alongside groups of inquisitive international and local tourists and distraught victims and survivors. The park also reaches beyond on-site visitors by providing a virtual tour in English, German, and Spanish on its website. The virtual tour includes photographs of the site, testimonials from survivors, and comments left in the guest books at the physical and virtual sites. At the end of the virtual tour, visitors are invited to send an e-card from the site.[18] The images convey the beauty of the site even as they provide evidence of human rights violations through the Torture Tower, the Railway Ties, and the Wall of Names. On the website, tourists may also book an actual visit to the park with a tour guide who speaks English.

The Chile Information Project, or CHIP, offers a human rights tour that includes Villa Grimaldi. CHIP's website emphasizes the importance of such sites to fight against the desire "to erase the memory of a very specific part of the country's history." It condemns forgetting by recalling Pinochet's 1995 words: "It is better to remain quiet and to forget. That is the only thing we must do. We must forget. And that won't happen if we continue opening up lawsuits, sending people to jail. FOR-GET: That's the word. And for that to happen, both sides must forget and continue with their work."[19]

Pedro Matta, a survivor of the Villa Grimaldi torture center and now a program director at Trinity College (Hartford, Conn.), has led hundreds of college students on international exchange programs through the Villa Grimaldi site. He has also hosted visiting dignitaries, scholars, and celebrities. With the English he perfected during his U.S. exile from Chile, he takes tourists through an intimate and personal journey, sharing his own experience of horror and his efforts at recovery. Recognizing the value of a survivor-led tour, one U.S. college student wrote: "I could sense that something terrible had happened to Pedro in his lifetime simply by listening to the way he spoke and watching the manner in which he carried himself. . . . Hearing his first-hand experiences in Villa Grimaldi was one of the most powerful experiences of my life." Its powerful impact did not seem to be enough to recommend the site, however, since this student did not include it on her travel blog list of top Latin American tourist destinations.[20]

The intense emotional experience of survivor-led tours has engendered some criticism from memory scholars and activists. Academic critics wonder whether the "routine makes the emotion suspect."[21] MacCannell might characterize these critics as "skeptical tourists [who] may think that they are not getting the 'authentic' experience but instead the staged authenticity."[22] Local activist-critics disparage such "memory entrepreneurship" by survivors, who they feel distastefully capitalize on their own experience with atrocity. This criticism may reflect resentment over the guides' personal and financial gains from the tours. It also demonstrates tensions within the victim and survivor community over the design of such sites, what kinds of tours should be offered, and how the past is narrated. In the view of some, intimate personal accounts of survival provide an emotional experience, but one without the capacity to link that experience to the broader, universal struggle for human rights protections. Indeed, as Carrie Murphy suggests, writing in her travel blog, the tour at Villa Grimaldi may bring closure on the past rather than serving as a catalyst to remember to not repeat: "Villa Grimaldi is a strange site, simultaneously sobering and uplifting. It is imbued with a sense of peace, due to the beautiful efforts to create the concentration camp anew as a place for reflection; there is also a sadness in the air, palpable and almost sinister. It is quiet, grassy, tiled in colorful mosaics with a beautiful fountain in the middle, as well as spaces for meeting and performance. A leafy Ombu tree rises, a testament to regrowth and regeneration. I left Villa Grimaldi feeling both deeply shaken and decidedly calm: the site is a fitting monument to those who were held there, as well as a beautiful and radical means of coming to terms with a dark chapter of Chile's history."[23]

Not all tours and guidebooks promote visits to this "dark chapter" of Chile's past. Some guidebooks ignore Villa Grimaldi altogether.[24] And tour developers may seek to provide political balance. Bicicleta Verde's full-day tour (part of CHIP) includes a stop at Villa Grimaldi, but also one at the Pinochet Foundation. Visitors thus get to experience the horror of the dictatorship along with its justification, which potentially keeps the past at a neutral and analytical distance, allowing tourists to observe and analyze without taking sides. *Moon* handbook calls Villa Grimaldi a "pilgrimage" site without "any overt political posturing."[25] By including the story of a businessman who was "inexplicably" detained at the torture center and who lived to publish his account, *Moon* handbook seems to accept the notion of human rights protections for the "innocent" while implicitly suggesting that those who supported revolutionary change in Chile may not have deserved such protection.

This question also arises at the *Ojo que Llora* (Crying Eye) memorial outside Lima, Peru. The artist Lika Mutal created the Crying Eye to fulfill the recommendation of the Peruvian Truth and Reconciliation Commission that there should be a memorial to acknowledge and condemn Peru's political violence from 1980 to 2000, and to deter future violence. Association Pro-Human Rights (APRODEH) describes the monument in this way:

> To live in peace and democracy, it is indispensable to know our history. It is necessary to look to the past to find the present and construct the future, and in this way to become conscious of the damage caused during the period of violence that we lived in our country between 1980 and 2000. One of the efforts to preserve memory and the history of thousands of Peruvians whose rights were violated for two decades is the Crying Eye memorial.
>
> This is a stone sculpture from which water trickles like tears. The stone represents the Earth Mother (Pachamama) fixed in the center of a labyrinth comprised of eleven circular paths lined with wide bands of smooth rocks. Thirty-two thousand rocks form these bands. Inscribed on 26,000 stones is the name, age, and year of disappearance or death of a victim of violence. It takes about 40 to 50 minutes to walk through the labyrinth depending on the time [of] the visitor's stops. The crucial moment arrives when the visitor arrives at the central [Earth Mother] stone. This stone represents each individual's central core. Once there, individual worries disappear and instead one confronts evil and its consequences for society. Then the visitor takes the return trip.[26]

Organized around the objective of national unity and the repudiation of human rights violations, the memorial did not intend to provoke controversy. Conflict erupted, however, when the Inter-American Court of Human Rights ruled against Peru's Fujimori government for human rights violations and ordered the Crying Eye memorial to include the names of Sendero Luminoso guerrilla prisoners killed in the Castro Castro penitentiary. Although the memorial had always included names of Sendero Luminoso and other victims of government human rights abuses along with the victims of guerrilla violence, the IACHR ruling exposed conflicts over how to remember the past. Supporters of the Fujimori government's fight against Shining Path vandalized the memorial, pouring orange paint (Fujimori's party color) over the center stone. Fujimori supporters, on blogs and in the press, called for the memorial's removal and for retaliation against the artist.[27]

The IACHR ruling and subsequent vandalism heightened local and international attention to the site and the conflict over memory of past violence in Peru. Rather than fuel the conflict with anticipated outrage, the memorial's website displayed the desecrated memorial without commentary. The NGO connected to the memorial remained true to its political neutrality on past violence.

Outrage over the monument's desecration did not prevent its trivialization, as this excerpt from a U.S. student's blog demonstrates: "Quite tragic to think that something like that could happen. It would be like an angry American mob destroying the Vietnam Memorial in D.C. It was a somber yet very interesting trip to the memorial. In other news, I completed my first trip to a Peruvian laundromat, or 'lavandaria' [*sic*], and I'm surprised I got my clothes back at all."[28]

The student's blog entry illustrates the tensions that can arise in marketing memory at tourist sites. The sites' "Never Again" project spread to an international and local audience after some challenged the meaning behind that call. Rather than building consensus for shared human rights values, vandalism and political conflict may attract the tourists. As the U.S. student's blog entry shows, often tourists possess little framework for making the experience universal. A simple, and no doubt unintentional, turn of phrase in the blog equates the unlikelihood of vandalism in the U.S. with the unlikelihood that Peruvian laundry service will measure up to U.S. consumer standards. The vandalism becomes part of the exotic day-to-day experience in Peru that also includes laundry. Rather than reflecting a global call to condemn human rights violations wherever they occur, the site represents a uniquely Peruvian past.

The U.S. student's experience reflects the more typical form of trauma tourism in Latin America—one stop on an itinerary—as compared to destination trauma tourism elsewhere. This student did not go to Peru to visit the Crying Eye, or to learn about Peru's authoritarian past, or to fight for human rights. Her trip was on the itinerary for her group tour, an excursion during her study abroad. Trauma tourism in Latin America sometimes forms part of a standard package or a set of options. Chile's Bicicleta Verde, for example, offers its Human Rights Legacy tour along with wine tastings, beach trips, and snowboarding. Trauma tourism forms part of the historical, educational, or cultural component of a tour package. It can even provide a rationalization for those who might feel guilty about spending their entire Latin American vacation in politically unconscious middle-class bliss.

To attract the casual visitor, Latin American guidebooks tend to promote "dark," rather than "trauma," tourism, to evoke shock and outrage instead of social responsibility.[29] The *Lonely Planet*'s guide to the site where Archbishop Oscar Romero, a human rights advocate in El Salvador, was murdered provides an example. Referring to the Hospital la Divina Providencia in the capital city of San Salvador, where Romero was killed by military officers while he delivered Mass in the chapel, the guide notes that visitors there will have the opportunity to "tour his modest quarters where his blood-soaked shirt and robes are displayed."[30] The text emphasizes the violence that was committed at the site, rather than the social responsibility of remembering to not repeat. Other guidebooks, however, do not even mention memory sites related to Romero.

Entries in other guidebooks on sites reflecting Latin America's traumatic past also reinforce national or regional stereotypes that fit the "dark tourism" model. Discussing the site of the 1968 Tlatelolco massacre in Mexico City, in which government forces killed hundreds of people, for example, the *Rough Guide* refers to "one thread of continuity between all Mexico's civilizations: the cheapness of life and the harsh brutality of their rulers."[31] The *Lonely Planet* uses a similar cultural stereotype in writing about Guatemala's violence:

> Here's a sticky one for you: take it as given that the Guatemalan justice system is broken, perhaps beyond repair. Lawyers get shot in broad daylight on downtown streets and nobody saw anything. Now translate that

to the villages, where the police drop in every week or so to see that everything's OK. Tired of living with known rapists, murderers, baby sellers and thieves in their midst, villagers often take justice into their own hands, rather than wait for a lengthy and often inconclusive court case. The most extreme form of "village justice" is the lynching—a mob grabs a criminal and strings them up from the nearest tree. And nobody saw anything. But there are less extreme forms. Traditional Mayan society had its own set of punishments—mostly along the lines of public humiliation—shaving women's heads, tying them to a post half naked, making them walk through town on their knees carrying a heavy rock. Which is all fine up to this point—in fact the Guatemalan constitution guarantees the indigenous population the right to continue with their customs as long as they don't conflict with national laws. And that's where it gets sticky—these same criminals have been turning up at the offices of the protector of Human Rights, claiming that their human rights have been violated. So the choice boils down to this: an ineffective system, which doesn't deter and rarely catches criminals, or a more improvised approach, without formal process, meting out punishments that, to the outside world, seem cruel and unusual.[32]

Demonstrating the capacity of guidebooks to take a different tone, the *Lonely Planet* portrays the Tlatelolco massacre entirely differently from its coverage of Guatemala's "village justice," and from the *Rough Guide*'s presentation: "Many Mexicans viewed the killing as a premeditated tactic by the government to suppress dissent, permanently discrediting the postrevolutionary regime."[33] Guidebooks, while inconsistent in their coverage of sites of past trauma, consistently sideline trauma tourism.

Guidebooks are not alone in their ambivalence toward international tourism at trauma tourism sites. Victim-centered sites sometimes share this attitude. The Women in Memory Monument in Santiago, Chile, provides an example. A stunning monument of light and glass, it is meant to represent women's struggles before and during the dictatorship. Located above a metro station at a busy downtown intersection, the monument could hardly be more visible or easy to find, yet few international visitors make their way to the monument. It is not marketed; other than the architectural prize it received, it is not promoted on any websites.[34] None of the standard tour guides include it. It forms part of the Santiago cityscape, and yet the significance of the monument remains exclusively on-site. Even then, visitors must search for a small plaque that identifies it, sometimes finding it behind visitors using the site for other purposes —hanging out or making out. Litter, including an Elvis Presley sticker affixed to the monument in June 2007, distracts the visitor. The monument's sponsors remain unconcerned about the alternative uses of the monument. They focus instead on the monument's very existence as its major accomplishment. They raised the funds for the monument themselves, without city or national government or international non-governmental support. By representing women as protagonists of political struggle, the monument challenges the typical depiction of women as victims. This political interpretation of past struggle, however, may render the project more controversial, and less visible in the tourist industry.

The Making and Unmaking of National Heroes

The tourist industry has only rarely and tentatively approached the processes of making and unmaking national heroes. The General Cemetery in Santiago provides an example. Like other national cemeteries, it celebrates the lives of the individuals who shaped that country's history. A walk through the beautiful and well-groomed General Cemetery thus provides an official story of political and social power in Chile. Guidebooks suggest a stop at President Salvador Allende's gravesite. As a popularly elected president (1970–73), such a suggestion would not seem unusual. However, controversy surrounds Allende's burial in the cemetery. *Moon* mentions that "after 17 years in Viña del Mar, following the end of the Pinochet dictatorship, [Allende] regained his freedom to travel to a monumental memorial here."[35] The tour books fail to mention that Pinochet, the dictator who took over after a military coup overthrew Allende, received neither a state burial nor a place in the General Cemetery when he died in 2006. It remains to be seen whether more recently published books will reflect on Pinochet's absence in the cemetery.

The legitimacy of Allende's leadership, represented in the cemetery, remains deeply contested in Chile. *Fodor's* only obliquely refers to the conflict when it remarks that the General Cemetery "is an emotionally charged place around September 11, the anniversary of the 1973 military coup."[36] The *Lonely Planet* merely states that "Chile's distant and recent history is on display here, where the tombs of figures such as José Manuel Balmaceda, Salvador Allende, and Orlando Letelier are reminders of political turmoil from the 19th century to the present."[37] The term "turmoil" downplays the violence of the Pinochet dictatorship. *Moon* handbook explains a bit more about that "turmoil," stating that Orlando Letelier was a "diplomat . . . killed by a car bomb in Washington D.C., by military intelligence agents under orders from Pinochet's henchman General Contreras."[38]

Burial in the General Cemetery transforms Allende's national status. A national villain during the Pinochet regime, Allende now has a "monumental" burial place that befits a national hero and respected political leader. Inscribed at the site are Allende's final words to the nation, delivered by radio from the Moneda Palace before it was bombed. The inspiring words circulated after the coup through underground tapes and on solidarity posters created by those in exile. The new official story represented at the General Cemetery subverts the authoritarian regime's version of Allende and his leadership.

The counternarrative to the Pinochet regime's version is further developed in other areas of the cemetery. Visitors encounter a "wall of remembrance," with the names of the dictatorship's victims inscribed in stone. Walls of names, like cemeteries themselves, are not new forms of remembering the fallen, but following the success of Maya Lin's Vietnam War Memorial in Washington, D.C., such walls have become the standard device for documenting the atrocity, rather than heroism, of war. They mark trauma to the nation. The wall in Chile's General Cemetery casts in stone a new perspective on the dead and disappeared. Rather than being "subversives," as they have been portrayed by the Pinochet regime, the wall identifies them as victims of human rights abuses. Their killers, once considered national saviors, appear in the cemetery as human rights violators.

Tourists might miss Victor Jara's gravesite on their walk through the cemetery because his tomb does not appear in any of the standard guidebooks. Jara was a folksinger killed by the military regime in the early 1970s, and his gravesite largely appeals to local, rather than foreign, visitors. Visitors to it leave flowers and notes attached to the tomb. Someone has indelibly inscribed on a tree trunk in front of the tomb the lyrics of a song written by this still famous folksinger and martyr of the Chilean military regime. This ongoing interaction with the site suggests that Victor Jara, and what he represents, remain vital to domestic visitors. Despite regime efforts to silence him, his songs live on in the daily lives of Chileans. The freshness of the flowers and the messages makes the site's meaning and importance to local people evident even decades after Jara's death.

Foreign tourists (and even some Chileans) would rarely know about the

Figure 1. Victor Jara's gravesite in the General Cemetery, Santiago, Chile. (Photograph by Laurie Beth Clark and Michael Peterson)

"N.N." (No Name) tombs of Patio 29, just beyond Jara's colorful site. This recently named National Historic Monument has not yet appeared in the guidebooks, but it is included in tours led by Bicicleta Verde. The field of simple crosses at the gravesite represents an important turning point in Chilean political history since it provides evidence of the dictatorship's summary executions of political dissidents and the disappearance of their bodies in clandestine graves.

Who ends up in official cemeteries after dictatorships end, and who does not, who visits them and who does not, can tell a remarkable story about past political trauma in a country. The gravesite aesthetic for national leaders seems unremarkable, until one understands how that representation challenges prevailing versions of the traumatic past. Tour books tend to ignore these local controversies, undervaluing the significance of the presence of Allende's tomb, for example, or the wall of names of those killed by the regime, or the clandestine graves, or Victor Jara's gravesite in the General Cemetery. Plaques mark, but do not explain, these shifts. Only tourists familiar with recent political events will grasp the significance of these controversies debated among Chileans.

Statues play a similar role to cemeteries in transforming national villains into heroes, and vice versa. Like gravesites, statues simultaneously enhance the historic power of past leaders and erase from public view the challenges to those heroic images. One of the first stops on the Bicicleta Verde tour is the statue of Salvador Allende in the public plaza in front of La Moneda

Palace, along with those of other statesmen from Chile's past. *Frommer's* mentions the importance of La Moneda as a memory site—"infamously, the Palacio is the site of the 1973 Pinochet-led coup that ousted Salvador Allende"—without discussing the post-dictatorship Allende sculpture.[39]

Rough Guide is the only guidebook that mentions the statue: "In front of the Justice Ministry is one of Chile's few monuments to president Salvador Allende, with his arm outstretched. This controversial work of public art pays homage to a man who died in La Moneda during the artillery and rocket siege that led to the installation of the military government in 1973." The guidebook skips the opportunity to discuss the controversy, and moves on to describe "another couple of impressive public buildings," including "the white temple-like Ex Congreso Nacional, set amidst lush gardens . . . where Congress used to meet, until it was dissolved on 11 September 1973, the day of the coup."[40] While *Rough Guide* does not hide political events, it does not explain them sufficiently for tourists to grasp their significance.

The statue of Allende represents him as a different kind of hero. Rather than appearing as a military victor, the proverbial man on horseback, Allende appears as a bespectacled intellectual statesman. His words, inscribed at the statue's base, speak to hope for a better future: "I have faith in Chile and its destiny." The victory represented is the existence of the statue itself, and the absence of Pinochet's statue, in front of La Moneda. It is a political victory: democracy's defeat of the dictatorship, human rights' ascendancy over atrocity. Ironically, Pinochet's call to forgetting has been heeded: his image and support for his regime have all but disappeared from public memorial sites.

One of the most well-known memorials of heroism is the living memorial that is the weekly protest marches of the Madres de Plaza de Mayo in Argentina. Every standard tour book for Argentina includes the group and describes the walk they have made every Thursday afternoon at 3:30 since 1977. *Lonely Planet* perhaps best captures the heroic nature of the group:

> In 1977, a year after a military coup trampled human rights in all domains, 14 mothers marched into the Plaza de Mayo in Buenos Aires, in spite of a ban on public gatherings ordered by the military government. They demanded information about their missing children, who had "disappeared" as part of the government's efforts to quash political opposition. The group, which took on the name Las Madres de la Plaza de Mayo (The Mothers of Plaza de Mayo), developed into a powerful

> social movement and were the only political organization who overtly challenged the military government. They were particularly effective as they carried out their struggle under the banner of motherhood, which made them relatively unassailable in Argentine culture. Their movement showed the power of women—at least in a traditional role—in Argentine culture and they are generally credited as helping to kick start the re-establishment of the country's civil society.[41]

Other tour books emphasize the details left out by the *Lonely Planet. Fodor's* describes the white headscarves that are painted permanently on the Plaza. These headscarves, with the embroidered words "We Want Them Alive," symbolize the diapers of the women's disappeared children. *Moon* handbook writes, "Most of the disappeared died at their captor's hands, but the mothers brought Argentina's shame to world attention."[42] *Rough Guide* provides an entire sidebar about the Madres, including the following information:

> Some [Madres] disappeared themselves after the notorious "Angel of Death" Alfredo Astiz infiltrated the group, posing as the brother of a desaparecido (disappeared). In 1982, during the Malvinas/Falklands crisis, the Madres were accused of being anti-patriotic for their stance against the war; a conflict that they claimed was an attempt by the regime to divert attention away from its murderous acts. With the return to democracy in 1983, the Madres were disappointed by the new government's reluctance to delve too deeply into what had happened during the "Dirty War," as well as by the later granting of immunity to many of those accused of kidnap, torture and murder. The group rejected economic "compensation" and both it and the respect in which it is held were critical in finally getting the amnesty laws overturned in 2005. The Madres continued to protest at the Pirámide de Mayo weekly until January 2006, when, after around 1500 protests, the Madres finally brought their long vigil to an end, citing confidence in President Kirchner. Now some of the Madres have branched into other areas of social protest: the emblem of the white headscarf was at the forefront of the movement to demand the non-payment of the country's foreign debt, among other issues.[43]

Not all of the information is correct. The Madres would not have used the authoritarian regime's language of a "dirty war," but rather "state terrorism." The reference to reparations ignores the fact that the Madres split into two groups, with one group accepting and another refusing to accept reparations. The entry suggests, moreover, that the Madres no longer walk once a week. In fact, one (the Association) group gave up the annual March of Resistance, but the other (the Founding) group continues to participate. Both groups, however, still walk on Thursday afternoons, separately, without speaking to each other, stationing themselves at different sections of the plaza. The casual visitor would not understand this arrangement, since tour books do not discuss it.

The politics behind the Madres de Plaza de Mayo is unexplored, despite their extensive coverage in tour books. Such books offer a simple interpretation: the Madres' bravery in the face of repression, and their consistent, visible, and active leadership in human rights since 1977. The guidebooks treat the Madres as unassailable, as "housewives and mothers turned militant activists" because of the disappearance of their children,[44] and thus ignore the controversies surrounding their split into two different groups.[45] The depoliticized portrayal of the Madres for foreign tourist consumption may sustain the groups' weekly walks, even as their numbers dwindle due to age, distance from the dictatorship, and disagreement over political positions.

Conflicts over national heroes might emerge more frequently if those who supported the regimes erected memory sites as well, but such sites rarely exist. The once public ceremonies to celebrate the coups that toppled the Latin American democracies of the 1960s and 1970s are now held privately and with little fanfare.[46] In the early 1990s, one could visit the Armed Forces Museum in Buenos Aires and find a plaque commemorating that country's wars, including the "War Against Subversion." It no longer exists. Some memory sites do glorify past political violence, however. The *Lonely Planet Guidebook* for El Salvador refers to the Museo de la Historia Militar (Museum of Military History) as "the other side of the story." According to the guide, it was in that place that "Colonel Domingo Monterrosa, alleged mastermind of the Massacre of El Mozote," wrote his "pages of glory for the history of the armed forces."[47] Another exception is the memorial to Jaime Guzmán, in the exclusive Las Condes neighborhood of Santiago, Chile. Guzmán, Pinochet's close advisor, head of the right-wing UDI party, and key architect of the dictatorship's 1980 constitution, was assassinated by a left-wing paramilitary group. The controversy over a memorial for Guzmán prevented its construction for years; it was finally completed in November 2008. Guzmán now also enjoys a prominent resting spot in the General Cemetery, although he shares that site with his erstwhile enemies.[48] Memorializing Guzmán has generated controversy; for example, the vandalism of an existing memorial to Guzmán in Viña del Mar in May 2008.

For the most part, authoritarian regimes and their supporters have failed to promote their perspective through trauma tourism. At memory sites, victims and survivors more often have the power to construct heroes and villains of the past authoritarian period. When vandalized or destroyed, these sites tend to gain visibility, as evident at the Crying Eye monument. Efforts to tear down Villa Grimaldi and replace it with high-rise condominiums have failed, due to the intervention of victims and survivors. A decree to demolish the infamous Argentine torture center at ESMA provoked intense opposition, and the eventual construction of the memory space there.

Examples of the erasure of memory sites do exist, however. In Uruguay, for example, the Punta Carretas detention center was transformed into an exclusive shopping mall. The significance of the site has virtually disappeared for the casual tourist. The reference to "jailhouse shopping" trivializes its history. As one visitor wrote: "I was told that this shopping center was formerly a jailhouse. Now it's a real great shopping center with lots of boutiques and a great food area. Don't forget to visit the fashionable 'confiteria' [*sic*] at the ground floor!"[49]

The former headquarters for the School of the Americas (Fuerte Espinar) in Panama has also been transformed into a commercial venture. *Rough Guide* at least provides a reference to the events that occurred at this "den of dictators": "The school graduated some of the worst human-rights violators of our time, including former Argentine dictator Leopoldo Galtieri, who 'disappeared' thousands during Argentina's Dirty War of the 1970s and El Salvador's Roberto D'Aubuisson, who led death squads that killed Archbishop Oscar Romero and thousands of other Salvadorans during the 1980s. In a bizarre twist of capitalism and ill-humor, a Spanish hotel chain has converted Building 400 into a giant resort hotel."[50]

Guidebooks deal uncomfortably with political conflict at sites of memory. In general, they segregate the political past from the sites themselves. *Rough Guide*'s historical overview provides significant detail about the various regimes, but entries on specific sites tend to minimize their charged political nature. The 2007 *Moon* guide for Chile segregates information by providing historical "background" sections and text blocks.[51] By segregating the information, the guidebooks seem to offer visitors the choice of whether to engage or avoid the contentious politics of Latin America's repressive past.

Cathartic Journeys

Journeys tend to involve discovery and the exploration of new places. They involve both foreign and "internal" travel. By "internal" travel, we mean not only the geographical locations of sites within particular countries, but also visitors' personal and emotional engagement and search for meaning at these sites. These are emotionally charged sites that often take the tourist on an exploration, or discovery, of feelings. These internal travelers, moreover, can include those directly affected from the country, exiled victims and survivors who engage in "return tourism," and tourists from within or outside the country. Memory site design reflects global tropes of memory culture, even if the sites take on a particular local specificity: the representation of victims through numbers and names; written and spoken testimonials; and expressive architecture.

Trauma tourism sites, for example, convey the magnitude of loss by representing the numbers and names of the dead and disappeared. The Crying Eye makes the tens of thousands of victims visible with names inscribed on rocks. Names of victims also appear on walls, trees, steps, and posts in the ground at other memory sites. Representing the number of dead and disappeared reflects the social losses. Naming gives identity to specific individuals who had lives, mothers and fathers, sisters and brothers, and friends.[52]

Despite the relatively commonplace appearance of lists of names, they sometimes generate conflict within victim communities. The Parque de la Memoria's wall of names in Buenos Aires illustrates this conflict. In its design the wall cuts into the ground like a jagged scar, depicting the injury to the nation and its imprint on society. The Asociación group of the Madres de Plaza de Mayo rejects the naming of the disappeared on the wall, claiming that it puts mothers in the role of symbolically killing and burying their children, since the state has still not produced the bodies of the disappeared or any evidence of their fate at the hands of the military regime.

While they object to the wall of names, the Madres display banners of photographs of the disappeared. These banners appear on commemorative days, and they show the children alive, the way they were before the regime disappeared them. Even casual visitors to the park pause to contemplate the photographs, which connect the viewer to real people, disappeared by the regime: people with faces, names, ordinary lives, and families.

Stories take a variety of forms at memory sites: plaques, recorded oral accounts played at the site, or tour guides who tell their own, or others', stories. In Paine, a small rural town outside Santiago that was targeted by Pinochet's repressive apparatus, the stories of the victims are told through mosaics. Family members of the many dead and disappeared prepared a collective memorial. Each family designed a mosaic to represent their dead or disappeared family member. Older generations used this opportunity to tell stories and remember the past. The younger generation learned about the town's past and their family's life during the dictatorship. Few of these stories or mosaics depict loss or death. Instead, they capture the individual's life: jobs, soccer team affinities, and political activism. The Paine memorial does not appear in international tour books yet; it is limited to those who are connected to the community in some way. Tourists who make it to Paine have the opportunity of learning from the members of the community about their ideals for the project. Some of the residents of Paine express hope that more visitors will come and learn about the stories. With a documentary film depicting the memorial's construction, "memory entrepreneurship" may make Paine a spot for certain trauma tourists.[53] The numbers, names, stories, and photographs allow those who were directly affected by the violence, and those who were not, a way to process the loss through personal engagement.

Sometimes visitors themselves create the sites for mourning. The Hornos de Lonquén, in a rural location outside Santiago, provides an example. Although access is now barred, the spot once marked the location of bodies discovered at the bottom of limestone ovens during the dictatorship. The ovens had been largely destroyed, but visitors who traveled to this distant and unmarked location created a folk monument, a makeshift shrine with a Virgin and an assortment of candles, rocks, flowers, and sticks. Tour books never guided travelers to this spot; instead, visitors discovered it through contacts within the Chilean human rights community. The secluded nature of the spot added to its personal and emotional intensity. At such makeshift shrines one can feel alone with the remains of the past atrocity and thus able to reflect on that loss.

On the surface, the Never Again Monument in Recife, in the state of Pernambuco, Brazil, looks little like the reflective spaces discussed above.

Its most striking characteristic, after all, is a depiction in stone of the infamous "parrot's perch" torture technique. Organized by the Torture Never Again Group, the stone denounces torture by depicting its inhumanity. It also acts as a reminder of the importance of remaining vigilant against human rights abuses. Like other sites, the memorial includes the names of victims and it provides a contemplative space to mourn and reflect on Brazil's repressive past. It thus represents political outrage of the past alongside personal reflective space. Undocumented in tour books, the site may be out of reach for most unaffected or uninvolved visitors.

These sites involve a cathartic journey from despair to hope, from silence and erasure to acknowledgment, outrage, and the call for "Never Again!" The Memory Spiral at the National University of La Plata, Argentina, recreates that journey on a small scale. It is not easy to find, but its elusiveness becomes part of the journey. The Memory Spiral does not appear in tour books, and only a few who live in La Plata know where it is. Marguerite Feitlowitz has written about it in her *Lexicon of Terror*, which may lead foreign visitors to the site.[54] The Spiral sits in the courtyard of the School of Architecture, a unit on campus particularly targeted by the regime's repressive apparatus. The names of students who died or disappeared appear in black granite on a spiral staircase that descends into the earth like an open grave. A tree blossoms from the bottom of the spiral, representing life and hope, or the fruitful possibilities that emerge from remembering the past. The Spiral is a beautiful and tranquil place that invites family members and friends to sit quietly and reflect. Its location in the center of the school's campus, however, means that current students use it as a social gathering place. Unconsciously, they reenact the daily lives of the students who were disappeared by the military regime, sharing their lives with the permanent presence of a traumatic past. The design of the monument attracts more than the conscious seekers of memory into it; it draws in accidental visitors and takes them on the journey down the spiral of horror and toward hope.

The power of these journeys suggests that some of the most personally meaningful memory sites are those that are not marketed. Most of these sites do not appear in tour books. Visitors find them with great difficulty, if at all. Catharsis and a personal connection come with the discovery of these unique, underexplored, and non-commercial sites. These sites provide an "insider" look at the country precisely because they are not part of a tourism "industry." MacCannell reflects on the heightened experience

Figure 2. "Memory Spiral," School of Architecture, National University of La Plata, Argentina. (Photography by Laurie Beth Clark and Michael Peterson)

derived from arduous tourist efforts: "The individual act of sightseeing is probably less important than the ceremonial ratification of authentic attractions as objects of intimate value, a ratification at once caused by and resulting in a gathering of tourists around an attraction and measureable to a certain degree by the time and distance the tourist travels to reach it."[55]

The former torture center DOPS (Department of Political and Social Order, a secret police organization), one of the only memorial sites in São Paulo, Brazil, challenges MacCannell's claim. No guidebooks identify the site. While members of the human rights community in São Paulo, and elsewhere in Brazil, know of the site, few have visited it or know how to find it. While a human rights activists' blog once mentioned the site, it did not provide its exact location. Since it is housed within an art museum, the entrance to the site is marked by only a small, easily missed plaque. A frequently malfunctioning video recounts the torture center's story. No other signs assist the visitor in understanding what took place there. The design of the site further complicates understanding; only four cells remain, each newly painted, with photographs on the walls depicting magazine covers and photojournalism from the time of the dictatorship. No direct connection exists between the photographs and the cells. The site is devoid of emotion or experience. Recognizing the failed opportunity of marketing DOPS, a reinauguration took place on 1 May 2008, with an eye toward catalyzing visits and contributing to human rights activism. The new center would "teach students about . . . history and hold civil society talks and debates." The organizers renamed the site the "Resistance Memorial . . . for the fight against tyranny and in defense of democracy."[56]

While these efforts might better market the site, a visitor wrote about the dissonance between the site's meaning and contemporary Brazilian human rights:

> I left the DOPS torture center wondering why I had spent so much time trying to find this place. No one knew where it was for good reason: there is nothing there and nothing to see. I headed for the Estação Luz subway. Despite my persistence, I could not convince anyone to tell me about it: what it meant, who came to it, what I should take from it. In an attempt to take a picture from the outside, I had to fend off a drunk who wanted to borrow my camera. I headed away from him only to have a police car pull up next to me on the sidewalk. The officer leaped out of the passenger seat and took aim with his gun at street children sitting on the sidewalk. Some had already fled as soon as they saw the car. Others scattered while the policeman took aim. Still others slowly ran away making sure the officer heard their taunts. This seemed like a pretty typical day for both the officer and the children. No one was surprised but me. I had just left a place aimed at remembering to not repeat. It was a mere block away. The existence of the memorial was not enough, particularly when it had no memories inside. It was devoid not only of memory but also political meaning. The police officer just outside the site could, therefore, act with impunity. Does the absence of memorials make a culture of impunity, or does a culture of impunity render empty memorials?[57]

Distance, the difficulty of the journey, and discovery do not guarantee a deep cathartic experience. A range of styles of memory sites competes on the memory market, each one fraught with tensions. Marketing thus can promote the sites' value, but it can also potentially undermine it.

Completing the Tour

Trauma tourism in Latin America presents a paradox: exposing sites of memory through mass marketing and global marketing to advance the

"Never Again" project risks trivializing and depoliticizing that very project. This chapter has explored how that occurs. No doubt appealing to a broad cross-section of tourists, guidebooks tend to minimize information and controversy around certain sites. Many sites are not covered at all. In others, the political significance or conflict is overlooked in favor of a simple "dark tourism" or "reconciliation and unity" narrative.

This process may be more acute in Latin America than in other regions, due to the lack of consensus over past violence. Dictatorships still hold some appeal in particular countries and around the world. Those who fear left-wing uprisings more than right-wing and pro-business dictatorships consider Latin America's regimes to have been necessary to the region's salvation. These individuals consider a very different "Never Again" project, one that emphasizes an end to the political Left rather than the promotion of a human rights agenda. Supporters of the past dictatorships constitute a significant minority in political opinion polls from the region. Forces within the region attempt to suppress memory to reduce conflict and move on. For the most part, however, attempts at demolishing or erasing these sites have failed.

Depoliticization is not the only constraint on trauma tourism; the victim community itself poses a significant obstacle. This community does not share a common view on how and why to remember the past, and for whom. Some groups within the region, responding to international funding opportunities and support, adopt global memory models to their own sites. Walls of names, however, offend other groups, who see them as symbolically burying memory along with the disappeared. They regard the naming and closure these walls provide as antithetical to the remembrance project. Similarly, taking on an identity from the past—the passbook in the Johannesburg Anti-Apartheid Museum, or the passport in the U.S. Holocaust Museum—is unthinkable in Latin America, particularly in Argentina, where DNA banks have emerged to trace the bloodlines of the disappeared. Survivor tours in the Robben Island Prison-cum-Museum in Cape Town, South Africa, create an emotional bond and solidarity behind the "Never Again" project for some. In Latin America, this strategy has been criticized for manufacturing sentiment that creates only a temporary empathy with an individual, rather than a sustainable political project of "Never Again." Those who consider these sites sacred spaces for mourning and remembrance find their marketing to tourists an affront to their personal traumas.[58]

To advance the "Never Again" project, Latin America trauma tourism may require more, not less, marketing. Those who were directly affected by the trauma have constructed sites with intimate and sacred spaces. These sites remain nearly invisible to those who may most need access in order to understand past political violence. Attracting visitors to the Memory Spiral in La Plata does not take away from the personal pilgrimages by the families of the disappeared. The site provides for reflection; without accessibility, however, its social and political value is limited. The DOPS site illustrates the problems of making a site too hard to find and too empty to sustain visits by either the directly affected or the casual tourist. On the other hand, Jelin's notion of memory saturation or memory fatigue may result from too much marketing.[59] Visitors may consider the past effectively commemorated and move on to different sorts of political projects.

A recent edition of the guidebook *Time Out Buenos Aires* documents the evocative memorial ceramics that have been placed throughout Buenos Aires by the group Barrios por la Memoria y la Justicia. Arresting memorials like these, designed to draw individuals in, do not seem to saturate the market. Instead, they attract both the aware tourist and the unconscious tourist who wants to know more. The failure to explain a site, either in guidebooks or through narration at the site itself, forgoes an opportunity to build an understanding of the violent past. Intriguing memorials will sustain themselves beyond the directly affected generation, universalizing the experience to create the possibility of a global "Never Again" norm.

Many different ways of remembering occur on these sites. They exist for multiple, even contradictory uses, and those uses reveal a complex political story. Fear of commercialization of trauma therefore seems exaggerated. A memory theme park is an unlikely outcome of global marketing. Few international visitors will seek the "all-inclusive" memory tour. On the contrary, marketing will draw those visitors off the beaches, away from the volcanoes, ecoparks, and ski resorts, to experience something new and powerful. In order to make the past visible to the politically unconscious tourist and attempt to build awareness of human rights violations around the world, some marketing may prove imperative. It will expose these pasts to those new generations or to foreign visitors who do not yet bear the social responsibility to remember and not to repeat.

A marketing solution does not exist to resolve these tensions. Instead, the political debate surrounding these sites seems to shape their meaning and purpose. Neither the sites nor the conflicts can achieve the elusive

"Never Again" project alone, but they can contribute to an awareness of the past and the possibility of developing a human rights consciousness, even among those who do not already have it. While some visitors may be overly concerned about their laundry, putting human rights into the itinerary of the casual tourist enhances the opportunity for shaping consciousness.

NOTES

Many thanks go to various individuals who helped to formulate thoughts and provide criticism on this project, particularly Rebecca J. Atencio, Ksenija Bilbija, Jo Ellen Fair, Alexandra Huneeus, Stephen E. Meili, Alice Nelson, Kathleen Pertzborn, Michael Peterson, Andrew G. Reiter, and Erika Robb.

1. Palmerlee et al., *Lonely Planet: Argentina*, 36.
2. Audra Felix and Piper Smith conducted research for this project, summarized in their report, "A Database of Military and National Sites from the *Lonely Planet* and *Rough Guides*: The Emergence of Trauma Tourism and Its Ties to the Colonial Past" (unpublished, 2008).
3. Clark began using the term "trauma tourism" in a 2002 conference paper ("Peripatetic Memory," International Federation for Theatre Research, Amsterdam, The Netherlands). For an extended discussion of its usage, see Clark, "Coming to Terms with Trauma Tourism." "Trauma tourism" is used pejoratively by some mental health practitioners to refer to volunteer counselors and professional therapists who flock to disaster sites to facilitate psychological debriefing (see Gist and Lubin, *Response to Disaster*).
4. Nora, "Between Memory and History"; Tumarkin, *Traumascapes*; Bickford, "Memoryscapes."
5. Seaton, "Guided by the Dark."
6. Lennon and Foley, *Dark Tourism*; Yuill, "Dark Tourism."
7. Lippard, *The Lure of the Local*. See also www.grief-tourism.com.
8. Rojek, "Fatal Attractions."
9. "Voluntourism" combines traditional travel with volunteer work. "Impact tourism" provides opportunities for visitors to engage in local social justice work.
10. MacCannell, *The Tourist*, 7.
11. Ibid., 10.
12. See Williams, *Memorial Museums*; Hirsch, *Family Frames*; Hirsch, *The Familial Gaze*; Bruner, "Tourism in Ghana"; Young, *The Texture of Memory*; Braxton and Diedrich, *Monuments of the Black Atlantic*; Yoneyama, *Hiroshima Traces*; Schwenkel, *The American War in Contemporary Vietnam*.
13. Sites of Conscience website, www.sitesofconscience.org/sites/villa-grimaldi/.
14. Sites of Conscience website, www.sitesofconscience.org. See also Liz Ševenko, *The Power of Place: How Historic Sites Can Engage Citizens in Human Rights Issues*, Minneapolis: Center for Victims of Torture, 2004 (available at www.sitesofcon

science.org/wp-content/documents/publications/power-of-place-en.pdf).

15. Latin America is one of four regional networks in the coalition and has one founding member. This region includes only nine of the sixty-two institutional memberships within the coalition.
16. Carillet et al., *Lonely Planet: Chile and Easter Island*, 103.
17. Corporación Parque por la Paz Villa Grimaldi website, www.villagrimaldicorp.cl.
18. Viva Travel Guides: Chile website, www.vivatravelguides.com/south-america/chile/santiago/santiago-articles/villa-grimaldi-chile/.
19. Derechos Chile website, www.chipsites.com/derechos/index_eng.html.
20. "Thousands of Zombies in Chilean Society," Calliope's Odyssey blog, at World Nomads.com, http://journals.worldnomads.com/homersmuse/post/6625.aspx.
21. Taylor, "Trauma as Durational Performance."
22. MacCannell, *The Tourist*, 101.
23. "Thousands of Zombies in Chilean Society," Calliope's Odyssey blog, at World Nomads.com, http://journals.worldnomads.com/homersmuse/post/6625.aspx.
24. *Lonely Planet* and *Moon* cover Villa Grimaldi; the other standard travel guides (e.g., *Fodor's*, *Frommer's*, *Footprint*, and *Rough Guide*) do not.
25. Bernhardson, *Chile*.
26. Memorial "El Ojo que Llora," www.aprodeh.org.pe/ojoquellora2006 (our translation).
27. See YouTube video, description of the site, and negative commentary at La Voz del Edén, el blog de Beto Serquén, http://blog.pucp.edu.pe/item/10272. See also "Perú—El Ojo que Llora," Expreso de Lima, 5 January 2007, www.lahistoriapara lela.com.ar; and Hite, "'The Eye that Cries.'"
28. Melissa Lulofs, 27 May 2008, TravelBlog website, www.travelblog.org/South-America/Peru/Lima/blog-280959.html. The responses to Lulofs's entry focused on issues unrelated to the monument: "Megan" commented that she would be unhappy if she had to drop off her clothes for someone else to clean; Lulofs's uncle wrote about his "Peruvian TV dinner."
29. For social activism in Germany, see "Germany for the Jewish Traveler" (Germany National Tourist Office, March 2008), www.cometogermany.com/pdf/jewish_traveler.pdf. Of course, there are also other publications in the "Germany for . . ." series, including Germany for Honeymooners and Germany for Young People, which do not include a social activist dimension (see www.cometogermany.com/ENU/culture_and_events/germany_jewish_traveler.htm).
30. Chandler and Penland, *Lonely Planet: Nicaragua and El Salvador*, 323.
31. Fisher et al., *The Rough Guide to Mexico*, 463.
32. Vidgen, *Lonely Planet: Guatemala*, 284.
33. Noble et al., *Lonely Planet: Mexico*, 106.
34. See Basulto, David, "Monumento Mujeres en la Memoria / oficinadearquitectura," Plataforma Architectura website, www.plataformaarquitectura.cl/2006/12/28/monumento-mujeres-en-la-memoria-oficinadearquitectura/.
35. Bernhardson, *Chile*, 56.
36. *Fodor's Chile*, 22.
37. Carillet et al., *Lonely Planet: Chile and Easter Island*, 100.

38. Bernhardson, *Chile*, 56.
39. Kueffner and Schreck, *Frommer's: Chile and Easter Island*, 88–89.
40. Graham and Benson, *The Rough Guide to Chile*, 107.
41. Palmerlee et al., *Lonely Planet: Argentina*, 40.
42. Bernhardson, *Argentina*, 39, 42.
43. Aeberhard et al., *The Rough Guide to Argentina*, 103.
44. *Fodor's Argentina*, 19.
45. The group Asociación Madres de Plaza de Mayo is criticized for having applauded the efforts by the 9/11 terrorists in the United States and for supporting the ETA Basque Nationalist attacks. They are also considered to be too closely linked to the Kirchner government to be able to act autonomously for human rights goals.
46. Carvalho and da Silva Catela, "31 de marzo de 1964 en Brasil."
47. Chandler and Penland, *Lonely Planet: Nicaragua and El Salvador*, 324.
48. Wilde, "Avenues of Memory."
49. Virtual Tourist website, www.virtualtourist.com/travel/South_America/Uruguay/DepartmentodeMontivideo/Montevideo-1624243/Shopping-Montevideo-BR-1.html (accessed 21 April 2008).
50. Firestone, *Lonely Planet: Panama*, 250.
51. Bernhardson, *Chile*, 58.
52. Milton, "Naming."
53. Agüero, *Memorial de Paine*.
54. Feitlowitz, *A Lexicon of Terror*, 181–84.
55. MacCannell, *The Tourist*, 14.
56. Fórum Permanente dos Ex-Presos e Perseguidos Políticos do Estado de São Paulo, Boletim, 1 May 2008.
57. "Anna says:" entry, Trauma Tourism website, http://traumatourism.wordpress.com/share-experiences/.
58. Nancy Gates-Madsen, "Marketing and Sacred Space: The Parque de la Memoria in Buenos Aires," this volume.
59. Jelin, *State Repression and the Labors of Memory*.

SUSANA DRAPER

The Business of Memory

Reconstructing Torture Centers as Shopping Malls and Tourist Sites

What place does the city, with its multiplicity of spaces, rhythms, and times, have in a critical history of the transition from dictatorship to democracy? Addressing this question is crucial on at least two accounts. The material transformations that have taken place in urban spaces during and after the transition from a military regime to democracy have entailed the privatization of public space, but they are also part of an overarching effort that has sought to modify the experience of temporality. The impunity granted to military crimes resulted in an emerging, collective desire in the early 1990s to enter a new time, or new present, severed from the dictatorial past. The spatial history of life in the post-dictatorship era thus reveals a double movement: vis-à-vis both a nascent dream for this new time, demanding erasure of certain unsettling temporalities, and, as one expression of this impetus, the proliferation of spaces of consumption. Such transformations in urban areas have involved remodeling commercial spaces that come to specifically embody a new present for controlled freedom, and hand-in-hand with inducing homogenization across multiple temporalities.

My work addresses a neoliberal city's process of consolidation, reflected in several social and political negotiations tantamount to the Full Stop Law that attempted to bring closure to the past. This task transports us to the early 1990s, at the height of many shopping mall openings, considered part of the new imaginary of progress in an urban texture being altered in leaps and bounds.[1] I will reflect on an instance I consider fundamental for having consolidated a relationship between the market and the dictatorial past: the transformation of the Punta Carretas (PC) penitentiary into the Punta Carretas Shopping Center (PCSC), Montevideo's most exclusive mall. Engaging the urban texture of this dictatorial past and the present, I will focus on a second layered transformation in Buenos Aires, through the Escuela de Suboficiales de Mecánica de la Armada (ESMA) and a former secret detention center (*centro clandestino de detención*, or CCD), dubbed "El Olimpo" by military personnel.

Each of these movements carries out a unique temporal operation, which I approach by drawing from a counterpoint in tension between sites. On the one hand, I explore architecture of the transition that expressed post-dictatorship impunity. This consisted of a series of architectural operations designed to control the ways in which the city's past could be articulated in new spaces for consumerism (exemplified by PCSC). On the other hand, I turn to the idea of a "critical folding" evident in these spatial transformations, which interrupts the former architecture and leads us to question the ways in which certain layers of an unsettling, clandestine past can be differently evoked and engaged. Critical folding describes an operation that occurs within the very materiality, or texture, of an already existing site; it transforms a site that, contrary to the assimilation we see in architectural alterations during the transition era, generates a spatio-temporal void in which traces of the past civic-military regimes and the city's neoliberal present interact. This raises questions regarding the relation between justice and public space that the architecture of the transition systematically attempted to conceal.

Although my analysis of specific sites aims to bring forth a layer of the past that the architecture of the transition attempted to obscure, this does not imply that there lies an essential past awaiting discovery, unveiled to us only now. Rather, the various transformations of CCDs belie problematic and paradoxical instances in which territory and history are articulated—interrupting the architecture of the transition without offering a new truth about the past. By contrasting the processes that homogenized and assimilated unsettling temporalities in PCSC, and those that turned the Argentine CCDs into sites for memory capable of conjuring up past conflicts, I propose considering these operations in terms of temporality and spatiality.

Montevideo: The Punta Carretas Shopping Center

In the case of the Punta Carretas Shopping Center, the transformative context of the place and its marketing strategies have erased the building's sinister character. In this preservationist mall the past has acquired a distinctly commercial value. PCSC, highly esteemed for having been "recycled" from a prison, maintains absolute distance from any sort of honest expression of the site's past; all indications of its former use have been erased, thereby forging an architectural work governed by its potential for consumption. In other words, in order to advertise PCSC a simultaneous conservation and negation of the prison's past occurred, leading to an overappraisal of the architecture's historical features. The prison's transformation into a mall also grants us the chance to reflect on the camouflaged aesthetic of the transition more generally; the past, like the prison, required alteration before it could open with an empty function, both for and by its market value. The prison-mall's transformation therefore becomes a cosmetic operation of whitewashing a site—a conversion characterized by the unequivocal separation of its history and the logic of commercialization.

PCSC opened its doors within a neoliberal context, which conceives of the market and memory in opposition to each other. We cannot talk about a total erasure of the past, however, since the PCSC project aimed to preserve certain historical features that would give the mall a new appeal for potential shoppers and tourists. Instead, its process of restructuring acted as a metaphor for how the market makes a business of the past. In fact, the recycling of architectural forms in great part made PCSC the most important and exclusive mall in Montevideo. In PCSC consumption governed the conversion of the prison; this site came to explicitly articulate the market demands constituted by the city and its consumers, as well as the specific demands of tourism. A widespread publicity campaign in urban spaces marketed the prison-mall as a symbol of love, evidencing the very process of revamping the prison's former image. We can therefore see the prison's transformation as operating within a framework that idealizes and eroticizes consumption, where burns once branding a tortured body are now supplanted by commercial brands.

Buenos Aires: Escuela de Mecánica de la Armada and El Olimpo

While public spaces lost ground to the 1990s rise in consumerism, spaces for memory have again come to play an essential role in South American metropolises.[2] Some spaces for memory thus carry out an operation altogether different from the architectural recycling and consumerist renovation of PC. My second set of examples, drawn from the city of Buenos Aires, contrasts the PCSC and the appearance of spaces for memory in ESMA and Olimpo. Asking how spaces for memory bring back the past entails seeing the ways in which they can (or cannot) be differentiated from commercializing strategies that we observe in the extreme case of PCSC. The idea of "MERCOSUR Memory" also exemplifies the explicit relation between memory and market.[3] Toward this end, the counterpoint between a transitional moment crystallized in the form of PCSC and the return to urban space allows us to question the repercussions of dictatorship on the present. I propose engaging differences between articulations of the dictatorial past and the challenges that they begin to face when spaces of consumption, the market, etc., threaten to subsume spaces for memory.

That the proliferation of sites for memory in Buenos Aires would obtain such relevance perhaps arose from an analysis of the PC conversion, a hugely explicit indicator of impunity expressed by the urban texture beginning in the 1990s. If we further consider the impact that the process of commodifying history has had on reshaping the inhabitance of urban space in South America, we must ask the following questions: Can we say that patrons consume the past in ESMA or Olimpo? Do these sites commodify the past or do something else? If tourism of memory exists (something we can find, e.g., in the previously cited advertising campaign for "MERCOSUR Memory"), are struggles to create sites for memory still reduced to a commercial function with tourist appeal? While no clear-cut answers to these questions exist, the contrast between PCSC (as an expression of impunity) and the former CCDs in Buenos Aires allows us to differentiate between transformative processes.

Here we open up many folds that demand subtlety and an ability to analyze the difference between space and place, between evoking memory and its fetishization. With these cautions in mind, a brief visit to the spaces at ESMA and Olimpo will guide our discussion.[4] The fact that threats and even disappearances continue against opening sites for memory in Argentina at present speaks to something beyond marketing; it references a kind of opening toward a past that brings back unsettling memories. Not only does the military reveal its disturbance by these sites, but there likewise persists a general perception that insisting on the past slows the present course—the argument par excellence that defined the transition. The case of Olimpo seems particularly relevant for this reason; it poses a series of questions that together reference an essential element in the connection between the machinery of terror and the experience of the neighborhood's everyday life. This speaks to the present, demonstrating how years under dictatorship left an indelible mark on the urban fabric and on daily experience.[5]

Beyond Consumption: Site Restoration in Montevideo and Buenos Aires

It seems necessary to differentiate between the mechanisms that posit a hinge between market and memory so we may open a space of critical analysis for what lies beyond the measurable register. This entails unfolding moments that suspend the logic of transactions and all things quantifiable—as two fundamental functions of the market and the language employed in transactions—from within the urban texture. I argue that these spaces evoke a certain incalculable experience, further guiding my approach to the cities' critical folds, which work toward revising the established meanings and relationships between city and polis. Such problematic centers thus interrupt the neoliberal city of consumption. This induces an emergent critical view, potentially capable of approaching two different processes that frame this analysis: (1) the globalization of place as a marketing strategy; and (2) the potential force of place, understood as an unfolding that provokes a question of past and present, exceeding the quantitative logic of sales. In turn, this tension would have us question the presence of the market, whereby bringing back the past is, and is *not*, a sustainable project. The fundamental question of this task remains how the past becomes, and what it incites when, evoked.

My analysis of space here centers on the notion of restoration emerging as a central focal point both for mall projects carried out by Juan Carlos López, the Argentine architect in charge of transforming Punta Carretas, and for spaces of memory in Buenos Aires. What meaning can the restoration of a place obtain? Differing from Villa Grimaldi, where restoration became an official strategy of national pseudo-reconciliation, the question of restoration here becomes the focus of conceptualizing each site's function and its investment in a politics at/within the present. There thus exists a tension within PCSC as an expression of the city of impunity, characterized by the privatization and isolation of public space, with the dictatorial past (embodied in the prison) preserved as an ornament that grants added value to marketing the site. On the one hand, the opening of detention sites—or the process of excavations that take place within them—challenges the kind of temporality configured in the transition. Remembering the necessity to forget operates discursively as a market strategy; a free market cannot be opened up by looking back. On the other hand, as highlighted by my analysis, such sites may turn into non-calculable, critical folds, making their total co-optation by the state and market impossible.

Commodifying the Past: The Transformation of Punta Carretas

This section analyzes the transformation of the PC prison into PCSC from within its own temporal logic. I approach Punta Carretas both as a part of a political process that resolved matters of remembrance to forget the dictatorship, granting amnesty for the military's involvement, and as part of a "malling" process concerned with constructing a new city that articulates a particular kind of temporality.

PCSC can be read as the congealment of an emblematic moment in articulating the past-present. Forgetting by state administration, as Gareth Williams argues, did not encourage an overall amnesia, but rather a continual repetition of remembering that the past must be forgotten for the common good and interest of all.[6] There existed a perception in Uruguay that any strategy that engaged remembering the dictatorship interfered with the market. As Nelly Richard explains, the transition began to pay off as an entrance fee into the logic of pure profit: more market, more liberty, more consumption, assumed to embody almost equivalent values for more forgetting.[7] However, at this moment, history became a prime target of diverse market strategies, which can be observed at different levels. These include literary practices and trends within the general public, exemplified by the sales boom of historical novels; commercial architectural styles that begin to value older, recycled styles, giving way to the so-called preservationist trend; and the fashion of collecting antique furniture.

In the case of PCSC, the past played an essential role in the site's strategy for marketing and consumerism, forming part of an architectural vanguard that Juan Carlos López's team put into practice in several Latin American countries, but, most importantly, in a process that began with Patio Bullrich, Alto Palermo, and Galerías Pacífico, and that culminated with Punta Carretas and Patio Olmos. Bearing the brand name "Juan Carlos López and Associates," this series of malls valorized a preserved but modified past, on several occasions earning design awards from the International Council of Shopping Centers. A site's historical elements, however, become a prime commodity only if the past can be transformed to fit into the new exigencies of the market and its rules for purchasing power accompanying the city's process of transformation and rejuvenation. As Harvey states, "The artifices of advertising and image construction" constitute a key instance in the process of commodifying places.[8] This must be analyzed in depth in the case of PCSC, with the very history of the place (the prison) burdened by memories that needed to undergo a radical transformation in order to make it visitor-friendly. For PCSC, this juxtaposition of past and present in the form of a prison-mall also served to mark who could and who could not enter this site. Examining the prison's transformation into Montevideo's most visited shopping center therefore takes us through the history of the prison, its closure, and beyond, to complex marketing strategies employed for the new prison-mall.

Opened in 1910, the Punta Carretas penitentiary formed part of a monumental architecture that expressed the symbols of a modernized country. Throughout the century the penitentiary held many political prisoners captive, its walls witness to various dictatorships, spanning from fascism in the 1930s to the military takeover in the 1970s. In 1971, political prisoners who belonged to the MLN-Tupamaros escaped from Punta Carretas through a tunnel dug from inside the prison walls. They escaped again in 1972, through a tunnel burrowed from the outside. In reaction to these events, the authorities built the Penal de Libertad, a high-security prison for political detainees, cynically named "Freedom," where they transferred the majority of male political prisoners. After the release of the last prisoners, the site was closed in 1985 for its connotation as a symbol of prolonged physical and psychological torture of prisoners.[9]

In 1986, however, after a revolt of common prisoners, the PC prison closed and Libertad reopened for the purpose of holding PC's former prisoners. As discussed by the members of Service of Peace and Justice (SERPAJ), the reopening of Libertad—a symbol for torture and human rights violations—augmented the impunity that occurred during these years. The same can be said about the conversion of Punta Carretas, bought by a corporation (Sociedad Anónima) run by key figures of the transition (e.g., the Ministry of Interior, then juridical partner of Julio María Sanguinetti, president during the transition and minister of culture during the dictatorship). As Hugo Achugar stated, the history of Punta Carretas's transformation must be considered in conjunction with the referendum and plebiscite for the Law of Expiry, which amnestied military personnel for their human rights violations during the decade of terror. The opening of PCSC in 1994 therefore became part of a bigger process: history configured as a kind of prison transformed into "the country of the future." The overlapping of prison and mall not only marks a passage between different historical paradigms but also poses a question regarding the status of the past within this new system, inducted into an order of homogeneous global sites (among them Sheraton Hotels, McDonald's, and Blockbuster video stores).

Marketing for the site centered on two features: first, the architectural and historical value of the renovated building (highlighted to attract tourists); and second, the cynical fabrication of an advertising image for the site as a place for love—a strategic pitch to local consumers who, unable to see the magic of the prison-mall, could still remember the prison's dark history. Within the ideal of containment sustained by the image of an atemporal site, there arose a conversion of the past into a commodity fetish for consumption (but not for investigation or critical articulation). In other words, the preservation of history occurred without entering into a conflictive dialogue with its new function. As the architect in charge of the prison's transformation expressed in explaining his work, elements from the past should operate as a decorative element. In addition, architect Estela Porada stated, "We tried to preserve the spirit of the prison, but in a way in which this 'preservation' would not be an obstacle for the development of the new function." One can also read the architects' supposition about the site's physical expression in relation to the conversion taking place architectonically over time. Both the past and present of the place connected to the city in an unspecified temporality that dually characterizes the space of malls and the overall problem of time surrounding the process of "malling," a U.S. model followed by Juan Carlos López.

As this specific prison-mall suggests in its architectural metaphor, the process of "malling," which took place in tandem with the political transition, worked to enact a realm of controlled freedom. The mall emerged as the dream of a space in which people could have everything without expos-

Figure 1. Punta Carretas Shopping Center, main entrance.
(Photograph by Ksenija Bilbija)

ing themselves to the contingencies of time, weather, poverty, insecurity, etc. This points toward a certain erasure of temporality, something that we can see in the transformation, and in the way in which the head architect described his first impression of the prison: "I was shocked when I entered into the place [prison] for the first time . . . and . . . I saw this three-story building with all the floors leading to a central plaza, and I said to myself: '*This looks like a mall*, a mall of prisoners.' And I grasped a very special idea there, that I could never forget."[10] This demonstrates the very legacy that the dictatorship left on the city: the need for a freedom always under control that constitutes most marketplaces.[11] As Moulian argues in his classic *Chile actual*, shopping malls became a kind of utopia for a freedom of movement within a highly surveilled site that responded to the demands of a long-standing, paranoid convention of security. In short, malls came to represent "the guarantee of always being watched by a Big Eye"; the co-existence of market-based freedom and control that went hand-in-hand with an inculcated habit for surveillance naturalized by the dictatorship.[12]

During post-dictatorship times, the prison-mall constitutes a kind of architecture for the experience of the transition. It plays a relevant role in constructing an imaginary of what neoliberal democracy involves through a specific operation. Malls have become monuments that express the silent contradictions grounding the dream of a post-historical time in the environment of consumption, thereby staging a dual transformation: (1) in the exhaustion of time; and (2) in turning history into an object of consumption. Fabián Giménez and Alejandro Villagrán express this idea at the moment of the "boom" of malling in Montevideo: "The shopping center is the lifting of the city. . . . A non-place indifferent to traditions and customs of the city, an abrupt arrest of social temporality. At the shopping center time comes to a stop . . . the end of history is materialized in these spatio-temporal capsules . . . the realized utopia of neoliberalism! The secret of eternal youth . . . No one gets old, no one dies, stores do not close for mourning, death dies amidst the system of objects. . . . The shopping centers become metaphysical objects that are immune to criticism."[13]

The authors emphasize the connection between the mall and the denial of time, as if these spatial capsules came to stage the dreams of a post-historical life with no place for death. However, a critical analysis of this process will inevitably lead us to the tensions that such sites—created at a moment when dealing with past deaths and disappearances became highly relevant—have concealed.

The idea of marketing PCSC with the central figure of love further arose from a bid for forgetting: attempting to reestablish the illusion of a common ground where remnants of death "disappeared." This image of love implied overwriting the site's past with a slogan, advertised with banners located throughout the city and in a modified song used in a television spot entitled "In PCSC you will fall in love": "En PCSC, ¡te vas a enamorar! . . . Vas a vivir la sensación y la emoción. . . . Punta Carretas Shopping, te va a enamorar." Masking disturbing memories triggered by the site thus coupled with a discursive strategy to promote the mall. But what is love in PCSC? On the one hand, love emerged as the promise of a perfect encounter. Advertisements for the place played with the idea of the site as a container of plenitude, where a mandate of a new love found in the transaction itself replaced the bodies that formerly inhabited the prison (bodies in pain and marked by it): "Where do people go when it rains? To PCSC." By following the advertising campaign used to whitewash memories of the site as a prison, we see that selling the image of the prison-mall concentrated on creating an image for a space of containment in which all the contingencies of life could find a solution.

The site's television propaganda played with the idea of a great container, immune to any danger, like a bubble, sheltered from the dangers of the city's outskirts. This conversion, traveling from a site filled with conflict and tragedy to its reconstitution as a protective, warm environment, made the installation prize-worthy for the free-market world. The building's architectural recycling operated like a kind of wrapping in which the shopping center had undergone plastic surgery to cover the folds and wrinkles of its post-dictatorial time. Avoiding any allusion to ruin, the prison transformed its remains into a "happy ending," through elements that compose a kitsch aesthetic, characteristic of López's artistic-architectural project. This confronts us with a longing for a (postmortem, embalmed) "time after time" that makes the very "immaterialization" of history official (its conversion into a "mythical" history). The present turned an ideal for a prison-made-shopping-center into a compass that could guide a dream of progress toward an absolute future—characterized by the elimination of all incited struggle, of all possibility for dialectics. Within this context, the words of Uruguayan President Lacalle at the ribbon-cutting ceremony for the supermarket inside PCSC say it all: "This is how Uruguay will be in 2000."

Punta Carretas also turned into a fascinating center for tourists. Many web pages on the Internet suggest visiting the site for its past as a prison, and promote it as having the best stores for shopping in Montevideo. The site is understood not as a space of internment, but as one for enjoyment by the tourist gaze. On one web page, called "Virtualtourist.com," I found the following message that demonstrates the tourist gaze and the sensationalism of the prison to PCSC, giving it incredible flavor:

> Punta Carretas Shopping Center: *Jailhouse Shopping*
>
> I was told that this shopping center was formerly a jailhouse. Now it's a real great shopping center with lots of boutiques and a great food area. Don't forget to visit the fashionable "confiteria" [*sic*] at the groundfloor! You will find practically everything in the many shops, even all you need for your mate [infused herb tea] equipment![14]

PCSC, turned into a novel site for tourists, constitutes another link to the "country of services," where tourism has become an essential part of the fetishization of the historical. With this, the space begins to acquire an added value; for its placement within a tourist circuit, the site becomes a monument that serves dually to atone for its architectural faults and to demonstrate respect toward history while it turns into a fundamental marketing tool. Its historical features become, following this line of thought, an ornament. Historical features, however, cannot be completely stripped from the prison-mall for all. In contrast to such happy advertising for "jailhouse shopping," a tourist who went to Montevideo hoping to visit the prison-mall asked a taxi driver to take her to "that shopping center that used to be a jail." Looking for conversation, she asked the taxi driver if he liked the place or went often, to which the man replied, greatly irritated, "How could I go to that place, Señora, if my brothers were prisoners there!"

With the tourist site and the creation of the boutique district, the neighborhood around PC became esteemed with higher value. It shot up and forced many inhabitants to move to other areas of the city since they could no longer afford to pay rent. Graciela Martínez analyzes this phenomenon in detail, stating: "Many houses change hands to become commercial property, particularly for restaurants, while others are bought by new residents who are more suitable for the current status of the area." The prison-mall thus imposed "a new individualist lifestyle" that called for more security (e.g., "doors, doormen, fences and garages, elitist segregation contaminating the whole neighborhood"). Finally, Martínez expresses that "the message implied in the opening publicity for the shopping center—recover a lost place for the city. . . . This is Punta Carretas, once withdrawn and now successfully recovered by and for them, the shopping mall investors, and for the city that they and the mall represent."[15]

People who have been left devalued in the new area (after the rise in rent) migrate to other areas of the city, generating a wave marked by the rhythm of the area's new services (e.g., tourism and high-end restaurants). Engaging Achugar's argument, the transformation of PC articulates two effects: on the one hand, the installation of one kind of forgetting-memory, and on the other hand, the tourist shaping of a post-dictatorial Uruguay with a peaceful but paradisiacal imagery that "Nothing happened here": "Within the framework of the project for a modern Uruguay, looking for its new historical function through a process of integrating Mercosur, hegemonic discourse promotes a paradisiacal version of the country. The PC Shopping Mall forms part of this paradisification of the country to which the modernizing and "pacifying" discourse aspires by presenting itself as a 'safe' space where former violence has been eradicated."[16]

The new shopping center bubble, erected for the neighborhood's rejuvenation and recovery as an ideal tourist site for consuming history while one goes shopping, constitutes a kind of model that entails the shopping mall concept—a space that promotes the idea of recovering a site from its old age in rhythm with its new architecture. In *The System of Objects*, Baudrillard argues that antiques perform more of a signifying role than a practical one, with a specific function "to signify time." However, these "signs" carry with them a double paradox that simultaneously invokes and denies history.[17] Baudrillard associates the paradoxical act that drives the desire to collect with a demand or desire for seeking a complete or definite being—in other words, a closeness to change that assumes history, a kind of "present perfect" that opposes the (simple) present of functional objects. In a certain way, PCSC operates like a point of condensation for the transformation of post-dictatorial time, by emptying the converted and conceived past into pure value for its consumption.

Other Times in the City: Sites as Critical Foldings

If PCSC emerges as a project to recover a space for its new function as a tourist site, how do we contrast this with the recovery of detention centers turned into spaces for memory? In what follows, I will briefly approach two spaces in the city of Buenos Aires where I find a critical opening produced, as well as a kind of articulation about the past that in PCSC remains cancelled out, given its full absorption by the market. In contrast to the prison-mall, in which a repaired past stretches like a face-lift over the city's skin, the other proposed spaces evoke the preeminence of ruins. Neoliberalism problematizes the processes of capturing memory and forgetting, because these ruins evoke a radical finitude (a mark of transience and death) that opens critical folds within the neoliberal city of consumption.

In contrast to PCSC, two brief visits to ESMA and Olimpo will allow us to think about the ways in which these spaces suspend the constellation of issues articulated in the prison-mall. If PCSC, in fact, does operate like a face-lift for the city, as Villagrán and Giménez claim, then I propose reading spaces for memory as the folds in a city that highlight the very finality and exhibition of a problem centered on death. We should keep in mind that these spaces remain constantly threatened by tourist demands and appropriation by the state that could turn them into cultural heritage sites for their complex, polemical history.

As Laurie Beth Clark and Leigh A. Payne argue in their "Trauma Tourism" chapter in this volume, Villa Grimaldi exemplifies one of the most sophisticated advances in memory marketing in Latin America. By following more faithfully the demands of a global market for horror tourism, Villa Grimaldi has become a problematic center of reconciliation. We could even say by a modest stretch of the imagination that this site's marketing and architectural work of recycling and reconstruction would seem close to the kind of conversion strategy (and pseudo-reconciliation) carried out for PC prison. Given the context of its transformation and the way in which it functioned as part of an attempt for reconciliation, the Villa Grimaldi case also helped to form a series of prejudices about the proliferation of sites for memory. As Mauricio Lazzara explains, Villa Grimaldi embodies a key space for the negotiation of an idea of reconciliation that remains under suspicion.[18] The remodeling of the place speaks to a questionable critical imaginary, and ex-detainee Pedro Matta's bilingual tourist guide helps us see this site as one that promotes itself under a certain fascination with, or "hollywoodization" of, torture.[19]

The selective whitewashing of PCSC or the marketing of horror in trauma tourism found in Villa Grimaldi (both cases used by the neoliberal state in order to promote a certain advertisement for reconciliation) contrasts with ESMA and Olimpo. A visit to ESMA or Olimpo (or Club Atlético, for that matter) proves surprising, since they do not explicitly subsume memory into a marketing strategy or tourist destination. These sites avoid stirring the sensationalism characterized by marketing for horror and torture methods. Furthermore, neither of the sites charges an entrance fee, nor do they sell souvenirs or other merchandise. The cases of ESMA and Olimpo therefore offer a counterpoint to the transformation embodied by PCSC, posing a series of questions regarding the role that place plays in relation to alternative ways of thinking about temporality in the city and traces of the military past. Visits to ESMA and Olimpo should thus be distinguished for their involvement in a much larger scheme.

In these two cases, the very sites of extermination themselves show the conditions that make possible the market-based notion of democracy and controlled freedom characterizing post-dictatorship society. Whereas aesthetic renovation and recycling are key elements for "selling" places in neoliberal cities, the process of transforming ESMA and Olimpo sets before us a different and ambivalent strategy, since the manner of narrating the sites constantly changes in response to current debates. In a way, the sites' transformation creates history by stressing two key elements: (1) the ex-

Figure 2. ESMA, main entrance. (Photograph by Ksenija Bilbija)

termination of political dissidents, and (2) the connection of this policy to the history of the accumulation of capital. In order to analyze the contrast to PCSC, I will outline a brief historical background of these sites within a broader network of clandestine detention centers during the dictatorship and subsequent transformation to democracy.

ESMA constitutes one of the most emblematic sites among some five hundred clandestine detention centers in Argentina. Operating as a CCD before the military coup d'état,[20] ESMA remained the largest detention center during the dictatorship. Approximately five thousand detainees, a majority of whom were disappeared, passed through its doors. During the center's operation as a CCD, the entire school portion continued its normal operations, providing the most obvious example of complicity with the center's activities. ESMA also exploited its detainees for forced labor, working for on-site operations like falsifying documents and managing real estate transactions for property seized by the government from detainees. The center further served as a space for anti-subversive education, training military personnel on the (mis)treatment of detainees. After a long struggle, the site was transformed into a "space for remembering and defending human rights" in 2004.[21]

Military personnel named the CCD that operated between August 1978 and the end of January 1979 in the La Floresta neighborhood's office for the Automotive Division of the Federal Police, "El Olimpo."[22] Some detainees identified the same material used for the prison cell doors that they had encountered in Club Atlético, thus implying that it had been equipped for use as a CCD.[23] The utilization of cells at Olimpo also began with Club Atlético's anticipated closure. This information points toward Olimpo as having constituted one link within the underground circuit of "Club Atlético"—"Banco"—"Olimpo." After a long struggle characterized by high levels of participation from residents in the La Floresta neighborhood—where Olimpo and Orletti Automotives both operated—the government declared the grounds a Historical City Site, becoming a "site for memory" in 2004. Since then, many activities for public remembrance have been held on these grounds, including discussion workshops, several film series, and the installment of a neighborhood library that has undertaken a project collecting banned books from the dictatorship years.

Only guided visits are allowed at ESMA and Olimpo because of their links to the dictatorship and the struggle to recover and preserve these sites. In contrast to PCSC's transformation, which centered on erasing unsettling temporalities and selling an idea of a new (and controlled) market freedom, these sites create a series of holes within the urban texture. They bring forth many questions regarding the clandestine, systematic extermination of dissidence practiced, in order to put an end to any alternative idea of society. The proliferation of these kinds of spaces speaks to a complex current political apparatus and struggle against becoming a city of impunity, characterized by a history based on this network of clandestine sites used for detainment. They therefore open certain folds that make visible the clandestine past, providing a bleak history for the conditions of possibility in the free market. These folds become critical for their very impossibility of providing a truth or a clear answer with respect to the past. In contrast to the whitewashing performed in the transformation and messages that advertised "new time" in PCSC, these two sites in Buenos Aires emphasize a radical ambivalence.

Neither ESMA nor Olimpo embodies a museum as a collection of objects; both sites involved a debate over how to avoid remodeling or recycling the site's architecture.[24] This feature raises an essential point, since the task of recycling architecture operated for PCSC as a symptom of a society in which the past must be held at bay by negating its temporality. One finds the opposite tendency in these sites, where the architecture itself expresses years of terror without becoming objectified as a tourist fetish. Both Olimpo and ESMA avoid falling into the trap of promoting fascination for the kind of torture gallery that lies within them (something I find problematic in Villa Grimaldi). Differing from the preservationist recycling that conceals the past, I find it significant that these sites have been maintained without remodeling. They create a different temporal fold in a city that has been perpetually renovated and restored through recycling its older features. These sites problematize and perhaps even contest what I call the "architecture of the transition," expressed by PCSC's transformation into a monument for a city of impunity. They open a series of questions regarding the relationships between (post)dictatorship space and their complex set of multiple temporalities. The passing of time and their absence of monumentality, demonstrated by the guided visits without a specific, definitive script, make them stand out. Their lack of scripted narrative about the past—coupled with their lack of remodeling—tends to highlight these sites' complex and open character. The visit stresses uncertainty and visitors find themselves confronted with the very incompleteness that characterizes these ruinous spaces.

In the case of ESMA, the monumentality of the place lies in its military history; a visit emphasizes the coexistence of the Naval School of Mechanics and the clandestine center, further underscoring the proximity of the detention center to the urban life surrounding it. The position of ESMA must also be seen within a greater mapping of a systematic process to eliminate dissidence. This suggests the possibility of thinking about the site within a logic that reaches beyond its specific location—thereby forming a kind of experience that takes place concurrently within and outside of the prison. Tours highlight the absence of bars in the jail cells of this CCD, allowing a visitor to perceive the internalized terror that made it almost impossible to escape. Such was the case with the fugitive Horacio D. Maggio, who was killed after being recaptured and whose dead body was exhibited in the prison as an example and threat to other prisoners who might attempt the same.[25]

In the case of Olimpo, the site does not exhibit the same sense of architectural monumentality that ESMA offers. It instead presents a ruin that not only speaks to its brief run as a clandestine center but also sheds light on the site's destruction before the Police Headquarters turned it over—an explicit demonstration of the rage that this functional transformation provoked. As proof of this struggle, the windows have been covered with glass instead of renovated; one can still see the vandalism undertaken by the police before deserting the site. There are also plans to remove the floor, as occurred in Club Atlético, so visitors can see what is left of the jail cells after the center no longer functioned as a CCD. Removing yet another layer of flooring would reveal the marks left behind in the cells. This choice of preservation allows the site to evoke the structure of the CCD simply by showing the many floor layers that serve as a record of its former architecture. Akin to Club Atlético, the terrain itself reveals the temporal layers covered as part of its post-dictatorial concealment.

On the one hand, Olimpo establishes a relationship to the past not concealed by makeup or made eternal, but one that reveals the dictatorial and transitional process of covering. On the other hand, it expresses the incomplete character of the void that the ruin suggests through speaking—and at the same time, remaining silent—about a past alluded to in the site's different features, without placing a finished structure for a complete history before our eyes. The fact that the site's prison cells were not remodeled embodies an avoidance of transforming these spaces into sites for reconciliation. Alternatively, in Olimpo, a neighborhood library is being built with books banned during the dictatorship, where each book will relate its own story on censorship, further encouraging a discussion about the materials held there. Also, workers at Olimpo are debating whether to install an exhibit on labor history and its transformations both during and after the dictatorship, as well as rooms for other exhibits.[26]

What differentiates the city model entailed by PCSC from the city model that involves a completely new urban layer opened by sites to practice remembrance are the manners in which they grapple differently with temporality. In a way, PCSC embodies a strategy of erasure for the dangers of time, since it maintains the ideal of an absolute present between the mall and the prison. There the past can only hold decorative value, remaining subsumed by pure market function. In a perverse way, we can note the erasure of finitude expressed architecturally in the transformation of PCSC as an element that pervaded military practices within the CCDs by denying both life and death to prisoners. The name "Olimpo" itself exemplifies this, as a key expression of disallowing finitude as mortality (the place of the gods).[27] When visiting the sites, one perceives a certain inscription of death that brings a finality denied to the detainees at their moment of incarceration, when official discourse declared the detention centers an area controlled by the gods. Many testimonies describe, as Pilar Calveiro argues, that the torturers' self-aggrandizement became an essential feature of the concentration camps, something made explicit in the case of Olimpo, where personnel managed the site like "the place of the gods," or claimed, as one survivor remembered: "We are God."[28]

For this reason, the demand for finality expressed within these spaces can function as a manner of articulating the past, for not only does it problematize the events of the dictatorship, it also questions the way in which the past marks and configures temporal experience in the present. One of the goals for transforming the CCDs into spaces for memory is thus to evoke and problematize a sense of temporality strategically erased and overwritten by impunity—one that must be considered in connection with the finality evoked by the site's ruins. I find that even though commercialism threatens the most critical-minded and creative intentions surrounding discussions of these sites, the transformation of the CCDs also engages the neoliberal consumer city in an important way; it reintroduces the dead, made invisible at a time of progress negotiated through forgetting.

The Question of Place: Toward a Topology of Memory

If PCSC stands as an exemplary case for the city of impunity, performing an operation that homogenizes the multiplicity of time through neoliberalization and its de-differentiation of place, then the transformation of the CCD works toward opening a critical fold in which the multiple temporalities of past and present become problematic. Not only physical representations, but also the debate regarding the language with which a discourse on the sites could be created, expresses this critical fold. This leads us to think about the passage from site—understood as a specific location—to a typology of place as a mutilfaceted category that cannot be reduced to a physical location; and which additionally involves a series of changing social relations practiced within and around the site.

The texture and function of different sites for memory are constantly being debated. A majority of those who write about these processes, redefining or at least problematizing recent history from the spatiality of urban terrain itself, sense that everything said before us attains a provisional character. In this ambivalent area, expressed at the level of language, we find the following expressions used vaguely in the promotion of these places: "memory museum," "space for memory," or "site of remembrance." In an attentive critical analysis of these terms, the distinction between "museum," "space," and "site" becomes fundamental. The confusion among terms, however, gestures toward the challenges undergone by these processes of transformation, but above all to the perception of their function. I am interested in stressing different points raised in the above analysis as a manner of approaching a topology of memory that articulates a turn from the generic notion of "space" (understood as a container) to the idea of "place" as "topos." I believe that in this movement from "space" to "place," one can not only find the potential for problematizing "space-sites" for memory, but also the kind of urban and temporal experience within them, left by the dictatorship as its legacy.

The so-called recuperation of CCD centers promotes this idea, producing a kind of estrangement in the detention center's proximity to the daily life of its neighbors. Estrangement marks a definitive difference in these projects from the notion of a museum, where a collection of objects represents the experience of the dictatorship; or from the notion of recycling seen in PCSC's architecture and in Villa Grimaldi's renovation, with the past reconstructed rather than evoked. I do not mean to imply that the CCD sites house a more authentic exhibition of the past, nor that these spaces have gone untouched by construction projects, which reimagined what the grounds once looked like. Rather, I am interested in highlighting two ways of bringing back and thinking about the past in relation to the city. We must consider that the politics surrounding the dictatorial past and its manifestation in the present have become themselves an object of state management. Thinking about these places as the city's critical folds that speak to a genealogy of the present evokes an antagonistic, irreducible multiplicity that the market has attempted to conceal and homogenize.

In his classic study on the notion of place, Edward Casey analyzes the way in which place "has increasingly been seen as secondary to space—typically to a particular notion of space as homogeneous, measurable extension—and so reduced to a notion of position, simple location, or else mere 'site.'"[29] In a similar vein, Jeff Malpas distinguishes the idea of "space" (which refers to a measurable space) from the notion of "place" (as a topos) that rather infers a gathering and disclosure (like an unfolding). To speak of topology implies thinking about the area of encounter between "place" and language, which the author highlights as "the saying of place"[30] and, in the instances explored in this piece, would refer to how to think about this gathering. By contesting impunity in the architecture of the transition, topology becomes a problem of speaking about "place," not as something given but as a constant process unfolding a complex, layered problem. This gestures toward a deficiency of language and the difficulty in articulating the social history of a site that lacks certain critical discourse tools.

In the *lieux de mémoire,* Pierre Nora argues that "memory crystallizes and secretes itself," indicating an instance that refers to a historical moment when "there are *lieux de mémoire,* sites of memory, because there are no longer *milieux de mémoire*, real environments of memory."[31] Although I find this contrast between *lieux* and *milieux* problematic (since it assumes a certain nostalgia for, and transparency of, the *milieux*), the proliferation of lieux de mémoire encourages us to think about the ways in which memory becomes an object, particularly in circumstances that have produced the society of the spectacle. For this reason, the linguistic ambiguity that I mentioned above when naming the CCD "museums," "spaces," or "sites" would seem to invoke a constellation that articulates a common ground between notions of space, place, and memory. "What is being remembered? In a sense, it is memory itself."[32]

If we think of topology as the problem of speaking about place—a kind of site where the past unfolds as a problem—we face a challenge to problematize the sense of gathering once memory no longer refers to the encounter with an essence of the past, but rather to its irrecoverable events. These sites allow for a reflection on the connection that memory retains with a meaning acquired by the city's polis. As Derrida argues, these spaces open up a kind of place that engages a specific politics while still hosting an impossible, albeit sustained demand (universal and unconditional hospitality).[33] Derrida maintains that problematizing city politics remits to a potential experiment in which place (lieu) can be turned into an instance for reflection on the articulation between the city and a democracy-to-come.[34] For this, a topology providing an encounter between place and language that guides us toward thinking about memory—as a disruptive gathering that operates from its multiple, temporal layers emerging within these sites—could serve a key function to displacing the notion of "recuperation." If we associate the possibility of thinking about places for memory to critical folds—capable not only of provoking reflection about the past, but also about ways of linking the genealogical past and present—we could move from a remembrance of memory to a reflection on the ways in which the past and present constitute a problematic site.[35]

The possibility of taking this critical turn resides in insisting that by recuperating memory, nothing is "recuperated" in the sense of one who finds a truth waiting to be revealed. Rather, a question on how to articulate an open, unending gathering where the site speaks from its fragmentary, ruinous, and impossibly absolute character emerges. If PCSC subsumes the past in the form of marketing for a new consumer society, the struggle around the CCDs constitutes a topology that dismantles the city's acclimated violence to question the effects of the past in the spatio-temporal experience of cities at present. With their ruin-like character, these places make us face the legacy left by secrecy—the impossibility of knowing the past with any certainty—while they open up a new urban experience: the emergence of multiple sites where secrecy becomes partial and problematic, thus interrupting the market driven by a demand to bring closure to the past.

NOTES

I would like to thank Orlando Bentancor and Jon Snyder for their invaluable comments and help in the process of writing this article. Thanks also to Elisabeth Becker for her final editing.

1. Many debates among architects in the 1990s make reference to the urban problem, in which construction projects advocating commerce and their primary function for consumption supplant the state (see Tella, *Un crack en la ciudad*; and Welch Guerra, *Buenos Aires a la deriva*).
2. See Tandeciarz, "Citizens of Memory: Refiguring the Past in Postdictatorship Argentina."
3. This relates to a project of exchanging experiences and discussions about potential collective actions, which took place in Montevideo in April 2008. It was convened under the title, "Primer encuentro de Museos de la Memoria" (see www.uruguayos.fr).
4. I am referring to the cases of disappeared key witnesses like Luis Gerez and Jorge Julio López, and also to the kidnapping of Juan Puthod, a human rights activist. Both Gerez and Puthod turned up alive, while López is still missing (see the Proyecto Desaparecidos website, www.desaparecidos.org; and Andermann, Derbyshire, and Kraniauskas, "No Matarás ('Thou Shalt Not Kill')."
5. A visit to the former CCD begins outside, by reading the walls marked with graffiti that signal the territorial and symbolic struggle for this place. There, we can observe the conflict that forced the police to abandon this site, as well as present-day politics and the struggle among political parties. This includes a poster petitioning for Jorge Julio López to reappear alive and well (López was a key witness in the case against Miguel Etchecolatz, chief police commissioner of Buenos Aires, responsible for several CCDs); graffiti highlighting the internal struggle among those who maintain that the site should depend on the state (the government of Buenos

Aires); and graffiti concerning those who withdraw because they believe the site should remain autonomous (the graffiti reads, "the Government of Buenos Aires," and below it, "the people").

6. Williams, *The Other Side of the Popular*, 223–24.
7. Richard, Introduction to *Pensar en/la posdictadura*.
8. Harvey, "From Space to Place and Back Again," 8.
9. Its name also refers to the city where it was situated (Libertad). See SERPAJ, Informe realizado por SERPAJ para el IV seminario sobre cárceles: "El fracaso del sistema penitenciario actual: Realidad y reformas urgentes," www.serpaj.org.uy.
10. Quoted in Ruben Bulanti, "El shopping de Punta Carretas," www.reduruguaya.com/departamentos/montevideo/puntacarretas.asp (my translation).
11. In this sense David Harvey says: "The construction of safe, secure, well-ordered, easily accessible, and above all pleasant, soothing, and non-conflictual environments for shopping, was the key to commercial success. The shopping mall was conceived of as a fantasy world in which the commodity reigned supreme" (Harvey, *Spaces of Hope*, 168).
12. Moulian, *Chile actual*, 113 (my translation).
13. Giménez and Villagrán, *Estética de la oscuridad*, 121, 122, 123 (my translation).
14. See comment posted 13 March 2004, Virtual Tourist website, www.virtualtourist.com/travel/South_America/Uruguay/Departamento_de_Montevideo/Montevideo-1624243/Shopping-Montevideo-BR-1.html.
15. For the site to succeed, profits must compensate investment, and the surrounding neighborhood must feel the impact through a "network of revenue." The Punta Carretas neighborhood demonstrates this phenomenon, as it transformed into a place for the city's most exclusive patrons (see Alexander, "Can You Build a Downtown Shopping Center?" 2–3).
16. Achugar, *Planetas sin boca*, 226 (emphasis added).
17. Baudrillard, *The System of Objects*, 74.
18. I refer to Lazzara's analysis of Villa Grimadi dedicated to analyzing different narratives surrounding the site's transformation (see Lazzara, *Chile in Transition*).
19. See Matta, *Villa Grimaldi: A Walk Through a 20th-Century Torture Center.*
20. As the ESMA web page indicates, information from an ex-detainee confirms that the site was already used as a detention center before the military coup (see www.derhuman.jus.gov.ar/espacioparalamemoria).
21. From the outset, residents expected the proposal of a "memory museum," a concept that was later modified to an idea for an "espacio para la memoria y defensa de los derechos humanos" (space for remembering and defending human rights). In a special edition published in 2006, a key book based on conversations from women ex-detainees states that once civilians gained control of the ex-CCD grounds, former detainees would have less interest in the way the grounds were obtained than in having them express the struggle of those who were exterminated (see Actis et al., *Ese infierno*, 302).
22. The grounds are located between the following streets: Ramón Falcón, Lacarra, Fernández, Rafaela, and Olivera.

23. This information has been deduced from survivors' testimony. Detailed information can be found at www.institutomemoria.org.ar/exccd/olimpo.html.
24. In this sense, the matter differs from various proposals for a memory museum, such as the one found in Montevideo at dictator Santos's former cottage. This memory museum follows an approach more traditionally in line with collections of objects corresponding to the moment of the coup, exile, the prisons, and the transition (see González, "Las sombras del edificio," 76).
25. See "Se descubrieron dos inscripciones de un desaparecido de la ESMA," *Página/12*, 22 July 2008, www.pagina12.com.ar/diario/ultimas/20-108286-2008-07-22.html.
26. The idea that pervades the entire process of the Olimpo transformation responds more to a commitment to the present than to a museification of the past.
27. "Godliness" played a fundamental role within the CCD, not only making reference to the commitment that the Catholic church played in Argentina, but also to the fact that once detainees were admitted to the center, they surrendered their potential will to live and die. The artworks produced on the centers, as well as many survivors' testimonies, emphasize the fact that entrance to the grounds implied entering a limbo state. In this state, the detainee was usurped from his or her chance of life and death. This was part of the dehumanizing process, where disappearance (like depriving one of death) is the most final feature. For example, see the game that Marco Bechis plays in the movie *Garage Olimpo* (also see the text in *Filmare la violenza sotterranea*) and the detailed study on "godliness," analyzed as the deprivation of another's death in the logic of the detention center, appearing in Pilar Calveiro's work on concentration camps in Argentina (see Calveiro, *Poder y desaparición*, 53–60).
28. Calveiro, *Poder y desaparición*, 53–54.
29. Casey, *The Fate of Place*, 3.
30. Malpas, *Heidegger's Topology*, 33.
31. Nora, "Between Memory and History," 9.
32. Ibid., 16.
33. In his essay on cosmopolitanism, Derrida considers a transformation in our idea of the city and stresses the challenges of the "refuge cities" as moving in a space between the "Law of an unconditional hospitality" and "the conditional laws of the right to hospitality" (*On Cosmopolitanism and Forgiveness*, 22).
34. Ibid., 22–23.
35. Presently, the La Floresta neighborhood has a high population of immigrants, and cases of Bolivian immigrants living in a state of near detention and slavery there have been reported. The most significant case took place in the former clandestine detention center (Automotores Orletti) that was a key site for disappeared Uruguayan detainees in Argentina, which until recently operated as a site where Bolivian workers were held, working throughout the week as slaves (see Carlos Rodríguez, "Centro clandestino, esta vez de confección," *Página/12*, 31 March 2007, www.pagina12.com.ar/diario/elpais/1-82598-2007-03-31.html; and Susana Viau, "El epicentro del Plan Cóndor," *Página/12*, 31 March 2007, www.pagina12.com.ar/diario/elpais/subnotas/1-26579-2007-03-31.html).

NANCY GATES-MADSEN

Marketing and Sacred Space

The Parque de la Memoria in Buenos Aires

In 2001, shortly after the Parque de la Memoria was inaugurated on the banks of the Río de la Plata, a new advertising campaign was launched by Los Platitos, a popular restaurant located directly across the street from the park. Recognizing that the public memorial had the potential to draw more visitors to the northern section of the *costanera* river walkway, the restaurant owners distributed flyers that exhorted potential customers to remember its location. While several of the park's overseers found such a tactic distasteful, many family members of the disappeared were enchanted with the flyers, believing such publicity would help draw visitors to the park itself. The tension between those who believed a space for remembering past horror should not be associated with a marketing campaign, and those who believed such a space might benefit from the free advertising, illuminates some of the inherent and perhaps irresolvable contradictions involved in the "marketing" of memory. Given that the creation of any public memorial space can never remain ideologically pure—outside of market forces—does the influence of external factors that shape any memorial inevitably taint the honorable impulse to remember? Put simply, what is the role of profane market forces in a sacred memorial space?

The creation of the Parque de la Memoria, like all other sites dedicated to the memory of past trauma, is fraught with tensions between a pure desire to remember a difficult past and the inevitable external forces (both political and economic) that shape the form of memory. Located on the banks of the Río de la Plata near Ciudad Universitaria (the northern campus of the University of Buenos Aires), the completed park will contain a monument to the dead and disappeared victims of state terror, as well as a sculpture garden, intended to provoke reflection upon the difficult years. Additional monuments, including one to remember victims of the 1994 bombing of the Asociación Mutual Israelita Argentina (AMIA) building and another dedicated to the Righteous Among the Nations, will also occupy the space. To date, a little more than one third of the park has been completed—the access plaza, four of the sculptures, the Monument to the Victims of State Terrorism, and the Centro de Documentación (Information Center)—yet tension regarding the aesthetics and politics of this memorial space remains.[1] When one considers that the Parque de la Memoria is one of the few memorials dedicated to the victims of state terror in all of Buenos Aires, if not the entire country, the mere fact of its construction gains significance. Because the park has the extraordinary burden of provoking memory and reflection about a historical period that a significant portion of Argentine society would prefer to forget, its creation has embodied a struggle to "sell" the idea to those parties in a position to help the dream of the park become a reality, as well as to the general public. Yet, paradoxically, the inevitable marketing involved in creating this sacred space for memory both increases and decreases the visibility of the park and its capacity to realize its lofty goals.

Commemoration versus Commodification: The Challenge of Marketing Memory

The association of memorials and monuments to past trauma with marketing seems at best contradictory, and at worst somehow unethical, for it implies converting traumatic memory into a commodity. "There's no business like Shoah business" was a critical phrase that arose during the debates regarding the Holocaust Memorial in Berlin to call attention to the tension between the desire to honor a difficult past and the necessary business of getting a memorial built. According to Horst Hoheisel, an artist who has created many memorials to the Holocaust, "the longer I worked in this commemorative business, the more aware I became of the problem. Memory disappears in the commemoration!"[2] More precisely, the commodification of memory to a certain extent robs a memorial of its commemorative power, and this tension between commemoration and commodification arises in the Parque de la Memoria as well. Originally proposed by a group of former students of the Colegio Nacional de Buenos Aires and family members of the disappeared, the impetus to create the park responds to the pure ideal of honoring the victims of the dictatorship, of acknowledging their loss in a public manner. As the proponents explain, the Parque de la Memoria "will have the significance of testimony, of a s[y]mbolic remembrance and homage to those beings the dictatorship tried to erase and that the world knows now by the name of 'desaparecidos,' as well as to those who were murdered. . . . Future generations will face here the memory of the horror committed and will become conscious of the necessity to take care that these events will NEVER AGAIN be repeated."[3]

Thus, the park aims to realize the lofty goals of making present the suppressed memory of the dictatorship and of promoting a consciousness and connection to the past. Yet the minute any type of memory project becomes a public proposal, it is affected by inevitable personal, political, and economic factors that range from the creative (What should the space look like? What type of monuments should it incorporate? For whom is it being created? What effect should it have?) to the practical (What space can be used? Who will fund its construction?). At issue here is the struggle between commemoration and commodification, between the honorable impulse to remember and the mundane reality of making that laudable vision come true. In the case of the Parque de la Memoria, given that its proponents were fighting against entrenched cultural and societal amnesia, they had to take advantage of favorable forces that would help make it a reality, or risk having no memorial at all. This essay explores the way in which market forces affected the creation of the Parque de la Memoria, from the timing of the proposal and the selection of the site to its design and ongoing construction, and how this potential commodification of memory impacts the park's commemorative power.

Timing Is Everything

In 1997, a number of factors combined to make the moment right for the proposal of a park dedicated to the memory of the dictatorship. First of all, Buenos Aires had recently become an autonomous city. Independent from the executive branch of the national government, the city could make its own decisions concerning public spaces. At the same time, the country was experiencing a so-called memory "boom" (1995–98), ignited when Horacio Verbitsky and Adolfo Scilingo began speaking about the now infamous death flights, and followed by numerous testimonials and documentaries about the dictatorship. Increased public interest in the dictatorship years (even if of a voyeuristic nature) and a favorable city government suggested that the time was ripe to advance the necessary memory work that so many human rights groups had been tirelessly promoting since the return to democracy. The proposal for the Parque de la Memoria gained support from other human rights groups, and a total of ten organizations took advantage of this opportune moment to propose the construction of a place to honor and remember the victims of state terrorism.

But the memory "boom" and the change in city government status were not the only factors that affected the timing of the proposal. Around the same time, Buenos Aires was in the process of developing ways to reconnect the city with the river. The project "Buenos Aires y el Río" sought to develop the entire riverfront area and encompassed several ongoing initiatives. This idea of reconnecting with the river meant that on the one hand there was space along the riverbank in need of development, while on the other hand, the human rights organizations had a proposal in need of a space. Finally, at this time, the University of Buenos Aires was also soliciting proposals for development of some territory adjacent to Ciudad Universitaria—and the creation of the Parque de la Memoria was incorporated into this initiative as well. When the city passed Law No. 46, which mandated construction of the park, it therefore specified the park's location: "on the coastline of the Río de la Plata, a space designated as a public walkway where a monument and group of sculptures will be located in homage to the victims who were detained, disappeared, and murdered by State Terrorism during the 1970s and 80s, until the reestablishment of a State based on the Rule of Law."[4] A Pro-Monument Commission was formed to oversee the project, consisting of the vice-president of the city legislature, eleven city representatives (one for each political party), four members of the local executive branch of government, a representative from the University of Buenos Aires, and one member from each of the ten human rights groups involved, including Buena Memoria (the group from the Colegio Nacional), the Madres de Plaza de Mayo–Línea Fundadora, and the Abuelas de Plaza de Mayo, among others.[5] The desire to remember a difficult past was not in itself enough to propel the project forward; therefore, the human rights groups achieved approval for their proposal through taking advantage of favorable political conditions, as well as adapting their vision to fit within existing projects.

The original law specifies one monument and a group of sculptures dedicated to the victims of the dictatorship, yet the park will contain two additional monuments: one dedicated to the victims of the 1994 bombing of the AMIA building, and another in homage of the Righteous Among the Nations. The combination of monuments seems somewhat out of place, especially given the initial genesis of the park as a place to honor the memory of victims of state terrorism. As Silvia Tandeciarz explains in "Citizens of Memory: Refiguring the Past in Postdictatorship Argentina," "Separately conceived according to divergent aesthetic principles, [the three monuments] seem awkward in juxtaposition even at this early stage."[6] Tandeciarz emphasizes the tension created in the park as "representative of the fraught nature of recollection and the persistent difficulty of consensus in Argentina regarding the dictatorship years."[7] Her reading of the park views the tension as a "reflection of the unresolved issues" surrounding the nation's attempts to reconcile its difficult past.[8] I would add that it is not simply divergent aesthetic principles that divide the monuments, but divergent ideas regarding the purpose of the park as a whole, and that the tension created by the awkward juxtaposition of proposed monuments arises out of how to "market" the project to the city and to the general public.[9]

To guarantee the creation of this much-needed space for remembrance, the Pro-Monument Commission garnered the support of other parties interested in promoting historical memory and battling against cultural amnesia—in particular, the Jewish community associated with the AMIA. According to Ana Weinstein, the director of the Center, the involvement of the Jewish community in the creation of the park was somewhat accidental. The AMIA had not participated in the original proposal to create a space for memory, but in 2001 the organization became more closely associated with the project when Marcelo Brodsky, a visual artist and the founder of the human rights group Buena Memoria, discovered the remains of the façade of the AMIA building on the proposed site for the Parque de la Memoria. A member of the Pro-Monument Commission, Brodsky was aware that the pieces of the former Jewish Cultural Center had been taken to the costanera for disposal, but the discovery of what at that time he believed to be part of a Star of David seemed to be a sign. Although it turned out later that the piece he had discovered was part of the "A" on the original façade of the building, rather than a Star of David, he remained moved by the profound significance of the discovery and began to work with Weinstein to salvage the pieces of rubble. He and Weinstein also agreed to incorporate them, along with the photographs Brodsky had taken, into *Nexo*, his next show, and into the park itself, as part of the monument dedicated to the victims of the AMIA bombing. Weinstein also notes that, some years earlier, a member of the commission had told her that unless they could count on the support of the AMIA, the project might not be able to go forward.[10] The fortuitous combination of the discovery of part of the façade shortly before the park's construction was to begin helped to bring the AMIA into the project and thus raised its visibility among another sector of the population.

Money Talks

The involvement of the AMIA in the Parque de la Memoria raises two central issues regarding the park's creation: its sponsorship and its location. The park's construction is sponsored by the government of Buenos Aires; thus, continued progress on the project depends to a certain extent upon the economic and political climate. The 2001 economic crisis had a great effect on the project, as did the change in government in 2007. As Patricia Tappatá de Valdez, a commission member and executive director of the organization Memoria Abierta, explained in an article written about the park in 2002: "A project that had generated strong support when voted into law and during the initial phases of construction does not have the same support today. Weakened management, the change in political composition of the legislature, and the original group allegiances, now unclear or destroyed, accompany the political and representative crisis that has extended over the country."[11] While former mayor Aníbal Ibarra's government had collaborated with the commission's efforts, members now feared that the more conservative city governors who took power in 2007 would not place such a high priority on the Parque de la Memoria, and that, consequently, the project might not advance as quickly as they hoped.[12]

Yet the park's sponsorship by the city government poses other problems regarding the memorial impulse. Tappatá de Valdez has noted the inherent challenge of "a public space constructed and financed by the state to remember victims of state terrorism."[13] Given the past reluctance by government officials to acknowledge the violence, let alone memorialize its victims, it seems unsurprising that some human rights groups and some visual artists dedicated to preserving the memory of the past horror (the purported purpose of the park) have opposed the construction of an officially sanctioned space for memory. The branch of Madres de Plaza de Mayo led by Hebe de Bonafini, for example, has refused to collaborate with the project, arguing that its members prefer to honor their loved ones through working on initiatives that will continue their children's struggles for a better society. Although it may seem surprising that opposition to the park comes from the family members of the victims that the memorial aims to honor, Bonafini's group continues to resist any memorializing impulse sponsored by those whom they view as having contributed to the culture of amnesia and injustice. At one point, her group even threatened to physically remove the names of their loved ones from the monument. To these mothers, the creation of a park to remember lost loved ones is tantamount to closing a chapter of the past that can only be resolved when the government provides a full accounting of the fate of each victim. For them, any permanent installation will tend to fix memory at a certain point in time, precluding continued progress or further understanding. Such debates among the groups who share the central goal of promoting memory of the dictatorship, although they raise the visibility of the project as a whole, also call attention to the tensions that exist within the human rights community, and to the difficulty of arriving at a common memorial vision.

Location, Location, Location

The mothers' concerns signal a tension between memorial spaces that are marketed to and by official institutions and sacred sites of memory. While the park's proponents emphasize that the impetus to create this dedicatory space came from human rights groups, rather than from any official decree, Bonafini's group fears that its institutional nature precludes any true memorializing impulse. These differing opinions as to the extent to which the park is an "institutionalized" space raise the question of how official sanction affects the sacred space of memory.

Religious theory defines sacred space as either substantial (essential) or situational (somehow constructed). Mircea Eliade offers perhaps the best-known essentialist treatment of sacred space in his classic study *The Sacred and the Profane: The Nature of Religion*. According to Eliade, the sacred manifests itself in certain places, which are subsequently set apart from profane space. He explains, "Every sacred space implies a hierophany, an irruption of the sacred that results in detaching a territory from the surrounding cosmic milieu and making it qualitatively different."[14] Not only is sacred space set apart from the ordinary, but this break in homogeneous space also allows for passage between different levels of reality, in particular heaven and earth. In general, Eliade's position implies that humans do not choose these spaces; rather, they arise seemingly independently of human influence.

Later theorists have taken issue with Eliade's categorization of sacred space as somehow apart from human influence. David Chidester and Edward T. Linenthal explain in the introduction to *American Sacred Space* that places set aside to memorialize past events or express religious significance never possess an unproblematic relationship with the surrounding society or the historical context in which they are found or constructed. Rather than coming to being through revelation, space is made sacred through the hard work of cultural practices and ritual. The authors emphasize that the creation process often involves a struggle of possession (such as the contested ownership between the U.S. government and native peoples of much of the Black Hills), interpretation (Mount Rushmore as national symbol of pride or dominance), and use (the types of activities that are or are not appropriate in certain national parks, such as Pearl Harbor). This definition of the sacred recognizes the enormous amount of human effort invested in creating and preserving meaningful spaces for remembrance. As Chidester and Linenthal explain, "Not full of meaning, the sacred, from this perspective, is an empty signifier," one that depends upon human intervention and interpretation to grant it meaning.[15]

Chidester and Linenthal categorize the differing interpretations that may arise as a conflict between the "poetics" and the "politics" of sacred space, yet ultimately they contend that politics always plays an important role in the process of designating the sacred. Not only does a "politics of exclusion" operate in any meaningful space (which place is chosen, who finds it meaningful, what interpretations prevail at the expense of others), but the meaning of any sacred space is also inevitably linked to larger political forces. Given the impossibility that sacred space can ever be truly separate from the profane, Chidester and Linenthal offer their own definition of sacred space as ritual space, significant space, and, most important, contested space: "Since no sacred space is merely 'given' in the world, its ownership will always be at stake. In this respect, a sacred space is not merely discovered, or founded, or constructed; it is claimed, owned, and operated by people advancing specific interests."[16] While theorists such as Eliade advocate a separatist, essentialist view of sacred space vis-à-vis the profane, Chidester and Linenthal argue that "sacred space is inevitably entangled with the entrepreneurial, the social, the political, and other 'profane' forces."[17]

Chidester and Linenthal develop a compelling argument for the situational nature of sacred space, yet it is important to note that proponents of the Parque de la Memoria describe that location in more essentialist terms. According to Eliade, one cannot simply declare a space to be sacred—space becomes sacred through the revelation of some sort of sign, and Brodsky's description of the discovery of the pieces of the broken façade of the AMIA building fits within this type of revelatory discourse. In Brodsky's own words, "The detonated façade of the AMIA building was an incredible find, while we were taking photographs on the site of what will be the Parque de la Memoria. It could be a kind of exorcism of forgetting: getting the forgetting out of the park, the ground, the river. Forgotten bits and pieces, of a recent event, that come to form a star and an image."[18] Important here is not the fact of the discovery itself (part of the letter "A," rather than a Star of David), but its symbolic meaning.[19]

The park's proponents also foreground an essentialist reading by emphasizing the symbolic relationship between the park and the Río de la Plata. According to Brodsky, the river symbolizes "the nonexistent tomb" for many victims of the infamous death flights in which drugged prisoners were thrown into the water as one method of "disappearing" them.[20] Many others involved with the creation of the park similarly concur with the funereal interpretation of the river, including Tappatá de Valdez, who states that "the Río de la Plata can now be recognized as a 'historic site,' where victims' family members gathered to remember them and 'lay' flowers in the place that became the tomb for many victims."[21] The Holocaust memorial artist Hoheisel has even proposed taking one of the barbed-wire fence posts that surround the park, placing it in the river, and directing all the lighting toward the post rather than toward the sculptures, because in his opinion "the true monument is the river."[22] Finally, newspaper articles describing the park's creation and the inauguration of each construction phase similarly mention the river's significance. Taken together, such comments imply that the space occupied by the park is somehow set apart from the surrounding landscape, made sacred through both its significant location (next to the river) and the memory embedded in the land itself (the remains of the AMIA building).

Despite the predominantly essentialist discourse that describes the site's sacred significance, the location was not originally selected for its inherent commemorative potential. The coincidence of finding the broken pieces of the AMIA building on a site dedicated to remembering past trauma does suggests some form of revelation; nevertheless, the discovery occurred after the space had been set aside for construction. While the river's undeniable symbolism may add a poignant layer of meaning to the site, the park's proximity to the river arises from its integration into the existing project "Buenos Aires and the River" and from an impulse by the University of Buenos Aires to utilize the riverbank area near Ciudad Universitaria. In fact, the space ultimately designated to become the Parque de la Memoria was claimed by both the City of Buenos Aires and the University, and permission to construct the park was ultimately achieved by incorporating the university more closely into the planning of the space. The partnership between the city, human rights groups, the AMIA, and the university is, to a certain extent, a marriage of convenience, entered into in order to get the project off the ground, and one of the results of this cooperation was the designation of the riverbank site.

The emphasis on the importance of the river may also be viewed as a way to compensate for the park's relatively remote location. Unlike other national historical monuments located in and around the Plaza San Martín, including the monument honoring soldiers who fought in the Malvinas War, the Parque de la Memoria does not occupy a principal memorial space near the center of the city. The park could perhaps be viewed (albeit cynically) as a sanctioned protest designed to have a minimal impact—after all, assigning a relatively remote place for memory and mourning can be interpreted as an attempt to channel and contain calls for memory and justice to a place far from the center of the public eye. Thus, the public discourse of the park's proponents, who emphasize the sacred nature of the space, may also be an attempt to insert the park into an existing group of significant sites of memory (such as former clandestine detention centers) and thereby legitimize its categorization as an important place for memory.

To what extent are these "profane" forces at odds with the sacred memory work of the park? The "Buenos Aires and the River" initiative was designed to promote the natural beauty and recreational use of the waterway, so the insertion of a park designed to remind visitors of the river's funereal connotations seems somewhat awkward.[23] Despite efforts to rationalize the park's location alongside the river by emphasizing its integration with other geographical points of reference, the two projects do not possess the same emotional significance for all the users of this space. The park's location at the end of the costanera, a long pedestrian walkway extending north from the city, designed to facilitate recreational use of the riverbank area, may serve to detract from its solemn purpose. The river's significance as a sacred place does not permeate all aspects of the walkway, and many of those who walk or bicycle along the costanera seem unaffected by morbid thoughts of anonymous victims and unmarked graves. Eliade emphasizes the importance of the threshold of the land and the water as marking a break between sacred and profane space; nevertheless, given the fact that the river remains a multiple signifier, not all who enter the space of the Parque de la Memoria will cease to view the river as a pleasant vista and source of recreation, and see instead a sacred tribute to past horror.

By the same token, despite the city's attempts to emphasize the positive aspects of the river through the "Buenos Aires and the River" initiative, its solemn significance remains quite evident for those touched by the state's violence. For those who lost a loved one during the dictatorship, walking along the beautiful costanera does not make the river less menacing, and some mothers of the disappeared have chosen to have their ashes scattered into the river, to be symbolically reunited with their lost children.[24] Such actions suggest that the packaging of this particular natural landmark may matter less than the attitudes held by the people who view the waterway, and this perhaps implies some limits to the extent to which the "marketing" of a space can actually determine its interpretation.

Yet the fact that every newspaper article describing the park makes mention of the river's symbolism implies that its proponents have been largely successful in promoting the Parque de la Memoria in essentialist terms. Given the volume of material that makes reference to the significance of the park's location, either through mentioning the remains of the AMIA building or emphasizing the symbolism of the Río de la Plata, it appears as if the park's proponents are trying to make the space sacred through declaring it so. Unlike other sites that are inherently charged with the memory of a traumatic past, such as the former clandestine detention centers, or locations that have been appropriated by those dedicated to memory work, such as the Plaza de Mayo, the Parque de la Memoria, to a certain extent, has to "prove" its identity as a legitimate site of memory. Perhaps as a way to compensate for its more neutral character, or for its relatively remote location, or perhaps as a way to question the implied positive connotations of the park's inclusion as part of the "Buenos Aires and the River" project, the description of the park in essentialist terms—emphasizing its inherent symbolism and its "difference" from the surrounding area—appears to be aimed at creating a sacred space through discourse, or at least to frame the discourse about this space in sacred terms.

A comparison of the development of the Parque de la Memoria with that of a more spontaneous memorial can help illuminate the tension between "given" sacred space and space that appears to have to "market" itself. While the park constitutes the official dedication of a neutral area to the memory of the dictatorship, the memorial that has arisen at the site of the former clandestine detention center El Club Atlético represents a more spontaneous call to memory at a symbolically "loaded" location. Torn down by the junta for the construction of a highway in 1977, El Club Atlético served as a detention center for hundreds of prisoners during the early years of the dictatorship. Located under a highway overpass, the remains of the building now have become an active archaeological site dedicated to revealing painful memories, and the ruins themselves represent a different kind of memorial than the Parque de la Memoria. As James E. Young explains in his study, *The Texture of Memory: Holocaust Memorials and Meaning*, "the magic of ruins persists, a near mystical fascination with sites seemingly charged with the aura of past events, as if the molecules of the sites still vibrated with the memory of their history."[25] Feeling this magical pull, former victims of this clandestine center petitioned for its excavation, in the hopes of unearthing secrets the military had tried to bury, and many regularly gather at the site to commemorate lost loved ones.

Although the archaeological excavation of El Club Atlético is sponsored by the same government branch that oversees the construction of the Parque de la Memoria, official sanction in this case does not appear to have affected the sacred "magic" of the ruins. Young elaborates, "On the one hand, we're reminded that it was the state's initial move to preserve these ruins—its will to remember—that turned sites of historical destruction into 'places of memory.' On the other hand, we find that these sites of memory begin to assume lives of their own, often as resistant to official memory as they are emblematic of it."[26] The Club Atlético has indeed assumed a life of its own, becoming a space for informal memorials dedicated to the victims. The highway support that rises out of the dig is covered with figures who appear to be climbing out of the ruins. Other support columns that extend along the street have been covered with graffiti, including poems

Figure 1. Signs posted at former clandestine detention center Club Atlético, Buenos Aires, Argentina. (Photograph by Leigh A. Payne)

and drawings that depict faces or bodies in various poses of torment or resistance. A large outline of a human form lies on the embankment next to the excavation, and each month a group of ex-detainees lights up the figure in commemoration. Over the years, the site has changed, with fumes from passing traffic obscuring some of the artwork and indigents occupying the plaza and sleeping on the benches that proclaim "Never Again." Yet despite the fact that the site is aesthetically unattractive, or perhaps precisely because of it, the Club Atlético remains a powerful space for memory.[27]

In contrast to the Parque de la Memoria, El Club Atlético does not need to promote itself as a memory site, and the writings about this location emphasize its success as a local, spontaneous call to memory.[28] Untroubled by aesthetic issues, true to its original purpose of uncovering the crimes of the past, the Club Atlético has remained largely outside of the types of debates that have surrounded the Parque de la Memoria. As Silvia Tandeciarz notes in her description of the site, "The Atlético speaks in more subdued tones [than the Parque de la Memoria], as if the voices of the disappeared were finding their way out of a tomb to vie for interpretive power."[29] When the location speaks for itself, those advocating historical memory need not market its sacred nature.

Designing the "Product" of Memory

"Profane" forces affect more than simply the Parque de la Memoria's location. The design of the space itself also speaks to the way in which the park needed to "market" itself to become a reality. To determine the physical appearance of the space, the commission called for two contests, one for the Monument to the Victims of State Terrorism, and another to choose sculptures to surround the monument and populate the green space of the park. The first contest was held within the School of Architecture at the University of Buenos Aires, and the winning design, by Baudizzone-Lestard-Varas Arquitectos—a large, segmented wall of names of the disappeared—was inaugurated on 7 November 2007. For the sculpture contest, an international jury consisting of human rights activists, artists, art critics, and museum curators evaluated 665 projects submitted from all over the globe, selecting eight winning sculptures and four honorable mentions to be constructed in the park. To date, four of the sculptures have been placed in the space: Dennis Oppenheim's "Monumento al escape," William Tucker's "Victoria," Nicolás Guagnini's "30,000," and "Sin Título" by Roberto Aizenberg, an invited artist whose work did not figure in the competition.[30]

But the contests themselves can be viewed as to a certain extent contributing to the commodification of memory. In the case of the Monument to the Victims of State Terrorism, having the call for proposals within the School of Architecture, which had originally claimed ownership of the space eventually selected for the park, could be viewed as a way to bring the university more closely into the project. For the sculpture garden, the decision to hold an international contest seems somewhat at odds for designing a memorial space that is dedicated to remembering a national trauma. The fact that a majority of the winning selections (seven out of twelve) come from non-Argentine artists also seems to make the memory park less a local space and more of an international project. Finally, the decision to invite selected artists to place pieces in the space also speaks more to a desire to raise the visibility of the park than to the sacred impulse to remember past trauma, as seen by the following statement by the Pro-Monument Commission: "The organizers have begun working with national and international artists *of maximum international relevance* and whose work maintains a commitment to the Defense of Human Rights. . . . The presence of these works . . . will serve to elevate the artistic level *and international significance* of the Parque de la Memoria" (my emphasis).[31] Early newspaper accounts of the site boasted that the park would contain monuments by such artists as Maya Lin, a further indication that the commission hoped to promote the park through the presence of internationally acclaimed artists.[32]

According to Tappatá de Valdez, the international design competition "was one of the first tasks of the Commission,"[33] which suggests the fundamental importance of this particular aspect of the park's creation. The advantages of holding an international competition appeared obvious for a commission dedicated to garnering support for a potentially unpopular project. Locating the Parque de la Memoria within a larger artistic and human rights movement and inviting the participation of internationally known and acclaimed artists serves to increase the visibility of the project as a whole. The juxtaposition of the Monument to the Victims of State Terrorism with monuments remembering attacks against the Jewish population may also be interpreted as an attempt to insert the terrible actions of the military into the internationally recognizable context of the Holocaust. Yet at the same time, such diffusion of artistic impulses disperses the memorial impulse as well.

Another important factor affecting the park's ability to provoke memory and reflection concerns the type of artistic language used to promote its message. From the beginning, the Pro-Monument Commission had to wrestle with the difficulty of how to "package" its important message in the most effective manner. Given that the ultimate goal was to provoke memory and reflection, not only in visitors acquainted with the recent past, but in the future generations who will walk its paths, the commission carefully considered what mode of expression would encourage the desired reflection and memory about the dark years of the dictatorship. Using both aesthetic and ethical criteria, the jury selected sculptures that exhibited "contemporaneity, as well as poetic sense," for they believed that this type of expression would best fulfill the park's goals.[34] Consequently, each of the winning sculptures in some way questions or operates outside of traditional figurative language.[35]

Although the open character of modern art precludes any authoritarian fixing of meaning, contemporary modes of artistic expression are often unable to meet the demands of those they aim to honor. Young comments that while architects and artists often advocate abstract forms of expression for monuments to past horror, many times victims and their families prefer more traditional forms that utilize the human figure. As many Holocaust victims claim: "We weren't tortured and our families weren't murdered in the abstract. . . . It was real."[36] After all, art that is dedicated to a specific purpose must somehow make its goal apparent. In assessing these difficult issues, Young poses a telling question: "If the aim is to remember—that is, to refer to—a specific person, defeat or victory, how can it be done abstractly?"[37] In other words, how can certain memories that appear to defy representation ever be transmitted in artistic form? Perhaps most importantly, if the viewer fails to grasp the work's "message," has the memorial space of the Parque de la Memoria somehow failed as well? In the end, while international contests may raise the visibility of the project as a whole, the use of abstract art may unwittingly decrease the park's commemorative power.

Overt versus Guerrilla Marketing: Monuments and Escraches

A closer examination of one of the installations for the sculpture garden—the Grupo de Arte Callejero's "Carteles de la memoria" ("Signs of Memory")—can further illuminate the challenges of successfully marketing the Parque de la Memoria's message through the selected artwork. The members of Grupo de Arte Callejero (GAC)—young artists who, as the name of their group suggests, generally work outside of traditional artistic spaces—are perhaps best known for their collaboration with H.I.J.O.S. (Sons and Daughters for Identity and Justice against Forgetting and Silence) in the presentation of escraches, performance protests designed to "out" the perpetrators of state terror. During these street demonstrations, GAC will place warning signs alerting residents that "a torturer lives 400 meters ahead," or speed limit signs with a military cap above the words "trial and punishment." For the Parque de la Memoria, the group created a series of oversized street signs designed to call attention to past troubles (the image of a pregnant woman behind bars, e.g., or a home invasion) and current issues (a sign announcing the amount of the foreign debt). Although the central goal of GAC's work is to raise awareness of past atrocities in the spirit of "Never Again," the traffic signs that operate on a subversive level in the escraches become more overt in the park, prompting a consideration of the most effective way to market important memory work to the general public.

Figure 2. Grupo de Arte Callejero "Trial and Punishment" sign, Buenos Aires, Argentina. (Photograph by Leigh A. Payne)

While traditional marketing tends to be rather direct, the most effective marketing often operates in subtler and more subversive ways. As Robert Levine states in *The Power of Persuasion: How We're Bought and Sold*, "The term *hidden persuader* is a good one: the most effective persuasion often takes place when we don't recognize we're being persuaded. It borders on the invisible."[38] When it comes to calling attention to the crimes of the past, GAC's street installations indeed border on the invisible, for they blend in with the surrounding context almost perfectly. Thus, in one sense, GAC's work operates on an almost subliminal level, for viewers may be unaware of what they are seeing, at least at first. Yet by manipulating structures of power, such as traffic signs, GAC also aims to utilize the power of the system to their advantage, which allows them to reach a wider audience. In this sense, they transmit their message through what Jay Conrad Levinson describes as "guerrilla marketing." Marketing, according to Levinson, is simply "*the truth made fascinating*";[39] thus, guerrilla marketing involves using nontraditional marketing tactics to transmit the truth about a product or service. Employing a range of creative options allows smaller businesses with fewer resources to perform against their larger competitors, in much the same manner as an escrache or a GAC installation allows a protest group to challenge the establishment. Given the power of guerrilla tactics, one wonders what effect GAC's traffic signs may have in the more overt context of the Parque de la Memoria. Will they serve to increase the visibility and impact of the park's message, or might they simply lose their subversive power?

The power of subversive versus traditional marketing, of viewing GAC's signs during an escrache or in the memorial space of the Parque de la Memoria, becomes clear within Diana Taylor's framework of the archive and repertoire. In her book, *The Archive and the Repertoire: Performing Cultural Memory in the Americas*, Taylor defines the "archive" as comprising supposedly non-changing objects, such as documents, architectural structures, or memorial spaces like the Parque de la Memoria. The "archive" stands in contrast to the "repertoire"—embodied practices that serve to transmit information to a live audience in the here and now, such as a play, a gesture, or a performance protest like an escrache.[40] According to Taylor, while the "archive" may be considered more permanent, the "repertoire" is ideally suited to the transmission of traumatic memory, because it demands presence and involvement on the part of the spectator. But if embodied performance—the "repertoire"—is better suited to transmitting traumatic memory than the "archive," what happens when you take an installation such as the "Carteles de la memoria" that gets its meaning and subversive power from the "repertoire" and place it in the "archive"? Can a more subliminal message have the same effect in a context of overt marketing?

During an escrache, GAC's street signs provoke an embodied performance, for they unconsciously force viewers to situate themselves vis-à-vis the structures of power. By choosing either to join the group, watch from a distance, or retreat behind closed doors, spectators locate themselves in relation to the protest, yet even those who try to ignore the spectacle become reluctant participants through their non-action. The presence of GAC's street signs further involves all in the vicinity, for the mere act of reading the sign situates the spectator in relationship with the violence. No one can avoid this type of memory message—the subversive marketing reaches everyone.

According to Lorena Bossi, one of the founding members of the Grupo de Arte Callejero, the purpose of the signs is to "make visible through institutional means what the institution hides."[41] In other words, the signs reveal the subliminal messages all around us. Traffic signs are part of the official, invisible structures of power that we rarely consider—we see a sign declaring "No left turn," and we don't turn left; we see a speed limit sign, and at the very least we check the speedometer to see if we are within the limit. By calling attention to the sign itself—"A *torturer* lives 400 meters ahead"—GAC's work both implicates the structure of power in the attempt to ignore or forget past crimes, and also makes the viewer consider how the movement of his or her body through the city is mediated by such invisible power structures. In other words, it encourages viewers to consider how everyday actions constitute a "performance" of obedience to authority.

GAC's signs locate and implicate the viewer as a participant in the performance, which is precisely the point of their work. Politically committed performance art aims to prompt the audience member to leave the passive role of viewer, observer, or spectator, and move into the active role of participant or witness. This can perhaps best be seen in the "You are Here" information signs GAC has placed at the sites of former clandestine detention centers around Buenos Aires. "You are Here," through its use of the second person (singular or plural), automatically locates the spectator vis-à-vis the violence. Addressing the viewer directly and forcing him or her to take a position in relation to the crimes committed, the sign effectively prevents any type of protective distancing from the scene. GAC's sign thus brings the spectator into the action, or brings the action to the spectator—there is no fourth wall in the Grupo de Arte Callejero's world. To return to the division between the "archive" and the "repertoire," then, while the work of art itself may pertain to the "archive," the moment of viewing pertains to the "repertoire," for it demands participation on the part of the spectator, and, in this manner, the spectator becomes an unwitting "consumer" of the intended message.

The question remains of how (or whether) the Grupo de Arte Callejero's series of traffic signs in the Parque de la Memoria will provoke a similar performative moment in spectators there and force them to bear witness. In other words, can guerrilla marketing tactics work within a more traditional context? While it is easy to see how the escrache involves all participants in an "act" of memory in the present moment, the question becomes tricky within the context of the Parque de la Memoria. The park aims to provoke memory and reflection about the dictatorship years in a fashion similar to a performance protest, yet a fixed art installation is fundamentally different from a performance protest. In the context of the Parque de la Memoria, the "Carteles de la memoria" may appear out of place rather than provocative: a long series of traffic signs mingled among abstract sculptures may be less likely to involve the viewer. Perhaps there is a reason why artwork pertains to the "archive," for it may be less able to provoke the movement from viewer to participant, from spectator to witness.[42]

Another aspect lost in the translation from street to park is the signs' anonymous quality. Press coverage of the escraches tends to attribute the signs to H.I.J.O.S. or other human rights groups, and the Grupo de Arte Callejero seems to take some pride in the fact that its artistic interventions often puzzle viewers as to their origin. In the same manner that institutional street signs have no specific author and therefore serve to represent an unseen authority, GAC's modified street signs harness that invisible power for subversive purposes. The lack of author deliberately and paradoxically adds to a heightened sense of authority and an increased impact on the accidental observers who view the signs. Placing these same signs in an official artistic space such as the Parque de la Memoria, with the names of the artists displayed, automatically creates a distance between viewer and installation. Once the viewer reads the plaque announcing that this is the work of the Grupo de Arte Callejero, he or she moves into museum mode, ready to look at and perhaps interpret a work of art, but with a lessened impulse to leave the comfortable role of observer or viewer and move into the realm of participant or witness.

It is worth noting that the artists themselves feel conflicted about their participation in the Parque de la Memoria. They are highly critical of any memorial space that serves more to allow forgetting than to inspire remembrance, and they strongly believe in the "here and now" of public performance as the best way to raise consciousness and transmit traumatic memory. In a statement describing their artistic and political philosophy, they criticize recent governmental efforts to designate sites of memory: "What kind of memory can arise from a state based on extermination? from a state that was organized by crushing other people and that continues to polish the medals of its most obedient assassins?"[43] Accustomed as they are to operating outside official boundaries, the members of GAC debated whether to submit a proposal for the Parque de la Memoria's sculpture garden at all, and they only agreed to participate once they verified that no member of the legislature of the city of Buenos Aires had former connections to state terror or had voted for the Due Obedience or Full Stop laws. As Lorena Bossi states, frankly: "If our work wasn't there, the Parque de la Memoria would simply be another place for petrified memory."[44] Yet rather than allow another installation to take their place in the memorial space, GAC decided to employ a tactic Bossi described as "infiltrating the cracks in the system,"[45] in the hopes that their participation would to a certain extent undermine the institutional aspect of the park.

The fact that these participating artists do not appear to wholly believe in the park's ability to realize its goals does not necessarily speak well to the Parque de la Memoria's ability to transmit memory, to effectively "market" its message. In fact, it would be easy to dismiss the move from the street to the park as a loss of the essential context that gives the signs their subversive power. But at the same time, the difference between contexts may allow for hope that GAC's contribution will indeed provoke active memory in those who move through the memorial space. The difference between the spectators who come to the park and those who may happen to witness an escrache, for example, can be viewed as positive. One could argue that the observers who come specifically to remember or mourn loved ones participate in an intentional embodied practice: walking through the sculptures, finding the name of a loved one on the Monument to the Victims of State Terrorism—these are symbolic, embodied performances that do constitute an *act* of remembrance.

This is not to say that accidental observers will not move through the space. The location of the GAC installation is particularly fortuitous in this sense, for their signs line the portion of the path that extends along the river's edge, the natural continuation of the costanera walkway. Given the signs' prime location, visitors who enter the park will naturally pass by them. So GAC will perhaps be able to take advantage of the best of both worlds (overt *and* subversive marketing) and impact both the intentional and accidental observer.

Despite the challenges presented by the park's location and official sanction, the Grupo de Arte Callejero has designed an installation that attempts to provoke a similar performative moment as their artistic interventions on the streets of Buenos Aires do. The first sign in the series, a seemingly innocuous information sign, brings the viewer into the frame. The sign reads "YOU ARE HERE," and shows an arrow leading along the river walkway. As opposed to the "You are Here" signs located at the site of former clandestine detention centers, this sign does not force the viewer to locate him or herself vis-à-vis the crimes of the past, but it does call attention to the body, to the physical presence of the person entering the space of the installation. The line drawn on the map furthermore shows the visitor where to proceed, perhaps in an unconscious attempt to mirror the invisible authority of the street signs found outside the park. Following the trajectory of the line, the viewer is thus (subtly) compelled to continue along the path, his or her body guided through the exhibit.

But even the signs that do not address the viewer directly encourage those who see them to meditate upon the traumatic past. In another attempt to re-create the performative effect of their street installations, several of the signs make reference to the particular space and location of the park. At one point along the series of fifty-three signs, a green information placard announces the distance to other clandestine detention centers around the country.

This mileage marker locates the viewer directly in relation to the dictatorship's crimes; although the park itself may not occupy a specific site of memory—like a former camp, a protest space, or an existing memorial do—the observer is forced to notice the proximity to other sites. ESMA's location a mere two kilometers from the park invites meditation on the traumatic past, while the subsequent sign, showing a map of Argentina with the locations of hundreds of other detention centers, calls attention to the extent of the violence. While one can simply consider other signs in the series as interesting iconic references to the various stages of the dictatorship, the maps and mileage signs implicate the viewer in direct relation to the violence, another way the installation seeks to break down the fourth wall, even in the official memorial space.

While some signs attempt to re-create the power derived from their context outside the park, others only function within the space of the park, proof that the recontextualization of the exhibit can actually be powerful in itself. The first sign that greets any visitor proceeding along the series is an exact reproduction of a very common street sign: No Left Turn. While its location on a street would not cause any meditation on dictatorship or violence, in its new context within the installation, directly preceding a sign declaring "Doctrine of National Security," "No Left Turn" gains a richer meaning. Not only does it call attention to the targets of violence, but it also makes a direct link between the invisible, institutional power structures (as Bossi remarks, there is "nothing more institutional than traffic signs"[46]), and the systematic violence implemented by the military government. Furthermore, after viewing the street sign in the context of the Parque de la Memoria, it is possible that visitors will view the "No Left

Turn" signs outside the art installation in a more critical fashion, thus carrying the purpose of the park (to provoke memory and reflection) outside the immediate space of the memorial.

One final way in which the Grupo de Arte Callejero hopes to keep their installation from stagnating in the "archive" is through updating the signs at regular intervals. Bossi explains that the group plans to modify the installation to respond to the changing political climate, and in this way prevent the series of signs from becoming stale. She admits that the group is unsure how the overseers will react to their proposal, yet the impulse to allow change fits within GAC's "guerrilla marketing strategy" to call attention to past crimes and current woes, and may help their installation maintain its ties with the "here and now" of the "repertoire."

Of all the projected sculpture installations, GAC's "Carteles de la memoria" appears to offer the hope to increase visibility of the Parque de la Memoria's project, through their attempt to employ performative guerrilla tactics within the context of the "archive." The almost reluctant participation of the group also may contribute to the success of the space. Because they are so highly critical of what they view as "dead" memorial spaces, their participation tacitly sanctions the Parque de la Memoria as a legitimate memorial space, if not, perhaps, one as effective as the embodied practice of the escraches. The ability of the commission to attract the participation of GAC thus can be viewed as an effective strategy to garner support from those who might simply have been critical of the project as a whole.

The Paradox of Successful Marketing

From the timing of the proposal and the selection of the site to the design of the space itself, "profane" market forces have shaped the Parque de la Memoria. Yet in the final analysis, the successful "marketing" of any memorial space depends upon the experience of those who visit. In other words, the physical form or the impulse to create the Parque de la Memoria alone will not determine its ability to provoke memory or reflection in visitors. Rather, its efficacy lies in the interaction between visitor and space, which highlights the final challenge facing the Pro-Monument Commission. Memorial space always risks becoming "dead" space if no one visits; thus, the overseers strongly believe that the most important aspect of the park is that the space be actively used. They trust that the use of the space in a non-reflective way will eventually lead to some type of reflective moment in the visitor. Yet this hope leads to questions regarding use (and misuse) of memorial space, and there has been some debate regarding the type of activities that should be permitted inside the park's boundaries. For example, should this memorial space allow picnicking? Playing with soccer balls? Music? Vendors? In short, what types of activities are appropriate for a space dedicated to the memory of a horrific past? Opinions vary as to what types of activities constitute suitable behavior in this space, as evidenced by the differing reactions to the Los Platitos advertising campaign cited at the beginning of this essay, and such debate over appropriate use raises some difficult questions. Does allowing more mundane activities, such as bicycle riding or picnicking, effectively communicate the park's message? Does the association of the call to memory with a restaurant represent an "appropriate" response? According to many involved in the creation of the Parque de la Memoria, the mere use of the space will facilitate the memorializing impulse, thereby raising the visibility of the park. Yet at the same time, more "profane" activities may inadvertently dilute the power of such a sacred space. In short, the message risks getting lost in the marketing.

Under Construction

The tension between commodification and commemoration leads to inescapable paradoxes during the memorial-making process. For the Parque de la Memoria, the attempt to attract visitors both undermines and enhances the sacred aspect of the space, while the effort to garner support and funding can result in a memorial that is either aesthetically and ideologically disjointed or comprehensive in its treatment of historical horror. The attempt to deem a space "sacred" through rhetoric at once compensates for *and* calls attention to a potentially disadvantageous location; meanwhile, guerrilla marketing tactics may both falter and thrive in the more traditional context of the park.

Although it is premature to arrive at any fixed conclusions about a space that is still under construction, the paradoxes regarding the Parque de la Memoria demonstrate two fundamentally important points regarding the creation of this particular memorial to Argentina's difficult recent past. First, although marketing inevitably plays a large role in any public project, in an initiative such as this the stakes are much higher. Despite the memory "boom" during the past decade, the legacy of the dictatorship and its victims remains muted in the public consciousness. Thus the creation of one of the only memorials in the country dedicated to honoring the victims of the military violence seeks to fulfill very high expectations. A failed memorial to a less polemic event, for example, while perhaps a cause for dismay, would not impact the nation's interpretation of a dark chapter in its own history.

This first point leads to a second: the distressing truth that some memories are simply more marketable than others. While the recollection of a national triumph could easily find its way into monumental form, the issue becomes more complicated when the proposed monument commemorates violence against one's own people. When a sizeable portion of the population believes such a memorial is unnecessary, unpatriotic, or both, the path from conception to realization becomes marked with pitfalls. Seen in this light, the rather aggressive marketing by the Pro-Monument Commission seems eminently appropriate, as they essentially had to choose between moving forward at every stage (with necessary compromises) or risk derailing the politically fragile endeavor. Thus, while it may be very easy to criticize the way in which the project has strayed from its original ideals (a sacred space dedicated wholly to the memory of those kidnapped, tortured, and killed during the dictatorship), the mere fact that, despite the debates, the monument has been constructed and the space is beginning to take shape remains highly significant. There now exists a space dedicated to the remembrance of the victims of violence, a place that officially acknowledges the atrocities committed against them, and for this reason the Parque de la Memoria has incredible value. In sum, the necessary commodification involved in creating the Parque de la Memoria may taint the memorial impulse, but the alternative risks eliminating the commemoration altogether.

Successful marketing campaigns aim to make the marketing invisible by inserting the "product" so deeply into the national consciousness that the "consumer" is unaware of any influence. Recalling Levine's assertion that the best marketing "borders on the invisible," one could argue that successful marketing campaigns rely on seduction rather than force. The call for memory of the recent dictatorship has proved difficult to insert into the national consciousness to date, and the promotion of the Parque de la Memoria exemplifies the attempts by human rights groups to combat the widespread cultural amnesia. While one might wish that the sacred memory of trauma could remain untainted by mundane marketing forces, the park has required more explicit rather than seductive marketing. One can only hope that through initiatives such as the Parque de la Memoria and other memorials, eventually there will come a time when the importance of commemorating a difficult past does not need to be "sold."

NOTES

1. Information current as of June 2009. Many thanks to Cara Levey for providing updated information while this chapter was being prepared.
2. Hoheisel, "Algunas reflexiones acerca del arte de la memoria y de la memoria del arte," 122. All translations are the author's unless otherwise indicated.
3. *Sculpture Prize, "Parque de la Memoria,"* 8.
4. "Un paseo público para mantener viva la memoria colectiva," Parque de la Memoria website, www.parquedelamemoria.org.ar/parque/index.htm.
5. The ten human rights groups involved in the project are Abuelas de Plaza de Mayo; Asamblea Permanente por los Derechos Humanos; Buena Memoria Asociación Civil; Centro de Estudios Legales y Sociales; Familiares de Detenidos Desaparecidos por Razones Políticas; Fundación Memoria Histórica y Social Argentina; Liga Argentina por los Derechos del Hombre; Madres de Plaza de Mayo–Línea Fundadora; Movimiento Ecuménico por los Derechos Humanos; Servicio Paz y Justicia.
6. Tandeciarz, "Citizens of Memory," 153.
7. Ibid.
8. Ibid., 159.
9. The original guidelines for the contest to design the monument to the disappeared, sponsored by the university, describe the other two monuments as the "Paseo del Monumento a la Paz y la Convivencia," at the site of the proposed AMIA monument, and the "Monumento a la Concordia 'Monseñor Ernesto Segura,'" at the site of the future monument to the Righteous Among the Nations. Two of the three original monuments have therefore been significantly modified throughout the process. The Parque de la Memoria itself is referred to in this document as the Parque de la Paz.
10. Ana Weinstein, interview by author, Buenos Aires, Argentina, 31 July 2007.
11. Tappatá de Valdez, "El Parque de la Memoria en Buenos Aires," 108.
12. One of the reasons the Monument to the Victims of State Terrorism was completed during the last months before the transfer of power was to avoid any potential delays regarding its construction. It was felt that while the new government might reduce the funds actively dedicated to the park's construction, they would not be able to undo what had already been completed. Since the change in city government, funding has been somewhat problematic, and progress on the park was stalled from May until August of 2008. Nevertheless, at the time of this writing, construction continues, new sculptures have been installed and inaugurated, and a publicity campaign targeting the university and other schools of Buenos Aires has been launched.

13. Tappatá de Valdez, "El Parque de la Memoria en Buenos Aires," 104.
14. Eliade, *The Sacred and the Profane*, 26.
15. Chidester and Linenthal, Introduction to *American Sacred Space*, 6.
16. Ibid., 15.
17. Ibid., 17.
18. Brodsky, *Nexo*, 122.
19. Also present at the site were the remains from an earlier attack on the Israeli Embassy, which added to the site's perceived symbolic significance. As *Clarín* reported after the inauguration of the Monument to the Victims of State Terrorism, "The place has a very strong symbolic burden, even in the ground: the fill along the banks was created with the remains of the Israeli Embassy and AMIA building" (see "Frente al río, 8.875 placas recuerdan a las víctimas del terrorismo de Estado," *Clarín*, 9 November 2007).
20. Marcelo Brodsky, "La memoria junto al río," *Página/12*, 13 April 1999.
21. Tappatá de Valdez, "El Parque de la Memoria en Buenos Aires," 98.
22. Hoheisel, "Algunas reflexiones acerca del arte de la memoria y de la memoria del arte," 123.
23. The government website dedicated to this initiative emphasizes the recovery of the productive relationship between the city and the waterway. The Parque de la Memoria is categorized under "Ecological Reserve and Green Spaces," with a description of the numerous parks along the river—some "ideal for visiting with children," others "more wild and natural" (see Buenos Aires website, www.bue.gov.ar/especiales/?id=2).
24. E.g., Lola Weinschelbaum de Rubino, who lost a daughter during the dictatorship, decided to have her own ashes scattered in the Río de la Plata (information sent by the Fundación Memoria Histórica y Social Argentina upon Weinschelbaum's death on 29 February 2008). The ceremony took place in the Parque de la Memoria.
25. Young, *The Texture of Memory*, 119.
26. Ibid., 120.
27. As I have suggested elsewhere, the stark brutality of the memorial may actually be more effective in transmitting past horror than a more polished monument (see Gates-Madsen, "Ruins of the Past").
28. See, in particular, the analysis of the site in Tandeciarz, "Citizens of Memory."
29. Ibid., 160.
30. At the time of this writing, Grupo de Arte Callejero's "Carteles de la memoria" was in the process of being installed in the space.
31. "Estado de situación," 5.
32. "Homenaje a las víctimas," *Clarín*, 19 March 1998.
33. Tappatá de Valdez, "El Parque de la Memoria en Buenos Aires," 101.
34. *Sculpture Prize, "Parque de la Memoria,"* 20.
35. One example that makes evident the jury's decision to favor nontraditional representation is a comparison between one of the winning sculptures, the Dutch artist Rini Hurkmans's "Pietà de Argentina," and another "Pietà," submitted by the Argentine team of Mariana Fernández Semhan and Silvia Noemi Rielo. The

Argentine artists proposed a realistic imitation of Michelangelo's "Pietà" statue, with one significant change: the absence of the son's body; yet the jury selected Hurkmans's more abstract "Pietà," a transparent photo of a woman holding a pile of crumpled clothing in the shape of a body, with other piles around her on the ground (see *Escultura y Memoria*).

36. Quoted in Young, *The Texture of Memory*, 9.
37. Ibid., 11.
38. Levine, *The Power of Persuasion*, 3.
39. Levinson, *Guerrilla Marketing*, 4.
40. Taylor, *The Archive and the Repertoire*, 24.
41. Lorena Bossi, interview by author, Buenos Aires, Argentina, 5 August 2002.
42. Park overseers are trying to make certain that the GAC's installation is more interactive, and at the time of this writing they are experimenting with the ideal placement of the signs in order to provoke a more involved response from park visitors.
43. Grupo de Arte Callejero, "El anti-monumento: Resignación de la memoria histórica," 212.
44. Lorena Bossi, interview by author, Buenos Aires, Argentina, 5 August 2002.
45. Ibid.
46. Ibid.

JOSÉ RAMÓN RUISÁNCHEZ SERRA

Reading '68

The Tlatelolco Memorial and Gentrification in Mexico City

Although the 2 October 1968 massacre in Mexico City's Tlatelolco Plaza is a well-established historical fact,[1] there was never a proper trial of its perpetrators. Three decades went by before the state allowed scholars to partially explore archives related to those events. Almost another ten years passed before the Memorial del 68 finally opened its doors, allowing belated recognition of the student movement's importance. The massacre still does not appear in Mexican textbooks.

The Memorial del 68, which was inaugurated in 2007, is constructed almost exactly on the site of the massacre. The easiest way to reach the museum, housed in the former chancellery of the Ministry of Foreign Affairs (the Secretaría de Relaciones Exteriores, or SRE), is from the Tlatelolco Metro station, in the heart of a housing complex by the same name. At its founding in 1966, the Unidad Tlatelolco complex was touted as *the* urbanistic breakthrough for solving, or at least dramatically ameliorating, Mexico City's overpopulation problems. In contrast to traditional *vecindades*, large eighteenth- and nineteenth-century homes that were haphazardly subdivided to accommodate tenants, the *unidades habitacionales* of Tlatelolco's high-rise buildings would provide affordable and sanitary housing for much larger populations. Moreover, the complex included parks, schools, dentists' offices, pharmacies, theaters, and small supermarkets, along with various kinds of apartments. Tlatelolco was planned to be a self-sufficient, orderly utopia in the middle of a gargantuan city made even more crowded by a period of booming post-Revolutionary industrialization.

Figure 1. The new Ministry of Foreign Affairs (SRE) building. (Photograph by José Ramón Ruisánchez Serra)

Today, as one tries to find an exit out of the housing complex (a challenge for visitors, since there are no signs), it becomes clear that even utopias require upkeep. The grass could be greener, the small shops, more prosperous. The buildings have a dilapidated air about them, ominously bringing to mind images of the 1985 earthquake in which the Nuevo León building was destroyed. The previously imposing SRE tower, which closes off the Plaza de las Tres Culturas—so called because pre-Hispanic ruins, a Franciscan church, and modern buildings all share the same space—now noticeably lurches to one side. In fact, even before the SRE moved to its new offices next to Alameda Park, several of the building's top floors had been deemed unsafe, and were quietly closed down.

After abundant official speculation about how sound the building remained, the bottom floors of the former SRE were finally given to the National University (UNAM) and opened to the public. The small Tlatelolco Cultural Center (Centro Cultural Tlatelolco) houses both the Memorial del 68 and the Blanstein collection of art of the Mexican School. On 22 October 2007, during the Centro's official opening,[2] one presence seemed to sanction, perhaps even sanctify, the consecration of this memory site: Elena Poniatowska, author of the most authoritative narrative on the student movement, and the massacre that ended it on 2 October 1968, was the keynote speaker.[3]

Poniatowska's inaugural role is much more important than it would seem at first, for the very conception of the memorial is fashioned after the "multi-testimonio" of her *La noche de Tlatelolco* (published in English translation as *Massacre in Mexico*). Like Poniatowska's text, the museum attempts to replicate the intervention of a multitude of different voices, acting against the monolithic discourses of the state and the media who sought to silence this history. Poniatowska's narrative was a success not only symbolically, but also quite tangibly in terms of market sales. In Mexico, where the usual press run for a title is fewer than two thousand copies, Poniatowska's book has been reprinted more than sixty times. By structuring the memorial using Poniatowska's book as a narrative model, the museum could potentially capitalize on the book's blockbuster success.

Yet despite a genuine effort to create a site where the most crucial event of the second half of the twentieth century in Mexico could be commemorated, and despite the site's ratification by Poniatowska and other well-known leftist intellectuals, the museum receives few visitors, either by members of the '68 generation or by those of younger generations. So the question of silence remains. Why is this important memory site so little known, and why from the time of its opening has it been marginalized by the very government agencies charged with promoting museums and cultural events? It has not appeared on the *carteleras culturales*, poster-sized ads publicizing cultural activities that both the federal Consejo Nacional para la Cultura y las Artes (National Council for Culture and the Arts, or CNCA) and the local Secretaría de Cultura (Ministry of Culture) distribute on a monthly basis.[4] The former omission is quite easy to explain, as the CNCA depends directly on the right-wing PAN government, and thus is not very interested in underscoring the importance of the Left as a hotbed of dominant cultural figures of the late twentieth century. But what remains problematic is the fact that the left-wing, PRD-controlled Secretaría de Cultura has done exactly the same thing. This is especially striking, given that the PRD originated in the civil society movement that powerfully came together after the 1985 earthquake, a movement that in turn can be traced back to 1968. The actions that took place in 1985—the seemingly spontaneous brigades, the way public space was occupied and reorganized when the government faltered in the face of crisis—were all sown in the furrows left by the '68 student movement. The frequent feuds that currently divide the party could be blamed for the silence surrounding the Tlatelolco memorial, but I believe there is a much more interesting possibility.

On closer examination, the carteleras culturales show a marked preference for museums in the renovated downtown area; MUNAL (the National Museum of Art), the San Ildefonso Museum (the former Jesuit College, which later became the First National High School, containing famous mural paintings by Diego Rivera and others), and Bellas Artes (the Museum of Fine Arts) all share poster space with information about free concerts and exhibits that take place in the Zócalo (Mexico City's main square), and about sponsored radio and TV programs.[5] Although during 2008, especially around October, the Centro Cultural Tlatelolco *was* mentioned in this publicity, and posters were placed at some bus stops and mailboxes, soon after the fortieth anniversary, the hype dissipated and the museum again received only scant attention in these promotional materials.

My contention is precisely that this lack of official publicity reflects the larger geographic situation of the Memorial vis-à-vis the gentrification process of downtown Mexico City—from which Tlatelolco was excluded—and the new map of the city it proposes. Moreover, the future of the museum also hinges on the fact that its director and its curators have *mis*read Poniatowska's *La noche de Tlatelolco*. A comparison of the museum and the book reveals that the Memorial unwittingly offers only a limited version of its model text's less obvious, and more radical, historiographic intervention.

Realpolitik and Real Estate

Before analyzing the Memorial proper, it is essential to read it in terms of the changing city where it stands. Let us begin with the new offices of the

SRE, housed in an impressive building, designed by Legorreta + Legorreta Architects, that looms over the Plaza Juárez across from the Alameda in the renovated downtown area (the Centro Histórico). It is situated in the heart of a corridor that starts with the new Hilton Alameda and includes the luxurious Puerta Alameda apartment complex with its indoor pool and gym, ending at the offices of Sears Mexico, owned by Carlos Slim. I mention Slim, one of the wealthiest people in the world, quite intentionally. The gentrification of the downtown area, and its exclusion of Tlatelolco, is due at least in part to Slim's real estate investments over the last decade, as well as to the efforts made by the local government to expunge the area of informal street vendors and rid it of crime. This successful reconversion has, in turn, sizably increased the value of Slim's properties.

Of course, the relatively quiet process of restoration and revitalization of the Centro Histórico, the most architecturally valuable sector of the city, is important in terms of history and of preventing further sprawl in the metropolitan area. Yet the way the process has been forced upon its current dwellers, one of whose main occupations is precisely informal commerce, seems quite problematic. The removal of the street vendors requires further analysis, especially since it correlates with the planning and opening of the Memorial del 68, and with its notorious silencing, and thus presents an opportunity for more ample evaluation of its place in the cityscape.

Months in advance, Marcelo Ebrard, the *jefe de gobierno* (mayor), had announced a 12 October 2007 deadline for hawkers in the prime area of downtown Mexico City to leave the streets of the "first perimeter," as defined by the main avenues surrounding the city center, as well as the Zócalo itself. The operation, despite heavy police support, was nonviolent, largely thanks to the new *plazas*: unpretentious shopping venues throughout the Centro Histórico where street vendors were given spaces. It must be remembered, though, that measures of this kind had been taken before, precisely in the Centro Histórico, and the results were not encouraging. In fact, the streets had remained occupied by a large *tianguis* (open-air, informal market) with ever-growing touches of sophistication, such as credit/debit card terminals available for those short on cash. In the latest effort, the plazas were occupied, but the street vendors reappeared—newly equipped with walkie-talkies to avoid police raids—suggesting that not everyone got a place in the plazas, or if they did, that the plazas were not as effective for informal commerce as the street.

Ultimately, the idea behind the removal of street vendors is not actually to regulate commerce, but to exert economic pressure on the area's traditional dwellers, so that they will sell their spacious, if dilapidated, apartments for the creation of new prime real estate zones out of impoverished neighborhoods. The underbelly of this process needs to be examined as well, as it creates margins to which the less desirable businesses and inhabitants are forced to migrate. This relates directly to the ongoing marginalization of the Memorial del 68.

A classic text by Michel de Certeau, *The Practice of Everyday Life* illuminates this connection. De Certeau clearly distinguishes between *place* and *space*, the former being a fixed niche where things and people are permanently ordered, subjected to an immutable plan; the latter, on the other hand, implies a displacement. Space *is* always already *a use of* space, including, of course, all manners of abuses, that founds new spatial potentials and permanently re-forms topologies.[6] From this basic distinction, two interrelated operations follow: the representation *inside the museum* of the topological modification of civic space, and the spatial modification the museum performs *from its doors outward*, which is to say, the way the Memorial del 68 transforms the city.

Of course, the spatialization performed in 1968 can be read as a phenomenon replaced by the incarceration of several student leaders and the confinement of the rest of the *manifestantes* (protesters) to private space, as well as by nationalistic celebration of the Olympic Games' collective agonies and victories.[7] Yet it can (and should) also be read as the beginning of new liberties, of a rare cultural flourishing, of a more tolerant sexual culture—and a little more than a decade and a half later, of the 1985 civil society movement. On that note, to tease out the museographic texture of the Memorial del 68 more subtly, it is imperative to go back to *La noche . . .* , in this case, to the spatial practices that were necessary for the archival accumulation that was later delicately crafted into the book. I shall approach Poniatowska's work via Frazier and Cohen, who ably point in the right direction when they spatialize the 1968 movement. Furthermore, they highlight space's gendered dimensions by signaling Lecumberri Prison not only as the locus of enunciation from which the male leaders of the movement deployed their memories, but also as the site that makes the work of recollection possible and furthermore shapes it: "The space of the prison overdetermines all these accounts by reconfiguring leaders as spokespersons for an entire generation of activists. The space of the movement and the space of the prison are collapsed, as male leaders become the movement['s] historical protagonists."[8] With this move, Frazier and Cohen in effect gender the space of the movement, but they fail to see what is truly unique about Poniatowska's book, which after all was forged by a woman. Women's space during '68 was the street,[9] maybe for the first time ever, and this lens opens a much vaster map both of the city and of the participants, central and casual, from top and bottom strata, including antagonists to the movement.

In preparing *La noche . . .* , Poniatowska did visit the prison, a gesture that Frazier and Cohen read as consecrating the male leaders' centrality, but at the same time, she did two things that refute their assertion. While at times she uses the leaders' testimony as truly representative of what happened to other people, this same testimony simultaneously may be read as deconstructive criticism of the Consejo Nacional de Huelga (National Strike Council, or CNH). She also balances this would-be hegemonic locus with the family homes and streets, as sites of a battle of versions, and with the (formerly) sacred spaces reclaimed by the lay city of the unidad habitacional and vecindades as part of its just-found(ed) importance: the Zócalo, where the government is housed; the Cathedral; the University. Poniatowska includes both the meetings where the intelligentsia determined the strategies and goals of the *movimiento*, and the atomized *brigadas* where theory met reality, with sometimes glaring disparities. She hops on buses, enters factories, and haggles at the market—the places where the urgent but frequently overtechnical messages of the Consejo Nacional de Huelga were performed, translated, explained, and confronted by the people they supposedly addressed. Poniatowska's book takes in the whole cityscape so effectively precisely because of her actual mobility in search of testimonies.

In effect, Poniatowska maps into her book the voices and practices that top-down historiography—and I include in this category the personal counter-historiography produced by former male student leaders *and* (as we shall see) the Memorial del 68—leaves out, creating the possibility for more than an overtly political reading. Poniatowska thus opens the potential for understanding the lasting effects of '68 in terms not only of nation but of self, permeating not only the National Palace, but also the homes of common people, reshaping the traditional familial text. And this, in turn, subverts all kinds of "placing" with spatial practices.

Against the voice of President Gustavo Díaz Ordaz—the voice that justifies violence against students, sympathizers, and bystanders in terms of an historic necessity to eradicate communism, of the continuation of economic progress, of a need for calm to frame the Olympic Games and show the "Mexican miracle" to the (developed) world—surges the counter-historiography practiced by Poniatowska: itinerant and polycentric, at times contradictory, and always ambiguous, capable of containing opacities and mystifications without a compulsion to explain them away. Instead of reducing history to a linear explanatory model, this practice allows the proliferation of a myriad of registers and partial understandings. This counter-historiography not only combats the presidential model of top-down, good-versus-evil historiography, with its Cold War resonances, but also invites a powerful meditation on its patriarchal deployments in the home. Hugo Hiriart acidly describes this in a few masterful strokes: "Something similar occurred at Mexican dinner tables before '68: the sovereignty of the home resided with the paterfamilias, the picturesque autocrat with his double morality (one standard for himself and another for everyone else), the vociferous, categorical macho."[10]

Two tools prove helpful for approaching the archeology of ante-textual motion involved in producing this counter-historiographic text. The first is a host of interviews in which Elena Poniatowska, a veteran reporter herself, has magnificently shed light on the state of the city after 2 October, revealing her own nomadic crossings of city and class boundaries in resistance to state repression. The second is Frazier's and Cohen's illuminating insight regarding the porosity of space as a consequence of its gendering during and after '68 in Mexico, which provides an explanation for an essential characteristic of Poniatowska's spatial practices. They would not have been possible had she not been a woman. Let us begin with an exploration of the strongly knit links between invisibility/silencing and female gendering during the specific period of the movement and its aftermath. The link has been well established by feminist scholarship, yet the formulation about Mexico merits quotation. About the pre-October period, Frazier and Cohen tell us: "The same [macho] attitudes that inhibited women from voicing their ideas and denied them full political agency worked to their advantage in other moments, however, [as when] women mobilized gender stereotypes for the movement. Because they were defined [as] apolitical and thus seen as non-threatening to the state, women could make their way into spaces cordoned off to their male counterparts."[11]

Interestingly enough, this ability to penetrate, carry, link, and disrupt was not curtailed by the massacre and incarceration of the leaders. After 2 October, women were still able to move about the city, and even penetrate the "dark palace" of Lecumberri. This penetration of the prison by women at that time is masterfully thematized in José Revueltas's claustrophobic tale of (male) confinement, *El apando* (The Heist), in which the mother of an imprisoned addict smuggles drugs into the prison in her vagina. It may appear unclear why contact between the sphere of the penal institution and (potentially) that of the public (if not the political proper) was allowed. Once again, Frazier and Cohen shed light on the matter: "Given the Mexican state's chronic inability to finance a so-called modern penal system, both prisoners *and* the state relied on this unpaid labor [by women]. Since families, and not the state, bore the brunt of the cost of feeding and clothing imprisoned loved ones, women's labor ironically functioned as a critical resource for the state as well as for prisoners themselves."[12]

The testimony obtained in jail put Poniatowska among the ranks of women that visited Lecumberri. As she stated in a 1988 interview: "I used to visit the jail almost every Sunday. . . . I was interested in the testimonies of all of the boys, and they would tell them to me without a recorder, without a damn thing, without pen or paper, because I would be searched on entry, so I had to reconstruct everything they told me when I got home."[13] Poniatowska's gendered transgression of spatial boundaries was a necessary precondition enabling production of her multivocal, counter-hegemonic text.

As we shall see below, it is necessary to reflect more deeply on such spatial practices, for while the Memorial del 68 can be read as a new effort to commemorate the massacre and officially recognize the overall importance of the student movement, it can also be interpreted, and this is what I attempt to do, as perhaps the most intelligent re-territorialization of '68, or *placing*, in the full sense that de Certeau gives to the term: what is placed is also placated, placidly brought to peace. Commemoration has already taken place, somewhere *else* by somebody *else*, and thus important business, such as the gentrification of downtown Mexico City, can go on.

In the same sense that the streets are rid of those who may pose a danger to the free flow of capital to the Centro Histórico, the lesser revolutionaries of the sixties are concentrated together and, in the same stroke, relegated to the past; they are properly placed in a museum occupying the less-than-prime quarter of Tlatelolco in the same way that the *ambulantes* (street vendors) are forced to occupy the ordered (and quite well-hidden) plazas.

The message for the latter is clear: business will never be like it used to be in the Centro, so the best they can do is move out of the downtown area, sell their dilapidated but roomy apartments to real-estate firms like Bienes Raíces del Centro, and find their own backwaters, perhaps even in the once-middle-class Tlatelolco.[14]

It is precisely in this context of gentrification and of conveniently setting uncomfortable history to rest in faraway places that we should recall that back in the immediate months after the massacre, while the state was trying to control the movement of people, it also had to allow for a certain porosity, as we have seen. Poniatowska's spatial practice served to knit the city back together, bringing together stories that otherwise may have been lost, to un-silence the muted voices of everyday people. Even though *La noche . . .* is not about the heroism of Poniatowska, the moment has arrived to read that as well, to read what it takes to recover memories to create the archive of her kind of historiography. If we are capable of reading this individual movimiento/movement as a direct consequence of the student movement/movimiento, we have tuned in to the correct trope, because we allow ourselves to listen to everyone, and not just to one voice; we become capable of exploring alternatives to the "reestablished order." Thinking about how the book was made prepares us to better perform it, play it, read it—and to be better prepared to actively interpret the museum and city surrounding it in terms of spatial practices.

The Museum

The exterior of the Memorial del 68 is decorated with a bottom row of very large black-and-white photographs of young men and women with innocent expressions and appropriately sixties-style hairdos and eyewear, and an upper row of multicolored reproductions from the Blanstein Collection. No photographs of the army, the police, or the massive marches appear. There are no captions, no explanations. Inside, beyond a ticket counter that doubles as a coat check, a patio opens onto the Memorial, paved with black volcanic rock; a noiseless rectangular fountain, also paved with dark stone, crosses its longitudinal axis. Over the portico of the Memorial proper extend two extremely large photographic blow-ups, one a frontal shot of a march where smiling young men advance towards the spectator, the other a meeting with both young and older people raising their arms in protest, viewed from the side. It is as if the marchers are progressing toward the dark patio that memorializes their deaths. The effect, though, is diminished by the predictable sixties pop music that drifts out of the museum, lending a sense of familiar reenactment.

An opening statement at the Memorial claims that it houses multiple *testimonios* of student-movement participants, thereby pointing toward *La noche* . . . and suggesting that the narrative the museum presents involves a process of negotiation in which the visitor must intervene. Similarly, Poniatowska's book opens with a series of quite moving captioned photographs of the 1968 student movement, photographs that capture the spirit of the time, of the collectivity that organizes itself creatively, as opposed to the docile masses that march, for instance, every November 20th (the anniversary of the Revolution) or May 1st (Labor Day), obeying the interpellation of the state. Immediately after these photographs, the book announces itself as "Testimonios de historia oral" / "Oral History Testimonies," in the plural. This multiple testimonio approach clearly separates this book from Poniatowska's previous one, *Hasta no verte, Jesús mío* (*Here's To You, Jesusa!*) which she called a *testimonio-novela*. That text utilized the more traditional metonymic pattern of the testimonio, in which the story of a single character creates a certain exemplarity, positioning the *testimoniante* (person bearing witness) as a type representing an entire social class during a given epoch. By contrast, the multitestimonio invites various voices into the textual space, with all their conflicting individuality, rather than as reduplications of a single voice, that of the underprivileged individual. Thus, the text itself acts as the space of hegemonic struggle, of necessary re-narration on the part of the reader, of undecidability. Other voices are not just tacitly implied as those silencing the voice of the testimoniante, but instead are daringly juxtaposed; in Poniatowska's book, we hear participants from all sides of the conflict, along with bystanders and "experts." And precisely here is where the book and the museum begin to diverge significantly, as the Memorial offers only a certain subset of voices and perspectives, which in turn circumscribes interpretive possibilities much more narrowly than does the book.

The exhibit of the Memorial is divided into five parts. The first is devoted to the antecedents of the movement from 1958 to 1967 in Mexico and the rest of the world: from the repression of the local railroad workers' strike to the Cuban Revolution to events in Prague, Paris, and the United States.

Then three sections describe and discuss the Mexican student movement itself, and a final section spans to 1973. The pieces displayed can be divided into four main categories:

1. Didactic diagrams, dioramas, and charts. These attempt to state the facts in an objective fashion. Yet information about the state seems notably understated, especially given that a portion of its archives are now publicly available.
2. Artifacts from 1968. These include posters protesting the violence of the state and clippings from newspapers, as well as promotional materials about the then brand-new Tlatelolco housing project, "a city within the city," which Carlos Monsiváis once called the "modest utopia of a Mexico City without *vecindades*."[15]
3. Several contemporary art pieces that address the movimiento. Most use various video techniques as their medium, which blends them sometimes a bit too much with (4); and
4. The most prominent installation: a long series of video-interviews by Nicolás Echeverría.[16] These are shown both on individual screens and in several large projection rooms, where different angles of the same interview sometimes occupy two convergent screens. At other times, one of the screens is used to project filmed photographs or to show original footage from the marches, or even of the 2 October events. In the video-interviews, cross-cuts between different *sesentaiocheros* (members of the '68 generation) forty years later are frequent, and aspire to generate a dialogic effect.

Yet it remains only an effect, a replication of a formal mechanism, emptied (at least in part) of its contestatory potential by a questionable selection of content. This is what I mean by the Memorial's misreading, or at the very least its superficial reading, of the radical textual operations of *La noche*. . . . It is not simply a question of the fact that, despite all the multi-angled video presentations, there *is* a written timeline that attempts an old-style monologic "objective" presentation of the "facts" in chronological linear order, for *La noche* . . . itself also contains an "objective" chronology. Rather, and much more subtly, the census of testimoniantes is quite suspect. The vast majority of voices included are now prominent personalities in the political or cultural spheres, and sometimes both: from Monsiváis and Poniatowska themselves, to Pino (now a PRD member), to the famous pianist Mario Lavista, to the celebrated painter José Luis Cuevas, to Gerardo Estrada, a well-known administrator who has hovered for years in high cultural spheres.

Poniatowska's counter-historiography creates its authority by fraternal and sororal inclusions in a single textual space. It allows voices invested with traditional authority and those of the chronically silenced to cohabit within the same page, voices from both sides (or neither side) of the conflict, (con)fusing seemingly clear Manichean divisions in a series of subtle differences: "A soldier,"[17] "Artemisa de Gortari, mother of a family,"[18] "Esther Fernández, student at the Faculty of Sciences, UNAM,"[19] "Roberta Avendaño, *Tita*, of the CNH,"[20] "Margarita Isabel, actress,"[21] "Chant at the August 27 demonstration,"[22] "José Carlos Becerra, 'The Stone Mirror,' "[23] "María Luisa Mendoza, writer and resident in the Tlatelolco Housing Unit,"[24] and the zero-degree of them all: "A voice in the crowd."[25]

There are two aspects that must be taken into account when examining Poniatowska's much more inclusive selection of voices. First, we must again recall the ante-textual activity necessary to produce this multitestimonio text. At the very moment when people were ordered to stay home, Poniatowska took to the streets, quietly working to reunite the city with its past and to counter in the present the government's attempt to atomize and fragment the citizenry. These actions, coupled with the confluence of disparate voices gathered in the pages of *La noche . . .* , contrast with the static, single, studio-based filming of interviews for the Memorial. The geographic is not ancillary to the sociological, but central to it: as discussed above, Poniatowska's appropriation of the city is just as crucial as the ample spectrum of voices it produced.

Second, the fact that a complex demographic not only includes obvious attitudes—the reactionary upper classes, the libertarian youth—but also shows that the obvious is always a simplification that marginalizes the complexity of what actually happened. For instance, how might a member of the police or the military have a critical opinion about what the state orders him to do? Or how does a structure of feeling emerge and later articulate itself across society? It may seem apparent that a wider selection of voices allows for a more complex understanding of a historical process, but what *La noche . . .* demonstrates is how this complexity does *not* entail a strategic compromise vis-à-vis the reductive version offered by masculinist official history, informed by paranoid narratives of the Cold War period.[26] Instead, it founds something else entirely: a welcome practice of nuanced historiography, delicate and intimate, a *feminine* historiography in the senses introduced above.

This does not at all mean that the museum is totally disappointing. Halfway through the visit, the chronology breaks at the end of August 1968, and one descends to what was once the inaccessible basement of a government building. Emotion is already inevitable: overtones of everything from secret archives to possible torture chambers are suggested by a dark stairway that overtly connotes a crypt or tomb. After the descent, marking the increasing importance of the student movement, with a resulting escalation of state worries, the light is dimmer and visitors encounter images of the silent march of 13 September and footage of the 2 October massacre. Both sets of images evoke a powerful aura, not only because of what we, the observers, know about the fate of the movement, but also because of the now-seemingly-unattainable dignity and pride and hope of those marching and chanting. Something seems irreversibly lost, something that is not mere *bios*, but *zoe*:[27] the intersubjective texture of political life. In the final analysis, the brave stance of recovered memory, along with a kind of purity—a now seemingly forever-lost conviction that emanates from the faces of those marching, again, in growing numbers, reclaiming public space—creates a powerful affective link between the present and the now-familiar past.

While the basement offers such complexity, this is exactly what the rest of the memorabilia fails to convey. It is precisely because copies of the small posters exhibited in the museum are available for the public to take home free of charge that the aura of the artifacts is diminished: they seem entirely recoverable, for the posters on the wall and those seemingly abandoned in certain corners of the museum are identical. These posters provide only a banal reproduction of '68's most accessible meanings—one, for example, demands peace and shows a dove—in effect erasing the traces of social trauma under a veneer of facile remembrance. Thus, even when offered free of charge, the posters enter the circuit of "retro" commodity fetishism, for they seem to possess a value that emanates from the object itself. This is not the case with the images of the silent march or the footage of the massacre, for there is no way to take home what is beyond them. If the posters commodify the past, replacing the need to remember, the basement images underline the past's disturbing irreducibility, the founding trauma of a social project that remains alive today but whose value is immeasurable in any currency or exchange.

It is possible to clarify the effects of the posters' availability even further when we compare them to the initial fate of *La noche. . . .* After it was first published, the book was awarded the prestigious 1971 Xavier Villaurrutia prize "from writers to writers,"[28] which Poniatowska famously turned down. Her words, "And who will award prizes to the dead?," signaled her refusal to engage with the government of Luis Echeverría Álvarez (1970–76), who was the Secretario de Gobernación (Minister of Internal Affairs) in 1968 and arguably the direct intellectual author of the 2 October Tlatelolco massacre.[29] Poniatowska's statement made apparent the incommensurability between her homage to the dead and a sense of closure, or "moving on," that acceptance of the prize would have entailed. Similarly, the easy availability of mass-produced museum memorabilia lacks the minimum distance necessary to remain respectful. In their very accessibility, the distance that would mark them as signs of a *continuing* struggle for justice collapses.[30]

Likewise, the mediocrity of the art pieces at the museum should be read precisely from the point of view of their lack of *difference* vis-à-vis the past. They seem unable to assert their presence, in the potentially productive sense of being positioned at a vantage point in the present that at the same time makes the past clearer *and* unreachable. Instead, they fall into the banal category of the monument, in the worst sense of the term: they represent the event without incorporating into the work a consciousness of what the representation inevitably fails to convey.

Before analyzing what I believe are the two exceptions to this pattern in the museum, allow me to return to Poniatowska's book and to other textual sources on '68 that allow me to emphasize the importance of representation's limits in this context. This is crucial not just for understanding what is missing from the art exhibited in the Memorial, but also for bringing a new sort of critical attention to *La noche. . . .* As mentioned above, most of the mainstream work written on *La noche . . .* notes that Poniatowska's book shares many ambitions with the narratives produced by the (male) leaders of the movement—centrally in the form of memoirs—as well as those of many books published on the twentieth, and especially the thirtieth, anniversary of the movimiento, when the state finally opened its files to researchers, thus breaking a silence that had lasted for a generation. Paradoxically, it is perhaps this archival euphoria and male orthodoxy, acting concurrently with the need to relate the democratic victory of 2000 to a possible (if admittedly partial) 1968 genesis, that have marginalized (once again) other very important aspects of the text: precisely those that have little or nothing to do with this epic strand, the non-monumental ones.[31]

It remains imperative to read with a more open attitude passages such as this one from *La noche . . .* , in which María del Carmen Rodríguez, a literature student at the Universidad Iberoamericana, describes her feelings for her boyfriend:

> I suddenly saw him as I had never seen him before. I saw his very pale hands, as white as wax, with blue veins, his little goatee that I had kept begging him not to shave off: "Leave it, please!"—because it made him look older than he really was, twenty-one; I saw his deep-set blue eyes (they've always had a very sad look in them), and felt his warm body next to mine. Both of us were soaking wet from the rain and from having fallen into so many puddles every time we flung ourselves down on the ground, yet his arm felt nice and warm around my shoulders. Then for the first time since we'd been going together, I told him yes, that when the Army troops let us go I'd live with him, that we were going to die some day, sooner or later, and that I wanted to live, that I was saying yes, yes, I love you, I really, really love you, I'll do whatever you want, I'm in love with you too, yes, yes, I'm in love too, yes . . . [32]

Here, the Joycean intertextuality serves as a vehicle for transporting affections into the future, a line that points toward sexual liberties, a freeing of (hetero)sexuality that also gave rise to robust gay and lesbian activisms as well as triumphs such as the recent legalization of same-sex marriage in the Distrito Federal. The shattered middle-class prejudices in the intimate sphere coincide with a revelation of the true nature of the state as well as the institution (or at the very least a glimpse) of a new public sphere. Moreover, the body serves as a crucial mediator of these processes: not only is the body politic of the nation modified, but the human body as well, the body of citizens with new freedoms and unimagined potentialities, even if virtual, to be exercised later on, but not any less important because of that fact. Once that body is taken away from the streets and placed into a small museum, such liberties become narrated as a thing of the past: the libertinage of a bygone era.

These features of the multiple testimonios edited by Poniatowska—their capacity to convey successful personal, familial, and local change—seem to me (born, after all, in 1971—too young to vote in the contested and, arguably, fraudulent 1988 presidential election) much more important than the overt political struggle for the locus of enunciation afforded by the Revolution and institutional power, the usual starting point of conventional criticism.[33] Now, the fact that these strands of personal change, happening beyond or under or alongside the institutional-political, have remained for years unread—or worse, read and cast aside as unimportant, as sentimental and non-political banalities—merits further analysis. Such analysis is all the more necessary given these strands' prominence in the most important book produced by an author noted for her attention to silenced aspects of society. In the case of the Memorial del 68, where a crucial part of what should be memorialized is precisely this change in sensibilities, this misreading becomes especially unacceptable.

The following passage from de Certeau's *The Capture of Speech*, his book about the French '68, proves helpful for teasing out the finer aspects that have made *La noche* . . . absolutely decisive for understanding the Mexican student movement of '68 *and its implications in the following decades*. Its power bears extended citation:

> What was *positively* experienced could only be expressed *negatively*. The experience was the capture of speech. What was stated was a contestation that, by calling the whole system into question, could only be betrayed by every existing organization, by every political procedure, or by every renewed institution. A massive movement from below escaped from preexisting structures and frameworks; but, by that very fact, every requisite program and idiom were lacking. In this society that it denounced, the movement could only be expressed marginally, whereas, nonetheless, it already constituted an experience for society. Its own "refusal" thus also betrayed reality since it merely marked off a barrier without stating what the inner landscape was—that is, the experience itself. For tactical reasons, the contestation also camouflaged the disparity of experiences in order to have them assembled under the flag of an identical counteroffensive. . . . Moreover, every negation is content with inverting the terms of the affirmation it contradicts. It is its victim. . . . But the main problem today is posed by the disparity between a fundamental experience and the deficit of its language, between the "positivity" of something lived and the "negativity" of an expression that, in the form of a refusal, resembles more the symptom than the elaboration of the reality being designated.[34]

What this means, what this *has* meant for forty years now, is that a sizable part of what was experienced in '68 was never incorporated into its textualization—which is to say, its emplotment (the stories-becoming-history of '68), either because it was marginalized due to a seeming unintelligibility, or "lost in translation" to the language of the Revolution, heavily mediated by the social sciences. The lack of more radical art in the Memorial works directly against the aims of its curatorial project, as inclusion of more cutting-edge pieces could help reclaim precisely the "incomprehensible" marginalia that are essential to the movement's legacy. The Memorial's (mis)reading of *La noche . . .* leaves untapped the sort of discourse that has only regained its true importance through later developments that insist on the personal as political, on the new possibilities of social texture as reservoirs of political imagination. Most of the works of art currently included in the exhibit fail to convey the new: they simply represent what was already there in the first place. They remain incapable of conveying the lack of articulation of the moment and they do not propose a *re*articulation that profits from the narratives conceived later in the diverse fields where the struggle of '68 reshaped prior hegemonies.

With this understanding, it is possible to better explore the power of the exceptional pieces in the museum. The first is the room-sized safe where photographs of the just-detained students are posted in a single row that spans the walls. The heavy steel door of the safe, the very low ceiling, and bars that at times prevent entrance into the room effectively play off the expressions of the detainees. Many are stripped down to their underwear; others are visibly stained with blood; in all cases, their fear, their youth, their vulnerability, all infuse the setting, a former government office, with the implications of torture. (After the 2 October massacre, arrested survivors were taken to the Campo Militar 1, a large military facility in what were then the northwestern outskirts of the city.) This installation points powerfully toward the possibility of desanitizing the museographic space, and of reincorporating the specificity of the site into the work. This intervention allows the site to become part of the visit, thereby emphasizing the tension between past and present, the gap of what remains unresolved, that is so glaringly absent from most of the rest of the pieces on exhibition.

Another exceptional work is a very funny yet powerful piece by Francis Aÿlis: a video in which the artist himself turns around the flagpole in the Zócalo, first alone and later, with every complete circumnavigation, followed by an ever-increasing flock of sheep that then eventually decreases one sheep at a time to complete the loop. This video-installation directly refers to the reconsecration of the flag by bureaucrats forced out of their offices in 1968 to be present in the Zócalo. Unable to state their inconformity otherwise, they marched, bleating, making reference to the fact they were not attending out of their own interest but following a state interpellation. Shot in black and white with an unflinching, unchanging, open perspective, the film arguably offers the gaze of the state, as the Zócalo is flanked by the traditional sites of power: the Cathedral, the first financial institutions, and the seats of local and national government. The tolling of a bell, to imply that the Church played its part as an agent of the status quo, is the film's only soundtrack. Overall, the loop is both hypnotic and thought-provoking, creating a reinterpretation of the historical facts where the artist and his present are clearly part of the work, allowing for reflection on the re-narrative and creative energies unleashed by the events of 1968.

The end of the visit, back upstairs, is inevitably anticlimactic, even though the last room includes a small case with politically aware and aesthetically felicitous books written in and around those years, and narrates the final liberation of those in jail. Despite the fact that an epilogue is included here, where glimpses of the *present* importance of '68 are offered—for instance, José Woldenberg, whose brainchild is the IFE, the independent Federal Electoral Institute,[35] is one of the interviewees in this last video—it remains insufficiently developed. After the final room, the visitor confronts a view of the fifteenth-century ruins of Tlatelolco and famous poems by Octavio Paz and Rosario Castellanos, printed on the glass and on the wall opposite. The only remaining space is a "study room," where one can sit and read any of a handful of books on '68, from Revueltas to Volpi's recent *Cultural History of '68* (securely fastened to a round table by a thick cable), or watch one of the video interviews at a DVD station,[36] or play around with one of several computers that offer further information on the Memorial del 68. All of the furniture here resembles the now-retro "space-age" designs of Eero Aarnio, and especially the audiorama at Parque Hundido,[37] which is a nice touch in terms of design, although not the best option in terms of scholarly comfort. And one wonders why the vast archive made available to scholars is not here, along with other materials, so that the production of further scholarship on '68 is encouraged.

A guestbook fruitfully reveals quite a few facts about the visitors—or at least the pen-friendly ones. First, the younger crowd mostly comes from high schools, overwhelmingly state-funded institutions controlled by UNAM.

Figure 2. The street view of the memorial del 68.
(Photograph by José Ramón Ruisánchez Serra)

Interestingly enough, there seems to be very little evidence of organized school visits, although the handwriting and the text-messaging-inflected language of quite a few entries seem to evince the presence of even younger visitors. The members of this group share the impression of the high "cool factor" of the museum, created by the sixties music and the omnipresence of flat-screen televisions. Yet most of them also complain about the sheer volume of information, and some add the need for a guide to orient their visit. Someone who actually lived through the process could create a welcome intergenerational dialogue, as Southern Cone memory sites have shown.

Among the middle generation, those who did not live through the student movement but who are already past school age, the wealth of information seems much more welcome; in fact, some of these visitors even seem enthusiastic about a second visit, yet no one actually claims to be visiting a second time. The most encouraging entries come precisely from this age group: people who confess to having been brainwashed in school and/or at home about 1968, who finally "realize what really happened," and are thankful for it.

There are a few entries from former sesentaiocheros as well. They all appear to be sympathetic with the museum, and none of them seem to bear a grudge about the fact that the less-than-famous crowd is unrepresented in the video interviews.

Finally, the number of foreign visitors, at least those who leave their trace behind, is negligible. But the precious few seem to agree with the locals about the lack of information about the museum. "Why don't you advertise more?" is the most common question.

Although in May 2008 the Museum Guide was published and presented in a public act in which Carlos Monsiváis was the keynote speaker, and despite the fact that in as little as half an hour some ten visitors have for the price of the DVD interviews that are just available for in-house viewing, the museum shop, advertised on new signposts, only opens, as the guards informed me, "on special occasions." Recently, the shop's entrance was also blocked by a box presumably being used to transport a very large canvas from the museum proper to the storage area. The restaurant and cafeteria, also confidently signaled, remain works in progress, though nobody seems in a hurry to complete them.

The events of the fortieth anniversary of the massacre also echo several large patterns I have discussed. As happens every year, on 2 October 2008, people marched from the Plaza de las Tres Culturas to the Zócalo. Some 40,000 were assembled by the time the groups started moving, and several thousand more arrived directly to Mexico City's main square. Tellingly enough, the Memorial remained impervious to what it is supposed to commemorate. *Olimpia*, by Flavio González Mello, a drama about the infamous battalion responsible for the 2 October "operation" was playing that night, and the exhibit was open, but no link whatsoever was created between the exhibits and the "real world." Sadly, obediently, the Memorial remained confined to its marginal quarter rather than extending its influence into the gentrified heart of the city. Meanwhile, university and high-school students, young punks, parents, daughters and sons of the disappeared, teachers from the city and from all over the country, showed that the preferred way of memorializing is linked not with place but with space, and especially, with the occupation of the city. Bodies walked away from a Memorial that, at least in its first year, has lacked the spatial and affective imagination to become part of the living memory map of the city.

To conclude, I have tried to show in the previous pages what remains absent from the museum, and thus, what has been lost in the process of reterritorializing the '68 movement as something localized and immobile, at once in the past and in the margins of a renovated city (re)gained by the winners and takers of post-NAFTA Mexico. Paradoxically, this has been achieved using the Memorial's very model: Poniatowska's *La noche de Tlatelolco.*

First of all, the history of occupying public spaces including city streets creatively and in ever-changing patterns—so crucial to the whole '68 process—has become relegated instead to one lugubrious corner of the city, where everything has been placed so that directed visits can be accomplished. Given the almost complete lack of temporary exhibits,[38] the poor research facilities, and the absence of historiographic or museographic workshops at the Memorial,[39] such a visit is unlikely to be repeated, despite the good intentions expressed in the visitors book. No one stated: "This is my second visit."

Second, the capacity, or even better, *need* to create dialogue is simulated instead with atomized monologues in the Memorial. Even though this work was filmed in the decade of 2000, it offers little new, whether in terms of a continuity with the past or in terms of using a version of 1968 reexamined from present-day Mexico as a vantage point for reflection about what was achieved, what remains virtual, and what never was attained through the movement and its legacies.

Third and even more important, there is no link between the art pieces on exhibit and the fact that in many ways the events of '68 made possible their very existence. The same is true regarding most everything that was *won* thanks to '68. Although the place is a memorial, and as such, it commemorates a loss, at the same time it displaces, or rather, *bans*, the more felicitous articulations, in terms of policy and especially culture and affect, that the student movement and subsequent elaborations by '68 and post-'68 intellectuals achieved. I think here of writers from Héctor Manjarrez and Paloma Villegas—the foremost novelists in terms of the structures of feeling that take place in the 1970s—to Juan Villoro and Jorge Volpi and Fabrizio Mejía Madrid, the most gifted novelists and nonfiction writers in terms of present-day Mexico and its sociopolitical articulations.

Moreover, the use of space, its creative occupation, the dialogic mode, and the conceptualization of '68 as an event that opened up a very rich set of liberties had already been articulated in *La noche . . .* , the text that served as a model for the discourse of the Memorial del 68. The problem is that if the museum takes *La noche . . .* as its model, it does so only according to one of the least empowering of its many possible readings. To deem this unimportant would be to misread it a second time, and with even more dire consequences, for accepting the museum and implicitly rejecting the rest of the legacy of '68 blinds us to what is perhaps one of the richest archives in terms of uses of space conceived in contemporary Mexico. This allows the gentrification process to continue unchecked, behind the backs of the citizenry, rather than opening discussion of its terms and the tactics that drive it. The Memorial could and should be an important locus of reflection on the projects of the city, for Tlatelolco *itself* was once such an "answer."

Yet, luckily, there are other modes of appropriation both of '68 and of the intersubjectivity created during and after the student movement. Such appropriations stress what Arjun Appadurai calls a "third space": social formations whose main interest is neither state nor market. A poignant example is the yearly march on 2 October where old sesentaiocheros and youth born after '68, sometimes decades later, intermingle and cross the city, marking with their presence many of the recently gentrified quarters. The march is dialogic in more than the intergenerational sense, for it is also a vehicle for voicing new discontents, and for relating old injustices to the new. The march is not just a reenactment of the pioneering marches of the past, but also an exercise where memory—reexamined from the present—is handed down and used as a vantage point to contest hegemonic narratives of the present. One example would be the debate over reparations for victims of Mexico's dirty war, another, the fact that the Tlatelolco massacre is not part of the official history textbooks. An important topic in the 2008 march was the complicity between President Felipe Calderón and the permanent leader of the teacher's union, "la maestra" (schoolteacher) Elba Esther Gordillo, which has allowed for a continuing decline in the quality of public education and thus a widening gap between publicly- and privately-educated students.[40]

A different use of the creative energies liberated by '68 fueled another downtown-based project: the gallery/workshop/daycare center Casa Vecina (the House Next Door), which tried to incorporate the current neighbors of El Centro, especially the children of street vendors, into the understanding and production of culture. But even this project has an underside, as inevitably its efforts open the zone to what George Yúdice terms the "culture economy."[41] Paradoxically enough, the success of Casa Vecina in creating a more artsy neighborhood accelerated a gentrification process that would eventually expel its current population. Yet, it is worth asking whether utopian ventures such as Casa Vecina could offer alternative forms of gentrification, such as multiclass urbanscapes where diagonal activities incorporating actors from different backgrounds come together and generate a productive dialogue in terms of the political and cultural texture of the city. I believe that given an intelligent historicization of its conditions of possibility, the answer could be other than a categorical "No." One must also bear in mind that the actual house is owned by Carlos Slim, who enjoyed a win-win situation: no matter what the outcome of the project, his property was well taken care of, while steadily gaining value and producing good press for the "philanthropist"-businessman.[42]

As we move closer and closer to the moment that Beatriz Sarlo has explored in her *Tiempo pasado*, when it is no longer the witnesses of events, but increasingly their children and even grandchildren who are the bearers of memory, or rather, of the stories that come together as History,[43] decisions regarding the fate of public memorialization of the '68 movement will evolve into a different but still all-important intersubjective pact. The decision whether this crucial event of liberty-creation will be relegated to the obscure corner of the city where it officially wound up or will continue as a force instigating pacts of intergenerational, multiclass, and perhaps even international solidarity, will have to be made by subsequent generations, my own and those to follow.[44]

In keeping with this articulation of the chronological aspect of the pact offered by this radical activation of 1968, we must reflect on the economic consequences of *not* articulating more fully its spatial implications. How, for instance, in the huge downtown tianguis now seemingly in the process of extinction—or rather, exile to less attractive sectors of Mexico City—the most popular commodities sold are pirate copies of CDs, movies, computer software, as well as clothing boasting prestigious logos, surely added illegally by local manufacturers to entice buyers that otherwise would not be able to afford the magic ciphers and talismans of global capitalism. Is not the displacement of the peddlers of exactly those commodities that signify global consumption a move to make room for an elite whose trade is precisely the creation of culture as commodity?

The spatial consequence of this unchecked gentrification process is the in-migration of those who occupy higher echelons in the same culture consumption processes, thanks to the emigration of those in the lower strata, without any remaining common space for dialogue or reflection.

Ultimately, without room for maneuvering outside strict lines of economic fatalism, everything remains in place and no spatial activities seem possible anymore.

And back into the realm of the Memorial, one must think about how this very replacement, caused by the repartition of sectors of the city, parallels the contraction of a history explicitly made of histories, motion, multivocal assemblages, by something that is not quite History, in the rigorous sense that Sarlo demands, from second-generation narratives. Sarlo calls for a vigorous product of previous dialogue furthered by method, catalyzed by a degree of reasonable doubt that would have been considered unacceptable, for both ethical and tactical reasons, at the moment of memory's first employment. The problem is that the product exhibited in the Memorial del 68 is not a collectively accepted history, but rather sights and sounds that flash in their technological vehicles but dare not claim scientific status or a furthering of dialogue, and thus lack the power to found a true discussion of the financial messianism so prevalent in the decision-making of today's Mexico City.

Ultimately what is at stake is the very core of memory before its commodification, and with it, *the possibility of a memory of commodification*, the possibility of actively recording what is going on *now*, thinking of and *from* the consequences of the darkest side of the defeat of '68. To preserve the condition of possibility of that memory process is indeed very well worth marching for, re-reading for, writing for.

NOTES

Although this text was originally written in English, its readability comes from the incredibly thorough rewriting and editing work of Alice A. Nelson, who also brought to my attention a number of aspects that needed to be developed, and thus helped me further refine the argument presented in these pages. Of course, any limitations remain entirely my responsibility.

1. According to the official report, thirty demonstrators died at Tlatelolco of gunshot wounds, but nobody believes this number. Other estimates suggest there were as many as three hundred deaths. This contest over the number of victims is part of the ongoing struggle to interpret the events of 1968 from the present day.
2. The date obviously had to do with the end of Juan Ramón de la Fuente's tenure as the rector of the UNAM: he could not wait until the fortieth anniversary of the massacre if he was to inaugurate the museum.
3. On the student movement and the massacre, besides Poniatowska, *Massacre in Mexico*, see these more recent titles, which have shed additional light on what hap-

pened: Volpi, *La imaginación y el poder*; Aguayo, *1968*; Taibo, *'68*; and Scherer and Monsiváis, *Parte de guerra Tlatelolco 1968*. Still, despite the voluminous bibliography on the movement, generated both by professional historians and by novelists and militants, much still remains unclear.

4. It bears remembering that the Distrito Federal, which contains the majority of the area commonly known as Mexico City, now has an autonomous government, elected by the District's residents. Although parts of the greater Mexico City area sprawl into the surrounding State of Mexico, I will refer to the city mostly as synonymous with the Distrito Federal.
5. One telling example of this is the enormous success that the "nomadic museum," featuring photographs by Gregory Colbert, enjoyed in the first few months of 2008. For an intelligent critique of this exhibition, see José Luis Barrios, "El museo nómada: Una mentira disfrazada de arte," *El Universal*, 26 January 2008, www.eluniversal.com.mx/graficos/confabulario/nota-26-enero08.htm.
6. By "topology," I mean a kind of spatial representation that is opposed to "cartography." The former implies an organization formed around an "I" that is always inside the space represented; the latter is a representation of space that is meant to totalize and fix the spatial representation by enclosing it and offering the totality of the map to an "eye" that is outside its margins.
7. The inauguration of the Metro in 1969 marked a clear symbolic departure from the primacy of the buses that had been frequently used by students as means of transport, as surfaces of inscription, and as barricades; and although buses continued to serve most routes—as they still do—the invariability of the Metro tracks is a clear sign of this reterritorialization (see Ruisánchez Serra, "Historias que regresan," 9–13).
8. Frazier and Cohen, "Mexico '68," 627.
9. Ibid., 637–51.
10. Hiriart, "La revuelta antiautoritaria," 18 (translation of quote by Alice A. Nelson).
11. Frazier and Cohen, "Mexico '68," 645.
12. Ibid., 649n65.
13. Bellinghausen, "Los muchachos de entonces," 248.
14. Today, a 100-square-meter apartment in Tlatelolco costs between $30,000 and $35,000 US, while an apartment of comparable size in the Centro Histórico ranges from $125,000 to almost $200,000 US.
15. Monsiváis, *Entrada libre*, 54.
16. Echeverría is a documentary filmmaker who crossed over into fictional cinema directing *Cabeza de Vaca* (1991) and, later, *Vivir mata* (2002). A feature-length documentary on the events of 1968 was prepared for screening in October 2008, but it was shown only on TV-UNAM, which is available exclusively on cable. It produced practically no public reaction. (I learned about this production in advance through a personal communication with Juan Carlos Colín.)
17. Poniatowska, *Massacre in Mexico*, 239.
18. Ibid., 190.
19. Ibid., 236.
20. Ibid., 62.

21. Ibid., 50.
22. Ibid., 40.
23. Ibid., 274.
24. Ibid., 295.
25. Ibid., 238.
26. Even in the late 1960s and early 1970s, people were taught a masculinist history, in which (phallic) heroes battled for equally heroic causes, such as Independence or, crucial to the official textbooks that are mandatory throughout elementary school, the Revolution. These battles were characterized in Manichean, good-versus-evil terms. Thus, for example, Cuauhtémoc was good and Hernán Cortés bad, Miguel Hidalgo and José María Morelos deserved monuments, while the three centuries from 1521 (the fall of Tenochtitlán) to 1821 (the consummation of the War of Independence) are not worth our while, and so on. This Manichean quality was intensified by the compulsory masculinity of the *novela de la revolución* (novel of the Mexican Revolution), which can of course be read otherwise today, but was then made to oppose the "effeminate" cosmopolitanism of the elitist *Contemporáneos* magazine. This, in turn, was reinforced in the popular culture—primarily in films and television, but also on the radio and in popular magazines, from the comics to *Reader's Digest*—imposed by the Cold War, where the same basic good-versus -evil Manichean matrix was used. Moreover, until '68, rightist propaganda was answered with left-wing propaganda, and it seemed that to renounce the prevalent "us-versus-them" logic would be a strategic mistake. But the success of Poniatowska's complex work (in terms of the positions of enunciation it accepts and its decentered authority) shows otherwise.
27. In the shortest possible definition, a human being can be split in *bios,* or the mere biological, and *zoe*, or the socio-political role that the *bios* performs.
28. It is not without interest that only one review (by José Emilio Pacheco) was published after the first run of *La noche de Tlatelolco.*
29. Chevigny, "The Transformation of Privilege in the Work of Elena Poniatowska."
30. That is the difference between these copies and the "*El dos de octubre no se olvida*"/ "October 2nd is not forgotten" graffiti, omnipresent in the Mexico City of my childhood. By intervening in public space rather than serving as a souvenir (from *souviens*, "that which remembers in our stead"), the latter preserve the incommensurable.
31. I do not use the term "antimonument," favored by some scholars, because in this context it would be inexact: small triumphs are textually celebrated, just not epically, but rather in a lyrical fashion, quite appropriate to their non-overtly-political essence.
32. Poniatowska, *Massacre in Mexico*, 269.
33. The next president, Luis Echeverría Álvarez (1970–76), as well as a good percentage of his team, were younger than in the past, a central feature of their politics, which convinced key intellectuals, among the most notable, Carlos Fuentes, of their genuine intentions.
34. de Certeau, *Capture of Speech and other Political Writings*, 14–15 (emphasis in the original).
35. The transformation of the IFE from a citizen-controlled, autonomous organism in

the 2000 elections to a state-controlled office in the hotly contested 2006 elections, which retained the PAN in power, would be another instance to discuss from the vantage points afforded by this chapter.

36. Interestingly enough, the videos in this room are not cross-cut, but are available as single interviews, classified not thematically but under the name of the interviewed person.
37. This utopian project turned what was once an open-air mine used to extract sand and make bricks into a park; later, replicas of pre-Columbian sculptures were added, along with a small auditorium surrounded by trees (the audiorama).
38. At least this aspect seems to be changing now as Tlatelolco enters the orbit of "alternative" museums, where up-and-coming artists can show avant-garde work, if only for very short periods of time. The first temporary exhibition in the former SRE took place in April 2008. It lasted for a week. Unfortunately, the December 2008 opening of the impressive MUAC (University Museum of Contemporary Art) in the Pedregal, the posh south of the city that houses the main campus of UNAM as well as the most important art complex in Mexico, relegates the CCU-Tlatelolco even more to the backwaters of culture.
39. Although some conferences took place in 2008, nothing of the sort has been announced for 2009. Dishearteningly but also tellingly enough, the only workshops offered on a regular basis by the so-called academic unit of the museum are English and computer basics: precisely the tools to leave the pre-global world of '68 behind and enter the workforce as a pawn of transnational capitalism.
40. All these topics are part of the crucial political polemics of today and actively produce a tension that forces us to re-read '68 as a seminal part of an *ongoing* struggle, as perhaps the cornerstone of its loci of enunciation.
41. Yúdice, *The Expediency of Culture*, 16–21.
42. Another recently opened museum, the Estanquillo in the heart of the downtown area, houses Carlos Monsiváis's collections of popular artifacts and is financed by Slim.
43. Sarlo, *Tiempo pasado*, 125–57.
44. There are, in this regard, encouraging signs. An interesting international project involving scholars based both in Mexico and abroad is analyzing '68, privileging the study of utopian formations that survived the October 2nd massacre; this group presented its first findings at the LASA 2009 conference in Rio de Janeiro. Only a couple of the scholars in this research group were born before 1968. Also, *Elena Poniatowska ante la crítica* (Selected Criticism on Elena Poniatowska) is forthcoming from ERA.

CYNTHIA E. MILTON AND
MARÍA EUGENIA ULFE

Promoting Peru

Tourism and Post-Conflict Memory

Travel advertisements invite youthful backpackers or the wealthy older set who can travel in comfort to explore the Andes and the highland peoples: guidebooks and documentaries portray images of llamas chewing in highland pastures, rural folk wearing ponchos, majestic ancient civilizations and remaining ruins, all in the scenic setting of jagged, snow-capped mountain peaks.[1] Year after year, hundreds of thousands of tourists visit Peru in search of an Andean experience and adventure. For most, this means visiting Cusco and the newly named, in 2007, world wonder Machu Picchu, walking a few days on the Inca Trail, and spending a brief sojourn in Lima before returning home with photos and handicrafts as souvenirs of their voyage.

Despite aggressive advertising, Peru's tourism faced challenges during the country's recent decades of conflict. The worst times of Sendero Luminoso guerrilla activity (1980–83) brought a precipitous drop in the total number of tourists (273,000 during the three years). Periods of guerrilla resurgence (1988–92) further hurt the tourist trade.[2] Peruvian tourism rebounded, however, after the 1992 capture of Sendero Luminoso leader Abimael Guzmán. Steady growth in the numbers of visitors followed.[3] The government optimistically embossed on its 1997 official stationery the phrase "The Year of 600,000 Tourists." That same year, President Alberto Fujimori posed for a photograph in *Vanity Fair*, in which he stood below a portrait of the famous Indian leader, José Gabriel Condorcanqui Túpac Amaru II, who had led an anticolonial rebellion against Spain.[4] Fujimori appeared to appeal once again to international visitors seeking a unique historical and Andean experience in Peru. Yet the image may have taken on more meaning when Fujimori defeated the last remaining armed group, the Movimiento Revolucionario Túpac Amaru (MRTA), who had borrowed the eighteenth-century hero's identity for their movement. Through operation "Chavín de Huántar," named after one of Peru's most ancient archeological sites, Fujimori's forces freed seventy-one hostages held by MRTA members for four months in the home of the Japanese ambassador, killing all the hostage takers. Riding high on this "success" over internal conflict, Fujimori cloaked himself in ancient Inca symbols and declared Peru open for tourism.

Fujimori, and the governments of Alejandro Toledo (2001–6) and Alan García (2006–present) that followed, linked tourism to development, particularly job creation and infrastructure improvement, in poorer regions of the country. To promote the tourist trade, the Peruvian government forged an image of a nation unified by its pre-Columbian past. This image of "*lo andino*" promotes a majestic, if surreal, Peruvian past.[5] In the process, it draws attention away from a more recent—and violently conflictual—past. Guidebooks seem to comply by barely mentioning the recent internal conflict. Tourism has thus become a mechanism for reconciling the nation around a shared ancient past in the interest of developing that nation, presumably to ameliorate long-standing inequalities.

Not all share this perception of tourism, national identity, and memory. Individuals, human rights groups, and the Peruvian Truth Commission (CVR) call for the acknowledgment of injustices committed in Peru's extended civil war (1980–2000). While they share the government's development and distribution goals, they insist on justice and reparations for victims and survivors. Since the 2003 commission report on the 1980–2000 violence, human rights groups have created new sites that engage a more recent past—including monuments and museums now scattered throughout the country. Some countries that have constructed such sites—Germany, Cambodia, Chile, and Argentina, for instance—are often visited by "trauma tourists," ranging from concerned global citizens who seek an understanding of suffering to voyeurs of other countries' misfortunes. Few visitors to Peru, however, move off the beaten track to attend recent memory sites, let alone actually seek them out. Despite attracting fewer visitors than ancient sites, the presence and growing prevalence of these "alternative" tourist sites in Peru is an important aspect of the modern tourist industry, as they reveal the more recent, violent—rather than only the ancient, romanticized—past.

This chapter considers the meanings that these unintended tourist sites hold for both the managers of spaces of memory dedicated to remembering recent violence in Peru and for their visitors. While the government markets *Peru* to tourists, managers of alternative tourist sites wish to market *memory*. In what appears to be a strategic use of (rather than a deviation from) neoliberal government discourse to promote tourism for economic development, dating back to the Fujimori era, the managers of these memory sites seek the same audience to remember the past in post-CVR Peru. The development-through-tourism model inherited from Fujimori's regime dovetails with the objectives of the Peruvian Truth Commission to reflect upon Peru's internal war. This chapter considers two memory exhibitions: the exhibit *Yuyanapaq: Para Recordar* (Lima) and the Museo de la Memoria de ANFASEP "Para que no se repita" (Ayacucho). They involve very different designs: one is a photography exhibit that received direct financial and logistical support from the truth commission, and the other is an internationally funded NGO museum. They share, however, the objective of transmitting knowledge about the recent violent past to a present audience, and promoting the CVR's recommendations for symbolic reparations. The *Yuyanapaq* exhibit and the Museo de la Memoria count among the very few memory sites dedicated to the remembrance of the internal war, and until recently were the only two that attempted to curate "difficult knowledge" for Peruvian and international audiences in the form of museum exhibitions.[6]

Tourism and Truth-Telling in Post–Sendero Luminoso Peru

Peru forms part of a global culture industry in which it presents to the world its glorious pre-Columbian past. The state sponsors the Peruvian tourist industry, and local people perform this part of the past for a contemporary audience in events such as the Inti Raymi celebration of the solstice.[7] PromPerú, a government agency founded in 1993, promotes Peru as the "Land of the Incas" and as a place for newly (exotic) lived experiences.[8] Recent tourism campaigns aim not only at foreign tourists, but also encourage Peruvians to visit other regions of the country on long weekends.[9]

Most of the tourists, in fact, visit Peru's most stunning examples of the Inca past. Cusco, with the nearby ruins of Machu Picchu, attracts 80 percent of foreign visitors.[10] With such intense concentration, the economic benefits of tourism are unequally distributed across the country. Successive Peruvian governments have encouraged the diversification of tourism in the hopes that tourist dollars might trickle down to the poorer regions. Prior to the 1990s, governments envisioned tourism as a growth and redistribution measure that required state investment. Fujimori began a process of privatization of the tourism industry, however, reducing the role of the state to encourage entrepreneurs.[11] The greatest hindrance to tourism in the more remote regions has been the continuing lack of necessary infrastructure, such as roads and airports, and tourist services, specifically hotels and restaurants.[12]

The promotion of peace through tourism lay at the core of Fujimori's politics, as demonstrated by Ayacucho, the birthplace of Sendero Luminoso and the center of the counter-insurgency war waged by the state. In the aftermath of the internal war, the department and its capital city received support from state institutions to (re)build its infrastructure, along with international aid for the restoration of old colonial buildings—in order to change the face of the city from one of a war-torn provincial capital to a sought-after destination.[13] Participation opened a space for communities to develop their own comparative advantage for tourism; Ayacucho had long attracted tourists to its precolonial and indigenous past. In a recent promotional video of Ayacucho, wide-eyed peasants stand by candlelight outside of the local cathedral. With suspenseful music reaching a culmination, the doors of the church open, issuing a bright light and majestic statue of the Virgin Mary. Hush and wonder descend upon those gathered. This short Hollywood-esque video portrays Ayacucho as a region of nativistic, devoted Catholicism, worthy of a visit, rather than as a former Maoist hotspot.[14]

Aware of the boom in tourism and the opportunity it poses to teach foreigners about Peru's more recent past, human rights organizations and managers of alternative memory sites also court potential tourists as part of their "Never Again" projects. In origin, Peru's memory sites of the war are not meant for the foreign tourist, but rather for Peruvians. These memory sites ask all Peruvians, and *Limeños* (Lima residents) in particular, to examine and situate what happened in their own country. Yet by reaching out to an international audience, these sites may gain a legitimacy and a stability that might otherwise be undermined by the lack of state support for projects aimed at remembering the internal war.

Single monuments of, and plaques to, the violence are scattered about the country, though most are located in Lima. Some examples include the Oval to Memory; the Monument to María Elena Moyano, a monument in the affluent neighborhood of Miraflores at the site of a devastating Sendero Luminoso car bomb in 1992 (known as the "Tarata bombing"); and a garden at the Universidad Católica, called the Plaza de Memoria, to remember dead and disappeared students. One plan that never came to fruition entailed the conversion of the Banco de la Nación in downtown Lima, a bombed building many believe Fujimori destroyed in an attempt to discredit the organizers of massive public protests following fraudulent elections in 2000. The idea to create a museum for remembering the recent past in this place has since been abandoned, and the space now holds a cement-covered recreational park. In Lima, the still-to-be-realized Avenida de la Memoria project hopes to unite the Ojo que Llora monument in the El Campo de Marte park; the *Yuyanapaq* photography exhibit (explained below); a massive Inca-style knotted mnemonic cord (known as a *quipu*) made during a campaign of national unity that focused on not repeating the past; and an information center. In this broader context of remembrance, *Yuyanapaq* and the Museo de la Memoria have emerged as the first enclosed spaces in the style of museums to exhibit the past.

The emergence of memory sites in Peru closely links not only with the tourist industry but also with the construction of a 2001 truth commission inquiring into the preceding twenty years. After two years of investigation, the CVR submitted its final report to President Alejandro Toledo on 28 August 2003 in Lima, and the following day to the community of Huamanga (Ayacucho). Their findings were staggering, revealing that close to 70,000 Peruvians had died or been disappeared. Seventy-five percent of this group spoke mainly Quechua and not Spanish, and came from rural regions. The conclusions of the CVR constructed a historical narrative that pointed to the long-standing racism and centralism of Peru; the heavily gendered nature of the violence (75 percent of victims were men over the age of fifteen); Sendero Luminoso as the main perpetrators (accounting for 54 percent of documented cases of acts of violence); and the responsibility of Peruvian political leaders for having abdicated their authority to the armed forces and police (who were responsible for 35.6 percent of human rights abuses).[15]

The truth commission's mandate focused on truth-seeking as a form of justice and reconciliation; reaching the "peace and agreement" sought by the CVR entailed both symbolic and civil reparations.[16] The CVR promoted reparations as "compensation for the harm done to victims" rather than as a way to repair the country or meet developmental needs.[17] Memory sites to pay homage to the victims and to promote remembrance, along with public ceremonies and performances to recognize the victims and survivors, have acted as symbolic reparations.[18] The photography exhibition *Yuyanapaq* in Lima and the Museo de la Memoria in Ayacucho embody two such symbolic measures that take up the CVR's recommendations.

The Emergence of *Yuyanapaq* and the Museo de la Memoria

These memory initiatives emerged directly out of the work of the Peruvian Truth Commission in at least two ways: first, the CVR's recommendations for symbolic reparations gave much-needed moral and institutional support to establishing places to publicly remember and discuss the years of violence. Second, the social opening that gave rise to the truth commission also provided an opportunity for public discussion of the past, and a memorialization of that past, through memory sites.[19] Since few public spaces exist for reflection on the internal war, *Yuyanapaq* and the Museo de la Memoria serve as important forums for disseminating the work and findings of the CVR.

Yuyanapaq refers to the 2003 photography exhibit *Yuyanapaq: Para Recordar*, a selection of two hundred photographs taken by photojournalists, members of TAFOS (Social Photography Workshops), families, and others, documenting the twenty years of conflict. This exhibit originally opened for six months following the conclusion of the CVR in Lima, with smaller versions of the exhibit sent to the five cities where the CVR had offices; it later reopened in 2005 in the Museo de la Nación on a five-year lease. This exhibit emerged directly from the CVR's work. The CVR actively solicited the photographs from newspapers, NGOs, and branches of the Catholic Church. They received countless identification photos from the family members of disappeared loved ones. A team of photographers and archivists worked to mount the exhibit and related items in consultation with the commissioners.[20] Bookstores sold the companion exhibition book for the high price of 100 soles (around $40 US), with the images printed out and compiled into free teaching guides for NGO workshops and for schools. The curators also hoped to create a virtual archive of all of the images—not just the two hundred presented in the exhibit.

Two years after the end of the CVR, on 16 October 2005, the National Association of Kidnapped, Disappeared, and Detained Relatives of Peru (ANFASEP) inaugurated a museum for memory, the Museo de la Memoria, in Ayacucho, with the subtitle "In Order That It Not Repeat." While some former commissioners encouraged the project, financial support came from abroad, principally from the German government.[21] ANFASEP's Museo de la Memoria falls within the domain of symbolic reparations recommended by the CVR—in this case, paying homage to the victims of state-orchestrated disappearance and their families. These two memory spaces—the *Yuyanapaq* exhibit and the Museo de la Memoria—therefore share similar origins in the CVR's call for symbolic reparations; they share the educational objectives of teaching personally and politically difficult knowledge; and they share content, with some of the *Yuyanapaq* photographs serving as central pieces for Ayacucho's memory museum.

The Aesthetics of Memory: Building Appropriate Spaces for Reflection

Both *Yuyanapaq* and the Museo de la Memoria have had to face the question of how to represent violence. Does an appropriate aesthetic to communicate terror exist? How can museum and exhibit curators create spaces to elicit remembrance, to educate, and to pay homage to victims, which do not in a way re-create, make sacred, or sensationally trivialize the terror? How, as Jelin and Langland have asked, can one represent the disappeared? How can one symbolize the gaps, the unspeakable, which no longer exist?[22] Both the photography exhibit *Yuyanapaq* and the Museo de la Memoria attempt in their separate ways to represent absence through images, objects, and testimony. They strive to give dignity and humanity to those who suffered from the years of violence.

Yuyanapaq: To Remember

At the inauguration of the *Yuyanapaq: Para Recordar* exhibit on 9 August 2003, the president of the CVR, Salomón Lerner Febres, invited the audience to make a "moral decision," through sincere and brave reflection, to recognize the past.[23] *Yuyanapaq*, as a preamble to the CVR's *Final Report* published later that month, provided some of the elements necessary to make this moral decision. Through the presentation of graphic documents of the violence, this exhibition displayed "the faces of suffering, the visible proof of the injustices committed in our country."[24] For Lerner, the diversity of these photographs expressed the reality of Peru, perhaps more faithfully and with more urgency than "the routine images of our country, of museum pieces, archaeological wonders, mysterious icons found in tourism brochures and in encyclopedias."[25] While in appearance similar to a museum exhibit, *Yuyanapaq* offered more than the usual arrangement of patrimonial artifacts, giving visual proof to unknowing and doubting Peruvians of what had occurred in their country's recent past.

Yuyanapaq recognized the suffering of Peruvians during the previous twenty years, and the need for Peruvians to face this past. This Quechua word translates as "to remember" or "to wake up" in the infinitive form—as "remembering" or "waking up" in the active form. The images of *Yuyanapaq* foster remembering and waking up, seeking to "bring to light forms of recognition of our past and present situation, ways in which we gain control over our individual and collective lives."[26] Earlier possible names for the exhibit included *Manchaytiempo*, "Time of Fear," and *Yayanapayaq*, "Time of Truth," but organizers decided instead to focus on active "remembering" and "awareness" among visitors.[27] If the CVR's work centered on oral testimonies, this photography exhibit offered an important visual testimony, "a testimony that not even the most insensitive and stubborn person could dare to ignore."[28]

Yuyanapaq, in its original setting, provides a multisensorial experience, a graphic account of Peru's internal war that goes beyond the visual. The exhibit was housed in one of the elite Riva Agüero family homes in the outlying Lima neighborhood of Chorillos, now the property of the Pontifica Universidad Católica del Perú. The abandoned home, in a state of ruins, fostered what Giuliana Borea Labarthe has referred to as the "three-dimensionality" of *Yuyanapaq*:[29] one entered into the exhibition space (the abandoned home) and moved through the exhibit (through the corridors and roofless rooms); one could hear sounds of others whispering, recorded testimonies, the voice of the murdered activist María Elena Moyano at a demonstration; one could touch the crumbling walls; and one could smell the dampness of the earth floors underneath. The feeling of reconstruction from the ground up additionally pervaded the exhibit: physical gaps in the construction speak to the deterioration of the Peruvian nation and its need to rebuild. The photos, developed to various sizes (from small frames to larger-than-life size), hung on the walls as in a gallery, but with a careful use of white drapes meant to play with light, the cleanliness of white, and the idea of healing gauze. In the words of the curators: "The house speaks to us. Its walls and structures tell a history of destruction (of earthquakes, humidity, and abandon), allowing us to make an analogy between the

Figure 1. The reflecting pool at *Yuyanapaq: Para Recordar* in Chorillos (2003). (Photograph by Cynthia E. Milton)

home and Peruvian society. The graphic documents on its walls reaffirm for us the deterioration not only of this house but also of a larger home: our country. Both have suffered and now we find ourselves in a process of recovery and healing."[30] The exhibit thus did not produce just an imagined community, but a real place for meeting and the sharing of experience: a place itself shared by visitors and the victims of Peru's civil war.

Yuyanapaq appears to have several objectives: promoting a remembering and an understanding of violence; informing present-day youth and future generations through collective historical memory; and deterring future atrocities. It also promotes a message of reconstruction and, perhaps, reconciliation—not just with other Peruvians, but also with the past. The exhibit curators blended aesthetics with the disturbing images of suffering and violence, imparting both a narrative through graphic testimony and an implicit goal of reconstructing the nation. As Carlos Iván Degregori has written, a society and a nation need material objects by which to fix memories: signs, symbols, texts, images, rites, practices, places, and monuments.[31] Similarly, the exhibit pamphlet links objects and testimonies to memory: "To look, to understand, to process by way of images and testimonies implies a concern of Peruvian society to know the history, to get closer to the truth. In this sense the decision to walk through this house requires a decision to remember."[32]

Although minimal (and printed only in Spanish) information accompanied the images, curators did not let the images speak for themselves. Rather, they arranged the photographs in such a way as to present a clear historical narrative to the past in the twenty-seven rooms that housed the exhibit. The original *Yuyanapaq* exhibition divided the internal war of 1980–2000 into five chronological time periods: the "beginnings of armed violence" (1980); the "militarization of the conflict" (1983–86); the "national spread of the violence" (1988); the "extreme crisis: subversive offensive and the state counteroffensive" (1989–92); and the "decline of subversive action, authoritarianism, and corruption" (1992–2000).[33] A passageway linking the early rooms held a timetable locating key events along a time continuum. *Yuyanapaq* implicitly acknowledged the inability to place experiences solely in a chronological order by also displaying images organized around themes. Thematic rooms drew the visitor to specific experiences, some of which were also addressed in the thematic public hearings of the CVR: widows, children, prisons, self-defense committees (*rondas*), forced migration and return, the war in the jungle, and such specific cases as the Tarata bombing, the Japanese Embassy hostage crisis, and a room dedicated to the murdered community activist María Elena Moyano.

In 2005, *Yuyanapaq* found a temporary home in the Museo de la Nación. Since the publication of the CVR's *Final Report,* there has been little political will or government support for the diffusion of their findings.[34] Thus, the housing of *Yuyanapaq* in the Museo de la Nación lends legitimacy to recounting this past against the repeated attacks on the CVR's findings. Support from the Defensoría del Pueblo, the Ministry of Justice, the National Institute of Culture, and foreign sources (the U.N., the E.U., and the Canadian and British governments) makes possible continued public access to *Yuyanapaq*.

The new setting clashes with the message implicit in the abandoned and ruined home that housed the original exhibit—that of a nation needing to

Figure 2. *Yuyanapaq: Para Recordar* in its present location at the Museo de la Nación. (Photograph by Cynthia E. Milton)

rebuild and heal. The Museo de la Nación building, a fortresslike structure on the edge of downtown Lima, seems impenetrable, indestructible. Curators tried to maintain the feel of a nation in the healing process by using white gauze drapes; the room displays roughly correspond to the original exhibit, but with fewer rooms and fewer photographs displayed; and the curators added an information center and a room for reflection, where visitors can sit and read the comments of previous visitors, inscribed on the walls. *Yuyanapaq* organizers hope eventually to move the exhibit to a more permanent home as part of the Memoria de la Avenida project in El Campo de Marte, the location of the Ojo que Llora monument. The German government offered two million dollars for the construction of this Museo de la Memoria, after Chancellor Angela Merkel visited *Yuyanapaq* in 2008. President Alan García refused the donation, however, stating that the money could instead be used for reparations to communities. He implied that the *Yuyanapaq* exhibit, the work of the CVR, and the envisioned Museo de la Memoria put forward an elite and partisan memory. This conflict clearly reflects a division between the present government and memory promoters. After discussions with the Peruvian writer Mario Vargas Llosa, however, the president formed a new committee to review the possibility of opening a museum, or a place of memory.[35] If this project ever comes to fruition, *Yuyanapaq* will most likely be the centerpriece.

The Museo de la Memoria: A Memorable Place Where Peace Begins

On 16 October 2005, a date meant to coincide with the international conference "Historical Memory and Culture of Peace," the Museo de la Memoria opened its doors in Ayacucho.[36] Members of ANFASEP envisioned the Museo de la Memoria as a special place for mourning, truth, and remembrance because of the few extant memory sites.[37] In Ayacucho, this museum remains one of the few official territorial landmarks or monuments that connect the recent past to the present. There are some plaques that pay homage to the victims of violence in Ayacucho, such as the CVR plaque in the central plaza and one with a photograph of the eight journalists that died in Uchuraccay in 1983. The former prison that held the young *senderista* Edith Lagos, along with other members of Sendero Luminoso, has become an artisan market mainly geared for tourists; no plaque reminds people of this site's past.

The Museo de la Memoria does not try to reproduce the national experience of "*manchaytiempo*," despite a promotional description of the museum as "representing the memory of the period of political violence lived by the victims, not only of Ayacucho but of all of Peru."[38] Rather, it presents the experiences of the mothers of the disappeared by telling their stories. Steven Lavine and Ivan Karp argue that the very nature of exhibiting forges a contested terrain.[39] ANFASEP's museum demonstrates this, as members have debated both whose stories should be recounted and how to represent them. As a result of displaying selected mothers' experiences, this museum also acts as a critical response to the CVR and its *Final Report*. While *Yuyanapaq* became a visual expression of the larger report later issued by the CVR, the Museo de la Memoria aims to correct aspects of the *Final Report*. For example, in the *Final Report* the CVR named Sendero Luminoso as the principal perpetrator of violence. But for the ANFASEP mothers who met while searching for their disappeared family members outside of prisons, army headquarters, and police stations, their loved ones were victims of violence perpetrated by the armed forces. Thus, while *Yuyanapaq* attempts to illustrate a range of experience—including those of the families of the military and the police, unmistakably suffering in the photos of funeral processions—such diverse displays are noticeably absent in ANFASEP's museum.

About the time the museum opened, Heeder Soto, a member of the youth wing of ANFASEP (Juventud ANFASEP), explained that ANFASEP had held many discussions on what to include in the museum: which artifacts and images most effectively symbolized the violence and the organization. The museum coordinators considered their prospective audience in their decisions; they intended for the museum to have a strong impact on potential visitors. Aware of the little space in which to educate a visitor, they wanted the most representative stories of the Asociación to come forth, but not everyone's memories. Most experiences displayed in the museum are those of senior members of ANFASEP.[40]

The competing accounts on the origin of this museum illustrate some of the tensions inherent in creating a memory site.[41] In one version, the lawyer and main advisor of ANFASEP, Emilio Laynés, claims authorship for the museum. He says that he proposed the idea during ANFASEP's candlelight vigils to support the work of the CVR: "The ladies of ANFASEP had always used some flags (*banderolas*) and crosses written with their children's names and the dates of when they disappeared or died. So, during one of these candlelight vigils one of the ladies said that she would like to get rid of her old and worn out flag. But [Laynés] suggested that she should keep it. [Laynés] suggested that they should keep these pieces behind a glass in the main room [of their office]. And there the idea of the museum was born. Among the pieces exhibited in the museum there is the letter that Mamá Angélica's [the founder of ANFASEP] son wrote from prison."[42]

Heeder Soto instead describes the museum as a natural outcome of the organization's trajectory. For him, the idea for this project did not come from a single individual—rather, it developed as part of the group's work. According to Soto, questions arose among ANFASEP members as to what to do with their memory artifacts. "'Why are we going to keep these things?' someone asked. Another person answered: 'But, why? This is part of our history. We could keep them in a place.' That's how the idea of the museum started. So we thought of getting financial support for this purpose. And, we asked, 'Couldn't [the museum] be a little bigger?' And that's the formal history of how it began to work . . ."[43]

The Museo de la Memoria is a one-floor museum located on the third floor above ANFASEP's offices and a soup kitchen.[44] A mural adorns the building's walls, and a sculpture acts as the centerpiece of the "Memory Park" across the street from the museum. Together with the museum, the park has become a "sanctuary of memory, a symbolic place where relatives remember, leave flowers and candles, pray for their dead and disappeared."[45] The mural and the sculpture, by the Ayacuchan artist Wari Zárate, represent the "before" and the "after" of the violence. The Museo de la Memoria remains further unmarred by complicated aesthetics. Yet it has a striking initial impact: as one walks upstairs to the third floor, a large five-story *retablo*—a wooden box in the form of a triptych—separates the ANFASEP offices from the museum. The youth wing of ANFASEP built this Retablo de la Memoria, filling it with figures and scenes that recreate the 1980–2000 period of violence.[46] The sides of the wooden box are painted with various colors and contain phrases about death, justice, and truth. Photographs of the detained and disappeared during this period, mostly relatives of ANFASEP members, decorate the back of the retablo and the doors.

The Museo de la Memoria consists of three main exhibition areas. The first room divides into two sections, called "Chaos" and "Nostalgia," respectively, which "reveal the human rights violations that occurred in Ayacucho."[47] The second room exhibits photographs of ANFASEP's members, displaying the clothing and possessions of victims, as well as artwork. The third room recounts ANFASEP's history in relation to the political violence in the region and the subsequent peace.

The Museo de la Memoria uses these photographs, artwork, personal belongings of the victims, and testimonies to represent the years of violence. Its leaders have also re-created sites of terror based on testimonies in an effort to allow the visitor to see what happened. Equivalent memory sites to those in Chile and Argentina, where actual locations of detention and torture have been salvaged for memory sites, do not exist yet in Peru. Thus, members of ANFASEP have built replicas of torture scenes and mass graves somewhat in the style of wax museums. One ANFASEP member, now a museum guide, explained during her tour: "And here, ma'am, this is the chamber of torture where people were tortured. Yes, this room of torture has been built according to what people said about how they were tortured."[48]

In 2007, Peruvian tourist agents held workshops to train some ANFASEP members as guides for the museum, with the support of German cooperation funds. As a result of this training, a visit to the museum now includes a narration—a vivid testimony given by a victim of violence. The personal story of the ANFASEP tourist guide interacts with the exhibit artifacts. In the process of giving a tour in person, the tourist guide lives her story again, but this time not for a truth commissioner, not for a non-governmental organization, and not for a lawyer—but rather for a tourist. As one member/

Figure 3. ANFASEP guide sits before a reconstruction of a torture cell at the Museo de la Memoria de ANFASEP. (Photograph by María Eugenia Ulfe)

guide pointed to exhibit artifacts and spaces, she reflected upon the objects and her experience: "We remember the events that happened; we have lived them in our skin; it's not what others have told to us, no? And there are pictures of people who've been tortured. There are the clothes of the disappeared. Here, there are [the clothes] of a disappeared, clothes of the husband of our lady president [of ANFASEP] that have been torn apart by dogs, no? So, whenever I give a tour, I remember things, ah, [places] where I've found bodies. I remember. And when I'm like that sometimes I feel sad, but then it [the tour] is over."[49]

The survivor/guide emerges as a new public subject, politically repositioned in the social world where she can contest the state.[50] There may be a need to speak her version of truth to an audience, a truth that differs from the CVR findings in that ANFASEP places principal responsibility for harm, death, and disappearance upon state agents. The survivor/guide becomes a testimoniante, as in the public hearings held by the CVR to symbolically repair the victims of violence.[51] For instance, Adelina García, one of the museum's guides, commented: "Yes, ah, personally I feel glad because maybe with this museum we could tell [people in] other countries all the things that happened to us. That's why we need your visit . . . and that of our fellow countrymen; the ones who want to come from Lima; all of them. Some of them don't know about this [past]. I hope they would visit so [that] we could tell them about these things so [that] these things wouldn't happen from here onwards, no? So these [things] wouldn't happen to us, no?[52]

The act of documenting their particular history, speaking to others about their experience, lies at the heart of the symbolic reparations envisioned by the CVR. These aims of recounting and remembering, however, have joined with the desire to solicit tourist visits. This entails not simply seeking tourist dollars (indeed, entrance to the Museo de la Memoria costs a mere 2 soles, or 80 cents US), but rather seeking broader national and international support from visitors. Today, ANFASEP's Museo de la Memoria appears as Site of Interest No. 41 on the map of Ayacucho distributed to tourists at the information center; and a small room of the ANFASEP offices has been converted into a gift shop selling handicrafts made by the women (such as blankets, embroidery, and bags), the group's recent publications, postcards, posters, and T-shirts.

Visitors to Peru's Memory Sites *Yuyanapaq* and the Museo de la Memoria

There are at least three kinds of visitors to Peru's memory sites: individuals who lived through the experience of the internal war, Peruvians not personally touched by the violence, and foreigners. Each visitor to *Yuyanapaq* and the Museo de la Memoria has his or her own relationship to the past, and memory sites "manage [these] memories" in different ways.[53]

First, there are the direct survivors, individuals who experienced the war and decided to visit these memory sites. These sites offer them a place in which to confront the past and to remember. As one commentator wrote of the *Yuyanapaq* exhibit, "All of this makes me remember my own life."[54] For these visitors, the experience becomes one of shared trauma in that individuals might identify with others in their past experience and pain. These sites thus allow for the possibility of fusing and infusing individual memories with a collective past.

Some visitors have recounted elements of their own stories in the comment books at the exhibits' end, attaching a personal memory to the collective narrative on display. The contrary also occurs, in that individuals might find their specific experiences or aspects of their experiences absent from the exhibit, and thus choose to tell their story in the comment books. Alonso Calderón, for example, wrote about his experiences as "a survivor of terrorism" on 12 August 1981. He asks why more victims of this massacre are not present in the exhibit.[55] One visitor to *Yuyanapaq* in Chorillos felt disappointed by the exhibit, since he had thought that he "might find here the photograph of Modesta, but it isn't here either. Neither photo nor name. She was my mother." Today, this entry from the comment book now adorns the wall in the room for reflection at the new exhibit's end.

Most of the visitors to these memory sites are not Peruvians who experienced the violence directly, but rather those who experienced it peripherally. Sites such as the *Yuyanapaq* exhibition and the Museo de la Memoria make it possible for visitors to approach the suffering of others. They may promote reflection among Peruvians who know little about this past. These Peruvians are asked to confront the difficult knowledge of the tragedy that engulfed their country in the 1980s and 1990s.[56] Indeed, these memory sites originally intended to address unknowing or doubting Peruvians, both of the current and future generations, in addition to being places of remembrance and homage for the victims and survivors.

For many of these Peruvians, the exhibition of the internal conflict brings to their attention events of which they claim to have been unaware. "Thank you for opening my eyes," writes one Peruvian in the comment book for *Yuyanapaq*.[57] Another found it terrifying "to see things of which in reality [she] did not know."[58] Peruvian visitors might claim empathy for those who suffered: "For me, this was a very interesting exhibit, at once painful because I never imagined the pain and suffering of my fellow countrymen had been so great."[59] Another visitor wrote: "Daniel Posada was here and suffered. Peruvians among Peruvians killed each other, but my suffering will never compare with the suffering of the truly innocent. My wishes and sadness for the victims of the twenty years of violence."[60] The Museo de la Memoria visitors book documents a similar complex range of emotions: "I don't have words to express my profound indignation for this atrocity; I have mixed feelings of anger, rage at those who caused all this pain, and sadness for the victims, especially for the children."[61]

The display and recounting of Peru's past atrocities not only elicits sympathy for victims and survivors, it also evokes a message of "Never Again." This message was clearly received by visitors, as indicated by pages upon pages in the comment books that state "Nunca Más" and "Para que no se repita." Similar messages support the implicit argument justifying the CVR's mandate to delve into this painful past: "One has to know the truth, no matter how painful."[62] Or, as one visitor writes in the comment books of the Museo de la Memoria: "[This exhibit is] important to make memory in order to demand justice, reparations, to work toward peace and reconciliation. I congratulate this initiative for allowing us to remember, to work for a new social pact among Peruvians. In order that it never happens again, to live as humans among humans."[63] Some visitors tie the message of "Never Again" and the need for reconciliation to religious references, exemplified by an entry asking for God's forgiveness.[64]

As *Yuyanapaq* holds an expressly pedagogic purpose, aimed at educating groups of schoolchildren, youth account for many of the entries in the commentary books. Some children and adolescents have simply doodled hearts on the pages with the initials of amorous (or wished-for) couples. Other youths, however, have left comments that express both their confusion and understanding: "I think that it is a bit difficult to understand, because I am young. After seeing the video, I realized what had happened in Peru and I felt a great deal of pain. Maj [followed by a drawing of a smiling face] 9 years old."[65] Some youth seem conscious of the importance of their age in creating a brighter future for Peru, such as eighteen-year-old Ana Cecilia Uribe Arce, who wrote "I was here . . . I plead that all of us realize that even in such evil there is always hope and that we, the youth, are part of this. With truth and honesty, we can build a better country."[66]

The comment books further provide a place for current political messages and the presentation of counternarratives to the CVR. Visitors take the opportunity to tell their compatriots where to place their political energies. For example, "Enough already, let's support Toledo. He is just as *cholo* and stubborn as each of us," and "Alan [García should go] to prison."[67] In book five of the original exhibit, on the same page, among the more common remarks such as "Good work" and "Chévere!" (Cool!), one entry says "Viva el P.C.P.!" in support of the Peruvian Communist Party (connected to Sendero Luminoso), and another inscription reads "Viva el Presidente Fuji y Vladi" (a reference to Fujimori and Vladimir Montesinos, both subsequently imprisoned).[68] Pointed questions, such as "What is the truth about the CVR?" have also been inscribed in the books.[69] Some visitors read in *Yuyanapaq* only part of the CVR's story—commending, for instance, the CVR for showing the violence committed by Sendero Luminoso and the MRTA, while not making reference in their comments to the abuses of the armed forces. Some entries are extreme, with sentiments like "Death to *senderistas* and all of the terrorists."[70] Conscious of the different uses for which the comment books could be employed, a message directed at visitors from Lima to the Museo de la Memoria urged visitors to reflect profoundly rather than superficially: "To the visitor from Lima: I hope that you continue in your search for truth and that you do not write 'this is pretty,' 'I like it,' or 'move forward.'"[71]

The third kind of visitor is the foreign tourist. By looking at the entries for *Yuyanapaq* and the Museo de la Memoria, we can see that these tourists rarely intentionally visit the memory sites to Peru's internal war. Yet these sites presently try to draw more international tourists, as a means to bolster human rights groups' projects for recognition of the violence and the continued need for reparations. While the first wave of truth-telling through memory sites and museums has aimed at educating Peruvians about their own past, newer developments of linking tourism and trauma invite the reflection of foreigners on Peru's recent past.

Yuyanapaq's move to the Museo de la Nación placed the years of violence within a much larger historical continuum, since the Museo de la Nación houses exhibits of ancient Peruvian history. Guidebooks invite tourists to come to this museum to explore the ancient cultures of the Chimú, Chincha, Chachapoyas, Moche, and Inca, among others. Three floors of mainly ceramic artifacts, and a scale model of Machu Picchu, overwhelm the visitor. Then, suddenly, the visitor jumps centuries and arrives in Peru of the 1980s amid scenes of political violence, unmentioned in the guidebooks under the entry for the Museo de la Nación. Without much explanation for the intervening centuries, tourists unexpectedly scurry through the photos in search of more ceramics. Some tourists stay to walk through the exhibit. Many are left confused by the photos, since only the titles have been translated into English, which limits access to descriptions of the development, and specific moments, of the internal conflict.

Despite such limits, the conversion of memory sites into possible international tourist destinations offers an opportunity to speak to a non-Peruvian audience about the internal war, and in so doing, to make this experience a more universal one. Among the comments by tourists, one finds interspersed reflections by foreign visitors who draw comparisons to the region's and their own countries' violence. For example, a tourist from El Salvador visited the Museo de la Memoria in Ayacucho and saw this history as one of the region as a whole: "Your history is the history of all Latin

Americans that serves to remind us and to always know that many of us have been violated; but even more [the exhibit reminds us] that we survive, we grow, we dream, and we keep standing."[72] "Colombia and its wounded memory are reflected in this museum," stated Claudio Jirón after his visit to the Museo de la Memoria.[73] A Uruguayan places Peru's experience in the context of his country's traumas from 1970 to 1983.[74] María José Alarcón remarked, "As a Chilean who has lived in a country that had a situation of terror, genocide and injustice as well, [it is important] to show the ignorant this history of the very real face of terrorism."[75] An Argentine visitor felt that his own country's history prepared him for Peru's: "It is truly depressing, the sickening *senderista* history in the history of Peru. Good thing that I am Argentine."[76] As Santiago, from Argentina, wrote on 22 February 2008: "History gave us similar violence in Argentina, and thirty years later many people prefer forgetting, covering up the past that has tormented us and left open wounds. This exhibit brings tears to my eyes, to reflect upon the suffering of my country and that of Peru."[77] One visitor compared the Peruvian terror to that of 9/11 in the U.S.A.: "I have read the names, the groups, the stories, but these photos made what I read real to me. It's difficult enough to live with one threat of terror as we do in the USA. I can understand how it was with multiple threats—this exhibition allows me to feel the reality of that horrible situation."[78]

Foreign tourists also expressed sympathy for Peru and hopes for a better future, such as John and Veronica from the United States, who "pray that Peru recovers and unites to prevent these horrible manifestations from occurring again."[79] "Very interesting exhibition, though so sorrowful. We cannot understand why nothing is said about the extrajudicial killings at the Japanese Embassy by the armed forces of Fujimori," remarked Isabel Ally and Daisy Simpson.[80] One Russian visitor to *Yuyanapaq* in February 2008 also wrote in broken English about his sadness to see images from his country used for violent ends in Peru: "Thank you for exhibition. It's really last chance for us to know about this Peru drama. It's so sad how many pain and horror came with our Russia 'legend'—one of the symbol persons to Sendero Luminoso—Lenin. We should remember about victims because it's our last chance to not repeat their lives."[81]

Reading the visitors books for the *Yuyanapaq* exhibit and the Museo de la Memoria, it becomes clear that most of the visitors are from Lima or abroad, and that few of the individuals who leave comments directly experienced the violence themselves. In the case of the Museo de la Memoria, few Ayacuchanos come to the museum, outside of local school classes and university students from across the central plaza. Adelina García, one of the museum guides, explained that *Ayacuchanos* do not like to visit the museum. She thinks that besides university students from the Universidad de San Cristóbal de Huamanga, they do not agree with ANFASEP's and the museum's description of the process of violence. The museum has become controversial, since it places emphasis on state agents as the principal perpetrators of violence instead of Sendero Luminoso; it thus provides a counternarrative to that of the CVR's *Final Report*. Some Ayacuchanos, however, disagree with the museum's willingness to consider reconciliation in line with the CVR's mandate.[82]

Marketing the CVR to Tourists

The memory sites of *Yuyanapaq* and the Museo de la Memoria are promoting narratives of the internal war found in the work of the CVR. *Yuyanapaq* closely follows the CVR *Final Report*, whereas the Museo de la Memoria wishes to correct aspects of that report by putting the emphasis on the violence committed by state forces against Ayacuchanos. These narratives are both, however, being marketed primarily to individuals and groups who did not experience the violence firsthand: Limeños who claim to have been unaware of the scale of the violence; schoolchildren, either too young to remember or born after the worst of the violence occurred; and foreigners who have only (if ever) read or heard about the war. In the absence of direct survivors, these memory sites become more about educating others on this difficult knowledge about Peru's recent past than about providing a space for catharsis or collective reconciliation among the survivors of the violence.

The uses and abuses of memory and memory sites are manifold. For both domestic and foreign tourists, exhibitions such as *Yuyanapaq* and the Museo de la Memoria raise moral problems for visitors. What role do tourists play in these sites? Are they to take away souvenirs of their experience of witnessing the painful experience of others? While these sites may promote a kind of appropriation of pain, such a misuse of these exhibitions has been outweighed by other uses of these sites. Memory sites allow for the diffusion of memory and knowledge, a strong impediment to public forgetting and silence. Indeed, visitors to these sites receive and often reiterate the message of "Never Again," the need to remember and not to repeat, three of the refrains most commonly found in these sites' comment books. Thus, the testimonials, eyewitness accounts, photographs, artworks, and memory objects become resources and strategies in the survivors' and affected communities' quest for recognition and participation in society. They also directly challenge efforts to negate their experiences, either because they are too painful for society or because they are politically inconvenient.

In the case of *Yuyanapaq*, the exhibition's managers did not initially prioritize drawing foreigners to the exhibit. However, in 2005, when the photography exhibit *Yuyanapaq* moved to the Museo de la Nación, foreign tourists became a likely audience. This move lent important legitimacy to *Yuyanapaq*, housed in a government building, open to the public for a nominal fee of one sol (around 40 cents US). Having a place to continue the exhibit improved the prospects of keeping open a visual account of the years of violence. Likewise, the Museo de la Memoria in Ayacucho indicates the struggle to keep memory of this period active and the importance of representing the period of political violence, "in the absence of social and political commitment."[83] The possibility to recount the past to tourists and to continue their political work makes tourism an intriguing avenue for developing and strengthening memory sites, particularly when government support is not forthcoming. Hoping to build upon the success of Ayacucho's Museo de la Memoria, small museums have opened in Lucanamarca, Huanta, Puttaca, and Huancavelica.

Thus, tourists can—and do—play a role in making the Peruvian experience a broader one, shared by many nations when the managers of these memory sites capitalize on the government's attempts to market Peru to tourists in order to market memory. Tourists' presence in these museums lends legitimacy to those individuals and NGOs who struggle to keep alive public discussion of Peru's recent past. In these ways, speaking to foreigners may help in the creation of symbolic reparations by providing an audience willing to listen. This has motivated the creation of traveling exhibits of *Yuyanapaq*, which has gone abroad when invited, attempting to educate others about the Peruvian internal war. For example, a smaller-scale exhibit traveled to Eugene, Oregon, in winter 2008.

A key issue now faced by Peruvian memory sites remains how to promote these memories for the tourist market, and what this means for the original objectives of remembrance and reconciliation among Peruvians as solicited by the CVR. In July 2007, a one-day workshop at ANFASEP entitled "Sueños" asked ANFASEP members to express their dreams for the future of the museum and how they could best reach these dreams. The workshop revealed a generational conflict between the younger members of the Association who would like to see the museum transform into a business-like enterprise, and the older members for whom the museum should remain a "sanctuary," a place for remembrance.[84] Younger members of ANFASEP believe that if the museum became more entrepreneurial it would receive more visitors, accessing a larger audience with whom to engage in their political work. In addition, as a business enterprise marketing memory to tourists, tourist dollars would help fund the work of the Association.

ANFASEP members are aware, however, of the infrastructural barriers to this dream. What would they do if a large group of tourists suddenly arrived at the museum? The museum remains ill-prepared to receive a large number of visitors at once. What if these tourists do not speak Spanish or Quechua? Should they train English-speaking tour guides? Should the ANFASEP mothers learn English? As questions regarding the practical aspect of marketing memory emerge, what happens to the initial aims of remembering and reconciling with the past? As these sites become more geared toward non-Peruvian visitors who have traveled to Peru for an "Andean experience," the message they impart or inspire—of remembering and reconciliation among Peruvians—may diminish in importance. The tourists, however, still might leave with a better understanding of Peru, beyond that of ancient ruins, fine cuisine, and wildlife, adding a human rights narrative to the stories they take home.

NOTES

1. One example is a documentary shown in 2005 on the Travel Channel, "The Royal Tour to Peru." Peter Greenberg, a journalist, led the tour, along with the former president of Peru, Alejandro Toledo, and the first lady, Elaine Karp (see Vich, "Magical, Mystical").
2. Silverman, "Touring Ancient Times," 899. Different statistics are available for tourists visiting Peru. According to *El Comercio* (4 April 2001), Peru received 410,000 tourists in 1999. According to a database on Peruvian tourism, 944,000 tourists came to Peru in 1999 (see Observatorio Turístico del Perú website, www.badaturperu.com.pe/mapas/trhistorico.htm).
3. O'Hare and Barrett, "Regional Inequalities in the Peruvian Tourism Industry," 53.
4. Silverman, "Touring Ancient Times," 882.
5. Indeed, Peruvian tourism promoters have tried during difficult political times to "forget Peru," inviting visitors to come to "the Andes," as a safer alternative. Such efforts included direct international flights that would avoid Lima altogether (see

James Brook, "Cuzco Journal: Drumming Up Tourism is Aim of 'the Safe Peru,'" *New York Times*, 17 November 1990.

6. Britzman uses the term "difficult knowledge" to refer to traumatic histories that require the learners to situate themselves within this new knowledge (see Britzman, *Lost Subjects, Contested Objects*, and Lehrer and Milton, Introduction).
7. Cadena, *Indigenous Mestizos.*
8. The promotion themed "Wake up your six senses" started in 2004 and was aimed at potential tourists from the U.K., the United States, Spain, and Brazil. In 2005, the campaign was extended to Germany and Italy, and in 2006, to China and France (see PromPerú, *Memoria 2001–2006*, 11–12; see also the videoclip at the Perú: Vive La Leyenda website, www.peru.info/peru.asp).
9. As exemplified by PromPerú's "Leave your Routine: Discover Peru" campaign (see PromPerú, *Memoria 2001–2006*, 11–12).
10. This is according to statistics from PromPerú's *Manual de importancia e impacto del turismo en el Perú*. In 2007, the average daily number of visitors to Machu Picchu was 2,192, and hence "putting at risk one of the newest wonders of the world" (see Observatorio Turístico del Perú website, www.badaturperu.com.pe/mapas/impne.htm).
11. For instance, Fujimori's government permitted the exchange of private bank loans for the purchase of public firms, a swap that included the government-owned EnturPeru's forty-seven hotels (see Casado, "Peru's Tourism Industry: Growth, Setbacks, Threats").
12. For instance, the journalist Mario Cueto Cárdenas has remarked: "Tourists are shocked by the poor care given to tourists and the excessive costs [for these poor services]. Therefore, we have to take care of the quality of our services: restaurants, lodging, transportation" (conversation with María Eugenia Ulfe, Ayacucho, Peru, 11 November 2007).
13. Ulfe, *Itinerarios y ciegos caminantes.*
14. See the videoclip at Perú: Vive La Leyenda website, www.peru.info/peru.asp.
15. Comisión de la Verdád y Reconciliación, *Informe final*, www.cverdad.org.pe/ifinal/index.php (accessed 11 December 2005).
16. Article 1, Decreto Supremo no. 065-2001-PCM, published in *El Peruano*, 4 June 2001.
17. See Point 9, "Propuesta de política de reparaciones," under "Balance CVR," in Comisión de la Verdád y Reconciliación, *Informe final*, www.cverdad.org.pe/lacomision/balance/index.php.
18. Among the possible symbolic reparations, the CVR listed "official apologies and requests of forgiveness, tombs for victims, name change of public places, monuments, commemorative dates, acts of homage, and spaces dedicated to the memory of victims" (ibid.).
19. Milton, "Public Spaces for the Discussion of Peru's Recent Past."
20. The Centro de Información para la Memoria Colectiva y los Derechos Humanos, in Lima, houses the correspondence of the CVR team that worked on the *Yuyanapaq: Para Recordar* exhibit (see File 150305, "Proyecto Fotográfico").
21. See the Asociación Pro Derechos Humanos, Sitios de Memoria website, www

.aprodeh.org.pe/sitiomemoria/anfasep.html. For more images and information on the Museo de la Memoria de ANFASEP, visit http://qillqakuna.iespana.es/ANFASEP,%20madres.htm.

22. Jelin and Langland, *Monumentos, memoriales y marcas territoriales*, 2.
23. Lerner Febres, *La rebelión de la memoria*, 140.
24. Ibid., 136–37.
25. Ibid., 138.
26. Ibid.
27. For an example of the internal debate regarding the exhibit's title, see Centro de Información para la Memoria Colectiva y los Derechos Humanos, file 150305, "Casas de la Verdad. Organización e implementación," 018.
28. Lerner Febres, *La rebelión de la memoria*, 139.
29. Borea Labarthe, "Yuyanapaq."
30. *Yuyanapaq: Para Recordar* (exhibition pamphlet), 2003.
31. Carlos Iván Degregori presentation at Pontificia Universidad Católica del Perú on *Yuyanapaq*, 2003.
32. *Yuyanapaq: Para Recordar* (exhibition pamphlet), 2003.
33. Deborah Poole and Isaias Rojas-Perez argue that the *Yuyanapaq* exhibit conveys a "self-evident" historical narrative that "closes off the possibility of articulating a more democratic (or plural) vision of reconciliation as 'an agreement to disagree'" (see Deborah Poole and Isaias Rojas-Perez, "Photography and Memory in Postwar Peru," unpublished paper, 2005). A short video of some of the *Yuyanapaq* photographs is available on YouTube, www.youtube.com/watch?v=MjTWHmnm20Q&NR=1.
34. Barrantes Segura and Peña Romero, "Narrativas sobre el conflicto armado interno en el Perú."
35. "Vargas Llosa convenció a García de aceptar Museo de la Memoria," *La República*, 27 March 2009, www.larepublica.pe/politica/27/03/2009/vargas-llosa-convencio-garcia-de-aceptar-museo-de-la-memoria-0.
36. Asociación Pro Derechos Humanos, Sitios de Memoria website, www.aprodeh.org.pe/sitiomemoria/ayacucho.html.
37. Angélica Mendoza and a group of Ayacuchan women looking for disappeared relatives at Los Cabitos military base in Ayacucho founded ANFASEP. About ANFASEP, see Muñoz, "Derechos humanos y construcción de referentes sociales"; and Tamayo, "ANFASEP y la lucha por la memoria de sus desaparecidos (1983–2000)." For the role played by women during the period of violence, see Coral, "Las mujeres en la guerra."
38. Asociación Pro Derechos Humanos, Sitios de Memoria website, www.aprodeh.org.pe/sitiomemoria/anfasep.html.
39. Lavine and Karp, *Exhibiting Cultures*, 1.
40. Interview by Silvana García (research assistant) with Heeder Soto and Jhon Sifuentes, Ayacucho, Peru, 25 July 2007.
41. Funding for the project came from various sources, most importantly from the German Academic Exchange Service (DAAD) and InWent, which provided technical assistance, expertise, and money. Peruvian support came from the Servicio de

Cooperacion Social Técnica (Cooperation of Social Technology), the Ministerio de la Mujer y Desarrollo Social (Ministry of Women and Social Development), and the Dirección General de Desplazados y Cultura de Paz (General Direction of Displaced Persons and the Culture of Peace) (see the Asociación Pro Derechos Humanos, Sitios de Memoria website, www.aprodeh.org.pe/sitiomemoria/anfasep.html).

42. Conversation with Emilio Laynes Luján and Maria Eugenia Ulfe, Ayacucho, Peru, October 2005.
43. Interview by Silvana García (research assistant) with Heeder Soto and Jhon Sifuentes, Ayacucho, Peru, 25 July 2007.
44. For a virtual tour of the museum, see YouTube, www.youtube.com/watch?v=rzJ7aSkx4uM.
45. Asociación Pro Derechos Humanos, Sitios de Memoria website, www.aprodeh.org.pe/sitiomemoria/anfasep.html.
46. The youth members of ANFASEP made the memory retablo in 2002 for the 10 December celebration of the Universal Declaration of Human Rights, with the financial support of the artist Jorge Baldeón (see ANFASEP, *Hasta cuándo tu silencio?*, 42).
47. Asociación Pro Derechos Humanos, Sitios de Memoria website, www.aprodeh.org.pe/sitiomemoria/anfasep.html.
48. Adelina García, member of ANFASEP, to Silvana García, 27 July 2005 (in authors' possession).
49. ANFASEP Guide to María Eugenia Ulfe, 10 November 2007 (in authors' possession).
50. Ulfe, "Reflexiones sobre los usos del testimonio en la esfera pública peruana."
51. This transformation into a witness who testifies to an experience is present in ANFASEP's recently published book of its members' testimonies (see ANFASEP, *Hasta cuándo tu silencio?*).
52. Interview by Silvana García, 27 July 2007.
53. On the idea of "managing atrocity" for tourism, see Ashward and Hartmann, Introduction to *Horror and Human Tragedy Revisited.*
54. *Yuyanapaq* "Cuadernos de comentarios," book 7, in the archives of the *Yuyanapaq: Para Recordar* exhibit, File 150305, "Proyecto Fotográfico," at the Centro de Información para la Memoria Colectiva y los Derechos Humanos, Lima.
55. *Yuyanapaq* "Cuadernos de comentarios," book 1.
56. For instance, Peruvians (and Limeños in particular) account for most of the entries in the "Cuadernos de comentarios" for the original exhibit in Chorillos.
57. *Yuyanapaq* "Cuadernos de comentarios," book 1.
58. Ibid.
59. Ibid.
60. *Yuyanapaq* "Cuadernos de comentarios," book 2.
61. Visitor from Lima, Museo de la Memoria, "Libro de visitas," ANFASEP.
62. *Yuyanapaq* "Cuadernos de comentarios," book 1.
63. *Yuyanapaq* "Cuadernos de comentarios," book 5.
64. Ibid.
65. *Yuyanapaq* "Cuadernos de comentarios," book 1.

66. *Yuyanapaq* "Cuadernos de comentarios," book 5.
67. *Yuyanapaq* "Cuadernos de comentarios," book 1 and book 6.
68. *Yuyanapaq* "Cuadernos de comentarios," book 5.
69. *Yuyanapaq* "Cuadernos de comentarios," book 1.
70. *Yuyanapaq* "Cuadernos de comentarios," book 6.
71. "Libro de visitas," Museo de la Memoria.
72. Ibid.
73. Ibid.
74. *Yuyanapaq* in the Museo de la Nación, "Cuadernos de comentarios," 25 February 2008.
75. *Yuyanapaq* in the Museo de la Nación, "Cuadernos de comentarios," 26 February 2008.
76. *Yuyanapaq* "Cuadernos de comentarios," book 1.
77. *Yuyanapaq* in the Museo de la Nación, "Cuadernos de comentarios," 25 February 2008.
78. *Yuyanapaq* "Cuadernos de comentarios," book 6.
79. *Yuyanapaq* "Cuadernos de comentarios," book 1.
80. Ibid.
81. *Yuyanapaq* in the Museo de la Nación, "Cuadernos de comentarios," 28 February 2008.
82. Interview by Silvana García with Adelina García, member of ANFASEP, 27 July 2005.
83. Asociación Pro Derechos Humanos, Sitios de Memoria website, www.aprodeh.org.pe/sitiomemoria/anfasep.html.
84. Interview by Cordula Strocka, DAAD scholarship recipient, with Jhon Sifuentes, 11 November 2007.

CATH COLLINS

The Moral Economy of Memory

Public and Private Commemorative Space in Post-Pinochet Chile

Chile has seen a notable and highly visible resurfacing of the "memory issue" in various manifestations since the late 1990s. A seemingly endless transitional amnesia, in which the human rights legacy of the Pinochet dictatorship of 1973–90 was never definitively addressed, has been interrupted.[1] The Chilean courts have belatedly begun to investigate seriously, and in some cases to prosecute, past human rights crimes that took place under the seventeen-year military regime.[2] The figure of the pre-coup president, Salvador Allende, architect of the ill-fated socialist Popular Unity government that was overthrown in 1973, has been rehabilitated in official discourse, and a statue to him was finally erected in the main square in front of the presidential palace.[3] There has been a veritable avalanche of official and unofficial activity, including the production of testimonial literature, memoirs, filmmaking, and other cultural and political events, to commemorate significant dates in Chile's recent past, including the thirtieth anniversary of the 1973 military coup.[4] In addition, monuments and memorials to the victims of human rights violations have begun to spring up across the country. Plaques have been placed in public spaces such as town squares. Former clandestine detention centers have been identified and, in some cases, recovered. Human rights organizations, individual activists, victims' families, trades unions, student centers, some political parties, and a whole range of other social actors have begun to reclaim "their" victims, commemorating individuals through plaques, sites, installations, and anniversary events.[5]

These twin-track efforts at prosecution and memorialization were in the beginning a largely private affair. Nonetheless, the state has increasingly been brought in to the circle of actors. Initially at best a reluctant partner, the Chilean state, or at least some parts of it, now appears to be grasping the nettle and involving itself in both justice and memorialization activities. Although parts of the state, including the executive, have been demonstrably perturbed by the prospect of high-level prosecutions reaching as far as Pinochet and his intimate circle, lawyers at the state-sponsored Human Rights Program of the Interior Ministry began in 2003 to take an active part in prosecuting those accused of having responsibility for the disappearances. Another state legal entity, the National Defense Council, became a co-accuser in some emblematic cases, including those brought against Pinochet himself and some members of his family for alleged human rights and financial crimes. In 2004, Chile became the only country in the region to have undertaken a second official truth-telling exercise. Complementing the original Rettig Commission Report of 1991, the so-called Valech Report details thousands of cases of torture and political imprisonment. President Michelle Bachelet (2006–2010), expressed at least a rhetorical interest in advancing the cause of human rights remembrance and commemoration upon taking office in 2006, and her personal stamp is on several recent official memorialization projects, including the National Museum of Memory and Human Rights. These changes should not be overstated, however. State leadership over the human rights legacy in Chile has in general remained notably absent, and policy is still markedly ambivalent. Nonetheless, there is some evidence that private memorial initiatives have formed part of the catalyst for a small shift toward acknowledgment of official responsibility, which goes beyond the passive acknowledgment of or limited practical support for activities proposed and/or carried out by those who have been directly affected or by the ideologically committed.

This chapter focuses initially on a selection of the non-state actors who have led the recent shift from amnesia to memorialization. It asks principally who in civil society has organized over the use of public and private space in this way, and how they have done so. The chapter discusses the complex dynamics and struggles that have arisen over the legal and moral ownership of spaces and buildings, but also over the political legacies of individual figures, in this sudden and apparently urgent collective desire to remember. Next, the chapter discusses state entities which have become the necessary counterparts, or dialogue partners, of the memorialization enterprise. Finally, the prospects for a "mainstreaming" of human rights remembrance in Chile are explored. Public denial and defense of the dictatorship's human rights record on the part of the political Right and the armed forces has certainly diminished, and the December 2006 demise of Pinochet certainly marked a tipping point in that direction. However, there is still a way to go before human rights in general, and the commemoration of past human rights violations in particular, can be regarded as uncontroversial democratic practices in Chile, rather than as ideological and/or political partisanship.[6]

"Hand-Made Dreams without Permission": The Obstinate Will to Remember in Post-Transitional Chile

Chile's transitional and post-transitional period had until recently seemed unpropitious for the emergence of the kind of sustained memorialization activity described above.[7] An official preference for silence and the preservation of impunity for past human rights abuses made itself apparent soon after a highly managed transition to democracy in 1990. The political coalition that presided over the return to democratic rule was of the center-left persuasion, its ranks including many emblematic opponents of the previous regime who had experienced its repressive activity firsthand.[8] Nonetheless, continuing political polarization and the maintenance of high levels of political influence for military and right-wing actors into the post-transitional era helped to make Chile's "human rights deficit" a controversial and virtually untouchable issue. After an initial valiant but limited foray into accountability, in the form of a truth commission, successive Concertación administrations did their best to avoid or downplay human rights–related controversies that might have thrown the prevailing consensual political arrangements into disarray.[9]

After Chile's first, and to date its only, official memorialization initiative, a wall of names of the disappeared installed in the capital's General Cemetery in 1993, some private groups and activists did continue to carry out occasional, and largely isolated, commemorative initiatives. One group managed to reclaim Villa Grimaldi, a notorious former secret police torture center, as early as 1996. However, the year 1998 is the more useful dateline from which to delimit a new period. That year is significant for various reasons. In January, the first two domestic criminal complaints were submitted in what would later become a wave of judicial activity and investigation surrounding former dictator Augusto Pinochet.[10] Moreover, September 1998 marked the twenty-fifth anniversary of the military coup, in the run-up to which both the political Right and the armed forces began to show signs of wanting to finally address ongoing criticism over their past human rights records. Finally, and most unexpectedly, it was in October 1998 that the aging dictator was finally brought to book: he was arrested in the U.K. under an international warrant, the result of judicial proceedings undertaken against him in Spain. Pinochet's arrest marked the beginning of an intense period of national judicial, political, and diplomatic activity that put both Pinochet and his regime's human rights crimes definitively back on the national agenda. It was also indirectly the catalyst for the formation of activist groups that would later campaign around the issues of sites, memorialization, and commemoration. These groups, many of which initially took up judicial action, such as lodging criminal complaints on behalf of the disappeared or torture victims, joined others, such as the Villa Grimaldi Committee, who had had a longer record of organizing and campaigning over places linked to past repression.

Groups, Their Memorial Projects, and What They "Really" Want

What follows is a necessarily selective, but hopefully illustrative, discussion of several of the many recent Chilean "private" memorial initiatives. These have been selected to reflect different dimensions of state-campaign group dynamics, and they range from the most to the least "state-friendly" ideology. Nonetheless, it is remarkable that in a setting marked by strong domestic-actor criticism of recent Chilean governments as being uninterested in, even cowardly about or actively hostile to, the impulse for memorialization, all the site-linked groups discussed here have received some kind of state assistance. Many are in active negotiations with various government departments over the design, implementation, or funding of existing or desired memorial projects. The exception is the non-site-linked group Funa, whose participants are generally opposed to any direct contact with the state.

The first site directly associated with repression to be reclaimed and rehabilitated in Chile was Villa Grimaldi, a former country house on the outskirts of the capital that had been commandeered by the DINA (National Intelligence Directorate) secret police in early 1974. Although the building's relatively isolated location shielded it from publicity, its supposedly clandestine activities were known to local residents as well as at the church school almost opposite its gates. Once the DINA was disbanded in the late 1970s, the site was transferred to the agency that replaced the DINA, the CNI (National Information Center), and it later fell into disuse. Shortly before transition in 1990, the then head of the CNI had ownership of the Villa transferred to his wife. His plan was to sell the site to property developers and make a tidy profit. Those plans were frustrated when a small group of local residents, survivors, and activists approached the local mayor, who was sympathetic to their cause, with a petition to save the site. They presented plans, drawn up by a recently qualified young architecture student, to transform Villa Grimaldi into a commemorative "park for peace." The then minister for housing and urban planning saw the plans and was persuaded to expropriate the site by compulsory purchase. During the ensuing legal battle to transfer ownership the original buildings were razed by the military, to remove all traces of their previous use. In 1993–94, the original architect's project was chosen as the blueprint for the park's development in an open public contest. Work began in 1995, and the park, although incomplete, was partially inaugurated in 1996, making Villa Grimaldi the first repression site to be recovered and opened to the public in the Americas.[11]

Now perhaps the most institutionalized, best known, and most developed of Chile's private memory projects, the recovery and redevelopment of Villa Grimaldi has raised many of the issues and dilemmas common to such efforts. First, the debate over preservation versus accretion has grown increasingly acute over time. The initial architect's plans called for preservation of the lineaments of the demolished house, and used rubble and tiling recovered from the demolition to create a mosaic installation and explanatory plaques guiding visitors around the site. Later developments included the reconstruction of an original wooden water tower at one end of the property and a tiny (2 meters × 1 meter) wooden cell, one of many which the DINA had constructed in the gardens to house groups of prisoners for weeks or months at a time. The reconstruction impulse was resisted by some, who felt it was inauthentic and distracted from the park's initial aesthetic as a place of serenity and restorative beauty. Those in favor, however, argued for the need for something that would transmit more forcefully the realities of repression at the site.[12]

The tower was later "beautified" by painting its original wooden exterior. A separate controversy arose in 2006 when the entire tower was virtually obscured from view by the installation of a large, permanent roofing area over a stage and events space constructed immediately in front of it. The development compromised the original design, which was meant to include a clean sight line linking the original entrance gates with the tower. The then president of the survivors' and friends' association which now administers the site defended the decision, saying, "If the options are to keep it like a museum or to be able to hold events here that bring people in, we'd rather people came."[13] The site has continued to grow, almost beyond its limited physical capacity, and it sometimes seems that no group, survivor, or relative can resist the desire to leave some trace. The most recent initiatives have been a rose garden commemorating women who were disappeared or killed, and the construction of a copper-faced cube that houses a display of train rails, which were used to weigh down prisoners who were then killed by being thrown into the sea.[14] The Villa has now become, in effect, the "container," or physical location, for layer upon layer of discrete commemorative events, rather than a single design that transmits a single story.

Each modification or innovation has meant debate, disagreement, and a certain amount of confrontation over who "owns" and who is entitled to speak on behalf of the site, its design, and even individual victims commemorated there. Some (though certainly not all) relatives of victims tend to downplay the political activities and affiliations of their loved ones, preferring to focus on other aspects of each individual's history and character. Theirs were among the voices who, early on, opposed ceding four plots in the site to political parties for the commemoration of their militants. The form in which disagreements have been settled has also led to a gradual reduction in the diversity of voices represented in the Villa's ongoing activities. One longtime committee member stated, "Oh, of course there have been disagreements, but we settle everything by consensus." When pressed, the same person acknowledged, "Well, what usually happens is there's a row, the people who don't like whatever it was leave, and so those who are left all have the same view."[15]

Aside from these particular design and ownership issues, the presence of the state in what is essentially a private initiative is another major characteristic of Villa Grimaldi as a memory site. Even though it was the first site developed, before a perhaps more benign attitude toward such efforts became evident in parts of central government, the explanatory plaques dotted around the terrain show that almost all the major phases of the site, as well as its acquisition and physical upkeep, have been at least partly financed by the state. The entities involved are many and varied, ranging from the Housing and Urban Planning Ministry, which originally purchased the site, to the local Parks Department (upkeep), the National Arts Fund (roofing of the events stage), and the Council for National Monuments, which placed the site on its official register after a successful petition drive in 2004.

Over time, Villa Grimaldi has become an international referent among memorial sites. An active member of the International Coalition of Historic Site Museums of Conscience, it receives regular visits from overseas delegations and has hosted various international conferences.[16] This has conferred on it the status of older sibling among similar national and regional organizations, and the group has acquired a certain air of respectability, making its representatives perhaps more welcome in official circles than other, more combative site-related campaigners. The international attention received by the Villa has not gone unnoticed in government circles: ministers attended and spoke at international conferences held there in 2006, and Bachelet chose to make a visit to the Villa one of her early public engagements once in office.

A certain official readiness to partake in any reflected glory available through successful initiatives is also visible in the case of Paine, a rural community outside the capital, where a memorial site was recently developed. Paine is notorious for having experienced particularly concentrated and targeted repression.[17] Although, again, the impulse to commemorate the victims of Paine essentially originated with a Relatives' Association, the site became the object of a government-sponsored design competition in 2004. The largely positive response to the competition, along with progress in the related legal case, brought a highly visible commitment from the higher echelons of the government, and in 2006 the community was asked to plan a (basically fictitious) pre-inauguration ceremony, so that outgoing president Ricardo Lagos could be helicoptered in and photographed shaking hands with relatives of the disappeared at the yet unfinished site. In general, though, the Paine site is remarkable, precisely because the victims' relatives managed to keep control of the project, even though they had to rely on outside entities, both private and public, for financing and expertise.

The central memorial, a commemorative installation in a public setting, was opened to public competition by the relevant government min-

Figure 1. One of the 70 memorial mosaics completed by relatives to remember the disappeared campesinos of Paine. It reads: "It's not the distance that kills me, nor the absence of a heartbeat, nor the sadness nor even their arrogance. Only being forgotten could kill me." (Photograph by Leigh A. Payne)

istries once it had been accepted in principle. Here, another repeated pattern comes into view: that of the occasionally insensitive and apparently high-handed behavior of state officials in dealing with victims' relatives and survivors. The five-person jury appointed to adjudicate the competition selected a project that was strongly opposed by the jury's only local representative, the president of the Paine Relatives' Association. Not even the sympathy vote of another member, the secretary-general of the national Association of Relatives of the Disappeared, was enough to prevent the design being imposed against local wishes. In the end, the local group came to accept the winning design, which did have the virtue of allowing for significant input from relatives. Family members went on to design and construct individual commemorative mosaics for each of the seventy victims, working collaboratively with professional artists over a period of more than twelve months. Nonetheless, certain aspects of the original project, such as the proposal that university psychology students interview the families, had to be abandoned when the victims' relatives proved unwilling to accept interventions they perceived as unhelpful.[18]

Finally inaugurated for real in May 2008, the Paine memorial is, on the whole, regarded positively by those who participated in its development. Members of the local Association see themselves as having grown in their capacity and willingness to retain control over their own process while negotiating with the authorities.

A less comforting tale is told by the various civil society groups who claim an interest in the recovery of Londres 38, a former secret-police detention and torture site in the center of Santiago. Unusual precisely because of its central location, the site was coveted by three separate organizations, some interested precisely in the potential offered for present-day political (oppositional) activity, given the site's proximity to the presidential palace, ministry buildings, and the central courts. The original organization, a small campaign group headed by a professional archivist/librarian, used individual political connections to have the site declared a national monument. The initial proposal was then to move ahead toward a Villa Grimaldi–type arrangement, with the state taking formal ownership of the building through compulsory purchase but then allowing private groups to administer and manage its everyday use. However, once the original group was joined by a more combative "collective" (which later split into two factions), the authorities became notably more reticent, and the pace of discussions with the relevant ministry slowed considerably.[19]

Finally, after eighteen months of negotiation, the building's existing occupants accepted a government offer to exchange their stake in the property for ownership of a suitable one nearby.[20] The exchange was completed in early December 2007, and the groups involved in the recovery campaign anticipated the promised announcement of a public contest for proposals for a memory site/archive/commemorative intervention. Instead, the Ministry informed them that the government now planned to use the site for offices for the newly announced national Human Rights Institute. This proposal succeeded only in uniting the three campaign groups, plus practically the whole of the rest of the human rights community, in a chorus of protest. The ensuing acrimony led to the cancellation of a planned ceremonial opening of the site to former prisoners on International Human Rights Day in 2007. Less than an hour before the official event was due to begin, the Ministry decided it was not prepared to run the risk of a protest derailing the ministerial speech and photo opportunity. Predictably, the last-minute cancellation generated considerable resentment against government policy—seen as high-handed and insincere—and prompted a spontaneous occupation of the building by the invitees to the event.[21]

Two final civil society groups should be mentioned, as they represent still more radical positions with regard to interaction with the state. The first, the Colectivo José Domingo Cañas, recovered and is now developing another clandestine repressive site, in the eastern sector of Santiago. This group has a clearly segmented composition, with a larger cohort consisting of young (teenage and early twenties) social and political activists, and a smaller, older cluster made up of relatives of the people who were detained or disappeared at the site. Like one of the Londres 38 collectives, the José Domingo Cañas group is interested primarily in commemoration through the kinds of grassroots political mobilization they associate with the memory of the disappeared. However, the José Domingo Cañas group is, if anything, much more combative in its denunciation of any association with the state. It considers that recent administrations have betrayed their responsibilities for justice. Nonetheless, contradictions are again visible. The group first succeeded in having the site declared a national monument, which required petitioning the Council for National Monuments, although not before demolition of the site had been completed. In early 2008, they signed an agreement with the relevant Ministry to occupy a contiguous building until the site could be purchased—with state funds—from its existing commercial owners.

The lineage of groups, from Villa Grimaldi to José Domingo Cañas, reveals a spectrum of goals for memorialization. These range from the personal to "museological" to political activism. The Funa takes on a different—and arguably counter-memorialization, or even anti-memorialization—purpose. In a direct-action public display, the group Funa "outs," or publicly denounces, former torturers at their homes or workplaces. Successfully gathering dozens, even hundreds, of people at short notice and in previously undisclosed locations—by using word of mouth, text messaging, and similar informal channels—this group raises questions about the conventional focus on absent (i.e., dead or disappeared) victims, considering it more important to turn the memorial gaze 180 degrees, from the victims to the perpetrators. Consciously modeled on the escraches of Argentina, a similar movement of earlier origin, the Funa maintains a deliberately "countercultural" and anti-official identity, although, in the context of improved judicial receptivity, participants have recently pronounced themselves in favor of the operation of formal justice through the courts.

The Funa has also moved away from its origins in anonymous or semi-clandestine on-street collective organizing, and more in the direction of an increasing internal institutionalization over time: the group now has a website and official spokespersons and has successfully defended legal actions brought against it by targeted individuals.[22]

We have seen here that among Chile's varied universe of private agents of memorialization there are common themes and dilemmas to be confronted. To what extent is the desire for individual/personal commemoration compatible with the desire to reinterpret or revindicate political commitment and collective identities? Who, if anyone, speaks authentically for victims: their relatives or their former political comrades?[23] How can diverse individual perspectives be preserved in the elaboration of common memorial design or aesthetics? What margin needs to be left for changes in the appearance and use of the chosen site or object(s) over time? Finally, what is the right relationship with the state? Most groups have been forced to negotiate with the state at some stage, whether it be to obtain permission to install a plaque in a public space, to find an arbiter to act in disputes over ownership, or to acquire and finance the reclaiming of a private or public site. In a context where the majority of the Chilean public at large can be considered at best indifferent to the memorialization impulse, it is perhaps logical that these small groups should rely on the state both for resources and for legitimation of their aims. In this sense, some groups also see a need to press the state to first acknowledge and then fulfill wider responsibilities toward society as a whole. Memorialization here is to be understood not as an essentially private transaction, requiring solely the delivery of reparations to victims and relatives, but rather as part of a long-postponed public act of acknowledgment and repudiation. In this sense, official involvement in memorialization can be regarded as more properly a truth and/or a justice measure.

The Political Economy of Chilean Memorialization: The Professionalizing Dynamic

This chapter argues that despite signs of a change in perspective in some state circles, present-day memorial practice in Chile still operates according to a largely privatized understanding of what ought to be done, and by whom. In this regard, it is notable that in one very practical sense, state involvement in the recuperation of sites has introduced a specific privatizing dynamic. The insistence on contracting out publicly funded design and construction projects through open public contests has itself been a source of discomfort for some. At times, the discomfort has had to do with the nature of the person or group behind the winning project. Thus, for instance, the contract for a statue of deposed president Salvador Allende was awarded to a sculptor who openly confessed his own right-wing political sympathies. The fact that the national Museum of Memory and Human Rights, a project pushed ahead with such haste that national human rights groups were unaware of it, was constructed by a Brazilian firm also initially attracted criticism in some quarters. The logic of market competition and "subcontracting" is by no means particular to the memorialization field. On the contrary, it is an increasingly common practice for much of Chilean state activity, ranging from pension provision to social policy intervention.[24] However, since this pattern was part of the economic model introduced by the dictatorship, its continuation has been one of the aspects of the Chilean transition most distasteful to the Left. It tends, therefore, to be unpalatable to the more politically minded members of relatives' or survivors' groups, who are generally located well to the left of both of Chile's increasingly centrist mainstream coalitions.

Independent of political persuasion, the act of handing over executive control of memorialization projects to architects, artists, and/or engineers also limits campaign groups' perception of their own margin of independent action and control. Thus, in the case of Paine, discussed above, the contract was awarded for a project not initially desired or approved by relatives. For some, this is particularly frustrating, as it mirrors their experience in the legal sphere. In the aftermath of Pinochet's U.K. arrest in late 1998, a plethora of newly formed and existing organizations—survivors' groups, trades unions, university associations, and the like—took action in the courts. Dozens, and eventually hundreds, of new legal claims against Pinochet and others were lodged. All were eventually parceled out to special judges, where they sat with pending cases dating back to the 1970s and 1980s. Finally, this large and unwieldy universe of cases began to work its way slowly, very slowly, through the equally unwieldy Chilean court system, and it is still for the most part in progress. The investigative magistrate system under which the cases are being processed, moreover, tends to reduce to a minimum the involvement of witnesses or complainants once a case has begun.[25] Cases are processed through the cumulative generation of a written case file. There are no oral hearings, and thus there is no public "day in court," for either plaintiff or defendant. Dependent on the personal preferences, accessibility, and competence of their respective lawyers to keep the complaint active and their own knowledge of it up to date, some group and individual plaintiffs therefore have turned their attention to memorialization activity as an alternative or complementary field of action. This relatively new and therefore thinly populated arena initially offered the prospect of immediately rewarding hands-on engagement, with the satisfaction of waging and winning early battles for recognition of sites as national memorials and so on. Once projects reach the formalization stage, however, protagonism has to be relinquished, or at least shared. The state brings in its own professional cadres, or indirectly appoints others through a bidding process. Although there is nothing to prevent campaign groups from taking part in the bidding, to do so on equal terms means accepting an essentially similar logic of involving third-party professionals in the project. As most campaign groups go to the state in the first place because they lack independent funds, they also tend to have to rely for the initial drawing up of a bid on architects and artists who can be convinced to contribute their expertise for free.[26]

The "Mainstreaming" of Memorialization: State Counterparts to Civil Society Memorial Initiatives

Six state entities are presently more or less engaged in or affected by memorialization initiatives in Chile. Of these, the main, and perhaps most enthusiastic, one is the Human Rights Program of the Ministry of the Interior. Originally formed after the Rettig Commission, the 2003 reorganization of the program expanded its legal operation and formed new areas of work. One of these involves the support and promotion of memorialization. The program's website accordingly contains a partial register of what it calls "works of symbolic reparation" constructed since 2002. The stated aim is to support or promote at least one memorial in each of Chile's thirteen regions.[27] When it began work in this area, the program discovered it was working after the fact, drawing up a central register of already existing private projects. Most new projects supported by the program also came about through approaches from relatives or other private actors, rather than at the program office's own instigation. In any case, with only two staff members in the memorials section, much of the necessary expertise and paperwork requires collaboration with other state entities or departments. The view of the section's director in early 2007 was that responses from these other entities still tended to depend excessively on personalistic factors and political coloring.[28] Organizations and campaign groups largely confirmed this perception, reporting in interviews that their relationships with the different government ministries or departments are unpredictable and have to be established anew after each change of personnel. There was, however, a stable perception of some improvement during the presidency of Michelle Bachelet (2006–10).[29]

The Human Rights Program has long been a bastion of progressive human rights activism within the state apparatus. Since 2003, it has attracted personnel who combine long careers in the human rights field with a track record of outspoken criticism of previous state inaction.[30] It is therefore perhaps understandable that other government entities, with a less specific scope, would be both less well informed and less committed to this particular subject area. Nonetheless, the cooperation of these other official agencies is often indispensable to get a planned project approved and built. In the case of large works in public spaces, financing has to be sought from Ministries with budgets on an appropriately large scale. Five other official institutions, therefore, are regularly called on to contribute to memorialization projects in some way. These are the Ministry of Housing and Urban Planning; the Ministry of Public Works; the Ministry of National Patrimony (Bienes Nacionales); the Council for National Monuments; and, since 2006, the Presidential Commission on Human Rights.[31]

Of all of these instances, the Council for National Monuments, although exceedingly junior in terms of budget and real influence within the government, has perhaps responded in the most positive way to the challenge to contribute to human rights memorialization. Although the council has no independent authority or budget to carry out memorialization projects,[32] it tends to be one of the two common points of entry for campaign groups seeking state assistance or advice.[33] Thus, the council had issued, as of May 2008, thirteen declarations protecting sites associated with past repression.[34] The experience of growing involvement in the memorial arena through this process also led the council to take the initiative of calling together the six state entities presently most involved in memorialization. A coordinating entity was set up, and since 2006 representatives of each institution have met periodically to share information or coordinate activities. All involved, however, are at pains to stress that the entity is precarious and voluntary, with no authorization to take a stronger steering role or to attempt to influence policy.[35] Tellingly, not even the group members interviewed were able to spell out clearly what steps a civil society group would have to take to prepare and present a new memorial project to official agencies. Individual members disagreed about where the proposal would need to be taken first, and what its progress around the circuit of institutions would then be. One of the interviewees noted: "Well, the question of who would shepherd [the proposal] through the system kind of depends on what it's about. There again, if you take it to Public Works but they just don't like it, they'll tell you they're the wrong people, or that there's no money left."[36] The same individual did however perceive recent change, stating that personnel within these six state bodies seemed to take memorialization increasingly seriously as a state commitment rather than as a private cause.

One might argue, therefore, that one outcome of the "professionalization" of Chilean memorialization activity in and through the state has been the gradual sensitization of certain functionaries and/or their institutions. Thus, the Interior Ministry's Human Rights Program, once it added memorials to its previously circumscribed legal activities, necessarily drew in other state bodies to provide resources and expertise it did not have in its own right. Meanwhile, the desire to protect sites from further deterioration or deliberate obliteration has driven campaign groups to begin petitioning the Council for National Monuments to make use of its faculty for preventing innovation or alteration to listed buildings. This apparent "mainstreaming" of memorialization concerns, moving toward becoming part of the everyday agenda of many state bodies rather than being solely a special-interest issue, is exemplified, since 2006, in the evolution of renovation plans for Chile's National Stadium. This major overhaul of an iconic site of mass detentions, torture, and executions in the very early days of the 1973 coup made no initial reference whatsoever to the site's human rights legacy, and was motivated rather by the proximity of Chile's 2010 bicentenary celebrations. However, a group of former detainees engaged in dialogue with Chile's official sports agency, Chiledeportes, to ask them to include a commemorative dimension and/or explicit reference to human rights principles in the renovation plans.[37] The group felt that its concerns met with an unexpectedly positive reception from the beginning. Despite hiccups caused by the replacement of the agency's director, on the one hand, and technical considerations on the other,[38] the group eventually saw at least some of its wishes respected in the final design.[39]

The Moral Economy of Memorialization: The Role of the State

How far does the reality described above reflect broader state culture and practice over memorial policy and human rights in post-transitional Chile? The trends discussed above seem to move in the direction of an increasing state acknowledgment that memorialization is a legitimate and/or a necessary activity. In funding or facilitating particular private projects, the state is undeniably fulfilling one part of its moral or legal responsibilities to victims. In Chile, however, the fact that the initial attitude of many state functionaries was, at worst, grudging, and at best, semi-clandestine, has served to perpetuate the privatization of the memory issue. In this approach, relatives, survivors, and campaigners were effectively treated as minority interest groups to be placated. At least publicly, their claims were not afforded any particular validity or prominence over and above those of their counterparts on the Right. Nor was their desire for commemoration treated as a possible plea, not for inclusion of their version of events alongside every other, but for a declaration of collective social recognition of and revulsion at atrocities, such as can only be validly done by or through the state. It is therefore perhaps fair to conclude that the Chilean state, in both an aggregated and disaggregated form, has to date been largely reluctant to conceive of its own memorialization activities as anything more than an often grudging concession in the face of persistent private pressure. This is quite in keeping with the Concertación's broader approach to human rights policy as a whole, which for most of the 1990s seemed to be quite deliberately not to have a policy. The absence of specific commitments allows for constant renegotiation or shifts of emphasis. If each initiative stands alone, rather than responding to a coherent plan, any action that attracts particular controversy or criticism can be quietly dropped or abandoned.

The March 2008 launch of an official survey of human rights memorials in Chile was revealing in this regard.[40] It was asserted during the launch that "the purpose of memorials is the honoring of victims by relatives."[41] The possible denunciatory or accusatory function of the memorials, whether public or private went unrecognized. Moreover, there is no sense that it may be considered a necessary or a proper undertaking for the state to repudiate officially, in its own voice, past atrocities committed in its name. The contention that state, or state-sponsored, commemoration and memorials ought perhaps to declaim and defend an official narrative, irrespective of what private groups may also desire or achieve on their own behalf, is not addressed.[42] The report text itself states that "governments have to avoid conflict."[43] This view also seems to be visible in a marked tendency on the part of the Concertación to defend human rights–related initiatives in the weakest possible terms, as "the promotion of democratic dialogue." The implication here is, again, that it is not the state's role to take any active stance in defining the limits of acceptable or unacceptable versions of the recent past. At the most, it can be called upon to facilitate or channel the expression of one private version or voice—here, that of relatives' associations or similar groups. Under the same logic, there is nothing to prevent voices from the other end of the spectrum, seeking to "contextualize," justify, or even deny past human rights violations, from seeking and obtaining state support. This implied moral equivalence, under which almost any and all views regarding past political violence are valid, has since the 1990s been a common mode of discourse between Left and Right in Chile. It is the grammar through which mutual recriminations are exchanged, and accusations and counter-accusations are levied, over the whole question of political and/or juridical responsibilities for the 1973–90 period.[44] In this sense, it is perhaps no surprise that the newly emerging memorialization field has initially taken on a shape characteristic of debates over other aspects of the human rights legacy of the dictatorship era.

There are, however, various aspects of the memorialization field that make it a particular case. The apparent official desire not to offend any side is certainly visible in this arena as in others. However, memorialization, when treated as an essentially private, reparatory movement, can appear to be a "softer" option for the state than, for example, supporting justice measures through the open pursuit of perpetrator prosecutions. This is particularly true when the design or content of memorials, or even the physical location of recovered sites—typically remote, as befits their previous clandestine status—promotes ambiguity and/or allows them to be ignored by possible critics or opponents. This becomes clear if one compares three major Chilean state actions in the transitional justice sphere since 1991. The truth commission report (the Rettig Report) of 1990 drew sustained and sharp condemnation from those criticized within its pages for their actions or inaction. The participation of state bodies, and therefore of state-employed lawyers, in the attempted prosecution of Pinochet and other perpetrators in the post-1998 period awakened the ire of the military and of the Right. And political maneuverings over the faculties to be granted to the newly established National Human Rights Institute basically represent a desire on the part of the Right to eliminate this activity. By contrast, the proposal for a National Memory Museum, with ill-specified content, was initially largely ignored. Particularly when treated discursively as essentially the continuation of reparations policy through the final meeting of time-limited, private demands by a small group, the funding of memorials can appear to be a relatively less politically costly concession than others being demanded by human rights activists on a newly invigorated post-transitional justice stage.[45]

The fact that this stage, since October 1998, has been an international one is certainly relevant. The delivery or denial of national-level justice for human rights crimes was a major cause of disagreement in the legal struggle over extradition or repatriation that went on after Pinochet's U.K. arrest. Although the intense outside scrutiny to which the Chilean process was subjected has of course declined over time, its effects in reinforcing a certain national sensitivity to outside perceptions of Chile's human rights record are still visible. Thus, Chile's recent difficulties in winning a seat on the U.N. Human Rights Council, together with outside criticism of Chile's policy toward indigenous communities, have clearly caused resentment in official circles. On this stage, too, memorialization policy can be a useful alternative to more internally conflictive actions. Between 2006 and 2010, the survivors' and friends' committee that now administers Villa Grimaldi was gratified by an increase in practical as well as symbolic executive support and approval of their activities. This was evidenced in 2008 and 2009 by an apparent policy decision to make the Villa a destination for foreign dignitaries on official visits. Although certainly a new and, to human rights organizations, a welcome departure, this policy was not exempt from the potential double reading suggested above in relation to other official actions in this area. First, although without a doubt the most developed of all the memory or memorialization sites in Chile, and therefore in a sense the most obvious destination, the Villa also has the particularity of being a site better known to, and more frequently visited by, overseas visitors than by Chileans. Accordingly, it is susceptible to being used as a canvas where international sensitivities can be deferred to and outside agendas met, without any necessary impact on domestic realities. In addition, while international interest in Chile's human rights legacy may now be better dealt with where it already exists, it is not necessarily cultivated or actively promoted.

Thus, while official visitors concerns or agendas regarding Chile's human rights legacy may be met by a visit to Villa Grimaldi, private travelers or tourists trying to get access to the site report that official agencies and tourist information centers claim to be oblivious to the site's existence.

In these various senses it can be argued that despite the combination of apparent recent mainstreaming at a lower level with increased sensitivity on the part of the executive, memorialization as a policy area is still subject to shifting and deliberately ambivalent trends. The overarching logic seems to be the desire to satisfy particular private national and international agendas at the lowest possible domestic political cost. Renewed official activity in the truth and memorialization spheres since 2000 should therefore not be automatically interpreted as having been willed rather than imposed. A more skeptical reading might depict it as arising from the desire to channel, manage, or co-opt the growing weight of demands for further legal accountability in a less confrontational direction. Thus, looking to the higher (executive) level of the state apparatus, it is difficult to see evidence of proactive, coherent, or orchestrated memorialization policy underlying the mid-level, apparently ad hoc, initiatives already described.

Executive Discourse and Practice over Memory since 2000: Lagos, Bachelet, and Memorialization

It has been argued so far that memorialization dynamics in Chile have in general been overdetermined by the insufficiency or even absence of an overall human rights strategy or policy in the post-transitional period. The little that was done, particularly in the early 1990s, proved reactive. It consisted of more or less successful attempts to manage the human rights issue back into obscurity, in response to periodic and unplanned "irruptions."[46] Over time, however, these same irruptions, combined with changes in the justice system and the gradual entry into the medium and upper levels of government of individuals sympathetic to the human rights cause,[47] appear to have initiated the kinds of gradual change described above. Although countersigns and contradictions are not difficult to find, it is true that former presidents Lagos and Bachelet both presided over significant shifts in Chile's truth and justice trajectory, and that both administrations made specific innovations in this regard.[48] As far as specific memorialization is concerned, we have seen how an increased number and range of state entities are now involved in the design and execution of projects, even though the impetus still largely comes from civil society. Parts of the state apparatus have apparently been colonized by sympathetic individuals prepared to "do good by stealth": deploying resources and influence on behalf of justice and/or memorialization without drawing undue or unwelcome attention to the fact.[49] The possible mainstreaming effect of the progressively closer involvement of new agencies, or of previously neutral individuals within existing agencies, in human rights–related justice or memorialization initiatives has also been discussed.[50] However, a question mark remains over the extent to which these changes reflect genuine enthusiasm at the executive level.

Certain high-profile executive initiatives, often cited as evidence of a new pro-memory agenda in Chilean politics, need in fact to be distinguished from the broader thrust of memorialization policy. Activities such as the 11 September 2003 commemoration of the 30th anniversary of the military coup[51] responded to a somewhat different and more explicitly political agenda.[52] The flurry of protagonism around this significant date by then President Ricardo Lagos—not coincidentally, Chile's first officially Socialist president since Allende—was in fact an unusually bold step. Lagos's administration, like those which preceded it, had been more usually characterized by an excessive caution and a reluctance to make strong direct or indirect statements concerning what still tended to be referred to in official discourse as the "military regime" (never "dictatorship"). Nonetheless, its focus was principally the political symbolism surrounding the coup itself, rather than the human rights legacy surrounding its aftermath. As regards the specifics of memorialization, the unfolding of state involvement in response to private requests was, as described above, exceedingly gradual during this period. It is also worth noting that certain changes which proved key, such as the expansion of the Interior Ministry's Human Rights Program, came about because the Lagos administration felt forced by circumstances to announce new policy initiatives over truth and (to a lesser extent) justice.[53] Nonetheless, although Lagos's "flagship" human rights intervention took the form of a truth-telling initiative (the Valech Commission) rather than memorialization, he did, as described above, take pains to associate himself with the successful Paine Memorial as almost his last official engagement in office. He also announced the framework under which the Human Rights Institute and Museum proposed by Bachelet would come about.

When Michelle Bachelet first emerged as the most likely candidate to succeed Ricardo Lagos after Chile's 2005 presidential elections, profiles of her in the English-language foreign press almost invariably highlighted her status as a former political prisoner and exile. Her domestic campaign, however, placed markedly less emphasis on this particular aspect of her identity. This dual treatment of anything connected to the question of Chile's human rights legacy, with a more prominent and bolder treatment reserved for outside consumption, is arguably characteristic. Under Bachelet, it is hard to deny that human rights, in its fullest interpretation, genuinely achieved a higher demonstrable priority or urgency on the national agenda.

Symbolically, however, it is also correct to say that the question of the past, although more prominent, was particularly more likely to be associated with site and memorial projects. Bachelet, after all, agreed to inaugurate a memorial to the so-called Degollados as one of her first acts in office, in March 2006.[54] Six months later, she made an official visit to Villa Grimaldi, where she herself had been detained more than three decades previously.[55] She subsequently pressed ahead with plans for two human rights institutions that seem destined to become her personal political legacy.[56] The first of these, a National Human Rights Institute, was mentioned by then President Lagos in a speech welcoming the Valech Report in 2004. He referred to "a National Human Rights Institute which will promote respect for human rights through education and will also take charge of . . . the information accumulated in Chile, from the archives of the Vicaría de la Solidaridad through to the work of this Commission."[57]

Once inherited by Bachelet, the proposal was redesigned. The function of safeguarding archives was peeled off and reassigned, while the Institute notion resurfaced as a legislative proposal in 2007. This, however, ran into trouble at the committee stage, when right-wing senators introduced alterations that would have prevented the Institute from taking legal action in the courts. In practice, this would have represented a significant step backward when compared to the existing program of the Interior Ministry. The next controversy arose when officials let slip that the government was considering locating the new Institute in Londres 38. The resulting outrage sent the proposal back into official limbo, where it languished until late 2009.

The star proposal in Bachelet's human rights firmament was, however, without a doubt the National Memory Museum, first proposed in 2006. The museum is supposed to house the official archives mentioned by Lagos, and also to gather existing private and NGO human rights archives into a single, professionally preserved and maintained educational and research resource. Built according to a competitive design on a public site in the capital, the museum will also host as-yet-undefined temporary exhibitions on memory and human rights issues. The future direction of this venture, whose construction phase was completed in early 2010, seems somewhat uncertain. The public announcement that NGOs would be handing over their own collections to be incorporated into the museum caused surprise and not a little annoyance. Not only had NGOs not been informed in advance of the announcement, but also, under the former administration, a corporation formed by eight NGOs had been actively pursuing an earlier, and almost identical, proposal of its own. Under that arrangement, the state would have funded the NGOs to form and run their own single archive collection. The discussions had gone as far as to identify a site and to design the architectural competition, and disquiet over the apparently high-handed appropriation of the project caused four of the original eight corporation members to withdraw. Several of them subsequently declared themselves unwilling to hand over documents to the state museum.

The early naysayers included FUNVISOL, the archive of the iconic former church human rights organization, the Vicaría de la Solidaridad. This is the best-administered and most complete private human rights archive in the country, and its non-inclusion would be a serious blow. Furthermore, there was a sense even among the three-person committee entrusted with the project of a certain unseemly haste, caused by the fact that then-president Bachelet wanted to personally inaugurate the museum before leaving office, and therefore set early 2010 as a deadline. The museum was accordingly announced, and an international architectural competition to design the building held, adjudicated, and concluded, before any decisions were made about content, technical requirements, or the role, if any, of human rights organizations and relatives' or survivors' associations. The first stone was laid on International Human Rights Day in 2008, during a somewhat improvised ceremony.

Meanwhile, the improved but still uncoordinated patchwork of state niches of memorialization activity and funding continues to operate largely unscrutinized. It is at least possible that the new institute and museum might in the medium term serve as a much needed center of gravity around which an official memorial impulse or strategy could coalesce. For the present, however, official attitudes seem to lack consistency and continuity, and explicit recognition and unambiguous voicing of a specific state responsibility or role remains pending.

The Moral Economy of Memory

This chapter has described how certain civil society groupings in Chile have recently—since around the late 1990s—turned their attention to the reclaiming of public or private spaces to use for commemoration of (the victims of) past repression. These groups are varied in their composition, origins, and purposes, and demonstrate, as might be expected, dynamics of conflict and contestation over representation, ownership, and resources. Although often motivated to take up memorialization activity by the desire to find a field of direct, unmediated action, relatives' and survivors' groups quickly found themselves driven to engage with state authorities. The need to negotiate permission, ownership, and resources to transform sites has led in some sense to a "re-professionalization" of the commemorative impulse. Architects, museologists, and other professionals are needed to provide technical advice for increasingly ambitious projects, such as those that involve the reclaiming and transformation of former repressive sites, rather than the simple placing of a commemorative plaque.

An increasing official insistence on state-run and state-adjudicated public bids for major site projects has also replaced an earlier, more ad hoc system whereby sympathetic individuals within the state apparatus would find ways to support or finance campaigners' own projects. This has resulted in a certain loss of protagonism by relatives' and survivors' groups and is, accordingly, resented by some. Nonetheless, there are signs of a largely unintended but possibly welcome secondary effect. As state entities are drawn one by one into the memorialization field, some have begun to develop a sense of the state's own necessary, and distinct, responsibilities in what was previously regarded as a largely private field of endeavor. There is thus an increasing mainstreaming of memorialization discourse and activity as a legitimate, and indeed a necessary, activity for the state to engage in. Nonetheless, it is questionable how far these low-level and mid-level developments are matched or met from above by unambiguous executive commitment.

NOTES

1. The track record of democratic administrations is not negligible, including two large-scale official truth-telling exercises and some efforts at official reparations. However, the chances of securing justice and/or unambivalent public rejection of the dictatorship were limited from the beginning by the highly pacted and conditional nature of the Chilean transition, in which the outgoing regime retained both symbolic power and considerable political support.
2. Figures supplied by the Human Rights Program of the Ministry of the Interior in December 2010 showed that 778 ex–state agents, mostly former members of the Chilean armed forces and police, were under investigation in 689 cases relating to dictatorship-era repressive crimes. Seventy-one ex-agents were serving confirmed custodial sentences at that date.
3. See Hite, "El monumento a Salvador Allende en el debate político chileno," for an account of the political horse-trading that saw the Right permit this initiative in return for authorization for a privately sponsored monument to the right-wing ideologue and key regime figure Jaime Guzmán.
4. See the Chilean publisher LOM's "September Collection," developed specifically to publish reactions and responses to the political violence that was unleashed on Chile's own September 11th (1973), at www.lom.cl.
5. The causes of such a complex and largely unpredicted resurfacing of various aspects of the human rights legacy, nearly a decade after the transition to democracy, are varied. Very real contemporaneous events, such as the early retirement in 1998 from the army and entry into the Senate of the former dictator Augusto Pinochet, provoked specific reactive justice initiatives aimed at blocking this otherwise effortless transformation from demagogue to democrat. Apparently unrelated structural transformations, including judicial reform, had meanwhile made it more possible for such initiatives to find fertile ground in the national courts, even before, but particularly after, the spectacular events of October 1998 and their fallout, generically known as the putative "Pinochet effect." For detailed accounts of how particular synergies of the structural with the symbolic and apparently incidental have shaped Chile's post-transitional human rights landscape, see Sebastian Brett, "The Pinochet Effect: A Decade on from London 1998," Universidad Diego Portales, www.icso.cl; Wilde, "Irruptions of Memory"; Roht-Arriaza, *The Pinochet Effect*; Joignant, *Un día distinto*; and Stern, *Battling for Hearts and Minds*.
6. Roberto Saba, in "El movimiento de derechos humanos y el trabajo actual en Derechos Humanos en Chile" (report prepared for the Ford Foundation, 2002, cited with permission), and Lira and Loveman, in *Las ardientes cenizas del olvido*, are representative of many analysts who underline Chile's continuing predilection for politicized and polarized discourse about the concept and definition of human rights.
7. The phrase "Hand-Made Dreams without Permission," which appears in the subhead, is taken from the slogan of the Funa, one of Chile's newest and more combative pro-justice groups. To wit: "We make the dream real with our own hands and without permission: where there is no justice, there's the Funa."

8. These include, as is often noted, former Chilean president Michelle Bachelet, who was briefly held at a clandestine secret police detention center, together with her mother, in the 1970s. They also include her two immediate predecessors. Ricardo Lagos, president of Chile from 2000 to 2006, was arrested in a sweep of opposition politicians after a failed assassination attempt was carried out against Pinochet in the mid-1980s. Eduardo Frei Ruiz-Tagle, the president immediately before Lagos, was generally poorly regarded by human rights organizations, who found him unsympathetic to or uninterested in their cause. However, it now seems clear that his own father, another former Chilean president, was poisoned by regime agents to speed his death from an apparently innocuous postoperative infection in the early 1980s.
9. The launch of the truth commission's report was overshadowed by the assassination days later of regime ideologue Jaime Guzmán. For the tendency to crisis-manage subsequent unavoidable "irruptions of memory," see Wilde, *Irruptions of Memory*; Cavallo, *La historia oculta de la transición*; and Salazar, *Contreras*.
10. See Collins, "Grounding Global Justice."
11. ESMA, in Argentina, had been recovered earlier, but it was not developed until 2005–6.
12. Although even among the latter group, some resisted the specific choice of the tower, which had been used in effect as a dumping ground for detainees who were to be killed. Very few people survived an extended period of detention there, and it was accordingly considered a particularly stark choice.
13. Interview, 16 January 2006, Santiago.
14. The rose garden was originally conceived to commemorate women who had passed through Villa Grimaldi, but was later extended in phases. The names displayed now include that of Ronnie Moffitt, a U.S. think tank staffer who was killed in Washington, D.C., alongside her colleague, the prominent Chilean exile Orlando Letelier. Moffitt herself never set foot on Chilean soil. The cube's contents were donated by the now retired Chilean judge Juan Guzmán, who was looking for somewhere to house the artifacts recovered as judicial proof during an investigation into an unrelated episode.
15. Interview, 16 January 2006, Santiago.
16. The international seminars held at Villa Grimaldi include "A Museum for Villa Grimaldi," in August 2005, and "Meeting of Sites for Memory," in late 2006.
17. With the active participation of local landowners, a total of seventy men from the community were rounded up and executed/disappeared in a single episode. Motives included the exaction of revenge on those who had been involved in land reform activities under the Allende government or its predecessor.
18. "They sent us these young students who knew nothing about life, really, and didn't even know what had gone on here in Paine. We sat them down and told them how it had been. . . . They would end up in floods of tears and we would have to comfort them. After a while we said it might be better to stop that part of the project" (Relatives' Association member, interview, 22 November 2006, Paine, Chile).
19. The Ministerio de Bienes Nacionales (Ministry of National Patrimony) oversees the acquisition, use, and management of state property (see www.gobiernodechile.cl).

20. Negotiations were complicated by the profile of the building's existing owners: it had been occupied since the 1980s by a right-wing historical society with strong military connections. Known as the Instituto O'Higgiano, the group had used the building as its headquarters, going so far as to change the building's street number to 40, in an effort to obliterate all traces of its former use. Understandably, this history complicated negotiations with the relatives' association.
21. The proposed national Human Rights Institute soon became mired in considerable controversy in its own right. In late 2008, a committee was therefore appointed to reconsider the site's future—a favorite government displacement tactic. After an internal wall collapsed at around the same time, informal access to the site was suspended, and the building fell into disuse, at least in the short term.
22. Interview with founding member, 30 January 2008, Santiago.
23. One project for Londres 38 ran into difficulties when some relatives objected to the inclusion of known political affiliations on name plaques.
24. Market competition and subcontracting is increasingly carried out on a competitive-bidding basis by domestic NGOs, many of whom, in the face of declining international support, now rely on such government projects for financial viability.
25. Under new judicial reform provisions that have introduced a public prosecutor system with oral trials, this system is now obsolete. However, preexisting cases, including human rights–related investigations, are still dealt with under the old structure.
26. Thus, for example, the later superseded NGO memory museum idea described above, as well as the initial Villa Grimaldi design, were drawn up for free by university undergraduates working on thesis projects.
27. "Support" consists for the most part of limited financial support. The list of projects in April 2008 mentions eighteen existing and five partially completed memorials—defined as plaques and similar installations, as distinct from full-blown site recoveries or interventions. However, some regions are overrepresented, and not all are yet covered (see www.ddhh.gov.cl/proy_construidos.html).
28. Interview, 3 January 2007, Santiago.
29. Interviews carried out between 20 November and 5 December 2006 and between 2 and 7 January 2007, Santiago.
30. The program's legal staff in early 2008 almost all fit clearly into this profile.
31. The latter agency began life when a personal adviser was appointed by Michelle Bachelet to resolve a crisis over the misidentification of remains by the medical forensic service. Later evolving into a three-person commission, the group was given additional tasks, including the drawing up of plans for the recently announced National Memory Museum. Its mandate however expired in 2008.
32. The council's budget consists of the modest annual sum of approximately US $20,000, which is earmarked for site management projects. This sum is, moreover, shared among all categories of monuments dealt with by the council.
33. The Interior Ministry's Human Rights Program, described above, is the other point of entry (interview with Council for National Monuments staff member, 23 January 2008, Santiago).
34. These include Villa Grimaldi, Londres 38, and José Domingo Cañas.

35. Interviews with two ex-officio members, 29 January 2008, Santiago.
36. Interview, 23 January 2008, Santiago.
37. This group was one of several formed to take legal action in the aftermath of the 1998 Pinochet arrest.
38. The stadium had been used in 1973 as an open-air holding cell, and the group asked for a section of the original communal bench seating to be preserved; but FIFA regulations now require stadiums to install individual seating.
39. Interview with group president, 26 June 2007, Santiago. In this instance, the work will not be submitted for bids but is due to be directly overseen and carried out by government architects and the Ministry of Public Works.
40. The survey was carried out by FLACSO Chile (the Facultad Latinoamericana de Ciencias Sociales) at the behest of the Interior Ministry's human rights program.
41. Remarks made by the report's presenter at the launch event, FLACSO Chile, Santiago (my record and translation).
42. Here, Argentina, admittedly with the historical advantage of a more propitious transitional context, seems to have advanced much further toward the idea of unequivocal, and if necessary, controversial, official repudiation of past human rights violations. The action of former president Néstor Kirchner in removing the portraits of *golpista* generals from the gallery of the military academy is a case in point. So too are the pointed comments of a longtime Argentine human rights activist, living in Chile at the time, who was perplexed by the official handling of Pinochet's funeral in December 2006. First, he asked, why had the Chilean defense minister agreed to attend the private, military-organized ceremony at all? And second, why had she not responded to the hostile reception she was given by Pinochet supporters with a few well-chosen and combative words to call them to order? These possibilities, perfectly reasonable to an Argentine, were equally perfectly inconceivable to this author, presumably socialized for too long in the Chilean habit of excessive official circumspection.
43. "Los gobiernos tienen que evitar el conflicto" (FLACSO, "Memoriales de derechos humanos en Chile" [Santiago: FLACSO, 2007], 10). The phrase appears in a passage paraphrasing Jelin—but she does not make this statement in any such unqualified form (see Jelin, "The Politics of Memory").
44. The balance of this discourse has shifted over time, with the Right now prepared to acknowledge at least the existence of massive human rights violations on the part of the military regime. Nonetheless, the debate discussed in endnote 55 over the possible role of Bachelet concerning the Guzmán memorial is a particularly stark recent example of this trend.
45. Some of these include the derogation and/or annulment of the Self-Amnesty Law of 1978, a demand given supposedly binding legal force by a verdict in 2006 of the Inter-American Court on Human Rights (see the Almonacid case verdict of September 2006, at www.corteidh.or.cr/docs/casos/articulos/seriec_154_esp.doc; and analysis contained in the versions from 2007, 2008, and 2009 of the "Informe Anual Sobre Derechos Humanos," at the Universidad Diego Portales website, www.derechoshumanos.udp.cl/).

46. See Wilde, *Irruptions of Memory.*
47. The migration of human rights sympathizers into the government is in part generational and in part exacerbated by the evolution over time of Concertación administrations and cabinets. The initially centrist Christian Democrat presidencies (those of Aylwin and Frei Ruiz-Tagle) were followed by two socialist presidential periods (under Lagos and Bachelet).
48. These innovations included a major policy announcement in 2003 culminating in the Valech Commission, in the case of Lagos, and the announcement in 2007 of the National Museum of Memory and Human Rights and the Human Rights Institute, in the case of Bachelet.
49. A member of the Presidential Commission charged with initial planning of the national memory museum openly welcomed the relative obscurity and uncertain legal status of the group, stating that it protected their work from the scrutiny of the opposition. She suggested that a certain haste perceptible in recent presidential announcements owed much to a desire to try to secure irreversible advances ahead of a future change in government (interview, 29 January 2008, Santiago).
50. For details of similar dynamics at work in recent government forays into the justice arena, see Collins, "State Terror and the Law"; and Hilbink, *Judges beyond Politics in Democracy and Dictatorship.* One interviewee told me, "[Human rights] patrimony is 'in.'" Another claimed: "When you asked before about people's credentials [for being involved in decisions about memorial projects] you would be told, 'Oh, we appointed X because she's an ex-political prisoner, so the relatives' groups won't give her such a hard time.' Now they're more likely to say, 'He's an architect,' or 'She's got a diploma in museum studies.' This is a good thing: human rights is turning into something normal for the national museums, or the library service, or whoever, to deal with; just like they appreciate it's their job to deal with every other bit of national history" (interviews with state functionaries, 4 April 2008, Santiago).
51. See Joignant, *Un día distinto,* for a description of the constantly changing meanings attached to, and projected onto, the celebration of September 11th over time.
52. A succession of highly charged and symbolic activities in and around the 2003 anniversary, including the remodeling (effective "demilitarization") of the public square opposite the Moneda presidential palace, seemed to add up to a virtual crusade on the part of the Concertación to rehabilitate the figure of Allende. The deposed president's personal courage and integrity were emphasized, by contrast with an apparently cowardly and venal Pinochet.
53. Both the Valech Commission of 2004 and the reorganization of the program's work were products of a major new policy document, launched by Lagos in 2003, called "No hay mañana sin ayer" (No tomorrow without yesterday). The text of the proposal and accompanying presidential message can be found at www.ddhh.gov.cl/ddhh_propuesta.html.
54. This installation, a sculpture, commemorates three Communist Party members who were kidnapped and virtually beheaded by security forces in 1985. Bachelet, who had known the three men, departed from official protocol so far as to intervene in an unscripted oral tribute during the inauguration ceremony.

55. On the negative side of the same balance sheet, she initially accepted (and later declined) an invitation to preside at the inauguration of a memorial to right-wing ideologue Jaime Guzmán, founder of the UDI party and perhaps the single most emblematic figure of civilian involvement in the dictatorship. Assassinated shortly after the return to democracy in 1990, Guzmán is regularly invoked by the Right in a kind of moral equivalence game which suggests that they, too, have their victims.
56. It seems to have become almost de rigueur for recent Chilean presidents to leave behind some major infrastructural project as a personal legacy. Frei Ruiz-Tagle was the first, with a major road project. Next, Lagos created a five-story subterranean exhibition center adjacent to the presidential palace. Bachelet gave strict instructions that the National Museum of Memory and Human Rights be completed before she left office.
57. Televised address by President Ricardo Lagos, 28 November 2009, broadcast by the domestic channel TVN (my translation).

CARMEN OQUENDO-VILLAR

Dress for Success

Fashion, Memory, and Media Representation of Augusto Pinochet

On 11 September 1973, a political earthquake rocked Chile, a country shaped over the eons by quakes of a more geological nature. From the shaken earth and architecture of the September coup, the strongman General Augusto Pinochet Ugarte emerged. But Pinochet, who until 1973 had been a non-actor on the national public stage, and practically unknown to the majority of Chileans, did not produce the coup: he was produced by it. The General emerged from the vacuum of power engendered by the coup, with the media serving as his principal scaffold. A close-knit group of media advisors, against whom Pinochet would rebel once in power, designed the coup's communications strategy and stage-managed the overall mise-en-scène. In 1973, the principal forms of media—radio, television, and the printed press—gave corporality to his image, projection to his voice, and relevance to his words, generating a body for the dictator, upon which post-coup law would be constituted.[1] After the coup, Pinochet led the longest government in the country's history (1973–89), known both for its neoliberal economic model and for its massive human rights violations whereby thousands were killed, imprisoned, tortured, exiled, or "disappeared."

The regime would have been able neither to gain nor to hold power so long by force alone. It needed to manipulate perceptions and ideologies, and, to this end, clothes, in particular, made the man. The new regime aspired to a theatrics of order and discipline, where bodies—both civil and military—would be defined through signifying garments. The manner in which Pinochet, via the media, was able to exert authority by manipulating these symbols throughout his military and political career was not a static process, but rather one of transformation. One might think that the military uniform, because it served as a symbol of the strongest continuing institution in the country, would have been a stable referent in Chile. Yet it was through the very mutability of the uniform that Pinochet effected his migration from non-acting persona to persona of power, and it was that uniform which enabled him to prevail as a symbol of authority until his death.

The word "avatar" derives from *avatara*, a Sanskrit term that breaks down into *ava*—"down"—and *tarati*—"he goes, passes beyond." Together with his economic policies and successful institutionalization of the regime, the transformed uniform and the constantly evolving garments allowed Pinochet to create avatars that would allow him to "pass beyond" and adapt his image in a series of shifting historical-political contexts. However, as fellow Junta leader Fernando Matthei once stated, using fashion terms to refer to the 1980 Constitution: "Even custom-made shoes bind."[2]

This chapter explores the transformation of Pinochet's figure between two salient media events of his history: the 1973 military coup (the first media coup in Chile's history and in Latin America in general) and his 2006 funeral (a mixed media event, in which emerging technologies and older ones appeared in a dynamic field). I pay particular attention to the role of military fashion in the iconic emergence of the dictator in 1973 televised and print media, and then in the 2006 public display of his embalmed body in both old and new media. Between these two dates (1973 and 2006), the uniform of the Commander in Chief went from being an autonomous entity, distinct from its wearer, to being indistinguishable from him, and then finally to achieving an autonomy that turned into a symbol in and of itself, detached from the specific body of the dictator. The uniform, which Pinochet alternated between civilian clothes and other garments, was a strong marketing device when he was alive, and played an equally great role in the disputed process of packaging the *caudillo* for posterity.[3]

The difference in mediascapes from 1973 to 2006 dramatically altered the way in which audiences related to the uniform. In 1973, Pinochet's body, as well as his garments, was "self-generated," displayed and disseminated in a unilateral manner by the Military Junta through a controlled media. Throughout much of his time in power, Pinochet himself rearranged his wardrobe and his public persona to adapt to new political contexts. In

2006, however, because Chile was no longer under dictatorial rule, and because emerging technologies enabled consumers to archive, annotate, appropriate, and recirculate media content, Pinochet's image was no longer generated exclusively by his entourage, but rather was customized by active audiences. There was, to be sure, an official staging of his body according to strict military etiquette, which the traditional media disseminated to the citizens, with varying degrees of independence. Now, in the process of transitioning from an "imagined community" to an "imagining community," Chilean audiences intervened directly in the fashioning of Pinochet's body during "live" public performances on the streets, and also by redressing and photoshopping images of the strongman.[4] New technologies—despite their still narrow reach in Chile—provided citizens with a limited yet important role in creating the memory market of Chile's recent history.

The Televised Emergence of the General's Body: Uniforms at a Table

Audiences first "looked at" Pinochet on television at 6 p.m. on 11 September 1973 on a *cadena nacional* (mandatory national television broadcast), the stage on which the four *juntistas* were visually identified for the audience.[5] After a very long day of sheer radio noise and military communiqués, the television networks finally broadcast the long-awaited images nationally. Replacing the usual evening-news anchor and edited sequences, the emerging leaders addressed the nation during peak evening television viewing time.

The scene opened with four military men, their faces stolid, seated at a nineteenth-century bureau placed for the occasion in the Central Hall of the Military School. Uniforms figured prominently in the national broadcast. The authors of the coup, rather than being recognized leaders, were mysterious apparitions in the ghostliness of television. Not among any of the usual suspects of Chile's political scene, they were unknown political actors with virtually no prior media exposure. Only two of them headed up their institutions—and their appointments were very recent ones at that. The men's anonymity and their unknown faces made their uniforms all the more semiotically potent. Although their garments communicated specific information, such as branch of service (army, navy, air force, or *carabineros*—Chile's gendarmerie-style national police) and rank (most wore the uniform of commander-in-chief), the viewing audience would have registered only the basic fact that these were military men. The uniforms mitigated the anxiety that arose from their anonymity, establishing their membership in one of the strongest and most authoritative institutions in Chile—the armed forces.

At first, then, the new leaders figured as four uniforms, with no salient personal traits or characteristics, their individuality subsumed by the institution to which they belonged. The uniforms of the army, navy, air force, and the carabineros figured as stable referents in the vertiginous changes that swept the national scene that September. During the hours of confusion and radio noise, the visualization of the uniform provided an indispensable placeholder for a recently lost and currently unrecognized and unrecognizable authority. Uniforms provided a familiar sense of order in the face of the vacuum of power that followed the demolition of the old order and the known leadership.

The military uniform, it is worth noting, had long been a charged topic for Chileans. Uniform create many types of expectations, especially as related to the bearer's appearance and conduct; but those expectations are related both to the ideology of the wearer and to the eye of the beholder. There had been many debates about uniforms in Chile, including a particularly heated one that occurred just before the September coup. That debate turned on two related questions. There was the question of *who* wears the uniform as a legitimate representative of the institution, springing from a need to separate the military from civil society. The idea was to define who, by wearing the uniform, belonged to the group entrusted by society with weapons, and thus with the legitimate use of force. But the question of *how* was also important in the debate. It related to an obsession with the meticulous protocols of uniform-wearing. References to the cleanliness and propriety of uniforms were constantly made in the media as a means of judging the wearer's adherence to the institution's moral and professional conduct.[6]

On the question of how, there were two lines of thought within the military, each advocating a particular use of the institution's official garments. One side of the debate was represented by the supposedly long-standing tradition in the Chilean military of loyalty to the constitution, and thus to the president—exemplified foremost by Navy Commander Arturo Araya, Army Commander René Schneider, and Army General Carlos Prats, all members of the national armed forces who had either resigned, or been killed, for allegedly defending the president. According to this line of thought, called the Schneider Doctrine, being a soldier excluded one from any possible activity against the government. Any such activity carried out by someone in uniform would constitute treason and would be to *manchar el uniforme* (stain the uniform).[7]

It was President Allende's assumption and hope that this attitude would prevail within the military. But in the 1970s a different belief developed within the ranks of the armed forces. In this view, the true soldier served not the president, but the nation. Military men confronting social chaos, such as in the antebellum period of the early 1970s, had a national duty to restore order. This was not "staining the uniform," but properly "wearing the pants" (*llevar los pantalones*) and rigorously tightening the belt. This gendered view of the role required by the uniform had resulted in the public scorning of some military officers who had been individually singled out by their peers' families for not adhering to their proper role. Such was the fate of General Carlos Prats, Pinochet's predecessor as Commander in Chief of the Army, whose manliness was questioned during a public protest in front of his home on 21 August 1973. A group of three hundred officers' wives had marched to his house to demand his resignation. They considered him to be an obsequious and unbearably servile commander-in-chief, now merely "bootlicking" a dangerously incompetent president. The clamor condemned Prats for his softness and for being the president's straw man, head of the army in name only, unable to muster the courage to uphold the autonomy of the armed forces in front of the government. More broadly, they accused him of being generally ill-equipped and unable to restore civil order in Chile.[8]

The officers' wives threw corn in front of Prats's house, shouting "Maíz para las gallinas" (Corn for the hens)—a common disdainful expression in Spanish that associates hens (the female of the species), not roosters, with cowardice. As evident by the wives' protest, Prat had lost the confidence of a considerable sector of the military, and he resigned from his office as commander-in-chief. A day later, Allende accepted his resignation, along with the resignations of other officers who also favored a constitutional, and not a military, solution to the political crisis. Thus, one of the salient images circulated by pro-coup forces was that of stolen uniforms and illegal weapons possessed by extramilitary groups loyal to Allende. This was the context in which the uniforms worn by men who had directly intervened in the political scene held significance during the televised cadena.

Yet the most effective uniform and the true protagonist of the cadena was one invoked from a more distant past. On the wall behind the bureau, projected onto the television screen, hung a large-scale oil painting of Bernardo O'Higgins, one of Chile's forefathers. Its painter, José Gil de Castro, had not only painted portraits of the Latin American aristocracy and the politico-military elites of the independence movements, he had also designed the army uniforms in neighboring Peru.[9]

The placement of the juntistas in front of a portrait painted by de Castro is a first instance of the use of visual language to create legitimacy in post-coup Chile. The presence of the Father of the Nation symbolically legitimized the new historical protagonists. Through the use of careful camera framing, however, a particular visual relationship was established that placed the other three juntistas into Pinochet's shadow. Proximity to the Father singled out Pinochet as the new leader of the drama, who would become the lone ranger of Chile's mountainous geography, the solitary leader and eager protagonist in what would prove to be a prolonged one-man show.

The visual impact of the Gil de Castro portrait in this televised ritual of power is evident in figure 1. Strategically placed above Pinochet, the painting not only established an affinity between the two fatherly warriors, but it also emphasized a number of other iconic images in Chile's history. The Battle of Chacabuco, which took place during Chile's War of Independence, is depicted in one of the corners of the portrait, creating a correspondence between the 1973 coup and the events of 1810, the year of Chile's independence. A scene similar to that in the oil painting was now being played out anew, for the entire nation, in the proclamation of the new, de facto Junta. In this interplay of the present and the past, Augusto Pinochet molded himself into Chile's second liberator. If O'Higgins was the founder of the original republic, Pinochet, by metonymic association, became the founder of the modern one.[10] He was placed in mythic time, not just as a figure of the present, relevant only to the vicissitudes of the 1970s, but as a reincarnate Father of the Nation, a recovered lost presence, and a perennial transubstantiation of the country's salvational figure.

The Captain General's Uniform: Between Cinematic Superheroes and Villains

Such is the first picture we have of Pinochet and O'Higgins. Having invented a tradition of memory defined by O'Higgins's portrait, Pinochet

Figure 1. The Junta's national broadcast, 11 September 1973. *Left to right*: Navy Commander in Chief Admiral José Toribio Merino Castro, Air Force Commander in Chief Gustavo Leigh Guzmán, Army Commander in Chief Augusto Pinochet, Carabineros General César Mendoza Durán. (Photograph by Chas Gerretsen, Gamma Press Correspondent)

then invents himself, as the lead in the new national epic, by continuously attempting to look like the man in the portrait. This was not, however, an entirely straightforward process of referencing the past.[11] For all the correspondences in the 11 September picture, O'Higgins and Pinochet were not wearing uniforms in the same tradition. O'Higgins wore the Spanish Captain General uniform, while as commander in chief of the Army, Pinochet's uniform was fashioned after the Prussian uniform. This misalignment between O'Higgins's emblem of power and Pinochet's own would eventually constitute a problem for Pinochet. The difference in the uniforms was a visual manifestation of a difference in military systems in the two historical epochs, as well as of a difference in political regimes under each military system.

The Prussian military system was established in Chile in the late nineteenth century after the Prussian victory in the Franco-Prussian War (1870).[12] Prior to the French defeat, most American military attire, including Chile's, was fashioned after the Napoleonic. The Chilean army decided to fashion itself after the new Prussian victor. It declared obsolete the military fashion of the vanquished, and abandoned all the fusty remnants of the ancien régime, now considered to have an unprofessional, old-fashioned feel to it. Thence began in the Chilean army a process of modernization and professionalization, effectively a Prussianization. Experts from Charlottenburg's military school were brought to Chile to teach Prussian military culture, which involved a specific discipline, along with, of course, the uniform. By 1899 the Chilean army had already adopted the pointed Prussian helmet, and in 1905 the entire uniform was modeled after the uniform of Germany.[13]

After the coup, Pinochet's compulsion to legitimate his regime in relation to O'Higgins led him to refashion everything after his predecessor, even if it entailed changing the very military institutions (for instance, the army) that had provided the legitimating framework for the coup. Although Prussian emblems represented the modernization of the Chilean army, Pinochet prioritized the ranks, titles, and uniforms from a very remote past, and in 1981 finally decided to modify Chile's Prussian military to recuperate aspects of the Spanish/Continental military system, such as the rank of Captain General and the accoutrements and emblems that went with it.

There was, however, more than pure fashion fetish behind Pinochet's copying of O'Higgins. Because of Chile's colonial status as a *capitanía general*, the rank of Capitán General was typical in Chile under Spanish rule and during the early Republican era. The rank was reserved for a leader who was simultaneously head of the government and of the army.[14] After arranging for a popular vote to ratify his new constitution in 1980, Pinochet aspired to further validate his position as both president and commander in chief. In September 1980, a *Time* magazine article, "The Dictator's New Clothes," used a clothing metaphor to suggest that the 1980 Constitution represented Pinochet's way to legitimize his rule, the underlying assumption behind the metaphor being that, even while wearing different covers, the regime remained in essence unchanged.[15] What the *Time* magazine article fails to note is that the change in clothing was also literal, that Pinochet actually changed his military uniform around the time that the new constitution was ratified. Returning to the title Captain General comported with the assumption of two simultaneous ranks, one military and the other civilian, and the new uniform registered this new layer of military and political legitimacy very clearly.[16]

Figure 2. Goosestep march. (The *La segunda* photographic archive)

The uniform now exhibited five stars, rather than four, over a red field. Four of them were military stars, reserved for commanders in chief, and the fifth star stood for the presidential power. Now, when Pinochet appeared in full-dress regalia, there was a surplus of presidential signifiers, since a presidential sash would be placed on top of an already saturated wardrobe. This change in uniform, requiring an enormous military hat capable of holding yet another star, inspired a number of caricatures in clandestine publications.

Associations abounded also in other aspects of the Captain General's new clothing. Having only ceremonial value in most European armies, the title Captain General had been retained in Spain and used by General Francisco Franco, a dictatorial figure after whom Pinochet modeled his military persona.[17] But the return of the old uniform, adapted by the use of an especially long, somber cloak, brought out other, presumably unintended associations.

Had Pinochet used image advisors, they might have advised him to create a link between his new look and that of other "positive" cloaked superheroes, like Zorro and Superman. Pinochet, however, refused to hear the comments related to the projected image of his new avatar. Pinochet's entourage, unable to comment on the emperor's new clothes and their hands tied, could only watch as the new cloak of power summoned up various incarnations of Count Dracula, and more recent ones, like Darth Vader (ranked third on the American Film Institute's list of the top-fifty villains of all time), as well as the memory of the goose-stepping aesthetics of the Third Reich.[18] Such was the case of the *La segunda* photograph, in which Pinochet walks toward the photographer wearing the five-starred cap and leaving behind the other three commanders in chief of the Junta and their aides de camp. The cloaked Pinochet slightly pans his head, acknowledging the neat horizontal line of subordinates, who hold their arms upright in a salute. The disproportion between Pinochet's acknowledgment of the troops and their total body orientation toward the Commander in Chief graphically represents the vertical nature of power within the armed forces. The long somber cloak, rigid military salute, and the accoutrements of the soldiers' dress (such as the shining black goose-stepping boots) resonate with imagery from Nazi Germany.

In fact, allusions to this aesthetic would continue until Pinochet's death, as his supporters, taking their adoration of Pinochet to its logical extreme, saluted his corpse in the Nazi style during the funeral. Meanwhile, satirical newspapers drew parallels between Pinochet's bloated postmortem face and the faces of those other monsters of the contemporary literary and cinematic landscape: Frankenstein and Jabba the Hutt.

This act of refashioning speaks clearly of the hierarchies of power writ in clothing that Pinochet tried to appropriate in his image. The previously quoted words of Fernando Matthei—referring to the very same 1980 Constitution that legitimized Pinochet's power—are prophetic: "Even custom-made shoes bind."[19] The unintentional allusions created by an obsession with grandiose military etiquette came to haunt Pinochet in the latter part of his life, when the final stripping away of his Captain General's uniform dramatically corresponded to the stripping of the immunity that had prevented his being tried for crimes committed during his dictatorship.[20]

Such actions are alluded to in a cartoon by the Peruvian caricaturist Manuel Loayza. The symbolic connotation of this caricature emerges precisely from a juxtaposition of contrasting garments. From the waist up, Pinochet is portrayed in his Captain General's uniform and the famous five-starred cap. From the waist down, he is portrayed in shorts, sitting in a kneeling position on top of an enormous bag of money, with a chicken "hatching" his egg of money. He is holding a storyboard illustration—an x-ray of sorts of the body and of the civilian wardrobe of a senile man with a walking stick—as if it were a protective shield. The implication is that the hybrid image of this political-civilian and his ailing persona's old age (a garment of sorts) are part of a performance of illness through which Pinochet and his entourage seek to make his illegal monetary actions unnoticeable.

Having stepped down from the presidency (1989) and from the military (1998), Pinochet increasingly wore civilian suits, as he had done previously, during a 1988 plebiscite campaign that sought to dissociate him from authoritarianism. In such a suit, adorned with a pearl, he elegantly appeared in the famous 1998 interview in the *New Yorker.* But in Loayza's caricature, as in "real" life, his civilian clothes were not large enough to conceal the scandalous body of evidence against him. After his arrest in 1998 (the first time in judicial history that a dictator had been arrested on the principle of universal jurisdiction), and after five hundred days of detainment in London, what British doctors deemed his "imminent death" ultimately protected him from international law, since he was judged to be too frail to stand trial in Spain. England, at Chile's request, extradited him to Chile so that he could be tried in his own country. The world was doubtful that Chile would indeed follow through with a trial; on their television screens the international community had witnessed Chile's armed forces welcoming the General home as a hero.

El País and other international newspapers recorded the entire Pinochet saga, including his welcoming ceremony by the armed forces, in photographs. In the photos, Pinochet emerges from the plane in a wheelchair and is lowered to the pavement in a truck with an improvised elevator. His first action is to miraculously get up from the chair to triumphantly greet the audience and to throw himself—dressed in civilian clothes—into the arms of a group of (mostly retired) army generals and family members, who have impatiently waited to greet "Mi General" in person. Photographs capturing the moment of embrace were displayed prominently in Spain, where Baltasar Garzón had waged an important part of the legal battle against Pinochet. But Chile did follow through; from 2000 until his death, Pinochet was forced to wear a scarlet letter of sorts—a suit that he violently resisted and periodically struggled to take off: a lawsuit.

A Floating Uniform: The Dictator's Corpse

It is not surprising that postmortem efforts to come to terms with the memory of Pinochet had a high visual component, and that clothing and image played an important role in it. Iconic status and iconography have accompanied Pinochet ever since he emerged as a political actor. The dictator's persona, initially generated through media images and words in 1973, would project itself over and over again into the memories of thousands of people, with an expressive force that is capable of striking spectators down to this day. Few icons—in uniform or in civilian gear, in success or in shame—have dominated Chile as Pinochet did. He has been Chile's celebrity. During the period of his arrest in London, there were more Internet pages devoted to Pinochet than to Princess Diana. Indeed, as Carlos Franz has observed, Pinochet became an "icon of contemporary pop culture."[21]

His 1973 image, with stern countenance and sunglasses, certainly struck spectators in 1998. When he was arrested in London that year, an event that foretold his political funeral, international perception was still tainted by the prevalent 1973 media images of the strongman.[22] This is shown in a caricature by the Swedish cartoonist and illustrator Riber Hansson, in which the 1973 Pinochet, in Prussian uniform, is pushing the senile, wheelchair-bound, 1998 Pinochet over a cliff—a premonition of his real death. In Hansson's caricature, it is the Pinochet of 1973, in his image as the austere military leader, who is pushing the old man to the edge of the cliff, suggesting Pinochet's desire to be perceived in 1998 as that old man, too frail to stand trial. But behind the old man, there still remains the dictator who, among his other failings, is not above an act so vile as to push a crippled old man over a cliff.

The army's official staging of Pinochet's 2006 funeral, scheduled to be broadcast live on local television channels and on the web in streaming video, sought to break free from both the overpowering 1973 image of Pinochet in his Prussian uniform and the image of an old man, his decrepit body covered in lawsuits. It was one more manifestation of the symbiotic relationship that he had exploited in life, not always successfully, between projected image, perception, and social control. In December 2006 Pinochet's body lay in public display in the Central Hall of the Escuela Militar. This image made the front page of many national and international newspapers (*El Mercurio*, *La Tercera*, *El País*, etc.), both in their printed and online editions.

Figure 3. Pinochet's funeral. (Photograph by Luis Hidalgo Parra)

Although his person had been stripped of legal immunity, two of O'Higgins's uniforms were draped over his body. This gala uniform of the Capitán General was the outfit in which he had been portrayed so many times, including in the official presidential portrait. A second, identical uniform lay unfolded alongside O'Higgins's sword, neatly covering the national flag, and all displayed on top of an open casket that revealed the General's bloated face. There was a reason for the placement of the funeral props. Infuriated by the government's refusal to honor the strongman with a state funeral, Pinochet's supporters symbolically repudiated the Bachelet administration by superimposing the military uniform over the national flag.

Given the polarization that followed Pinochet's death and that accompanied his funeral, it was as if the uniform itself were attempting once again to restore order. The country dedicated itself to processing its perceptions about the caudillo, and to reaching closure with regard to this leader who had never been tried for his crimes. Various judgments were discussed—divine, historical and legal. Public debate mostly weighed Chile's economic prosperity and political stability, which, arguably, had been one effect of the military government, against the human and social costs of that government: the assault on democracy and humanity. The strongman's defenders pressed their version of history, which emphasized the country's economic prosperity; his detractors expressed their discomfort with the idea of progress as catastrophe, and argued that the bright economic picture needed to be seen in an ethical mirror. To some, Pinochet was and is a symbol of ruthless dictatorial rule; to others, a revolutionary leader. The casket with the uniform on top was honored by a long procession of followers, some of whom even gave the Nazi salute, while his detractors gathered in the Plaza Italia, celebrating Pinochet's death yet lamenting that he had never been brought to justice. His cadaver was spat upon by the grandson of Carlos Prats, the former military commander who was murdered in Argentina on Pinochet's orders.

Pinochet's funeral wove together publicity codes and military protocols, as is evident both in the numerous articles in national newspapers detailing the military etiquette of the funerary rituals and in the obsession with iconographic representation of the deceased manifest at the grand event. Thousands of people, polarized by their ideology, took to the streets, icons in hand. Even though a ratings-driven media exaggerated the extent to which Chile had become repolarized by Pinochet's death, people did carry images of the brutal dictator in his Prussian uniform, while others preferred images of him as the benevolent founding father of modern Chile, Capitán General Pinochet.[23]

Clothing functioned in key ways in the photographic portrayals of Pinochet. Newspapers and magazines, such as *Ercilla* and *La Segunda*, published special issues remembering Pinochet's trajectory in images carefully selected according to the publication's predominant ideology. In some cases, though, opposing factions used the same images, imbuing them with different meaning.

While it is true that the media created a "Pinochet reality show" that "allowed spectators to follow Pinochet's illness, death, wake, funeral, cremation, and burial step by step and in such minute detail that . . . [it] generated the illusion of *being there*,"[24] one must ask where the "there" is really located during a media event such as this one. Perhaps audiences were not inside the military hospital where the strongman died surrounded by his close group of family and friends, or inside the military school where the wake occurred, or even invited to the cremation and burial in Los Boldos, but they were for the first time able to penetrate the mediatic "there," previously reserved for official and sanctioned transmitters of information.

The current hyperaccelerated news cycle, driven by new players on the mediascape, represents a cultural shift that breaks away from the traditional way audiences received information. Better informed and more skeptical audiences questioned the information supplied by both the formal sources and rumormongers—in contrast to the acceptance of the mystery surrounding Allende's murder/suicide at the time of the coup—but audiences also actively created content. In order to remain competitive, traditional media venues—like *El Mercurio* or TVN, media outlets that once transmitted information unidirectionally, from media creator to media consumer—have slowly begun to include some interactive options for an audience now in the process of getting used to having some input on content.

In fact, as Henry Jenkins points out in "Interactive Audiences": "The new participatory culture is taking shape at the intersection between three trends. 1. New tools and technologies enable consumers to archive, annotate, appropriate, and recirculate media content. 2. A range of subcultures promotes do-it-yourself (DIY) media production, a discourse that shapes how consumers have deployed those technologies. 3. Economic trends favoring the horizontally integrated media conglomerate encourage the flow of images, ideas and narratives across multiple media channels and demand more active modes of spectatorship."[25]

New media have created the possibility of what Mark Poster has called the "netizen," a subject that resembles "neither the autonomous agent of citizenship, beholden to print, nor the identity of postmodernity, beholden to broadcast media."[26] This netizen is part of a larger shift from the "imagined community" of print to the "imagining community" of new media.

Despite the fact that media conglomerates in Chile, or anywhere else in the planet, are not interested in promoting a "semiotic democracy" at the expense of their own economic interests, the fact remains there has been a shift in the way audiences around the world question expertise and sources, and hence, also in the way the public relates to the political process and acts upon political discourse.[27] Chileans are far from being the "netizens" that Poster theorizes. They are still informed about national events primarily through traditional venues. Media consumption occurs in this order in Chile: television first, then radio and the printed press, and finally, new media.[28] Still, in December 2006, the audience had a crucial role in the political staging of the strongman's corpse, despite officialdom's highly protocolized and schematized funerary rituals. People were able to participate "live" in the staging of this public performance of Pinochet's death, by bringing their own icons and images to places like the Plaza Italia or the

Military School, something they had not been able to do back in 1973 when Pinochet emerged on the national scene amid curfews and a strict state of emergency. Unlike the controlled social and media landscape of 1973, the 2006 landscape allowed audiences to consume the event through traditional media, but also permitted a very limited interactive participation in the event through new online media.

When I state that the media in Chile in 2006 were "uncontrolled," I mean that the new Internet media are still relatively "uncontrollable," because, unlike the unidirectional and controllable technology of 1973, today's media allow are for somewhat anonymous and at times unmonitored audience participation. I also mean, however, that the Bachelet administration, like all post-Pinochet administrations, has been much less invested in exercising control over the media than the military regime had been.

Emerging technologies have shifted the way in which Pinochet has circulated in the public sphere, allowing for a surfeit of Pinochet images to float around cyberspace. Opinions about his persona proliferate on blogs and in e-mails; the independent Internet broadcaster *YouTube* has received an avalanche of Pinochet-themed videos, uploaded by users around the world. Recent technologies of access to, and preservation of, the dictator's body (such as online newspapers, web-based archives and blogs, instant-messaging programs, and mobile locator technologies) have added unprecedented immediacy, and also ephemerality, to the creation of a shared memory about the man and his legacy.[29] End users create content to be consumed by themselves and others, sometimes uploading content during street demonstrations with mobile phones. This has allowed other users not only to view these images but also to crop and make composites of them, picking and choosing their preferred outfits for Pinochet, as if he were a virtual paper doll ready to be dressed and undressed by audiences.

The death of Pinochet shook civil society's public opinion, but it also shook the government and the armed forces, who were considered important actors in the funeral, but who, unlike in the Chile of 1973, no longer held the technological and dictatorial monopoly over the creation and dissemination of the most widely circulated images of the caudillo. Public debate gravitated toward issues about the cadaver's accoutrements (i.e. national flags, military flags, Captain General uniforms), but also asked about the proper use of military uniforms in general. For example, two army officers, one of them Pinochet's grandson, Augusto Pinochet III, demonstrated sympathy for Pinochet during the funeral, verbally expressing, while in uniform, their political affinity with the coup as a viable instrument. These remarks alarmed those who believed that twenty-first-century Chile could never endorse a coup, and eventually the remarks were interpreted by the government and the top army leadership as "political opinions," unacceptable for uniformed officers. Both men were dismissed from the army.

"The death of General Pinochet has caused an earthquake among the army rank and file," noted a journalist from Catholic Channel 13 with undue alarm, underscoring what the media portrayed as a turbulent situation faced by President Michelle Bachelet and the army. But in fact, both the government and the army had prepared in advance for Pinochet's death. Their position had been determined ahead of the event: despite their differences—because the army did indeed mourn its former commander in chief—both institutions agreed to maintain a sober distance from the ceremonies.[30] Two top army officials (Juan Emilio Cheyre, Army Commander in Chief from 2002 to 2006, and Oscar Izurieta, Army Commander in Chief from 2006 to 2010), not the fanatic retired generals who still now defend Pinochet, controlled the honors to be bestowed on the former Commander in Chief. Perhaps pressured by La Moneda, the army decided that only its flag (but not those of the other three branches of the service) would be held at half-mast.

The polemic of the time concerned questions like the granting of a state funeral and military honors, but soon escalated into impassioned arguments about the possible construction of a monument in Pinochet's memory, or the placing of an oil painting in his honor in the Gallery of the Presidents in the presidential palace, La Moneda. Raquel Correa, a noted journalist known for having conducted daring interviews with General Pinochet during the harshest part of his regime, reported the reaction of Minister of Defense Vivianne Blanlot, the only government official present at the funeral, wearing a white suit to signal that she was not attending the event as a mourner, because in Chile, unlike in other countries, white is not the typical color of mourning. Even so, Correa argued, Blanlot thought that Pinochet deserved, if not a state funeral, then at least a space among the Chilean presidents in the Gallery of the Presidents.

Thus, civil society, the government, the military, and the media industry as well as media users, all sought to dress the dictator and former president, in an attempt to inscribe their political projection and historical memory by either covering or stripping the cadaver.

The Evolution of a Fashion Image for Posterity: Empty Mausoleums, Fancy Clothiers, and Cyberspace

Even after Pinochet's body had been cremated, public debate continued about the historic inscription that was to be bestowed upon the caudillo's body. The dead man's body, its packaging, and the symbolic location and decor of its final resting place comprised the stage and battlefield on which memory was being shaped in the public sphere. In those December days, the debate was, and continues to be, about the image that will be monumentalized in the imaginary mausoleum of Augusto José Ramón Pinochet Ugarte (1915–2006). In a 1998 pre-arrest interview, Pinochet had many thoughts about death and commemoration in relation to China's Mao Zedong, an ideological rival that he nevertheless admired:

> They took me to a large temple, immense, how can I tell you? Like the American Congress building. Where, every day, thousands of people take flowers to Mao. I went to that temple, but Mao isn't there. Mao is in a second temple further on, where all the walls are of black marble. In the middle is Mao's catafalque. What a monument!—of silence . . . Dark . . . half-light, and the catafalque. . . . I had a very simple thought . . . I remembered the verse of Bécquer . . . which says, 'Only the dead remain.' Because the grandiosity of the place—the mausoleum, Mao's catafalque, the darkness—is imposing. All Mao's power has been reduced to that. And I think it's a matter worthy of further study and reflection: how, after having possessed such impressive power in China, after having disposed of the lives and deaths of human beings, he ends up in a catafalque, alone, in a place the size of a stadium, completely covered in black marble.[31]

All of Mao's power had been reduced to a mausoleum. But Pinochet's own fate would not even amount to a stone monument. After the funeral at the heavily guarded Military Academy, the Pinochet-Hiriart family decided against a multitudinous land procession toward his final resting place. They instead chose to fly his body in a helicopter—to keep him, not in Santiago's General Cemetery, but in the chapel at the family property of Los Boldos, away from public access. Alexander Wilde reflected on his exclusion from the General Cemetery:

> Broadly speaking the General Cemetery has historically been inclusive rather than exclusive—much more defined by all that *is* there, socially and politically, than by what is not. From its beginnings as a *panteón*—

> the resting place of its heroes—it quickly became a broader representation of Chilean national identity. As the construction in stone and mortar of historical memory, it contains the tombs of an extraordinary array of Chile's most famous men and women—painters, sculptors, writers, playwrights, musicians, athletes, trade union leaders and a wide range of political figures from before Independence into the current millennium. Every president of republican Chile is buried there except O'Higgins, González Videla and . . . Pinochet.
>
> When Pinochet died in December 2006, his ashes were interred on a family property in Bucalemu on the coast, not in the General Cemetery. According to cemetery officials, his family did not ever approach them about burying him there. His absence, and that of the many prominent civilian officials of his regime still alive, means that to a visitor, the cemetery's story is largely that of the victors of 1988 (who were the vanquished of 1973). Whether the victors of 1973 will yet see their day remains in the future. With so much precedent, it would be bold, indeed, to predict with confidence that Pinochet will never find his place there.[32]

Gonzalo Cornejo, the mayor of Recoleta, believes the family's decision not to bury him in the family mausoleum, arranged at Pinochet's request by his cousin and former Minister of Justice Mónica Madariaga,[33] was motivated by the attempted profanation of the Pinochet-Hiriart family tomb in 1986.[34] The fact that Pinochet's body ended up on a private estate (and not in the national cemetery, or even on military property) represents the distance most parties adopted in relation to the General, now an inconvenient persona non grata.[35]

With no mausoleum to his name in the national pantheon, Pinochet's memory has been compressed onto his garments. Unlike lonely Mao, or Napoleon, whose former power—Pinochet lamented back in 1998—has been reduced to mere buildings, in 2006 Pinochet's remains did not have even that. So far, he has no monument but his clothes. These are one of the few publicly visible marketing devices of his persona. The uniform and his civilian suits played a role when he was dictating politics in Chile, and now they do so again in the battle over his historical legacy. No synthetic viewpoint or consensus on his persona has been reached: his detractors still show images of a relatively young general in Prussian uniform, while his followers offer images of him in either his O'Higgins uniform or his civilian clothes.

Pinochet's official biographer, Gonzalo Vial, addresses the fundamental question that is still being debated: how will Pinochet be remembered in history? Vial, a law professor and historian who closely collaborated with the regime by serving as minister of education and, some say, by anonymously authoring the infamous *El libro blanco*, concludes his two-volume, 759-page biography of Pinochet with the following statement: "The first indicator of Pinochet's importance is how little his enemies have been able and willing to modify his *oeuvre*. . . . Chileans keep playing politics in the Captain General's field and he still sets—fundamentally—the rules of the game. The terrifying memory of repression also belongs, and justly so, to him. I think this is the way in which history will register the darkness and brightness of the Augusto Pinochet era."[36]

According to Vial, who published his authoritative biography while the General was still alive, Pinochet will be remembered both as the man with a stern authoritarian countenance and dark glasses, and as the man who was the founder of modern Chile. According to this view, Pinochet's image will not be many, but an amalgamation of several images. In Chile's memory he will at once wear the 1973 Prussian uniform with dark glasses and five-star cap, the conservative business suit with a tie and discreet pearl pin that he began to wear in the late 1980s and '90s, and the Captain General's uniform with which he was draped, twice, during the funeral. Despite the presumptions of the 2002 title, *Pinochet: La biografía*, this biography and Vial's words are far from being the final say on the strongman's legacy.[37] Recent polls indicate that, in spite of the "Pinochet factor" (the General's continued popularity decades after leaving power in 1989), Chileans are increasingly thinking that Pinochet will go down in history as a dictator—63 percent thought so in 1996, 78 percent in 2005, and 82 percent in mid-2006.[38]

Technologies of Memory

Pinochet's image may be going through a "post-heroic phase," as Steve Stern argues in the forthcoming third volume of his trilogy *The Memory Box of Pinochet's Chile*. According to Stern, the year 2004 marks the beginning of the strongman's post-heroic phase, when the combination of the Riggs Bank controversy, the Valech torture commission, and the continuing indictments in human rights cases forced sympathizers of the regime to create a stronger separation between a defense of what they thought the military had accomplished, economically and politically, and of their sometimes blind loyalty and admiration to Pinochet as an unstained hero and noble architect of Chile's salvation. Stern goes as far as to say that "Pinochet as hero is no longer viable. The defense of his work must rely on a 'post-heroic' sensibility—the idea is that he did the indefensible, and may have been a corrupt *mafioso*, but that the overall work of the regime was good for Chile anyway, in its economic and modernizing aspects."[39] If Stern's assessment is correct, one cannot help but wonder which garment will dress the public monuments and memorials of the post-heroic Pinochet, now that his "custom-made shoes" have indeed bound him?

Stripped of exclusive rights to forefather O'Higgins, and having lost his status as heroic superstar, Pinochet was unable to figure in death as the Chilean dictator of fashion. He was dressed to kill, but unable to dictate a reading of his persona and his legacy.[40] Imprisoned in a casket during the multitudinous wake, he was exposed to the gaze and interpretation of all Chileans, in fact of the entire planet, appearing once again before a public incapable of reaching consensus.[41] But he was unable to enforce one by a uniform. In fact, it is now—in this post-heroic phase—that audiences, either by holding banners in live demonstrations during funerary rituals or by posting photoshopped images online, enforced or stripped him of garments.

Days before his arrest, when the *New Yorker* reporter Jon Lee Anderson could still consider him the "rarest of all creatures, a successful former dictator," Pinochet explained: "I was only an *aspirante* dictator. . . . History teaches you that dictators never end up well." What, according to the 1998 Pinochet, is the history lesson of success? A semiotic reading of the use of garments by this "*aspirante* dictator" helps explain not the history lesson itself, but at least Coco Chanel's dictum about successful yet fatal fashion checkmates. "Les vraies réussites—according to Coco Chanel—sont fatales."[42]

As noted in the *Oxford English Dictionary*, the English rendition of *shāh māt*, which is Persian for "the king is helpless," signals that the game is over. Months after the funeral, the game was still far from being over; his body long gone from public sight, Pinochet ended up like the leading character in *The Emperor's New Clothes*: naked. Alongside selected items of his civilian wardrobe, the everyday suits of this "*aspirante* dictator" and equally aspirante father of the nation were put up for sale by his son, Augusto Pinochet Hiriart. *Pinochetistas* paid up to $2,000 for each suit, sold at a fancy clothier in Santiago.[43]

Though his suits have been put up for sale, and postmortem Pinochet regalia and memorabilia still abound, Pinochet's actual uniforms remain unsold at the Fundación Augusto Pinochet, where the most radical pinochetista version of his memory is being staged for posterity. It is worth remembering Patricio Navia's comments about Fernando Matthei's notion that the constitution, like custom-made garments, binds: "The new institutional order [born with the 1980 Constitution and the Captain General uniform] was both custom made for Pinochet but designed for a post-Pinochet Chile."[44] Is the uniform—I ask, thinking alongside Navia—waiting for a post-Pinochet political hero to wear it? Or has the Captain General uniform, unlike fairy-tale garments, turned into an untransferable object that, once detached from the General's body, can be worn by no one else?

Given that hard-core supporters are likely to buy almost anything related to *Mi General*, one cannot help thinking that the profit his circle hopes to make by not selling the uniform (and thereby letting others wear it) will be on the memory market. Just as Pinochet's remains may eventually make it to Santiago's General Cemetery and a bust in his likeness may even make it into La Moneda's Gallery of Presidents, his military garments may also migrate to more official sites of memory. Though for the moment his uniforms remain at the seldom visited Fundación Pinochet, in time they may land in the Museum of the Military Academy along with other historical objects associated with the 11 September coup and the former commander in chief—or even in La Moneda itself.[45] The potential museification of the uniform suggests its hightest value is in the public inscription of Pinochet's image onto Chile's collective memory.

While the uniform still stands metonymically for his person, 2006 marked the year when it was permanently detached from his physical body, now ashes. It is as if the shaken earth has swallowed the body of strongman General Augusto Pinochet Ugarte and spit out a naked post-heroic persona, to be dressed by the audience as president, savior, dictator, or to be stripped as criminal and thug. Competing inscriptions of his memory will range from permanent material renditions of his persona in public spaces, which could be personified effigies in full-dress regalia (his body natural) or abstract monuments symbolizing the Chile born in 1973 (his body politic), to virtual, dematerialized icons constantly re-dressed by media users.

There has been much debate over whether the Internet is to be seen as a new public sphere, especially in the case of Chile where its reach is still limited, but the fact is that the Internet has created the possibility of removing historical memory from being the exclusive domain of officialdom, be it the government, the military, or media conglomerates.[46] During the funeral, emerging technologies and older ones appeared in a dynamic field; and the battle over historical memory was waged—and it is still being waged—through what has been called "phenomenotechnics" (technologies of memory, consciousness, individuation).[47]

The long-term success of Pinochet's fashion statements is yet to be proven. The dictator is now dead and his body has turned into ashes, but his image has been kidnapped and "jacked into" several online networks. Now inhabiting not a mausoleum, but the virtual ontology of the avatar, Pinochet will perhaps be forced by users to reincarnate—in a not very distant future—as a re-dressed hologram capable of being judged and sentenced, and, why not, also judged and absolved from charges—in an imaginary parallel world. He is not to be *un desaparecido más* (yet another disappeared), at least not until users tire of him, turning his image into an obsolete icon, trivial or trivialized in online memory sites.

Perhaps no such oblivion will occur. The global data communications system called the Internet, and especially the World Wide Web—the collection of interconnected documents and resources linked by hyperlinks and URLs—provide users with enormous amounts of memory space that could yield new kinds of technologies of memory related to Pinochet, the historical figure, and his technological avatars. This technologized "memory" has the potential of becoming an über-archive, a privileged site for what the filmmaker Patricio Guzmán once called Chile's "obstinate memory."

NOTES

1. Oquendo-Villar, "Chile 1973."
2. Fernando Matthei quoted in Barros, *Constitutionalism and Dictatorship*, 255.
3. Cárcamo-Huechante, *Tramas del mercado*.
4. Anderson, *Imagined Communities*, 6; Levy, *Collective Intelligence*, 217.
5. Marita Sturken and Lisa Cartwright establish a difference between the act of seeing, an "arbitrary process of observing," and the act of looking, "actively mak(ing) meaning of the world in order to communicate, to influence and be influenced" (Sturken and Cartwright, *Practices of Looking*, 10).
6. Montalva, *Morir un poco*, 340.
7. The series of military coups in 1932 and the events which led to the formulation of the 1969 Schneider Doctrine, which included troop mobilization against the Frei Montalva government (1964–70), reveal a less-neutral Chilean military than is commonly assumed. I thank Patricio Navia for this insight.
8. Power, *Right-Wing Women in Chile*, 15–20.

9. Mariátegui Oliva, *José Gil de Castro "el mulato Gil"*; Benson et al., *Retratos.*
10. Alexander Wilde discusses the 1979 decision by the Pinochet government to move O'Higgins's tomb from the General Cemetery, where it had existed for over a hundred years, to the square in front of La Moneda: "The symbolism was patent: the dictatorship represented a 're-founding' of the nation based on its most traditional historical values, with Pinochet as a second O'Higgins" (Wilde, "Avenues of Memory," 165).
11. O'Higgins provided Pinochet's main source of inspiration, but Pinochet also fashioned himself—rhetorically and politically, though not in garment—after another historical figure, namely, Diego Portales, known as El Padre de la Institucionalidad, the Father of Political Institutions.
12. Patricio Quiroga and Carlos Maldonado, in *El prusianismo en las fuerzas armadas chilenas*, refer to four stages in the Prussianization process of the Chilean armed forces from 1885 to 1945. See also Nunn, *The Military in Chilean History*; and Nunn, *Chilean Politics, 1920–1931.*
13. Ejército de Chile, *Historia del ejército de Chile*; Márquez and Márquez, *Cuatro siglos de uniformes en Chile.*
14. Arriagada, *La política militar de Pinochet, 1973–1985*, 123–35.
15. "The Dictator's New Clothes," *Time*, 22 September 1980, www.time.com.
16. Interview with Pinochet's Minister of the Interior Francisco Javier Cuadra, 20 August 2004.
17. Jon Lee Anderson, "The Dictator," *The New Yorker*, 19 October 1998; Vial, *Pinochet*, 365–66; "The Dictator's New Clothes" (editorial), *Time*, 22 September 1980, www.time.com.
18. Those close to Pinochet contend that he refused to hire media advisors (interviews by the author with General Cortés Villa, Santiago, 22 August 2005, and with Francisco Javier Cuadra, Santiago, 23 August 2005). The rare occasion when the regime brought in consultants did not constitute a coherent strategy (Sapag and Sepúlveda, *¡Es la prensa, estúpido, la prensa!*, 9, 23, 24, 25).
19. Fernando Matthei quoted in Barros, *Constitutionalism and Dictatorship*, 255.
20. Peter Kornbluh, "Pinochet Stripped," *The Nation*, 27 September 2004, 32.
21. Carlos Franz, "La muerte del ícono," *La nación*, 13 December 2006, 26.
22. See Sapag and Sepúlveda, *¡Es la prensa estúpido, la prensa!*, 9, for a discussion of the impact of early images of Pinochet on Judge Garzón's opinion of him.
23. See Joignant, *Un día distinto*; Lazzara, "Pinochet's Cadaver as Ruin and Palimpsest," 83.
24. See Joignant, *Un día distinto*, 181.
25. Henry Jenkins, "Interactive Audiences," *The New Media Book*, 157–58.
26. Mark Poster, "The Net as a Public Sphere?," *Wired*, www.wired.com/wired/archive/3.11/poster.if_pr.html.
27. Jenkins, *Convergence Culture*, 208.
28. Arriagada and Schuster, "Consumo de medios y participación ciudadana de los jóvenes chilenos," 38, 39.
29. Informal interview with Arturo Arriagada, 12 November 2008. On Chilean blogs, see also www.tendenciaspoliticas.cl.

30. Lazzara, "Pinochet's Cadaver as Ruin and Palimpsest," 187.
31. Jon Lee Anderson, "The Dictator," *The New Yorker*, 19 October 1998.
32. Wilde, "Avenues of Memory," 155, 142.
33. Lazzara, "Pinochet's Cadaver as Ruin and Palimpsest," 184.
34. Wilde, "Avenues of Memory," 166.
35. See the discussion about the meaning of Pinochet's burial in the Escuela Militar, in Politzer, *Chile*, 68.
36. Vial, *Pinochet*, 741.
37. See Vial's discussion of the title of the book in Vial, *Pinochet*, 9.
38. Angell, "The Pinochet Factor in Chilean Politics." For polls about the inscription of Pinochet in history, see Huneeus, *Chile*, 59–92. For more recent polls, see www.cerc.cl. I thank Cath Collins for providing this information.
39. Personal communication with Steve Stern, Madison, Wisc., 12 April 2008. For a discussion of the body politic and the body natural, see Lazzara, "Pinochet's Cadaver as Ruin and Palimpsest," 177.
40. See "Christian Dior: Dictator of Fashion," *Reader's Digest*, May 1957, 128–32. For the significance of President Ricardo Lagos's act of returning O'Higgins's tomb to civilian control in 2006, see Larry Rohter, "O'Higgins the Liberator is Reclaimed from the Military," *New York Times*, 10 March 2006.
41. See Benstock and Ferris, *On Fashion*, 1–17, for "dressed to kill" and "prey to the look" concepts.
42. Morand, *L'allure de Chanel*, 43.
43. Manuel Délano, "Un hijo de Pinochet saca a la venta trajes de su padre," *El país*, 13 August 2007; Manuel Vega O., "Augustito puso en venta trajes del 'Tata' porque necesitaba espacio en el clóset," *La Cuarta*, 12 August 2007. For more efforts by Pinochet's son to profit from his father's image, see Mónica González, "Ahora Pinochet tiene un vino con su nombre," *Clarín*, 22 July 2001, Edición Domingo. Other attempts were made to sell "Capitán General" wine and "Don Augusto" pisco as fundraisers for Pinochet's detention in London. Consider this radio advertisement for the wine: "A native stock of grape, pure and traditional, is the origin of this robust wine. *Captain General*, an exclusive wine with immortal lineage. *Captain General*, a wine that consecrates the great milestones of history, our history" (www.ua.es/up/pinochet/imagenes/curiosidades.html). Pinochet tended to appear on these bottles in his Captain General uniform.
44. Navia, "Pinochet."
45. Wilde discusses the relative mobility of tombs in and out of the General Cemetery in "Avenues of Memory," 136. Changes in the Army Museum inventory and displays reflect an evolving historical memory within the military (see Jon Lee Anderson, "The Dictator," *The New Yorker*, 19 October 1998). For the army's new image under democracy, see Politzer, *Chile*, 15–72.
46. Poster, "The Net as a Public Sphere?"
47. Emily Apter, "Technics of the Subject: The Avatar Drive," www.iath.virginia.edu/pmc/current.issue/18.2apter.html.

KSENIJA BILBIJA

Tortured by Fashion

Making Memory through Corporate Advertising

Photography [is] a message from time past," wrote Susan Sontag, referring to the fact that photographic images taken in the past bring to the viewer in the present recall or reminiscence about the instant when the snapshot was taken.[1] At the moment when the real is long gone, and sometimes repressed, it resurfaces through the photographic image in front of the eyes of the viewer as a reminder of some kind of loss. "Like a footprint or a death mask"—Sontag concluded later in her essay, as she searched for an appropriate metaphor to convey the association between the photograph and death.[2] The snapshot is made as the light inscribes the contours of the photographed, and the outcome is a specter, a ghostly visitor from the past who reminds the viewer in the present of his own mortal and fleeting existence.

What gives meaning to every narrative is its ending, and one of the puzzles of human existence is precisely the impossibility of positioning oneself at the moment of life's end. We cannot describe our own death; we can only imagine it as something inevitable in the future. And so one is left conjuring up the image of a death with the discursive aid of those who have witnessed it and, of course, the imagination of those who write about it.

Survivors of atrocities often prefer to cast memories of violence out of their consciousness. They become too overwhelmed by the trauma of what they have endured to access the symbolic realm of language, so they silence it and push it toward the unpredictable and quite unmanageable creases of the unconscious. At times the magnitude of the trauma is such that it leaves a whole generation, a collective, or even a nation, wounded for years

Figure 1. "Underwater and Bound," Diesel advertisement, 1998.

to come.[3] Societies, just like individuals, need to mourn their losses and undo the violence of repression.

So what happens to a society when an image associated with the collective trauma, an image that was never recorded, a snapshot that was never taken, gets unknowingly and carelessly re-created with a purpose completely foreign to any commemorative function?

On 9 April 1998, some three years after Retired Navy Captain Adolfo Scilingo publicly confirmed the rumors that had circulated in Argentina regarding the "death flights" and the tragic fate of hundreds of victims thrown alive from airplanes into the Atlantic Ocean during the military dictatorship (1976–83), readers of the right-leaning Argentine magazine *Gente* were faced with Diesel advertisements for a new collection of jeans.

The ads portrayed several young men and women sporting Diesel apparel underwater, bound at their wrists and ankles and chained to cinder blocks pulling them down. The one closest to the viewer seems to be still alive, since there are bubbles of air coming out of his mouth. The photographic image shows the actors' hands tied behind their backs. The bluish light that comes from above fades with the depth of the water, gradually turning into black. A tagline in English that accompanies the "Different Washes" ad reads: "Over 10 styles of legwear, 8 weights of cloth, 24 DIFFERENT WASHES. Everything from streaky to sandblasted. They are not your first jeans but they could be your last. At least you'll leave a beautiful corpse."[4]

On 4 March 2006, only three years after Judge Alejandro Solís issued the first sentences in Chilean judicial history for crimes committed during the military dictatorship against the former DINA director Manuel Contreras—crimes that included torture in infamous detention centers such as Villa Grimaldi and Londres 38—readers of the Chilean newspapers *El Mercurio* and *La Tercera* interested in the new fashion styles of the season found what they were looking for in the advertisements of the multinational company Ripley, one of the largest department store chains in the country.

Entitled "Jeans Parade," the advertising campaign that, in addition to the print media, also appeared on TV and billboards, featuring photographs of beautiful young models bound, shackled, or harnessed and hanging from hooks in the ceiling by their feet, their heads in many cases covered with sacks. These hoods were reminiscent of the *capuchas* used to cover the faces of the victims tortured during the dictatorship.

In one of the ads, a woman resembling a sadistic dominatrix stands firmly grounded next to a tied-up male body that hangs upside down. One of her arms is behind her back, allowing for the possibility that a hidden weapon such as a whip might be part of her attire. While there is no tagline accompanying the images, there is the price of the pictured jeans, the Ripley logo, and brand names of models featured in the catalogue, such as Lois Jeans (Spain), Naf-Naf (France), Ellus Jeans (Brazil), Index Jeans (Brazil), BB2 Jeans (Chile), Rider Jeans (USA), and Wrangler (USA). The "Jeans Parade" campaign also featured a fashion show inspired by VH1's fashion awards and the popular British show *Fashion Rocks*.

In both cases, human rights organizations protested and the ads were soon removed from circulation. Because of their trivialization of recent history, the ads were seen as a direct insult to the victims of state violence and their families, and they were particularly criticized for promoting sales of something so trifling as a pair of jeans through references to human suffering.[5] Argentine newspapers such as *Clarín* and *Página/12* immediately condemned the "macabre ad" for "emulating one of the methods of extermination used during the last military dictatorship." Organizations such as Fundación Memoria Histórica y Social Argentina, as well as Madres de Plaza de Mayo, presented a complaint not only to a Diesel representative in Argentina but also at the company's headquarters in Italy. The ad, designed for Diesel by the internationally renowned agency Lowe-Howard Spink (now an entity of Lowe & Partners Worldwide), targeted "the deeper, darker, more disturbed recesses of the mind!" and was sent to different national markets.[6] The Argentine representative of Diesel Marketing, Marco Marini, blamed the provincialism of the Argentines for their "misreading" of the message. He informed Diesel headquarters that "in advertising, the story of a global village doesn't work."[7] Marini further argued that the ad had not only been accepted by "the entire world," including "the countries that have also suffered the unfortunate experience of human rights violations," but that it had also been approved by local advertising firms. "They [the foreign public] don't care about the message, but like to see the strange, the exotic, the unusual."[8] In order to show that there was some thinking involved in the publication of this ad, he also pointed out that his local team had rejected two other ads in the same Different Washes series, the first of which was ultimately discarded on ethical grounds, for portraying an elderly couple sitting on a sofa with the grandmotherly figure grabbing the grandfather's genitals. The image was accompanied by a tagline that read: "The result is ANTIQUE, DIRTY, DENIM which has an aged, vintage appearance. A bit like your grandmother."[9] The second ad had been rejected because it could have offended the Church for showing nuns in jeans. The inscription that accompanied that photograph read: "Pure, virginal 100% cotton. Soft and yet miraculously strong. Our jeans are cut from *Superior Denim*, then carefully assembled by devoted Diesel followers."[10]

In Chile, the Ripley department store received numerous complaints, and eventually Amnesty International, as well as the Council of Advertising Ethics and Self-Regulation (Consejo de Autorregulación y Ética Publicitaria, or CONAR), voiced their objections. The Internet became a forum for a discussion about freedom of expression and the advertising agency's choices in presenting their jeans selection. "Ripley banalizes torture methods used during Augusto Pinochet's dictatorship" read one blog posting, authored by columnist and torture survivor Pedro Matta.[11] Along with fellow columnist Javier Campos (*El Mostrador*), Matta charged the creators and promoters of the campaign with using torture as a marketing technique. In addition, Matta accused Ripley of further muddying the already murky waters of Chile's path toward "recognizing and culturally internalizing atrocities committed" during the dictatorship.[12] There was also an urgent call for social action against Ripley's ads, but it ultimately failed.[13] It was determined that nothing could be done legally, since the ads represented neither a case of deceptive advertising nor did they suggest that "by employing means of violence and/or torture the consumer will obtain some kind of advantage and/or benefit."[14] Nevertheless, Amnesty International contacted CONAR, but they decided not to pursue the claim against Ripley's advertising campaign because it was not in violation of the Chilean Ethical Advertising Code. It seems that they accepted the defense of the Ripley department store, that there were no explicit images of violence and torture in the ad. The ad did not contain "an explicit or tacit message that induces the general public to commit or support acts of violence and/or torture."[15] A less official social action that did not bring the expected results included a call to all consumers who had a Ripley's charge card to destroy it at a public gathering. However, most cardholders could not do this, since they had outstanding balances that they needed to take care of before destroying their cards. Another call for social action included assembling the e-mail addresses of all the companies whose brands were featured in the contested catalogue and requesting that they denounce the offensive Ripley ads directly by expressing their outrage.[16]

Guido Puch, the creative director of the McCann Erickson advertising agency, which designed the ads for Ripley, declared that the ads did not display "any torture in hoods and ropes" and that those who read them in that way were demonstrating an "exacerbated sensibility."[17] He also added that the offending advertisement was "just a fashion ad, with a graphic design very much belonging to youth, associated with MTV. It never occurred to us that it was going to provoke such a reaction and [the company's] intention was never to provoke this."[18] Furthermore, he explained away the hoods and ropes as elements of modern dance, going so far as to claim that the inspiration for the ad had come from a certain "Argentine circus."[19] Puch was referring to the world-famous Argentine theatrical troupe De la Guarda, which is quite popular in Chile. Somewhat resembling the acrobatics of Cirque de Soleil, the Argentine group distinguishes itself by inviting audience participation, including strapping volunteers into harnesses, thus allowing them to mimic the acrobatics of the professional—just as the models seen in the Ripley ads were doing. Interestingly, following the argument of his Argentine colleague, Puch underlined a certain provincialism, seen as a lack of global perspective among those who read the ads, as actually offensive to the victims of human rights abuses because those ads were part of a "world trend."[20]

It seemed that the advertising executives were claiming that certain Argentines and Chileans are not literate in the new global rhetoric. To whom are they referring?

Diesel is an Italian-based clothing company that targets urban, casual, fashionable young adults who are wealthy enough to pay a high price for a pair of jeans and who see themselves as sophisticated, original, irreverent, flamboyant, ironic, sexy, witty, and more than anything else, as "debunking the status quo."[21] According to statements made by owner Renzo Rosso and the company's marketing directors, Diesel is more interested in targeting consumers who share a lifestyle and philosophy than in targeting a specific age group.[22] However, most of their customers are between eighteen and thirty-four years old. Their logo, "Diesel for successful living," carries a promise of a fulfilling, well-off, and dynamic lifestyle.[23] Every six months, the company launches a new collection through an original advertising campaign. And that is precisely the vehicle Diesel used to differentiate itself from its competition: their ads generally display colorful, provocative, weird photographs that grab viewers' attention with an ambiguous, phantasmagoric, ironic, or humorous story that requires a very involved and active participant. By creating controversy through indeterminacy and the intentional ambiguity of their message, they are allowing for multiple points of view and showing irreverence for any kind of authority and stability. Diesel's representatives, including Renzo Rosso, all insist on the same philosophy: they "sell dreams," and do not hold anything as sacred: "The intelligent part of our advertising is to inspire people to think in different, alternative ways about our world. But we don't want to tell them what to think. We're not being political, we want young people to think and interpret for themselves."[24] Diesel is making the point that they are not interested in politics, that they speak to young, irreverent people (18–34), and that nothing is untouchable. They do not want fashion victims, Diesel's representatives insist, but it appears that they do not want their clients to identify as victims in any sense. They want them to feel empowered and capable of reading against culturally prescribed interpretation.[25]

Ripley also portrays itself as "customer-centered," but, being a department store, it strives to attract a somewhat less age-specific clientele than Diesel. However, "youthfulness" is one of the principal elements of the company's "philosophy." For example, a very brief home-page profile emphasizes that the average age of Ripley's executives is forty. The company is aware of the importance of publicity and advertising for placing their products, and that is why they contract the most well-known, most experienced, and biggest international agencies, such as McCann Erickson, which claims to be able to "uncover key customer insights and develop direct and interactive platforms to connect to our clients' customers."[26] It appears that the controversial ads that McCann Erickson designed for the Ripley's Jeans series were inspired directly by the Abu Ghraib prison abuse scandal that shocked the world two years earlier with images of degrading, unlawful torture that U.S. soldiers perpetrated on Iraqi prisoners. McCann Erickson's "translation" of the Abu Ghraib images lacks blood, or expressions of pain, suffering, and trauma in general. What is left in their staging of violence are "clean," exquisite bodies, torture props, and an air of transgression that surrounded the original photographs. Transposed from those original snapshots taken by American soldiers is also a sense of power, immunity, and arrogance. Such visual rhetoric mimicking torture trophy photographs is a kind of strategy that places the viewer in the position of a perpetrator, a sadistic voyeur, a complicit bystander, or even a victim. In that sense, McCann Erickson's marketing specialists are not offering a critical comment on Abu Ghraib, nor trying to cultivate socially conscious citizens. Cynically and gratuitously, they are using the air of empowerment and irreverence from the Abu Ghraib frame of reference in order to promote sales.

Sales and the market are perhaps the key link between the authoritarian past and the democratic present. Can the Ripley and Diesel advertisements help us to understand that linkage? Chile and Argentina's became free market societies through processes that call into question the divide between dictatorship and democracy. During the dictatorship era, Pinochet's Chile went through neoliberal restructuring, while Argentina shift to the economic right occurred after the transition to democracy, under the government of Carlos Menem (1989–99). In Argentina, anticipating Menem, the 1987 Full Stop Law put an end to military prosecutions for human rights violations—and to the process of mourning—by resisting "any kind of transaction or substitution," thereby placing societal moralities under a cold, neoliberal umbrella.[27] In her snapshot journey through fin de siècle Buenos Aires, the cultural theorist Beatriz Sarlo writes about the differences that the last few decades have wrought. She argues that Buenos Aires is in the hands of those who have neoliberalized culture, who care only about "the lessons of the rhetoric and philosophy of exchange. . . . Advertising pedagogy is more powerful than any other image or fantasy of the city."[28] As a result, the past and the present "are comfortable embracing each other because the past has lost its density and the future has lost its certainty."[29]

It was into Menem's Argentina that Diesel launched its advertisements. *Menemismo* did not deny memory so much as it reinforced the connections between neoliberal economics, violence, and the triumph of dictatorship ideologies. Marked by a free market, by "savage" capitalism, Menem's Argentina (1989–99) was in many respects a product of what democracy was meant to have defeated, the Proceso. The violence, for example, of economy minister Domingo Cavallo's policies echoes that of his dictatorship-era equivalent, José Martínez de Hoz.[30] A still more poignant case of *proceso-menemismo* is represented in the figure of Alfredo Yabran, a powerful entrepreneur who committed suicide in 1998 (the same year Diesel launched its campaign) when faced with accusations of having murdered the news photographer José Luis Cabezas. The trajectory of Yabran's career had benefited from a number of factors: his murky, thuggish dictatorship origins; unaccounted-for sources of wealth from the Proceso era; Menem-era business triumphs; close links to the government; the overlap between organized crime and "legitimate" business; and violence.

Michael Schudson, a communication and media theorist, has coined the term "capitalist realism" to capture the concept of symbolic structure produced by market-oriented societies. He contends that "abstraction is essential to the aesthetic and intention of contemporary national consumer-goods advertising. It does not represent reality nor does it build a fully fictive world. It exists, instead, on its own plane of reality, a plane I will call capitalist realism. By this term, I mean to label a set of aesthetic conventions, but I mean also to link them to political economy whose values they celebrate and promote."[31] Capitalist realism does not strive to represent reality as it is, but as it should be. It is "either cool, relishing understanding because it relies on common understanding with its audience, or sentimental, appealing openly to basic human feelings it is certain are already in place," and it "glorifies the pleasures and freedoms of consumer choice in defense of the virtues of private life and material ambitions."[32] Schudson concludes by parodying the "ideals" of "socialist realism," by claiming that the satisfaction that these ads should bring is not based on collective, but on private, values.

The Diesel and Ripley ads comply quite nicely with the demands of capitalist realism. They are communicating with an audience that is young, mostly 18–34 years of age, with whom they assume a mutual understanding. This understanding is based on the fact that the multifaceted and quite abstract decontextualized message will be read properly by those who "know" how to read. Consumers should feel unrestricted in their interpretation, and will feel empowered by that freedom. Chilean and Argentine consumers will also feel superior for being included in a global trend vis-à-vis their local reality of being members of a marginal nation. In other words, by absorbing these ads, and hopefully buying jeans that will help them look like the models portrayed in those ads, they are shaped by an MTV aesthetic that lifts them instantly from their own, never as interesting and always inadequate local reality. This satisfaction comes from what the MTV segment of the population finds in values associated with sexuality, hedonism, youth, beauty, and even irreverence to death. Thus, the inscription in the Diesel ad—"They are not your first jeans but they could be your last. At least you'll leave a beautiful corpse"—mocks loss in a most profane and eerie way. The tied-up, hanging upside down, and sensory-deprived bodies featured in the Ripley ads communicate with those young consumers, who feel defiant, provocative, and superior to the local social collective and its moral concerns.

When Diesel and Ripley marketing representatives expressed their surprise that human rights organizations should advance such a wrong reading, both companies emphasized that the local was not up to the task of interpreting the global. And so the global perceived the local in a paternalistic manner and tried to "help" it. For example, when a Diesel representative was asked if the company had ever been in trouble because of the theme of one of its campaigns, the answer was: "Yes. One campaign was for a new system of stone washing denim. In the ad, we showed models under water, with cement blocks tied to their feet. When we broke the campaign in Argentina, many people were sad and upset because during the *revolution*, young people were massacred in this way. But, we explained that it was not our intention, that this style is who we are. In the end, after we communicated in this way, they thought maybe it was good, because years later, we brought new attention to the tragedy."[33] The brutal military dictatorship, the state terrorism that resulted in shrouding the destiny of some 30,000 victims of the regime in the ambiguous folds of the term "disappeared," was labeled as "revolution." And the global fairy tale concocted by Diesel representatives also has a happy ending because allegedly their ad served as a positive memory trigger. This is not to say that Diesel's creative team and its marketing department purposefully intended to invoke the atrocities committed during the Argentine dictatorship. It does, however, suggest that they may have been careless in not understanding that a specific historical context (in this case, the atrocities committed by the state on its citizens) can leave profound emotional scars on survivors. The ad, then, becomes an attempt to capitalize on tragedy, and a cynical assertion that violence can be used to boost the sales of jeans.

In her research on memory in general and generational memory in particular, Elizabeth Jelin quotes Norbert Lechner's and Pedro Güell's proposal that "the politics of memory don't contribute in dispersing the ghosts of memory."[34] These ghosts of memory at times persist through photographic images, such as those of the ads in question, that still haunt the middle-class and elite sectors of Argentine and Chilean society. When Adolfo Scilingo publicly confessed his involvement with the gruesome practice of pushing live political prisoners out of planes during the military dictatorship, a rumor that had circulated in Argentina regarding the destiny of many of its citizens was finally confirmed. The rumor became fact. Phantoms that had haunted the nation became truth. Scilingo's exact words—"They were stripped naked and thrown into the waters of the South Atlantic from the planes during the flight"—became part of a discursive memory of the horror that the repressive state apparatus had employed.[35] However, there were no visual records of this practice and citizens were "free" to imagine the ghastly act for themselves. When the Diesel ad appeared, only three years after the confession, it functioned for some as a visual trigger of that discursive memory log, even though the photograph was staged, not the actual recording of the real moment of death, and it was models performing torture and death. In spite of the claim that the ad was "bringing new attention to the tragedy," Diesel cannot be considered a socially conscious marketer, and this "reading" is packed with aesthetic as well as ethical problems.

The stunningly beautiful Diesel images, along with Ripley's attractive and twisted models, exhibit bodies that should be in pain. Yet neither pain nor suffering is in evidence. The images are devoid of any visual marks of torture or distress, in spite of the context in which they are placed. In Ripley's case, the background does not reveal the location of the tied-up, heads-covered bodies, so they are decontextualized. Diesel, however, has established storytelling as part of its marketing strategy. But what is the story that Diesel is telling? The ad's visual imagery conveys the following: youthful, languid, and somewhat wistful human figures are underwater; their arms and legs are tied up and cement blocks are holding them down; some of them are already dead while others are close to dying. The tagline mentions death explicitly, thus confirming the visual impression. Furthermore, the verbal inscription is not even referring to bodies, but corpses. And while the visual image claims that it is important to be beautiful even at the moment of death, the verbal inscription underlies the significance of leaving behind an equally beautiful corpse. What leads to this kind of ending, in which it is not important that seven or eight models are elaborately staged to appear dead, but rather that they have left beautiful corpses? Is their death a consequence of violence or is it self-inflicted? Where are these decoding clues taking the viewer? How is the sadness of the dying youth to turn into pleasure for the viewer? Is the story completely arbitrary or is it open-ended? Or maybe the meaning is continually being deferred? After all, where is the referent?

For many middle- and upper-class readers older than those targeted by this ad, and especially for those who were the same age as the marketed segment—eighteen to thirty-four years old—during the dictatorship, the referent is ghostly.[36] To them, the Diesel ad mocks in the most profane and eerie way the loss associated with the rupture of their generation, with hundreds of bodies that were eliminated in such a way as not to leave any referential trace. The market that is fueled by this ad, consisting mostly of white, middle-class, elite, narcissistic, cynical, young, and blasé consumers, does not share this meaning. For them, the referent is behind the logo Diesel, and it denotes commodity: commoditized desires, meanings and images of the self. The past is not fashionable, they seem to say, let us live in the present and not search for any meaning beyond it. Every "next generation" strives to live better than its parents' generation. However, in societies that are marked by traumatic loss, the transmission of memory is often riddled with conflicts, particularly if the conflict occurred between different factions within the country. The Chilean dictatorship ended after a political pact had been forged between Pinochet, supported by the political Right (the military, a rich investor class, and many in the middle class), and the coalition of those who had opposed him on the basis of human rights violations. Since the specific terms of the pact were never made public, Chile's transition was problematic. The media emphasized from the beginning of the transition the need "to look forward and not look back, as well as portraying Pinochet as a figure of the past, as somebody who should be left by himself and forgotten."[37] This is clearly reflected in some of the blogs that appeared on the Internet as a response to a call for social action in regard to Ripley's ads. The blog posts are reproachful and critical of a historical interpretation that members of the previous generation, the one affected directly by Pinochet's dehumanizing measures, provided: "Whoever writes this is still stuck in the past," Mauricio Kris commented.[38] "It's a pity, instead, we should be living in the present and the future," he added. "We should stop looking towards the past," comments Jocelyn, while another Internet reader emphatically writes: "Enough with turning everything into an iconic past and relating it to what the country has been through. How should Chileans live? We, the children of democracy are fed up with stupid fights waged by all those who are filled with social resentment and who only want to divide and categorize people and mass media into *pinochetistas* and communists. How long do they want to go on with this? When will they stop poisoning us? Enough with nitpicking and searching for a secret message in a clothing catalogue! Enough is enough! Open your minds and let us live in peace!"[39] Ripley's representatives and CONAR pointed out that Amnesty International's reading of the ads did not reflect the opinion of the majority. In a recent interview regarding the use of these particular images in Ripley's advertising, Sergio Laurenti, a marketing executive, recognized that certain people, both young and old, past and present, are more sensitive to human rights violations, especially those who have experienced some form of it themselves. He quoted the popular Chilean refrain, translated as "When you burn yourself with scalding milk, you see a cow and cry."

Advertising campaigns, particularly those which use the kinds of shock tactics Diesel and Ripley engage in, make the targeted segment of the population believe that they are not only buying jeans, but also a way of life. What seems to be projected in these ads is a death appeal. However, when issues such as love, life, happiness, and even death are transformed into commodities, their meaning is lost. And when they are subordinated to consumption, it is because of the conviction that the investment of money, a simple exchange of pesos into jeans—the measure of how well one is doing—will bring the fictional moment portrayed in the ad campaign to the "investor." Consequently, every product has a symbolic value attached to its material value, and Diesel and Ripley strive to distinguish their jeans from those of their competitors by creating imaginary, fictional contexts and riddles. Intentionally or not (one can never neglect the ambiguous nature of postmodernism), they also tell the story of the violence of capital itself. Diesel ads in Argentina reflect neoliberal violence (most specifically, the economic links between the dictatorship and the years of the Menem government in the 1990s), and the history on which that violence is drawn. Nevertheless, the term "capitalist realism" also describes the aesthetic and ideology in which images, as an outcome of the imaginary, become the model of reality. The Diesel and Ripley logos establish a frame of reference that decontextualizes reality and, in the words of the postmodern theorist Jean Baudrillard, denotes the end of history. Fredric Jameson uses a more flexible term: the "weakening of historicity." In either case, the assumption is that in postmodernism, history becomes a reservoir from which anything can be extracted and interpreted according to the context established by the interpreter, and not the context in which the event took place. Ahistoricity leads to an obliteration of social engagement. So, for the target generation of eighteen- to thirty-four-year-olds, "death as a beautiful cadaver" is not a real death, but a provocative juxtaposition, and the reference to historically confirmed death flights is nonexistent.

Fredric Jameson noted that culture undergoes a transformation in capitalism when he wrote: "In postmodern culture, 'culture' has become a product in its own right. The market has become a substitute for itself and fully as much a commodity as any of the items it includes within itself. . . . Postmodernism is the consumption of sheer commodification as a process."[40] Thus, the logic of late capitalism constructs identity through consumption, and not through human relationships.

Sarlo supplies a number of Argentine examples in her volume of essays, *Escenas de la vida posmoderna*, and in *Instantáneas*, and concludes that her country, marginalized in relation to the First World, is going through a process of cultural homogenization, whose main characteristic is extreme individualism, manifested in what market forces have named "youth culture," and in the social imaginary, which contains two kinds of ghosts: "limitless freedom of choice as an abstract confirmation of individuality and programmed individualism."[41] One glance at the Diesel and Ripley ads shows that there is no communication between individuals. The faces of the group underwater in the Diesel ad are turned away from one another. While in Ripley's construction, each individual is focused on the contortions of his or her own body; even the dominatrix's gaze is directed toward the viewer, not toward the tied-up "victims" who are also within the frame, although they should logically be the focus of her interest. In some cases, for example in Diesel's emphasis on "different washes" of jeans—a technique that gives them the impression of being worn out—(imaginary and programmed) individuality is transposed through the idea that such jeans have already been broken in by someone (a beautiful model?), and thus have a certain (fictional) identity imprinted on them.

I have already mentioned that all the models in the Diesel and Ripley ads are beautiful. The identification that real Argentine and Chilean consumers establish with the realm of the (global) imaginary is partially conducted through beauty, and is based on the fact that beauty is just another consumable commodity. Elaine Scarry, a theorist who not only tackles the issues of torture, but of beauty as well, argues in her 1999 study, *On Beauty and Being Just*, that "beauty brings copies of itself into being."[42] While cynical consumers take eerie, hyper-real settings like those in the Ripley and Diesel ads as fictional, and not as a literal prescription for acting out in everyday life, they are, however, touched by the (digitally produced) beauty of the models in a more direct way. Consumers simulate the copies of the adjusted, somewhat altered, images of beautiful models (originals in that sense never existed), thus enacting the process of never-ending simulation, just as Baudrillard predicted.

In *Regarding the Pain of Others*, Sontag proposes that creating beautiful images in photographs "tends to bleach out a moral response to what is shown."[43] In his discussion of "moral and political concerns about conjunction of beauty and suffering," the visual critic Mark Reinhardt ponders if maybe "beauty breeds passivity." "Perhaps," he suggests, "by beautifying suffering, photographs cannot help but urge us to want the scene before our eyes always to remain just as it is."[44] However, Reinhardt tries to see if beauty is necessarily detrimental in provoking indignation. The kind of beauty that is depicted in Diesel's ad could fall into the category of elegiac photographic images, because this kind of representation and organization of beauty "gives sorrow public form and enables it to become shared, thereby helping to constitute a community of mourners. . . . This response can elevate death's importance and lend it meaning. It can prompt deep reflection."[45] However, even a quick glance at the ad in question will reveal the Diesel logo and an anything-but-elegiac tagline. Furthermore, there is no community of mourners that can ever be constituted by Diesel's ad, because the targeted community of shoppers does not reflect on the suffering of the other, as the elegiac depiction demands. Neither is the ad constructed in such a way as to solicit an acknowledgment of the suffering of the other. Reinhardt uses the work of the philosopher Stanley Cavell, who distinguished between the knowledge that one has of the suffering of the other and the actual acknowledgment of it.[46] He proposes that when one is confronted with human suffering, "the acknowledgement of another calls for recognition of the other's specific relation to oneself." This is in line with Elaine Scarry's theorizing of representation of pain. She contends that the presence of a weapon (such as those used in torture or war) in a spoken sentence, a written paragraph, or a visual image (such as in fashion photography or painting) "does not mean that there has been any attempt to present pain and, on the contrary, often means that the nature of pain has just been pushed into deeper obscurity."[47] In spite of what Diesel's representatives constructed, in view of the protests by human rights organizations, Diesel had no altruistic motives in representing dying, helpless (and beautiful) youth, nor were they soliciting outrage in their audience. No emotional affect was intended to be provoked, and no one was expected to shed a tear after looking at this image.

The images that constitute the advertisements for Ripley's jeans are ambiguous in presenting beautiful, athletic youth in gymnastics performance and torture spiced up with a domination scenario. Ripley's representational strategies are geared toward more "realistic" settings than Diesel's depiction of drowning youth. The three languid bodies extended from the hooks on the ceiling yet touching the floor, heads dangling to one side, as well as the image of a man with tied-up wrists and ankles, a sack pulled over his head, and hanging from the ceiling, are probably the most explicit references to torture techniques. The interpretation of these images purposefully falls to the viewer. Some will certainly embrace the domination fantasy. However, one should not neglect the fact that the purpose of advertising is to connect a particular product (jeans in this case) with the imagination of certain segments of the population. Market research determines what will attract that specific targeted group of most-probable consumers. And in the cases of Diesel and Ripley, it is definitely the age group portrayed in these ads, basically eighteen- to thirty-four-year-olds. Despite the statements that Diesel and Ripley issued after the controversy broke out, it is clear they are not proposing any change, nor are they assisting in the process of mourning. Corporations such as Diesel and Ripley are not in the business of raising social consciousness; they are in the business of promoting their brand. Shopping will not save the world, and wearing Diesel and Ripley jeans is not promoting the policy of remembering. And although the settings for their ads are surreal, imaginative, and even artistic, their fashion conventions remain unchallenged: their models continue to be beautiful, slender, and attractive.

The other segment of the population, Argentines and Chileans who have firsthand knowledge of the dictatorship or those who uphold an ethical imperative of remembering it, do not see the beauty in the ads, but possibly, the sublime. What complicates the reading of these images as sublime is their framing through particular brands. There is no doubt whatsoever regarding Diesel's and Ripley's motives in using these images: they are not intended to raise social consciousness, to mobilize rage. They are interested in raising profits. The rage that some readers of journals and newspapers felt after seeing the ads, and the disgust that prompted them to write blogs or articles in dailies, are in direct response to the fact that the ads are used in order to sell goods: jeans, to be more precise. They do not acknowledge the suffering that one would actually endure if one were actually tortured. But the Diesel and Ripley ads are not in the business of engaging the historical memory of Chile and Argentina. However, if we could see the pictures without an advertising framework, or only artistically, it might be possible to see them as the traumatic sublime.

Based on Kant's discussion of the category of the sublime, the moment in which a human being has reached the limits of his or her imagination, Kimberly Wedeven Segall has developed the notion of the "traumatic sublime" as "a troubling sensation that occurs when a painful event of the past is changed into a disturbing image."[48] This phenomenon occurs when "experiences of violence are changed into images of oppressed subjects and ghosts. These images of ghostly figures serve as troubling *memory sites*."[49] The sublime refers to poignant images that provoke fear and terror. The Diesel ad, with its somber, bluish tones and its uncanny floating figures that are either dead or dying, their heads unnaturally twisted away, has a ghostly quality inscribed in it. It is a morbid simulation, something Baudrillard cynically calls "the succulent imminence of death."[50] The verbal inscription reinforces the phantasmagoric nature of the representation by explicitly pairing the concept of beauty with the corpse. The ghostly quality of Ripley's ads lies in their aquatic backgrounds that disperse uncanny white light; in the positions in which figures defy gravity; in the robotic figures whose faces are covered with white face masks; and in the proximity of death, depicted in the ropes hanging from the ceiling. The effect that these images produce is particularly unsettling given the histories of Chile and Argentina—the fact that there are thousands of disappeared citizens whose bodies were never buried and who *are known* to have undergone a violent death. But there is a crucial difference between going through the ritual of burying a loved one and knowing that the person was killed, because he has not been seen alive. In that sense, paradoxically, what was taken away from the thousands of victims of state terrorism in Chile and Argentina is precisely their death. And whereas they were all deprived of their deaths as legal narratives—they were *disappeared*—their families were dispossessed of the right of habeas corpus. While, according to Kant, beauty is an objective experience, the experience of the sublime is subjective and related to the effect that is produced in the viewer. Thus, the identity of these nontargeted viewers, whose relation to the violent past is inscribed in the trauma of so many unresolved deaths, is altered by the ghostly depictions in the ads. The past comes alive in the present and haunts them through the images of imminent death. And unlike those other spectators, unburdened by the existence of the past, these viewers do "read" pain that is not reflected, but refracted, in the photographs. Edmund Burke, who also dedicated a significant part of his work to the discussion of the concept of the sublime, argues that the source of the sublime is "whatever is fitted in any sort to excite the ideas of pain, and danger, that is to say, whatever is in any sort terrible. . . . That is, it is productive of the strongest emotion which the mind is capable of feeling. I say the strongest emotion because I am satisfied the ideas of pain are much more powerful that those which enter on the part of pleasure. Without all doubt, the torments which we may be made to suffer, are much greater in their effect on the body and mind, than any pleasures."[51]

In a paradoxical way, the Diesel and Ripley photographs are a kind of historical evidence of the crimes that haunt Argentine and Chilean society and that were never visually recorded. As Susan Sontag brilliantly observed, they are impure, just like most historical evidence.[52] At the same time, that evidence may establish a role for the ads as countermonuments, or perhaps even true monuments, to the victims of the Proceso, where the monument does not build a wall between dictatorship and what came after, but rather, reflects on continuities through the fall of dictatorship in 1983.

The ads are apparitional, and as such, they produce emotional, affective recognition and animate certain segments of the society. They conjure up, evoke the "reading" that was not intended by the makers, an interpretation that is ghostly because it represents what is absent. The spectral language of the disappeared victims lingers in the present and future. It carries the message that does not fit comfortably in the mold of a utopian "Never Again."

"The memory of war, however, like all memory, is mostly local," wrote Susan Sontag in her essays *Regarding the Pain of Others*.[53] And while the state terrorism of the Argentine and Chilean past could be viewed through the prism of the local, as the advertising executives are suggesting, the problem seems also to be related to the transmission of intergenerational memory and the paradoxes associated with postmodernism, mainly its openness toward ambiguity and contradiction. Baudrillard argued in *The Illusion of the End* that in our postmodern society, "nothing is news if it does not pass through that horizon of the virtual . . . as real to be consumed as unreal."[54] Thus, reality is processed through the mass media ultimately turning into a simulacrum, which is devoid of any relation to reality. The past ceases to be "real" and it translates into a pure rhetoric. The advertising industry challenges reality by producing an unreal, simulated reality. It creates memory-free consumers of that simulacrum through abolition of the referent. The images created by Diesel and Ripley, devoid of any expressions of suffering, suggest that torture and killing by drowning are something natural for human beings. They imply that this kind of tragedy, even though it is provoked by other humans, cannot be avoided.

Photographs as a medium, on the other hand, displace the real and offer a possibility of remembering the referent at the fleeting moment in which the shot was taken. While staged photographs have a different relation to the real, the implication that the photographic medium carries the truth remains. In societies such as Argentina and Chile, where thousands of human referents were disappeared through the repressive state apparatus that used torture as a primary technique of domination, they haunt the present with their ghostly presence and resurface in memory, resisting assimilation into the narrative of loss. The question that remains is for how long will anyone remember? This question is even more relevant in view of the recent discussion in the *New York Times* regarding the interrogation methods and definitions of torture. A psychologist, Dr. Randy Borum, is quoted as saying: "We [the marketing industry] have a whole social science literature on persuasion. . . . It's mostly on how to get a person to buy a certain brand of toothpaste. But it certainly could be useful in improving interrogation."[55] And if interrogation can be improved, oblivion could also be accelerated, and that would definitely lead to a time in which there wouldn't be anyone to hear the calls from the past.

NOTES

1. Sontag, *On Photography*, 54.
2. Ibid., 154.
3. While not all sectors of Argentine society were equally shaped by the violence of the atrocities, the nation was affected by the trauma for years to come.
4. Diesel Denim, "Advertisement," June 4, 2007, www.motherjones.com.
5. Staff, "Catálogo de multitienda Ripley hace parodia de la tortura como instrumento

de marketing," *Clarín*, 9 March 2006. This is one of several articles that appeared in the Argentine and Chilean press voicing objections to Ripley's marketing techniques. In this particular example, the choice of words was "*banalización*." While there are often arguments regarding some problematic tropes of Holocaust art, such as those that dominated the press after the premieres of Lina Wertmuller's *Seven Beauties* (1975) or Roberto Benini's *Life is Beautiful* (1997), I found no evidence of anyone arguing for the subversive potential of Ripley's marketing techniques.

6. Mat Honan, "Death Squad Chic," *Mother Jones*, 26 May 1998, www.motherjones.com/commentary/columns/1998/05/honan.html?welcome=true>.Honan. When apprised of research for this chapter, one of the mothers from the Asociación Madres de Plaza de Mayo responded by suggesting that the study should be stopped: like the ad itself, an analysis of the episode would reopen old wounds unnecessarily. This is not the first occasion on which the Madres have positioned themselves as arbiters of present morality with regard to past human rights abuses. In 1999, the great anti-authoritarian rocker Charly García planned a concert for Buenos Aires in which he proposed to commemorate the Proceso-era dumping of half-dead prisoners by the military into the Rio de la Plata. García wanted helicopters to fly overhead, from which sandbags would be cut loose to fall into the river. When Hebe de Bonafini, the leader of the Madres, got wind of the plan, she instructed García that his commemoration was inappropriate (see Carlos Polimeni, "El deber de la amplitud," *Página/12*, 21 February 1999; and Juan Carlos Feinmann, "Charly, otro Argentino genial," *Página/12*, 21 February 1999, www.pagina12.com.ar/1999/99-02/99-02-21/pag27.htm).
7. "Ya no venderán jeans con una publicidad macabre," *Página/12*, 5 May 1998, www.pagina12.com.ar/1998/98-05/98-05-05/pag18.htm.
8. Quoted in ibid.
9. Quoted in ibid.
10. Advertising Standards Authority, Agency Lowe Howard-Spink, "Diesel Publicity," 2007, www.asa.org.uk/statistics/1998/top10/advertisers98/diesel_98.asp.
11. Pedro Alejandro Matta, "Chile: La tortura en Ripley como factor de ventas," *Piel de leopardo: Cultura y política latinoamericana*, March 2006, www.pieldeleopardo.com/modules.php?name=News&file=article&sid=1973.
12. Ibid.
13. While the mobilization did not permeate *all* social strata of Argentine and Chilean society, a significant action occurred among those who were in tune with human rights issues.
14. Rodrigo Albagli and Guillermo Rivas Sureda, "Chile: Case Report (1)," March 2006, http://gala-marketlaw.com/pdf/2006/Chile.pdf.
15. Ibid.
16. Amnistía Internacional, "Ripley retirará publicidad ofensiva," *El clarín de Chile*, 10 March 2006, www.elclarin.cl/index.php?option=com_content&task=view&id=2072&Itemid=45.
17. Patricia Kolesnicov, "El horror como materia prima: Usan la tortura para vender jeans," *El clarín*, 17 March 2006, www.clarin.com/diario/2006/03/17/sociedad/s-04201.htm.

18. Ibid.
19. Ibid.
20. Ibid.
21. "Debunking the Status Quo with Diesel," *One: A Magazine* 7, no. 3 (2004), http://www.oneclub.org/oc/magazine/articles/?id=18>.
22. Ibid.
23. Diesel website, 2006, www.diesel.com.
24. Quoted in Bonnie Tsui, "New Diesel ads put focus on Africa," *Advertising Age* 72, no. 6 (2001): 12.
25. It may be argued that irreverence to authority marks precisely the sort of cultural democracy that opponents of dictatorship once sought in Argentina and Chile. At the same time, this chapter makes no pretense of trying to determine democracy's scale, but rather to show how market-driven societies have created a sense of freedom of choice regarding historical events. This tendency might well be attributed to a deconstructionist approach, where "everything is a text" and where the truth can be found solely in the subject's account and accounting of it.
26. McCann Worldgroup website, 2006, http://www.mccann.com/.
27. The cultural theorist Idelber Avelar establishes a very pertinent connection between neoliberal politics and memory. According to his argument, "mercantilism denies memory because the goal of every new product is to replace the old one, send it to the dumpster of history. The market operates according to the logic of substitution and metaphor according to which the past is always about to become obsolete." Since transnational capitalism in Latin America took this logic to an extreme, "the past needs to be forgotten because the market requires that the new replace the old without any residue" (Avelar, *Alegorías de la derrota*, 285).
28. Sarlo, *Instantáneas*, 49–50.
29. Ibid., 59.
30. Sheinin, *Argentina and the United States*, 163–64.
31. Schudson, *Advertising, the Uneasy Persuasion*, 4.
32. Ibid., 6.
33. "Debunking the Status Quo with Diesel," *One: A Magazine* 7, no. 3 (2004), www.oneclub.org/oc/magazine/articles/?id=18> (emphasis added).
34. Jelin, *Los trabajos de la memoria*, 132.
35. Quoted in Verbitsky, *The Flight*, 8.
36. The voices that appeared in online discussions and blogs identified themselves as either activists during the dictatorship or defenders of human rights issues.
37. Pedro Alejandro Matta, "Memory across Generations: The Future of Never Again" (paper presented at the Memory across Generations Conference, Buenos Aires, 10–12 October 2002).
38. Quoted in Andrés Bianque, "La tortura como moda," *Granvalparaiso, Diario Libertario y Pluralista*, 11 March 2006, www.granvalparaiso.cl/publimedios/publicidad/tortura.htm.
39. Quoted in ibid.
40. Jameson, *Postmodernism, or, The Cultural Logic of Late Capitalism*, x.

41. Sarlo, *Escenas de la vida posmoderna*, 9.
42. Scarry, *On Beauty and Being Just*, 3.
43. Sontag, *Regarding the Pain of Others*, 81.
44. Reinhardt, "Picturing Violence," 29.
45. Ibid., 30.
46. Ibid., 31.
47. Scarry, *The Body in Pain*, 18.
48. Wedeven Segall, "Pursuing Ghosts," 42.
49. Ibid.
50. Baudrillard, *The Illusion of the End*, 55.
51. Quoted in Vieira, "Torture and the Sublime," 10.
52. Sontag, *Regarding the Pain*, 51.
53. Ibid., 32.
54. Baudrillard, *Illusion of the End*, 55.
55. Scott Shane and Mark Mazzetti, "Interrogation Methods are Criticized," *New York Times*, 30 May 2007.

SUSANA KAISER

Memory Inventory

The Production and Consumption of Memory Goods in Argentina

Thursday afternoon at the Plaza de Mayo, the Madres hold their weekly march, and several members attend to a stand around which a crowd gathers to buy products—ranging from books to key rings. On a sunny Sunday morning, tourists explore the street market of San Telmo, where an artist sells his photographs; one photograph portrays tango dancers, several others project the "memory theme" of the Madres' marches. Monday night after a performance of the Teatro X la Identidad (a project developed by the Abuelas de Plaza de Mayo), the public buys T-shirts outside of a downtown theater. On a windy Saturday afternoon, under the highway that replaced Club Atlético, a center for torture and extermination, dozens of people attend the inauguration of a new "espacio para la memoria," and activists from H.I.J.O.S. (Hijos Por la Identidad y la Justicia Contra el Olvido y el Silencio) concurrently sell T-shirts and calendars. The list goes on.

The above vignettes portray the city of Buenos Aires during the last months of 2007, the year that marked the thirtieth anniversary of the Madres and the Abuelas de Plaza de Mayo. Three decades of persistent and courageous campaigns by activists, and a series of political measures taken by the Kirchner administration, have brought human rights and memory issues to the forefront of Argentina's political agenda. A monument to the victims of state terrorism stands in the Parque de la Memoria. And society challenges the culture of impunity, both by prosecuting torturers and assassins and by recovering former torture chambers as spaces for memory

Figure 1. Madres de Plaza de Mayo bookstand at their weekly Thursday marches, September 2007. (Photograph by Laurie Beth Clark and Michael Peterson)

(e.g., the infamous ESMA, planned to house cultural and educational institutes run by human rights organizations).

The strong presence of this traumatic past in the public sphere, in an environment of trials and commemorations, creates a multilayered socio-political space for the production, giving, selling, and consumption of memory products/artifacts. This chapter inventories these products—a broad category of memory-message carriers that includes books, DVDs, videos, CD-ROMs, and appointment books, as well as souvenirs and memorabilia, such as T-shirts, key rings, calendars, mugs, posters, money clips, and magnets. It examines both the makers and the consumers of these objects, identifying who benefits, who buys, and what motivates the buying of these objects.

Framing the Discussion

This chapter focuses on the process by which these products come to embody the past; the messages transmitted through them; and the effects of buying, using, and collecting memory artifacts on both the construction and the transmission of memories. I argue that human rights organizations and institutions largely control the production of memory artifacts. While the marketing of memory messages may or may not include the exchange of money, identifying the makers and consumers of these memory carriers helps to explain the political economy of memory. The following questions guide my analysis: What do individuals, organizations, and institutions sell? What will they never sell? How do these memory products interlink with struggles for truth and justice? How do they contribute to maintaining the memories of state terrorism? Are memories of the dictatorship becoming a commodity? Should we categorize these items as memory prods or memory kitsch? To frame the discussion, I consider the historical/mnemonic context; the marketing of memory; the consumption of the past; and the producers of memory goods.

The Historical/Mnemonic Context

As memories evolve over time, memory as an ongoing construction process must be analyzed within a specific historical, mnemonic, political, and cultural environment—in this case, the year 2007. During the last months of 2007 many debates, talks, conferences, and workshops centered on memories of the dictatorship. Discussions focused on this area revealed recurrent subjects: revolutionary activism, monuments, museums, and memory's presence in film and the arts.[1] Moreover, in 2007 the official memory discourse mirrored that of the Argentine human rights movement, characterized by strong alliances with, and official fiscal support from, federal and local government.

This historical moment in Argentina confirms that there are waves of interest when remembering violent periods. The most important events in one's memory occur between the late teens and early twenties.[2] On average, monuments, exhibits, and/or films depicting historical events emerge 20–25 years after an experience.[3] One explanation for this phenomenon is that people try to distance themselves from devastating events immediately after they occur. A second, and compatible, explanation highlights the fact that after two or three decades, those directly responsible for the repression have withdrawn from public life.[4] I offer an additional explanation: the process of remembering develops not only as a consequence of time, but also in response to particular political events. In the case of the year 2007, efforts in Argentina to put perpetrators on trial reawakened memory around the events that had transformed citizens' lives thirty years earlier. Additionally, by 2007, the generation that had been terrorized by the military regime had acquired the political power to follow through on reengaging the memory project. In the broader political climate, however, not only does this particular generation remember, but also society as a whole has begun to reconstruct memory. Both the witnesses to the dictatorship and the younger generations have committed themselves to preserving its memories and thereby shaping the present wave of remembering. Youth has thus become central to societal organization, and new generations act as primary fabricators of mnemonic sites.[5] Activists, such as H.I.J.O.S. members and others belonging to the post-dictatorship generation, engage in reconstructing memories of this past, both producing and consuming memory messages and goods.

The Marketing of Memory

The marketing of memories of state terrorism calls for considerations of message and product consumption. The critical citizen of reasoned judgment has turned into a consumer of packaged images and messages; consumption is a trait of our identity.[6] Indeed, consumerism is so central to our culture that we pride ourselves on being politically correct consumers: we discuss conscious consumption and pay attention to how our buying affects our societies; and we buy green products, boycott sweatshop-produced merchandise, and shop for "red™ products," when profits go to causes in which we believe. As consumption in contemporary society has become a form of sociopolitical participation, we need to analyze what and why we consume.[7]

Beyond the consumption of material goods lies the consumption of ideas—the focus of both political and social marketing. In presidential campaigns, for example, candidates aim to sell their qualities and to convince citizens that their election will contribute to the well-being of the nation. Similarly, human rights activists aim to persuade society and governments that truth and justice are essential for democracy. Social marketing campaigns employ strategies similar to those used for selling soft drinks, but aimed specifically at consumption for the purpose of changing behavior. Likewise, the marketing of memories of state terrorism has several goals. In an environment where different versions of the past compete for hegemony, human rights activists aim to broaden support for their specific points of view and demands. Through consumption, they encourage the adoption of their ideological positions, hoping to modify behavior by prompting society to participate in their struggle.

The Consumption of the Past

The marketing and consumption of the past is done via "not-for-profit" and "for-profit" ventures. First, there exists a marketing of the memory message that does not involve selling goods. For example, the Asociación Madres de Plaza de Mayo organized an exhibit of books by disappeared writers at ESMA,[8] and the museum of memory in Montevideo owns a collection of objects that were made by prisoners as souvenirs. The proliferation of memorabilia sold around the world illustrates the profitable side of marketing and consumption, the focus of this analysis. "Souvenir society" thrives through the commodification of nostalgia. While this commodification proliferates around the world,[9] in Latin America, the effort to turn the image of Che Guevara into profit-making merchandise provides one key example. Alberto Korda's photo of the heroic guerrilla, one of the most-reproduced images in the world, can be found on tank tops, mugs, flip-flops, and beyond. Moreover, the public broadly allows for the business of profit-making through historical reproduction, as evidenced in storytelling products ranging from paperbacks to film.[10] Although I do not focus on books and films in this chapter, we should be aware of the business of memory in relation to such memory products.[11]

Producers of Memory Artifacts

The act of consumption, whether of ideas or material goods, requires two main actors: producers and consumers. There are several producers of memory messages and goods, including official representatives. The state shapes official memories and versions of history that may evolve or devolve, depending on the government in power. Its institutions produce messages that may or may not clash with human rights activists. In 1984 in Argentina, at the beginning of civilian rule, the rhetoric of "two demons" was the prevalent official discourse, which referenced the violence of the state as a response to the violence of guerrilla organizations. In 2007, however, official memory was advancing the agenda of the human rights movement, which emphasized that rather than "two demons," in Argentina there exists (1) the victims of state terrorism; and (2) those guilty of crimes against humanity, who must be prosecuted.[12] On the other hand, civil society is active in the production of memory messages that may support or counter official versions of memory. Producers range from human rights groups to the media, from artists to academics. The transmission of memories in a society devastated by state terrorism involves everyone, even those who promote amnesia. Memory battles thus take place in several cultural realms and through various media, including the products discussed here.[13]

This chapter focuses on a selection of producers from three main categories. The first category includes human rights organizations comprised of relatives of the desaparecidos. These include the Madres de Plaza de Mayo (the mothers of the disappeared), which has divided into two groups: the Asociación Madres de Plaza de Mayo—the group I analyze here—and the Madres de Plaza de Mayo Línea Fundadora, which is not part of this analysis. They also include the Abuelas de Plaza de Mayo (the grandmothers of the disappeared); and H.I.J.O.S. (the adult daughters and sons of the disappeared, murdered political activists, or activists forced into exile). The second category includes human rights institutions, illustrated by the Instituto Espacio para la Memoria (IEM) and Memoria Abierta. And the third category involves independent artists, consisting of photographers and a fashion designer.

Mapping the Memory Products/Artifacts

Human rights organizations and institutions actively pursue truth and justice. They link their messages, their activities, and the artifacts that they produce. Similarly, independent producers create memories with their work, both drawing on activists' campaigns and incorporating their own perspectives. A variety of symbols, images, and words transmit memory messages: discourses, events, and objects. They thus become the material carriers of diverse historical, cultural, and mnemonic meaning in which memory "takes root":[14] they are the "technologies of memory" through which "memories are shared, produced, and given meaning."[15]

A variety of cultural products represent memory of the dictatorship. These objects reinforce specific representations of this past, encouraging memory or forgetting.[16] Moreover, human rights organizations' messages are not frozen in the past, but are dynamic and dependent on the political climate and other surrounding circumstances. They make constant and changing links to the present. Human rights organizations thus avoid a nostalgic and sterile use of the dictatorship: theirs is a memory at the service of justice—the exemplary memory defined by Todorov.[17] Their products consequently reflect these evolving and interactive messages.

Human Rights Organizations

ASOCIACIÓN MADRES DE PLAZA DE MAYO. This group produces and sells the most memory artifacts. Their products link to the Madres' activism. Prompted by the military regime's illegal detention and disappearance of their children during the 1970s, the Madres demand accountability for the past and engage in new activities that continue the commitment of their disappeared children to social change. The products sold by the Madres include coffee mugs, T-shirts, key rings, magnets, postcards, posters, appointment books, buttons, and money clips. They also sell books and videos/DVDs, which are not all produced by or directly linked to the cause of the Madres. This merchandise is sold in two main locations: their bookstore and at a stand in Plaza de Mayo during their weekly Thursday marches. The memory merchandise that the Madres produce and/or sell must be further contextualized by their activities and projects, including: the weekly marches; a university, publishing house, bookstore, and coffee shop all founded in their name; their cultural center Nuestros Hijos in the School of Officers building of ESMA; and their housing construction program.

The white kerchief, meant to invoke the diapers of their children, has become not only a branding symbol of the Madres' struggle, but also the quintessential memory symbol of the Argentine human rights movement. Alluding to the strong mother-child link, the Madres wear it as a form of identification at all of their public appearances. This practice began with the annual pilgrimage to the Virgin of Luján in 1976, where they first collectively denounced the disappearances of their children by the military regime. Initially, they wore actual cloth diapers on their heads.[18] Later, they replaced the diapers with white kerchiefs. Posters, publications, and all the Asociación's products reproduce this logo. It is also drawn on sidewalks and other surfaces where the Madres hold public appearances: an inscription of their struggle that marks the urban landscape.[19]

Over the years, the Madres have employed some mottos, one of which, "We want them alive," they inscribe on their kerchiefs. This motto summarizes their raison d'être; it is a statement calling for truth as a first and necessary step to justice. This rhetoric embodies many meanings: their insistence that the desaparecidos taken alive must reappear alive; the expectation that those who kidnapped them, those who gave orders, and those who tortured and raped them must be exposed; and the idea that the respective families have a right to know the details of the desaparecidos' fate.[20]

As long as those guilty for the crimes against their children remain free, the Asociación says it will consistently refuse reparations, offers of exhumation, and monuments. Other mottos thus portray the Madres' continuing demands for accountability: "We won't forget, we won't forgive, we won't falter," and "No to exhumations; no to economic reparations; no to posthumous homages." In parallel with these mottos, which express their central demands, the Madres also employ mottos in solidarity with other causes and movements. Examples include "No to the payment of the foreign debt," "Freedom for political prisoners," and "Democracy with hunger and impunity is a joke."

The memory carriers produced by the Asociación employ both their symbols and their mottos. All are adorned with the white kerchief, either used alone or in multiples forming a semicircle. Most of the T-shirts, key rings, magnets, buttons, money clips, and coffee mugs sold by the Madres also portray this white kerchief, or a semicircle of kerchiefs, over a blue background, and bearing the organization's name. One example, the image of the kerchiefs marching around a stool with a military cap on it, implies a metaphorical trial of the military by the Madres. In 2007, some of the products (such as money clips and magnets) placed the semicircle of kerchiefs around the iconographic image of Che Guevara with his black beret and a red star. While the Madres have always publicly professed their admiration for this revolutionary leader, this design explicitly links the Madres with Che, thereby uniting two powerful icons of Latin American political imaginary in a single product. The Madres also link imagery with mottos; for example, they sell key rings with the kerchief and the motto "Not a single step backward," and T-shirts with the kerchiefs encircling the military cap and the motto "30 years of life defeating death."

The Madres' publications include coffee-table books, books about their history, books of poems, a magazine, and other printed material, such as appointment books, posters, and postcards. These products, containing photographs of the Madres, usually document different facets of their activism. Such images act as a reminder of the scope and style of the Madres' struggle, and the diverse arenas in which it takes place—for example, at marches, in confrontations with military officers, at meetings with world leaders, or at rock concerts. The Madres' images also adorn postcards and posters created by artists who have supported their struggle by donating these pieces.

The annual appointment books reflect the changes in the scope of the Madres' activism over time. In 1992, a time of weak prospects for justice, the inscriptions in the notebook reaffirmed the crusade for accountability. By 2007, the Asociación was endorsing the administration's official human rights policies, declaring that the government was no longer its enemy. On their thirtieth anniversary, the Madres' messages proclaimed their commitment to social change and the redress of injustice through the building of low-cost housing financed by the government. The site of the first of these projects, located in a shantytown, is called the "White Kerchief Neighborhood." Through this project, women and men are paid to develop construction skills and build their own houses. They thus become homeowners and also learn skills that will allow their reinsertion into the labor market.

The 2008 appointment book conveys the impact of the housing project "Sueños Compartidos" (Shared Dreams) on that community. Its images featured the neighborhood's transformation: mothers and workers/owners at the construction site, children at the kindergarten, a crowded cafeteria. Participants in the project, expressing how it had changed their lives, authored the inscriptions: "I am proud that, finally, I feel that I'm a model for my children"—"The Madres gave back to us the desire for living. I am 25 years old and never thought that I would enjoy so much waking up at 6 A.M."—"It's hard to tear down what is built with the heart." Participants also wrote mottos both about the past (the dictatorship), and about political matters affecting contemporary Argentina, such as "Jail for genocide," "The lack of jobs is a crime," and "We struggle for Latin American unity and against imperialism."

The white kerchief sometimes appears on construction helmets these days. The construction of the housing projects has emerged as one outcome of three decades of activism. This "manifesto" about teaching people how to build proclaims that, for the Madres, activism and memory link to contemporary issues and proposals to solve problems. It shows that their memory is not frozen in place or time, but rather connects past injustices with those of the present. This project also illustrates a fruitful collaboration between the organization and the government, which was absent in earlier eras.

ABUELAS DE PLAZA DE MAYO. For over thirty years, the Abuelas de Plaza de Mayo have searched for their stolen grandchildren, mostly born in clandestine detention centers to disappeared mothers. This search has involved the development of several strategies, including obstinate detective work and media campaigns. Since the seized babies have now grown into young adults (in 2007, most would have been around thirty years old), the Abuelas concentrate their efforts on reaching young people, encouraging individuals born during the dictatorship and doubtful of their identity to contact the Abuelas or CONADI (the Comisión Nacional para el Derecho a la Identidad). These first steps can then be followed by DNA testing and confirmation of identity. At the beginning of 2009, ninety-seven of the estimated five hundred children seized as the spoils of war had recuperated their identity.[21]

Identity is at the core of the Abuelas' activism and it remains the focus of their memory messages. Their goal is to create awareness in Argentine society that four hundred young people, many of them appropriated by military families, remain missing. A double task, of reaching the public with appealing messages and of educating the public about state terrorism, characterizes this search for identity. The carriers of these messages range from books to theater performances, from television programs to sports and music activities. Posters, print ads, radio spots, and television commercials promote these active campaigns through the slogan: "If you doubt your identity."[22] The official and private funding given to the Abuelas, including from foreign sources, makes possible the production of printed material, as this organization does not sell merchandise. The books and other publications produced by the Abuelas are provided free of charge.[23] However, collaborators do make and sell products designed to honor the Abuelas and to raise money for their cause.

The Abuelas have several publications, including their (print and online) monthly bulletin *Mensuario* and various books. In commemoration of their thirtieth anniversary, in 2007, they compiled data and images documenting the organization's history and achievements, which they published in three books. The first, *La historia de las abuelas: 30 años de búsqueda*, describes the varying political contexts in which the Abuelas' searches have taken place. The second, *Abuelas de Plaza de Mayo: Fotografías de 30 años en lucha*, is a small coffee-table book with scenes of family gatherings, recuperated grandchildren meeting their relatives, everyday work at the Abuelas' offices, marches, events honoring the Abuelas, and the For Identity projects (discussed below). A visual mosaic of the Abuelas' struggle, it combines the public and the more intimate moments of their activities. The third book, *Niños desaparecidos: Jóvenes localizados en la Argentina de 1975 a 2007*, documents the Abuelas' activism. This book visually conveys the continuing presence of the abducted and the emptiness left by their disappearances, through photos of the parents of the missing grandchildren and of the grandchildren themselves. It also includes photos of recuperated grandchildren and estimated dates-of-birth coupled with an empty space where a photo should be for children born in captivity. This combination of photos and empty boxes represents the fragmentation of families and the many spaces that the Abuelas hope to fill through their search.

The "For Identity" projects are a crucial component of the Abuelas' organization.[24] These projects have broadened the discursive and deliberative spaces of their struggle, particularly among younger Argentine generations. They incorporate strategies of entertainment education that involve designing messages to amuse, educate, create favorable attitudes, and change behavior.[25] For the Abuelas, memory is at the service of recovering their grandchildren; their campaigns thus entertain in order to promote investigations and gain allies for their cause. The pioneer venture of this sort was Teatro X la Identidad (Theater For Identity), an annual series of free performances launched in 2000.[26] As a collaborative project between the Abuelas de Plaza de Mayo and playwrights, actors, and directors, most of the plays address the kidnapping of babies and issues of identity. After each performance, the Abuelas and the actors give brief presentations that explicitly link the play to the campaign for identity.[27]

The latest "For Identity" project was Televisión X la Identidad (Television For Identity), a series of three programs honoring the Abuelas' thirtieth anniversary, broadcast in October 2007 by a major television network, Telefé. It presented the organization's work through fictional representations of real cases of recuperated grandchildren. The series was a success, demonstrating the potential of commercial television as a vehicle for transmitting memories of state terrorism. It both generated good ratings and prompted increased calls to the offices of the Abuelas by young people who thought that they might be children of desaparecidos.

"For Identity" projects involve the participation of individuals and organizations that independently produce memory artifacts. This is the case with the T-shirts that organizers sell at the theater performances.[28] These T-shirts bear the inscription "Teatro X la Identidad" and the group's logo (a mask with a smiling and peaceful face between the two faces representing Comedy and Tragedy).[29] The printed mottos focus on the Abuelas' relentless search, and include inscriptions like: "There are still 400 disappeared children; we have to find them" or "When you assume responsibility for history . . . you become part of it . . . until the appearance of the last appropriated grandchild." Hence, the T-shirts both help to cover the performances' expenses and serve as carriers of the Abuelas' message.

As noted above, there exist memory products whose sales benefit the Abuelas, although the Abuelas do not sell them. One month after the broadcast of Televisión X la Identidad, the network Telefé and the newspaper *Página/12* joined forces for the massive distribution of a DVD of the programs and donated the proceeds to the Abuelas. To commemorate the organization's thirtieth anniversary, three filmmakers offered the Abuelas profits earned by launching a special edition of their films: Luis Puenzo's *The Official Story*; David Blaustein's *Spoils of War*; and Andrés Habbeger's *(h)Historias cotidianas*. Both the television series and these films address the experience and effects of state terrorism on the children of desaparecidos. The films' distribution has multiple advantages: the transmission of memory messages; support (both socially and fiscally) for the Abuelas' search; and educating the public. Hence, while the Abuelas may give away what they produce, other groups and individuals involve themselves in the marketing of memory through the sale of several related artifacts.[30]

H.I.J.O.S. The members of this powerful and noisy group have gained recognition through an intense presence in the streets. H.I.J.O.S. was organized in 1995 by the adult sons and daughters of the disappeared, and became famous for its escraches, creative campaigns of public condemnation aimed at shaming torturers and assassins who benefited from impunity laws.[31] In spite of the nullification of these laws, certain criminals remain at large; in 2007, I partook in the renewed activism of H.I.J.O.S. through an escrache against a current prosecutor who had forged documents in order to steal property from desaparecidos.[32] While the group divided into separate factions in 2000, by 2007 the faction that split off (HIJOS—no periods) had ceased to exist. Over the years, H.I.J.O.S. has grown to include members that do not have disappeared relatives, thus incorporating a new generation of activists into the human rights movement.

H.I.J.O.S. markets memory through messages that reflect the group's goals and its support for other organizations. H.I.J.O.S. reproduces memory messages in banners and collage posters, which they bring to demonstrations and commemorations, that vindicate their disappeared parents' activism; denounce torturers, assassins, and their accomplices; and inform the public about legislators who have voted for the impunity laws. H.I.J.O.S. makes a point of providing precise data on those responsible for the repression and the legalization of impunity. Sometimes they sell memory artifacts, the proceeds of which help to cover their expenses. In 2007, these included a T-shirt with the image of the "Hear no evil, see no evil, speak no evil" monkeys, and the added inscription "Indifference is a pact with impunity." In pairing these sentiments, H.I.J.O.S. members hope to raise the sensibilities of bystanders to the terror and of those who remain indifferent to current struggles for accountability. H.I.J.O.S. also sells blank notebooks with the inscription "The impossible only takes longer" on the cover. A snail image also appears on the cover, symbolizing the very slow pace of advancement in the long fight against impunity.

This organization maintains close ties with the Abuelas. The cover of their 2008 calendar reads, "Abuelas de Plaza de Mayo, 1977–2007, 30 Years of Struggle For Identity and Justice. An Homage from H.I.J.O.S." Images of the Abuelas and a fingerprint, symbolizing identity, adorn the calendar. H.I.J.O.S. has inscribed the back cover with a letter praising and thanking the Abuelas for their work in leading the search for the desaparecidos, and their promise to continue this work. Additionally, every page of the calendar provides information on what individuals should do if they doubt their identity, including contact information for the Abuelas, CONADI, and Hermanos, a group within H.I.J.O.S. that focuses on the search for stolen babies who are sisters and brothers of its members.

The calendar, a public representation of H.I.J.O.S.'s alliance with the Abuelas, further honors the Abuelas by summarizing important facts regarding their three decades of activism; and it portrays H.I.J.O.S. as both their collaborators and their heirs. Photos of the Abuelas demonstrating, descriptions of their main triumphs, explanations of the organization's strategies, and their mottos fill its pages. Providing a chronology of the milestones achieved in the search for grandchildren, the H.I.J.O.S. calendar combines data on legal resolutions with slogans like "Let's struggle together against impunity," details on recuperated grandchildren, and information on the cultural projects/artists who collaborated with the Abuelas in the calendar. It both writes the memory of the organization and becomes another tool in the search for identity, an intergenerational collaboration exemplary of memory at the service of justice.

H.I.J.O.S. distributes memory messages through several carriers. However, selling memory artifacts is not integral to all of their public appearances; their disruptive and festive escraches remain the central carriers for their message. For example, while they offered T-shirts and calendars at the inauguration of a Space for Memory, H.I.J.O.S. members sell no products during an escrache; instead, they focus their efforts on chanting slogans against the target of the escrache, painting the sidewalks with mottos, and giving away flyers with information about the crimes perpetrators committed.

Human Rights Institutions

The two institutions that I discuss here, the Instituto Espacio para la Memoria (IEM) and Memoria Abierta, were developed in collaboration with human rights organizations and activists. Both institutions organize educational, academic, and cultural activities, including conferences, workshops, public talks, screenings, and the production of memory artifacts—demonstrating how actors in the field of human rights combine efforts for the preservation of memories of state terrorism.

INSTITUTO ESPACIO PARA LA MEMORIA. The IEM, created in 2006 by the government of the city of Buenos Aires, consists of several human rights organizations, members of the city's government, and public figures committed to the defense of human rights.[33] Its work, centered in Buenos Aires, denounces the crimes of, and the policies that originated and supported, state terrorism. Its memory products—useful educational devices—disseminate data obtained through investigations. The institute also coordinates activities, including visits to former torture centers, like ESMA.[34]

The IEM has several publications, many of which can be accessed through its website. Among the material that it distributed for free in 2007 was the *Sculpture Prize* book on the international contest for the sculptures created for the Parque de la Memoria. Photos of the winning projects and comments by the artists about their motivations to participate in the contest, as well as the rationales for their artwork, comprise this book. It therefore offers insights into the debates about representations of the past and decisions about what belongs, and why, at an officially funded memory site.[35] Another important IEM publication is a report of their activities since the institute's creation, which offers details of the nature and scope of its collaboration with different organizations and governmental institutions. IEM also provides postcards, bulletins, and posters, such as a giant map of the clandestine torture centers that operated in Buenos Aires.

The institute exemplifies the deliberative space between civil society and the state. The objectives of IEM's activities, the content of its messages, and the goods that it distributes result from interactions with an administration that supports policies developed by human rights organizations. Official funding is key to the organization of events and the free distribution of costly educational materials. The political will of future administrations could thus greatly affect IEM and make other actors responsible for its maintenance. A changed political context could mean that IEM will have to compete for alternative funding from national and international sources that support human rights causes.

MEMORIA ABIERTA. This organization represented the coordinated action of several groups: Asamblea Permanente por los Derechos Humanos (APDH); Centro de Estudios Legales y Sociales (CELS); Fundación Memoria Histórica y Social Argentina; Madres de Plaza de Mayo—Línea Fundadora; and Servicio Paz y Justicia (SERPAJ). Its mission is to preserve the memory of what happened in the period of state terrorism and to foment cooperation between different archives that contain information about the period.[36] As with the IEM, funding is central to the activities of this institution, which currently has the support of the government and several international foundations.[37] Memoria Abierta has more varied funding sources than IEM, however, and thus less dependency on official support.

This institution sells memory products that complement its work, as the means for distributing its research projects. A primary activity of Memoria Abierta is the writing of memory through interviews with human rights activists, opinion leaders, intellectuals, artists, victims of state terrorism, and average citizens who witnessed the terror. In 2007, the archive had over five hundred oral histories, an invaluable resource for researchers and educators.

Memoria Abierta produces knowledge aligned with its mission and the politics of memory put forth by human rights organizations. The products on sale serve as educational devices. At the end of 2007, it had published a set of three CD-ROMs entitled "De memoria: Testimonios, textos y otras fuentes sobre el terrorismo de estado en la Argentina."[38] Texts and testimony about the massive mobilizations and the growth of social and political movements in the 1969–75 period comprise the first CD-ROM, "La primavera de los pueblos." The second CD-ROM, "El 24 de Marzo 1976: El golpe y el terrorismo del estado," includes texts and documents about the social and political environment preceding the military coup and the consolidation of the dictatorship. The final CD-ROM, "1983: La transición democrática y el camino hacia la justicia," includes testimony, source material, and texts that address the beginning of civilian rule, the debates related to the search for truth and justice, and the different proposals promoted by human rights activists and the state. Another multimedia product of this institution is an interactive CD-ROM about El Vesubio, a former torture center; it combines testimony and source materials, including animated reconstructions of the demolished building. Drawing on the words of the poet Juan Gelman, we can say that the institution is helping to weave the quilt of the nation's collective memory.[39]

Independent Producers of Memory Artifacts

In addition to human rights organizations and institutions, several independent producers represent and transmit memories through a wide range of goods. To illustrate this category, I focus on creative entrepreneurs who sell objects with a memory theme.

PHOTOGRAPHERS/ARTISTS. In 2007 I identified several artists who sell photos of activists, particularly of their marches, that have become memory landmarks of Buenos Aires' landscape. In these photos, sold on the street of Buenos Aires, politicized portrayals of the Madres, Abuelas, and H.I.J.O.S. are juxtaposed with cultural portrayals of tango dancers. Turko Alí sells his pieces from a stand at the San Telmo neighborhood street fair, which attracts a large public packed with tourists. His photos depict many themes, including street scenes and architecture, and are framed in wood or mounted on wood to create *retablo*-style, three-dimensional displays. His memory-themed pieces include images of the Madres' marches and the H.I.J.O.S.'s escraches. Turko Alí is an artist/activist involved in several projects; his political ideology and support of these activists' work inspires this particular merchandise.[40]

Portrayals of the Madres, the Abuelas, and other memory activists are also part of the collections of photographers who sell images of tango dancers and additional scenes of Buenos Aires culture at the Sunday fairs at Plaza Dorrego, San Telmo, and at the Caminito in La Boca neighborhood, another common stop for tourists. These artists' appreciation of human rights action motivates their choice to incorporate such themes into their own work.[41] Some examples of the scenes captured by the photographs include the monument in the square facing the Congress building, with a large graffito of the words "Neither oblivion nor pardon"; and images of the Madres demonstrating, some with the banner of H.I.J.O.S. behind them.

While not the top sellers, these photographs represent initiatives of production and distribution of memory artifacts independent from those of the human rights organizations. Moreover, the photos that the artists sell in street fairs provide one of few opportunities to buy memory artifacts for tourists who cannot attend the Madres' marches or other "memory acts." These products—both through their production and in their final material form—support human rights memory and are an option for those seeking to buy "politically correct" souvenirs, which in Argentina link to known social movements.

FASHION HONORING THE ABUELAS DE PLAZA DE MAYO. The designer Teo Gincoff, who employs fashion as a communication medium, based his 2007 fashion line Moda X la Identidad on identity. The collection honored the Abuelas for demanding the right to identity and for their struggle in concurrently restoring memory and family to their grandchildren. When he approached the Abuelas, Gincoff had already produced fashion with an ecological orientation, using natural fibers and dyed cloth from indigenous communities.[42] The artwork chosen to decorate the 2007 T-shirts was from a series of paintings of the Abuelas wearing white kerchiefs by celebrated artist Milo Lockett.[43] (Most of the Abuelas are also Madres of desaparecidos, but they do not always wear kerchiefs in their public appearances.) This demonstrates a three-pronged link between committed artists who admire the Abuelas, socially responsible "green" fashion, and the human rights movement.

Gincoff used the Abuelas' photographs as a resource.[44] He designed 1970s-style raincoats inspired by images of the Abuelas marching in the rain. He produced orange garments, the color of the Abuelas' media brochures. His collection also included dark-colored clothing, which symbolized the years of terror; long collars partially covering the face, and thus hiding the identity of the wearer; and outfits with white hoods that represented kerchiefs. For the presentation of his line, Gincoff invited an actress who played the daughter of a desaparecido in a popular television series, *Montecristo*, to model. If we add to this picture the presence of several Abuelas and supporters at the event, and the fact that Gincoff gave away over one hundred T-shirts to the public, we see that the designer managed to perform an act of memory in the often frivolous sphere of the fashion world.[45] The fashion show, and its broadcast for over three months by a TV fashion channel, undeniably meant an opportunity to promote the Abuelas' struggle in a sphere that conventionally ignores the human rights movement.[46]

Figure 2. T-shirts honoring the Abuelas de Plaza de Mayo, produced by Teo Gincoff, artwork by Milo Lockett. (Photograph by Susana Kaiser)

While a unique and contributive production, the memory project behind the fashion line may not have effectively reached the public. Press releases sought to promote this collection in circles less familiar with the work of the Abuelas, but they only provided sound bites of the designer's rationale for his creations. While press coverage did involve a discussion of the meaning behind the garments themselves (e.g., that they "cover the face, representing the lack of identity"),[47] they lacked an explanation of the choices and motivation behind the design of specific items.[48] Media appraisals of the fashion line thus failed to reflect the diverse motives that led the designer, the artist, and the Abuelas to collaborate in this venture. This demonstrates a unique translation of three decades of searching for kidnapped grandchildren into products that must compete in a specific market.

The fashion collection certainly presents a new twist in the production and distribution of memory goods. Indeed, simply creating an association between the Abuelas and the fashion world is a bold move. The Abuelas' agreement to participate in the project further suggests a willingness to explore new venues to convey their message. Although it is the only case that I found with this kind of representation of an organization's struggle, it opens the possibility for similar ventures and products in the future. But the question remains: how can they contribute to transmitting memory messages, and who (if anyone) benefits from the monetary profits that are realized in such creative endeavors.

About the Consumption of Memory Artifacts

Since the consumer is at the other end of the production process, s/he must be addressed in understanding memory artifacts: Who consumes memory? How do people respond to memory artifacts? How do these representations of the past impact the user? Barbara Kruger's iconic image "I Shop Therefore I Am" became a motto symbolizing a society obsessed with consuming. Going beyond this general characterization of a materially preoccupied society, how does what we buy define us? Are we what we consume? Does the consumption of memory artifacts turn us into memory-keepers and transmitters? T-shirts, for example, as walking billboards decorated by numerous slogans and symbols, may become vehicles for people to voice their ideological positions. What does it mean to wear these messages?

We need to study the use of memory products in the same way that we study media audiences.[49] Media research today centers on the social act of consuming media, on the analysis of the encounter between the message and the people.[50] Whatever the intentions of human rights activists and independent artists in producing a memory product (the encoding), its meaning will have different interpretations depending on who uses and consumes it (the decoding).[51] While the encoding of the message is the point of departure, its circulation and reception are also moments of the production process. Who we are shapes our interpretations of what we read, watch, listen to, and, I would argue, the memory products that we buy, give away, use, and wear. Differences of age, gender, ethnicity, and knowledge of a particular topic affect people's diverse interpretations of messages. An Argentine teenager wearing an H.I.J.O.S. T-shirt and a Spanish tourist who attends a Madres' march and buys a money clip as a souvenir are very different.

The reasons why we buy and consume memory products vary depending on the individual engaged in this process, who can be a local or a foreigner, a supporter of the human rights movement, or someone simply looking for a special souvenir. Motives may include helping the cause, wanting a memento from a group or event, expressing a political position on the dictatorship, and actively promoting a human rights memory by using and/or giving away these products. The characteristics of the product also influence the motives of consumption. Books and CD-ROMS serve as informational and educational devices. Goods such as key rings and coffee mugs conform to a separate category of collection or gift-giving.

Differences also emerge based on the seller and location of selling these objects. Locations where memory acts take place reveal interaction between the public and relatives of the desaparecidos, moments with a strong presence of those who are absent—and where buying can imply a form of dialogue with them. This can be seen at the Plaza de Mayo during the Madres' marches; after a performance of Teatro X la Identidad, where the public is emotionally touched by a play; and at a commemoration where attendees have talked to members of H.I.J.O.S. These occasions compare to people's interaction with memorial sites, where dialogue between visitors and the dead may nurture a society's memories.[52]

While we ponder if memory-themed photos are just another souvenir for tourists, we might also ask if there is a way to contextualize the delivery of memory products as presents, for we may wonder how friends and relatives will appreciate and understand the meaning of these objects. As a woman from Buenos Aires shopping at the Madres' stand told me: "I buy one [mug] each time that I come here and then keep them for when I need to give a present." Irrespective of the familiarity of her friends with the Madres, whenever they use this mug at their homes or in their workplaces they will engage with the Madres' message, and thereby memory transmission will take place through this product.

Those buying from independent artists may not have attended any memory events. As the Madres and the Abuelas are well-known abroad, it is foreign tourists who buy most of their products.[53] According to the photographers I encountered, however, those who shop for memory-themed photos know about human rights activists.[54] With regard to items of fashion that honor the Abuelas, we can only speculate about decoding by those who bought garments. Despite their sell-out success, these products have not been the subject of any systematic market research about their consumers. Designer Gincoff speculates, however, that consumers are conscious of the political meaning behind his fashion memory goods.[55]

Hence, we should continue to explore the consumption of memory artifacts by realizing their complex interaction with consumers: whoever consumes them is at once decoding particular and different meanings and also contributing to the transmission of a message. Consumers thus become a link in the memory chain.

Memory Goods or Memory Kitsch

In Argentina, we cannot yet identify a commodification of memories of state terrorism. It is hard to imagine that the white kerchief will ever be for sale. While memory goods may be used primarily to expand knowledge and reawaken memories of the past, they may also be exploited to expand consumption. At this time, I believe that they are primarily produced and employed in the spirit of the former, more altruistic practice. Argentina is characterized by a strong commitment not to turn memory into a commodity.

The fact that human rights organizations and institutions dominate the production of memory artifacts suggests that these items do not have massive distribution or generate substantial profits to help cover expenses. It is too early to see how the organizations will run their projects at ESMA, or to know what types of memory products will be distributed there. We cannot ignore the possibility of museum stores, which can contribute to the sustainability of a museum's operations, something applicable to all spaces for memory. We should remember, however, that monetary profits do not monopolize or negate possible gains from selling (or giving away) memory products. The goods discussed here, whether sold or distributed freely, contribute first and foremost to the continued presence of this past in the public sphere, to the current construction and transmission of memories.

As for the production of independent artists, there is no indication that sales of these artifacts generate substantial profits. While sales of the many concrete manifestations of "Never Again" may generate revenues, I did not identify any cases in which the use of this past has resulted in profitable merchandising. There also exist instances of independent producers donating the proceeds of such sales to human rights groups. How these organizations assess the value of such contributions will determine their feasibility and incorporation into their projects. Since there is undeniably a commercial angle, this will require careful consideration, in order to avoid endorsing or co-opting the production of memory artifacts of no value to their cause.

There is, however, no simple distinction between memory goods for knowledge dissemination and memory goods for profit. Whenever sale transactions occur, we must differentiate between who controls the production and who profits from it. A manufacturer may profit monetarily, for example, from the massive distribution of the kerchief that is printed on all kinds of merchandise. Activists may, however, at the same time profit from expansion of knowledge of their cause. Additionally, symbols may evolve as commodified products. Over the years, the Madres have given away kerchiefs to thank key supporters; similar to Walter Benjamin's analysis of the work of art in an era of mechanical reproduction, the white kerchief became an award embodied with the aura of a unique object. The Madres may opt in the future to reproduce this object so as to fiscally benefit their cause. How can we analyze or judge if they decide to do a global sale of kerchiefs for raising funds? Who can question their authority to do so? How would we classify a project like this?

Based on the examples of political memorabilia and memory kitsch (e.g., the Che paraphernalia), we should, however, refrain from saying "never" to a shift in focus of memory goods production from knowledge to monetary profit. I am writing at a moment in which this situation could change along with social and political transformations. Human rights organizations and institutions do not control what independent artists produce and sell. More significantly, generational issues do and will affect the production and consumption of memory goods. After more than thirty years of activism, the Madres and the Abuelas are growing old and many have passed away. A younger generation may utilize different strategies of goods production in their wake, in the wake of this broad wave of memory, and in new waves of remembering.[56]

This chapter has discussed the marketing of memory in the year 2007, a snapshot into the ever-changing memory scenario during its latest wave. This wave must be contextualized by a government explicitly supportive of human rights causes, as well as by cooperation between victims of past terror and younger generations. Whether the projects of human rights organizations and institutions, or the initiatives of independent artists and corporations, the production of memory goods will continue. This production may focus in the future on the distribution of goods primarily for knowledge or for profit. The scene in Argentina in 2007, however, showed resilience, emphasizing the former and avoiding the transformation of memory goods into memory kitsch. Concerns and debates on this topic will continue, as will the different approaches for carrying out memory work that does not negotiate, let alone negate, its integrity.

NOTES

1. See the presentations at the panel "Memoria y Espacios Sociales," 1a. Feria del Libro Social y Político, Buenos Aires, 26 September 2007; and the presentations at the conference "Modernidad, Religión y Memoria," Buenos Aires, 10–11 October 2007.
2. Gaskell and Wright, "Group Differences in Memory for a Political Event."
3. Pennebaker and Banasik, "On the Creation and Maintenance of Collective Memories," 17; Igartúa and Páez, "Art and Remembering Traumatic Collective Events."
4. Igartúa and Páez, "Art and Remembering Traumatic Collective Events."
5. Nora, "Generations," 526.
6. Benhabib, "Models of the Public Space," 93; Warner, "The Mass Public and the Mass Subject," 391.
7. García Canclini, *Consumidores y ciudadanos.*
8. The event, held on 30 April 2008, celebrated the thirty-first anniversary of the first march at the Plaza de Mayo.
9. For some examples of memory marketing from around the world, see Andrea Stone, "Souvenir Invasion Turning Normandy into 'Disney World,'" *USA Today,* 3 June 1994, sec. A; Don Oldenburg, "For the Big Day, Cartloads of After-Dinner Mementos," *Washington Post,* 15 January 2005; Daniel J. Wakin, "Mementos from Postwar Prison Depict Turning Point for Japan," *New York Times,* 28 July 2004, sec. B; and Schrift and Pilkey, "Revolution Remembered."
10. Popular Memory Group, "Popular Memory," 208–9.
11. Even when the "for-profit" marketing of memory products was not significant in 2007, the consumption of the past, including state terrorism, remains at risk of commodification.
12. See Juaretche, *Violencia y política en los 70,* 23–24.
13. Ibid.; Fentress and Wickham, *Social Memory.*
14. Nora, "Between Memory and History," 9.
15. Sturken, *Tangled Memories,* 9.
16. Igartúa and Páez, "Art and Remembering Traumatic Collective Events"; Nora, "Between Memory and History"; Popular Memory Group, "Popular Memory."
17. Todorov, *Les abus de la mémoire.*
18. Bonafini, *Historias de vida.*
19. See Kaiser, "The Struggle for Urban Territories."
20. For the Asociación's communication strategies, see Kaiser, "The 'Madwomen' Memory Mothers of the Plaza de Mayo."
21. See Mensuario de Abuelas #78, March 2009, at www.abuelas.org.ar/comunicados.php?comunicados=mensuario.
22. Author's conversation with Rosa T. de Roisinblit, vice-president of Abuelas de Plaza de Mayo, 31 October 2007.

23. For example, the Italian government funded many of the publications that celebrated the group's thirtieth anniversary.
24. See www.abuelas.org.ar.
25. See Singhal and Rogers, *Entertainment Education.*
26. In Spanish, "X"—the multiplication sign—is expressed as "por" (= "for"); hence its use replacing the word "por."
27. In addition to Teatro X la Identidad, this chapter explores two other "For Identity" events—Televisión X la Identidad (Television For Identity) and Moda X la Identidad (Fashion For Identity). Other "For Identity" events have included Deporte X la Identidad (Sports For Identity); Rock X la Identidad (Rock For Identity); and Arte y Cultura X la Identidad (Art and Culture for Identity), through which the Abuelas have joined photographers, filmmakers, choreographers, and musicians to organize tango, dance, film, and photography contests.
28. Conversation with Rosa T. Roisinblit, 31 October 2007.
29. Teatro X la Identidad, www.teatroxlaidentidad.net/editables/TxItos.asp.
30. The Abuelas have also recently received one of the buildings at the ESMA compound to house a Casa de la Identidad. The creativity that the organization has shown over the years suggests that this project will set new parameters in the search for identity. This new center will probably incorporate the Abuelas' projects. It may also serve as an arena for the distribution of memory products.
31. For escraches, see Kaiser, "*Escraches.*"
32. Escrache to Oscar Hermelo, Buenos Aires, 28 November 2007.
33. The organizations involved are Abuelas de Plaza de Mayo; Asamblea Permanente por los Derechos Humanos; Buena Memoria Asociación Civil; Familiares de Desaparecidos y Detenidos por Razones Políticas; Fundación Memoria Histórica y Social Argentina; Hermanas de Desaparecidos por la Verdad y la Justicia; H.I.J.O.S. (Hijos por la Identidad y la Justicia contra el Olvido y el Silencio); Liga Argentina por los Derechos del Hombre; Madres de Plaza de Mayo—Línea Fundadora; Movimiento Ecuménico por los Derechos Humanos; and Servicio Paz y Justicia.
34. Instituto Espacio para la Memoria, www.institutomemoria.org.ar/.
35. This text has an English translation that is intended for distribution to foreign audiences.
36. Memoria Abierta, www.memoriaabierta.org.ar/.
37. Memoria Abierta's website lists funding sources.
38. "De memoria" means "by heart." The title implies a thorough compilation of accurate data.
39. "Qué manto de memoria colectiva se podría tejer con esos pedacitos" (Juan Gelman, "Del silencio," *Página/12*, 13 August 1998, Contratapa).
40. Conversation with author, 30 September 2007.
41. Conversations with photographers in La Boca, 14 November 2007, and in San Telmo, 4 May 2008.
42. See the 22 March 2007 press release at www.abuelas.org.ar/comunicados/varios.htm.
43. Interview with Milo Lockett, 1 July 2008.

44. Interview with Teo Gincoff, 5 July 2008.
45. The distribution of the line was limited to a few cities (ibid.).
46. "Moda X la Identidad," Comunicado de Abuelas de Plaza de Mayo del 22 de marzo, www.abuelas.org.ar/comunicados/varios.htm.
47. Ibid.
48. E.g., the reason for choosing the color orange (in the brochures) was not discussed, nor was the inspiration for the raincoats themselves (see "Moda X la Identidad," Comunicado de Abuelas de Plaza de Mayo del 22 de marzo, www.abuelas.org.ar/comunicados/varios.htm and "90+10: Diseño, creatividad y comunicación," 6 April 2007, http://www.90mas10.com.ar/moda/2007/04/tatu-diffusin-otooinvierno-07.html).
49. For the Argentine post-dictatorship generation's interpretation of media texts, see chapters 8 and 9 in Kaiser, *Postmemories of Terror.* Kansteiner also highlights that theories of media and cultural studies can help us understand the reception of memory artifacts (Kansteiner, "Finding Meaning in Memory").
50. Ang, *Living Room Wars*; Moores, *Interpreting Audiences.*
51. I am referring to Stuart Hall's classical model of encoding/decoding (Hall, "Encoding/Decoding").
52. Sturken illustrates this potential for communicability using the Vietnam Memorial in Washington, D.C., as an example (see Sturken, *Tangled Memories*).
53. Conversation with photographer in San Telmo, 4 May 2008; and ethnographic observation at the Madres' stand during Thursday marches, October–November 2007.
54. Conversation with photographer Turko Alí, 30 September 2007.
55. Interview with Teo Gincoff, 5 July 2008.
56. One area of further research is funding, as fiscal matters cannot be delinked from discussions of the political economy of memory in Argentina. The administration of sites that produce educational material, and allow for the giving away of memory products, is highly funding dependent. And while official funding in 2007 was central to human rights movements and institutions, private funding may become more important for the functioning of these entities in the future. It will be up to human rights organizations and institutions to evaluate the strings attached to accepting funds, just as they must evaluate the repercussions of producing, selling, and/or giving away memory goods.

CONCLUSION

ALICE A. NELSON

Marketing Discontent

The Political Economy of Memory in Latin America

In his essay "Memory and Forgetting," Benedict Anderson suggests that mechanisms for institutionalizing historical memory—whether textbooks, museums, maps, or even a name—always simultaneously carry with them modes of forgetting. The very call for memory implies that something considered essential is being forgotten: "Having to 'have already forgotten' tragedies of which one needs unceasingly to be 'reminded' turns out to be a characteristic device in the later construction of national genealogies."[1] Moreover, any representation will include some things and not others, which then do not figure in the official memory of the nation. Even more crucial, those very things that are included, once fixed, move toward a kind of stasis that itself becomes memory's opposite. The "modern accumulation of documentary evidence," Anderson writes, " . . . simultaneously records a certain apparent continuity and emphasizes its loss from memory."[2] Nevertheless, he contends, the nation's "biography" relies on the establishment of a narrative in which "violent deaths must be remembered/forgotten as 'our own.' "[3]

Clearly, which deaths and which people figure in this construction of what is "our own" are part of an ongoing contest of interests fully enmeshed in a given society's structures of power, in terms both of race/class/gender relations and governmental policy, and of the pervasive influence of the capitalist marketplace. In the current context of globalization, in which flows of people, money, ideas, and communications across borders all confound the status of the nation itself, national memory processes are bound up in transnational questions of human rights advocacy as well as in

Figure 1. Making reference to Mario Benedetti's poetry collection, *El olvido está lleno de memoria* (Forgetting Is Full of Memory), this installation at Villa Grimaldi in Santiago emphasizes the simultaneity of remembering/forgetting, presence/absence. (Photograph by Laurie Beth Clark and Michael Peterson)

globally structured inequities that have largely deepened over the last three decades. In this sense, memory formation is nothing if not a conflictual, mobile process: less a static repository of meanings from the past than a radically contested dynamic of rethinking relationships between the past and the present, potentially bringing out tentative links, new readings, or alternative interpretations. As Diana Taylor would have it, the "repertoire" of performed meanings, rather than the fixed "archive," more effectively conveys the multiple and potentially contradictory memories stemming from a nation's recent past, particularly in the context of political violence. At the same time, Taylor holds, "the archive and the repertoire exist in a constant state of interaction,"[4] defining themselves dialectically against and through one another. Memory formation is never innocent of the intersecting local and global power relationships it simultaneously enacts and rebuts, invokes and potentially rewrites.

Moreover, any gesture toward recuperating historical memory is always simultaneously about *two* moments and contexts: the moment remembered as well as the moment of remembering, the context of past events and the present context for their recollection. The historical and economic forces shaping those moments and contexts may be more or less similar, but both remain operative, even as some aspect of the present presumably has become different enough from the past to allow the emergence of signs/narratives/images once repressed. The unresolved tensions between the two contexts are enacted and replayed through the promotion of memory, including (but not limited to) its marketing; clearly, those tensions are as much about the present as they are about the past. (Per Rebecca J. Atencio, e.g., Globo's arguably self-serving promotion of the popular *Anos Rebeldes* miniseries had at least as much to do with revising the company's pro-authoritarian image in the present as it did with engaging the past.) To these two moments we should add a third: the moment of reception and interpretation, continuously evolving over time in relation to the other two. Consideration of memory processes and products by necessity involves examination of the tensions and contradictions within and between these three times and the conflicting political, economic, and social interests they involve.

Given this orientation to memory, what, then, is particular to the recent histories of remembering/forgetting in Argentina, Uruguay, Chile, Brazil, Peru, and Mexico, explored in this volume? Two aspects seem particularly crucial. One is that the contest over memory in all six countries forms part of their complex transitions from authoritarian rule (albeit with important distinctions among the six). The other is that this process has taken place within a particularly extreme economic context of late-capitalist globalization (the so-called neoliberal turn of the last three decades[5]), in which a culture-ideology of consumerism, transnational free market capitalism, and global mass media all pervasively structure world economic, social, *and* cultural relations.[6] In fact, these two processes—(transitions from/legacies of) authoritarianism and (ongoing) neoliberal capitalist expansion—are themselves inextricably intertwined, structures that have worked in tandem to consolidate the privilege of the few at the expense of the many on an increasingly global scale.

At the same time, however, from Seattle to Chiapas to Buenos Aires, flashes of dissent have continued to erupt and interrupt from the margins and interstices of the dominant socioeconomic order, shifting the political landscape over time. Since the late 1990s, Latin America has witnessed not only a resurgence of leftist governments,[7] but also an increasing momentum of grassroots social movements contesting the neoliberal free trade paradigms that have favored the global North to the detriment of the global South.[8] Nicolás Lynch argues that this "left-wing turn . . . unimaginable ten years ago," has created a context in which several countries have attempted to redistribute resources, alleviate poverty, diminish U.S. influence, and "(re)enter . . . globalization under their own terms."[9] While these developments are quite hopeful, the extent to which predominant inequities of the global economy may be renegotiated (or not) under neoliberalism will only become clearer with time.

Although versions of this story are familiar in so many places, examining one country's history in greater detail will help illuminate large trends more fully. Perhaps nowhere is the interrelationship between authoritarianism and neoliberalism's ascendant hegemony clearer than in the case of Chile, from neoliberalism's early manifestations under Pinochet in the mid-1970s, to its current, "normalized" role in the ongoing transition process. Manuel Délano and Hugo Traslaviña contend that only under a regime as violent as Pinochet's could such a radical version of Milton Friedman–inspired free-market economic experiments have taken place. Not only did the pervasive security apparatus ensure social order, but also the sanitized, technocratic appearance of the economic plan itself seemingly depoliticized subsequent policy decisions.[10] Pinochet's economic team gave free rein to private enterprise and the market, embarking on near-complete economic deregulation; slashed public spending on social services and privatized government-owned enterprises (e.g., schools, social security, health care, etc.); curtailed labor rights and reduced taxes on corporations and the wealthy; and emphasized individual (over public) responsibility for fulfilling basic material needs.[11] As a result, both economic and political power became concentrated within the hands of a very few Chileans (a fact obscured by official proclamations of an economic "miracle"), while extreme poverty further marginalized the same working-class people who were seen as the internal enemy of the military regime. Economic neoliberalism therefore served several of the regime's key political interests: the dominant classes were appeased and rewarded for supporting the military government, while economic inequity, unemployment, and hunger became the regime's *indirect* (and ostensibly legitimate) tools for excluding lower-income people from the formal exercise of political power. Quoting Willy Thayer, Idelber Avelar writes, "It was the dictatorship that made the transit from State to Market, a transit euphemistically designated as 'modernization.'"[12] Through modernization, underlying structures of domination and exclusion have carried forth in the post-dictatorship years, leading Avelar rightly to conclude that "*the real transitions are the dictatorships themselves.*"[13]

Since 1990, the conflictual aspects of historical memory and debate have been defused within Chile's institutional democracy, which has tended to repress its own contradictions in a seamless official discourse based on consensus and reconciliation. Within this context, "modernization" has become "naturalized" as the largely unquestioned destiny for both the country and its citizens. Not only have the successive center-left Concertación governments taken neoliberalism as a "given"—an unstated part of the political "pact"—but also daily life continues to be structured, and bodies disciplined, in function of economic utility.[14] Nelly Richard contends that the technologies of publicity and commercial discourse, which she terms "las tecnologías de la desmemoria" (technologies of dis-remembering), have only abetted this process, diffusing debate about the past and reducing social exchange to a kind of eternal present based on production and consumption.[15] That is, citizenship is no longer defined by political participation, but rather by consumerism itself.[16] At the same time, despite some change in recent years, the ability to negotiate social demands largely remains framed within the technical terms of neoliberal policies and assumptions, which Verónica Schild calls the "dominant grammar" functionally defining self and society in Chile today.[17]

Within this overall context, the debate about historical memory in the wake of authoritarianism becomes a debate about the costs of the transition and its unspoken contradictions, including neoliberal "modernization's" (not-so-)hidden underside. The post-dictatorship processes of Brazil, Uruguay, and Argentina, Peru's reckoning with authoritarianism and extended internal war (1980–2000), and Mexico's break from PRI hegemony in the wake of its incorporation into NAFTA, all offer variations on large themes from the Chilean case. Assessing neoliberalism's legacies across Latin America, George Yúdice, Jean Franco, and Juan Flores write: "The widely publicized economic 'miracles' of the 1970s made Latin America into an area beset by debt, informal economies, mass migration, and narcotraffic,"[18] with an attendant shift from predominantly rural to predominantly urban societies. As a result, daily life in the now overburdened cities involves "the increase in environmental diseases and urban violence; the criminalization of entire sectors of the population . . . [e.g., in shantytowns]; the increase of repressive surveillance; and the bunkerization of the rich."[19] We need only think of the massive protests and organizing in the wake of Argentina's late-2001 economic collapse to see an increasing social recognition that one of the deepest legacies of authoritarianism, forged within deep North-South inequities, may be neoliberalism itself. Yet any critique of neoliberalism, any gesture toward historical memory, is at once substantially framed by the "grammar" it seeks to contest. That is, offerings on the memory market are both produced by, and consumed within, neoliberalism's terms, even as they struggle (to a greater or lesser degree, with varying strategies and tactics) to disrupt that very paradigm.

What, then, might we expect from marketing memory in a neoliberal era, given the conflicting dynamics at play during the current phase of globalization? One central tension arises between marketing—promoting products within the capitalist marketplace, with what Naomi Klein calls a "corporatist" government/state role under neoliberalism[20]—and memory projects, often shaped (as Bilbija and Payne note) by anti-market sentiments. Such sentiments persist both because of the historic links between authoritarian regimes and the rise of neoliberalism resisted by victims/survivors, and because of the sense that ascribing monetary value to memory projects and products sullies or cheapens their moral value through commodification. Yet as Nancy Gates-Madsen and others observe, memory products that never reach an audience may fall into oblivion, or in the case of monuments or museums, never be built, without some "pitch" to funders and "advertising" to visitors to make their existence both possible and known. And as Ksenija Bilbija and Leigh A. Payne suggest, silence ultimately benefits perpetrators, not victims, of state-sponsored violence. Many of the preceding chapters reveal how this central tension around memory's marketing may lead to renegotiations of interrelationships among public and private funders, agents of the state and human rights groups, and local and international memory "consumers." Such renegotiations may at least partially reconfigure predominant neoliberal patterns, as discussed further below.

Another tension involves the interrelated "diacritics" of media and migration, in Arjun Appadurai's formulation, and their "joint effect on the *work of the imagination* as a constitutive feature of modern subjectivity"[21] within globalization. Migratory flows—whether voluntary or forced, whether motivated by global capital's never-ending need for cheap labor or the displacements of war and repression—may not be new, but are certainly exacerbated within the current context. Several of the preceding chapters show that, in addition to producing diasporas of economic and political refugees, globalization has enabled transnational activists seeking solidarity and new modes for building an international human rights culture (if not unproblematically). Appadurai persuasively contends that these intensified transnational patterns (or "deterritorializations"), coupled with the proliferation of electronic media, not only have restructured the communications field globally, but also have fundamentally reshaped the ways in which people imagine themselves and the communities to which they belong.[22] Electronically mediated forms of memory, and their attendant transnational markets, reconfigure not only the potential audiences for memory products (where does "local" end and "global" begin?), but also the very imaginative structures that inform what memories are thinkable and recognizable, and for whom, today. As Néstor García Canclini notes: "In an age of globalization, in which the city [or nation] is constituted not only by what takes place within its territory, but also by the way in which it is traversed by migrants and tourists, messages and goods from other countries, we construct what is ours with greater intensity against the background of what we imagine about others."[23] At the very least, then, migration and media have dramatically reshaped the imaginable communities—overlapping and diasporic, rather than strictly national—that have a stake in constructing "our own" version of "Never Again."

The authors in this volume grapple with a range of ways memory has been promoted and constrained by the market at this particular historical juncture. Although they overlap in generative ways, for the purposes of discussion, I have clustered the chapters into two groups: those examining the technologies of representation, or "mediascapes," per Appadurai[24] (explored in the popular cultural and media analyses of Atencio, Bilbija, Burt, Kaiser, and Oquendo-Villar), and those focused on memorials and museums, "memory sites," or lieux de mémoire in Nora's formulation (the subjects of essays by Clark and Payne, Collins, Draper, Gates-Madsen, Milton and Ulfe, and Ruisánchez Serra). To clarify terminology: although Bilbija and Payne consider "memory accounts" and "memorabilia" separately in their introductory chapter, I have found it useful, given my emphasis on local-global nexuses, to consider both together under the single "mediascapes" rubric, as it emphasizes the large mass media/communications aspects they share; the "memorysites" designation remains consistent with Bilbija's and Payne's usage. My discussion of both groups will address intersecting issues related to memory production and consumption in the context of neoliberal capitalist globalization.

Mediascapes

Rebecca J. Atencio, Ksenija Bilbija, Jo-Marie Burt, Susana Kaiser, and Carmen Oquendo-Villar all variously explore how particularly charged images/stories/signs reproduced on a mass scale (whether as media images, serial products, or both) promote particular political meanings about the past for and within the current context. Among these, Bilbija takes on advertising, "a main symbolic structure produced by market-oriented societies";[25] Atencio explores conflicting meanings of the Brazilian TV miniseries *Anos Rebeldes*; Burt and Oquendo-Villar examine how story spin and iconography project the very different figures of Afro-Peruvian community leader María Elena Moyano and Chilean dictator Augusto Pinochet; and Kaiser questions the relationship between Argentine "memory products" as "communications media" (from books and DVDs to keychains and coffee mugs) and commodification. These pop cultural phenomena connect both to the globalized economic context and the global mass media in complex ways: the memory images and accounts discussed by Bilbija, Atencio, and, to some degree, Oquendo-Villar, were produced and/or promoted by transnational corporations and advertisers, with varying degrees of (dis)connection from local contexts; in all five chapters, the consumers of memory products consist of overlapping local and global audiences, who have debated these products' meanings in mass electronic (blogs, YouTube, etc.) as well as traditional print forums. Again, we must bear in mind that the global and local overlap especially strongly in the context of exile and displacement caused by both authoritarianism and neoliberalism, such that some "local" publics themselves have become globally deterritorialized and reconstructed (via media and other means) over the last decades. Finally, the question of who profits from the production of memory in each case seems especially crucial: only in the case of the memorabilia discussed by Kaiser do the victims and survivors of human rights abuses have primary influence over the financing, content, and goals of memory products; in all four other cases, parties sometimes significantly removed from the survivors have benefited from reproduction of memories that arguably distort and decontextualize the past, promoting instead an amnesiac status quo. Taken together, these chapters suggest that "free trade" of memories, not unlike the dominant pattern for other products, has served to advance powerful transnational commercial interests over those of the bodies that suffered in their production.

In her analysis of torture imagery in Diesel and Ripley advertising campaigns (Argentina, 1998, and Chile, 2006, respectively), Bilbija pointedly asks: "What happens to a society when an image associated with the collective trauma, an image that was never recorded, a snapshot that was never taken, gets unknowingly and carelessly re-created with a purpose completely foreign to any commemorative function?" (292). It seems crucial, as mentioned, that the images in question were produced and reproduced by those representing transnational companies, people with no direct experience of the local realities invoked. Bilbija plumbs what it means to "capitalize on tragedy" (299), an apt phrase echoing the local response of human rights organizations in the two countries, who took the advertisements as an affront, a trivializing of past horrors in the service of corporate profit. In their own defense, Diesel and Ripley claimed their ads were open to a range of interpretations, dismissing the human rights critiques as provincial and short-sighted in the larger global context. Perhaps most disturbing, the ad agencies contended that these images formed part of a "world trend." If indeed they were based on the horrific Abu Ghraib torture photos stripped of their context for marketing purposes, then the ads not only do not fit comfortably "in the mold of a utopian 'Never Again'" (307), but instead do the exact opposite: they serially reproduce an idealized form of violence *again and again* across borders and times. This does indeed constitute a form of "cultural homogenization" under globalization;[26] it is, as Bilbija notes, the inverse tale of capitalism's violence and the "obliteration of social engagement" (303), in which torture becomes not only a trend, but also trendy.[27]

Bilbija's analysis holds deep ramifications, both in terms of the general ways late-capitalist market-driven societies serially produce mechanisms that decontextualize the past, and of the specific generational shift these ad campaigns presumed in Argentina and Chile. In terms of the former, Bilbija's notion of marketing and the market underscores its corrosive qualities; through commodification, she holds, "meaning is lost" (302), or perhaps more accurately, it is collapsed, ahistoricized, stripped of context. Images, she writes, "as an outcome of the imaginary, become the model of reality" (302). She continues: "They conjure up, evoke the 'reading' that was not intended by the makers, an interpretation that is ghostly because it represents what is absent. . . . [Yet, the process of simulation ultimately] creates memory-free consumers of that simulacrum through abolition of the referent" (307–8). In short, these ads aesthetically sanitize and displace the past, leaving in the present moment decontextualized, beautiful "corpses" framed by violent trappings but somehow unmarked by them, bodies upon which desires are to be projected and consumed. Yet they simultaneously invoke, through absence, the uncomfortable residue of a past to be rejected. Given that the advertisers' target audience is hip eighteen- to thirty-four-year-olds, the unstated assumption behind these ads is that irreverence toward human rights abuses *sells*, that youth today are all about moving on, that they are "superior to the local social collective and its moral concerns" (299). Quite simply, as Bilbija puts it, "the past is not fashionable" (301).

If advertising is one of the key symbolic structures of late-capitalist market societies, television and the mass media are not far behind in shaping—and yes, marketing—certain "mediated" versions of historical memory to the general public (or as Atencio so aptly puts it, "repression lite," in which one memory fits all). In her analysis of the Brazilian miniseries *Anos Rebeldes* (Rebel Years), Atencio argues that the TV giant Globo, with historical ties to the military regime, offered this program focused on the dictatorship years not to promote historical memory, but rather to refashion itself in the network's transition from "authoritarian ally" to "champion of democracy and model corporate citizen" (44) at the time of Collor's impeachment. The network clearly profited from both the series' popularity and its spin-off products. Atencio shows how the *Anos Rebeldes* phenomenon disrupted links with the past by offering largely decontextualized documentary footage embedded in the fictional frame, reducing the plot to its love story components in spin-off products, and through revisionist commentary by Globo's spokespeople about their motives. Just as revealing, Atencio contends that the series offered a kind of postmodern political education to the next generation, which consisted, in the final analysis, of the trappings of protest (face paint, songs, slogans) stripped of specific content, employed against Collor in a dehistoricized simulacrum of the 1960s. In this way, and despite the real political momentum the protests garnered for ousting Collor, the miniseries participated in the modes and mechanisms of a generalized amnesia that found further expression in the reelection of Collor to the very senate that had impeached him. Ultimately, Globo engaged in "memory merchandising" (52), Atencio argues, in order to "market itself" (63).

So, returning to Bilbija's notion that "the past is not fashionable," we might ask, what if the past *were* fashionable, or *became* fashionable, as it did in the case of the *Anos Rebeldes* tropes and anthems? Do those tropes and anthems (or, to posit another example, the ubiquitous and trendy Che T-shirts) actually count as "the past," or are they simply more evidence of the ways commodification collapses meaning into an eternal present? The Chilean cultural critic Carlos Ossa holds that the sheer act of repetition for marketing purposes, whether through media serialization or product commodification, evacuates images/objects/texts of their contestatory power: "The mode of erasure is to repeat the repetition, and in doing so, to make disappear the disappeared. This is not a metaphor; it is an operation that finds its design in electronic culture."[28] Historically, capitalism has neutralized points of opposition by incorporating them more deeply into the system, diffusing their most challenging meanings, but today's "technologies of dis-remembering" (to return to Richard) intensify this tendency. For Ossa, serialized memory equals a designed operation of forgetting built into the current, technological stage of globalization. Echoing this concept in their introduction, Bilbija and Payne discuss the notion of "post-memory" represented by the fictional "73" bar in Fuguet's appropriately titled *Por favor, rebobinar* (Please Rewind); there, photos of Pinochet in dark glasses coexist with TV sets projecting *La batalla de Chile* (The Battle of Chile) in an endless loop, emphasizing precisely how repetition may empty the past of its most potent political content.

Yet as the heterogeneous responses to *Anos Rebeldes* and the Diesel/Ripley ads suggest, nodes of dissent still do emerge from within the structures of globalization. As Yúdice, Franco, and Flores write: "In the interstices of these [global economic and communications] networks there develop quite specific and ephemeral protests, resistances, and social movements. . . . Globalization leads not only to new elites; it also gives rise to new particularisms."[29] These "particularisms" include political art actions such as the Argentine escraches and Chilean funas discussed in this volume, as well as the Andean indigenous, Afro-Brazilian, and Chilean squatters movements cited by Yúdice, Franco, and Flores; we should also consider the oft-noted ways new social movements like the Brazilian Movimiento Sem Terra (MST) and Mexican Ejército Zaptatista de Liberación Nacional (EZLN) have utilized the Internet and other media as one of many organizing tools to both imagine and advance their *particular* struggles in the *global* context. As Leslie Sklair has noted, "Although capitalism is increasingly organized on a global basis, effective opposition to capitalist practices tends to be manifest locally"[30] and "find[s] ways of globalizing these [local] disruptions."[31] In general, there has been an important, widening accessibility to media through the Internet, YouTube, blogs, and so forth, even as access issues remain for populations with fewer resources. This accessibility has had material consequences: Marisol LeBrón contends, for example, that Guatemala's "Twitter revolution" nearly "brought a presidency to its knees" in the wake of the recent murder of progressive attorney Rodrigo Rosenberg.[32] Even the seemingly amnesia-inducing Ripley and Diesel ads that Bilbija discusses are the target of a quite heterogeneous Internet discussion critiquing their significance: arguably, a discussion that itself constitutes memory, in the form of current debate about the conflicting meanings and interpretations of the past, while potentially fostering an international human rights agenda. As I will suggest in the case of monuments below, it may well be in all these spaces "in-between" or "surrounding" the marketed memory/forgetting that dynamic social remembrance actually occurs, if sometimes only ephemerally.

The essays by Burt, Oquendo-Villar, and Kaiser all make the point that who controls the story or image being promoted largely determines the interests it advances. For Burt, María Elena Moyano's memory has been "spun" for political purposes by both the state and Sendero Luminoso as part of a broader ideological struggle for winning the "hearts and minds" of Peruvians. Burt outlines three moments pertinent for analysis of the construction of Moyano's memory: the proliferation of accounts following her 1992 assassination by the Sendero Luminoso; a diminishing of stories after the Sendero Luminoso's 1992–95 defeat; and the current resurgent phase of memory formation in the wake of Fujimori's 2007 trial. While "spin doctors" on all sides have attempted to reduce the complexity of Moyano's critiques of *both* Sendero Luminoso violence *and* neoliberalism and "state terrorism" to one or another dimension serving their own purposes, perhaps the most insidious "spin" has come from a seemingly unlikely source: Moyano's sister Marta. Burt reveals how Marta Moyano, elected congresswoman for Fujimori's party in 1995, has traded on the Moyano name in support of a pro-Fujimori, pro-neoliberal project her sister surely would have repudiated. By casting *herself* as a victim of Sendero Luminoso violence, Marta emptied the category of human rights "victimhood" of its complexity in the Peruvian context, in effect casting out the predominantly rural, Quechua-speaking peasants systematically targeted by state repression. Promoting her version through powerful media and party structures, Marta Moyano capitalized on her moral authority as family member of a victim to uphold, rather than contest, the dominant authoritarian narrative—and tacitly, the neoliberal legacy it represents.

Similarly, Oquendo-Villar shows how Pinochet's image, via his iconic uniform, was carefully marketed and deployed within available media and other institutional structures to consolidate his authority. Arguing that "clothes . . . made the man" (265), Oquendo-Villar contends that Pinochet utilized the uniform as a "marketing device" serving the "theatrics of order" (265–66), in the early post-coup years. Over time, however, alternative images were employed by different groups to underscore opposing views of his regime: "detractors still show images of a relatively young general in Prussian uniform," associated with the Spanish dictator Franco, "while his followers offer images of him in either his O'Higgins uniform," suggesting parallels with the Chilean independence hero, "or his civilian clothes" (283). In the wake of Pinochet's death and cremation, only his clothing—and images thereof—remain. On the one hand, Pinochet's family sold off his user-friendly civilian suits, while the Fundación Pinochet has refused to sell his more symbolically potent uniform, ironically restricting circulation of the "real thing" on the market he helped "unfetter" during his rule. On the other hand, *images* of the uniform have proliferated, circulating widely in Chilean media and on the Internet, now the contested local/global terrain of a "disputed process of packaging the caudillo for posterity" (266). Although it is difficult to assess the meaning of monetary values assigned on the image market, it seems symbolic of Pinochet's tarnished legacy that a signed photo of him in uniform, offered for auction on eBay in 2008 with a starting bid of $360, remained unsold.[33]

Recalling Elizabeth Jelin's distinction between memory *emprendedores*, who promote public and social human rights projects, and memory *empresarios*, who are in the memory business solely for profit (Bilbija and Payne), Kaiser reminds us that in the context of a proliferation of memory products, "we must differentiate between who controls the production and who profits from it" (334). Kaiser argues that the fact that Argentine human rights groups themselves determine the forms, content, and price of Argentine memorabilia mitigates the market's corrosive impact—even in the most mediated case of Moda X la Identidad (Fashion For Identity). Many groups give away or distribute information free or at minimal cost, deciding what to reproduce on T-shirts or mugs; so far, they have benefited from both public and some private funding without excessive dependence or contingencies attached. Groups such as the Madres de Plaza de Mayo thereby have controlled the ability to *not* sell, for example, their kerchiefs, which retain the Benjaminian "aura" of what has not been mechanically reproduced. So while the *image*, or "logo," of the kerchiefs has been reproduced, packaged, and sold, the kerchiefs themselves have not . . . "yet" (as Kaiser tellingly adds). Whether or not they are eventually packaged and sold, for the moment they provide evidence for Bilbija's and Payne's assertion that while markets can certainly distort memories of past terror, not all marketing works categorically against memory. Likewise, Bilbija and Payne add, "profit is not inherently positive or negative in the memory market; the kind of profit is what matters" (12). Kaiser's case study of the Madres' and H.I.J.O.S.'s control of memory product production and (mostly non-)profits suggestively illuminates one possibility of a "fair (or more just) trade"[34] renegotiation of the "free" market terms so predominant today.

Memorysites

The questions surrounding how and whether to market memorysites (Nora's lieux de mémoire), whom and what should be represented in them, who should sponsor them and how, what audiences should be targeted, and so forth, are all bound up in complicated ways with the neoliberal context, as the discussions by Laurie Beth Clark and Leigh A. Payne, Cath Collins, Susana Draper, Nancy Gates-Madsen, Cynthia E. Milton and María Eugenia Ulfe, and José Ramón Ruisánchez Serra all variously play out. The process of monument- and museum-building in the cases these authors discuss all reveal ways that anti-market sentiment co-exists with market orientation, as Bilbija and Payne emphasize. In framing these tensions, Clark and Payne explore the ethical issues around "trauma tourism," particularly the sense that the packaging and promotion of sites of former atrocities risks turning them into one more commodity to be consumed on the international market. At what point, exactly, does viewing become voyeurism? When does repeated witnessing become performance—or more pointedly, serialized mimicry? When (to recall Carlos Ossa's words) does such serialization disappear the content of what is serialized? In short, what determines if a memorysite will elicit "authentic" understanding of the past and expand human rights cultures, or "cheapen" the human rights discussion through its decontextualized reproduction? *How* can one tell the difference? *Who* can tell the difference? Per our discussion thus far:

who has the power to determine the story told, and how are official versions contested from "around" and "in-between"?

In their introduction, Bilbija and Payne cite Vargas Llosa's celebratory assessment of the "disappearance of borders" under neoliberal capitalist globalization. As we consider the possible development of an inter- or transnational culture of human rights, especially in the context of Clark's and Payne's compelling analysis of "trauma tourism," we should recall that human rights frameworks, themselves products of the Enlightenment and classical liberalism, bear a complex relationship to capitalism and imperialist expansion.[35] It seems crucial, then, to recognize for whom borders have ostensibly disappeared under globalization, and for whom they categorically have not. There is simply no comparison between the flow of tourist traffic (the province of privilege) from North to South in the Americas, and the life-threatening South-to-North trek of migrants forced into ever more dangerous routes across U.S. Southwestern deserts to seek work in the age of the North American Free Trade Agreement (NAFTA). While some South-to-North tourism may also exist, those tourists are a minority, with resources to negotiate "across" the increasingly restrictive "borders" of anti-immigrant U.S. policies. For most South-to-North travelers, unlike their Northern counterparts, the border has become less porous rather than more: indeed, it literally has become a militarized wall. Thus, there is a Northern and privileged bias to international trauma tourism, which does not invalidate the whole enterprise, but may help account for easy blog elisions between human rights abuses and laundromats (Clark and Payne), as well as for the non-necessary correspondence between visiting memorysites and increased activism for social change.

Tensions between the local and the global frame trauma tourism in Latin America. As Clark and Payne show, the translation of local issues for the global (privileged North) tourist/patron/consumer in guidebooks and websites has involved varying degrees of reductionism and depoliticization of painful human rights history, as well as the stereotyping of entire national histories. While Clark and Payne acknowledge that "some of the most personally meaningful memory sites are those that are not marketed" (119), they also hold that "to advance the 'Never Again' project, Latin America trauma tourism may require more, not less, marketing" (123). For Clark and Payne, a sense of international responsibility for defending human rights will only occur with increased exposure and education of "global citizens," which means that "some marketing may prove imperative" (123). The question may be how to establish a greater congruence between the thick, contradictory versions of local history, and their (often thin) global versions, such that the "global citizenship" being imagined and created continues to "globalize [local] disruptions" (to return to Sklair), rather than isolating them or evacuating them of their most contested and contestatory meanings.

For their part, Milton and Ulfe focus tightly on the case study of two Peruvian memorysites—the photography exhibit *Yuyanapaq* and the Museo de la Memoria in Ayacucho—both part of symbolic reparations projects stemming from the Peruvian Truth Commission 2003 report, and on the "difficult knowledge" marketed through those spaces. Although the paradigm of tourism in Peru, dating from Fujimori's neoliberal project, made rural "development" dependent on tourist, rather than public, spending, Milton and Ulfe contend that human rights groups have strategically appropriated space within this overall project to advance their own agendas. Not only have human rights activists retained an impressive degree of control over these memorysites (along the lines Kaiser describes), but they have also promoted specific narratives about the internal war that emphasize the disproportionate state-sponsored violence against highland Quechua speakers, rather than a more relativizing official approach to violence "on all sides." Thus, these human rights groups have taken advantage of the neoliberal promotion of tourism to turn it on its head, countering the typical archeological "fare" of Cuzco and Machu Picchu, packaged and sold as symbols of an idealized past, to reveal instead the legacies of violence still impacting indigenous peoples/cultures today. Milton and Ulfe hypothesize that international tourists add stability and legitimacy to the sites, rather than emphasizing their more problematic potential as privileged consumers from outside.

In her analysis, Gates-Madsen asks if, in fact, the marketing of memory "taints" the "sacred" impulse to remember, even as she notes that memorysites like the Parque de la Memoria in Buenos Aires could not exist without concerned parties "selling" the idea to funders and governmental and/or non-governmental agencies who enable their construction, and serve to attract the public to the site. Gates-Madsen persuasively argues that, paradoxically, "the inevitable marketing involved in creating this sacred space for memory both increases and decreases the visibility of the park and its capacity to realize its lofty goals" (152). The "marriage of convenience" among government, university, and human rights groups led to the choice of its remote location on the costanera, marginal to the city center, as well as its disparate, conflicting aesthetic configuration. (I would add that the internationalization of the sculpture contest carried out in the park's design tensely illustrates the local's renegotiated status in the context of globalization.) While citing Silvia Tandeciarz's contention that the park is "representative of the fraught nature of recollection and the persistent difficulty of consensus in Argentina regarding the dictatorship years," Gates-Madsen simultaneously suggests that the remote costanera park "could perhaps be viewed (albeit cynically) as a sanctioned protest designed to have a minimal impact" (160). Although any work's reception as memory/forgetting is far from guaranteed, and Gates-Madsen conserves a strong sense of the park's various potential meanings, the park's location and institutionalization do seem to work toward dissipating dissent.

I am reminded here of a crystallizing moment in the essay by Clark and Payne, the haunting question posed by a blogger who recounts a perplexing journey to the Department of Political and Social Order (DOPS) former torture center in São Paulo. Seeking to reconcile the underwhelming content of this out-of-the-way memorysite with the overwhelming experience of having witnessed police brutality just outside its doors, the blogger asks: "Does the absence of memorials make a culture of impunity, or does a culture of impunity render empty memorials?" (121). Returning to the inextricable connection between authoritarian residues in post-dictatorship contexts (including impunity) and the ongoing hegemony of neoliberal "modernization," I would also ask: does an absence (or marginalization) of memorials reflect and abet neoliberalism's hegemony, or does a culture of neoliberalism render memorials empty? It seems clear that both processes take place, if unevenly, and as the authors in this volume expose, memorysites may not only become emptied of potential meanings through the processes of their funding, institutionalization, promotion, and consumption, all marked by the neoliberal context, but also through the very aesthetic of *fixity* that monumentalization itself entails.

Thus, as Clark and Payne, Gates-Madsen, Ruisánchez Serra, and others in this volume point out, a major limitation of many monuments is their static quality: once the past becomes concrete, it need never move again. A major dilemma for monument organizers is how to keep the process of memory formation alive and dynamic, given all the forces (market, political, institutional, aesthetic) pushing toward stasis. How can dissident and contradictory voices continue to perturb and disturb, to provoke memory repeatedly over time, without becoming ossified as one more museum artifact or experience to consume? It seems especially important to notice that, in the interstices of the processes producing and institutionalizing memorysites and their memory/forgetting, some other possibilities have emerged.

Draper contrasts two very different ways the past has become transformed both spatially and temporally in post-dictatorship cities. On one hand, she demonstrates how the Punta Carretas Shopping Center in Montevideo, an elite mall literally superimposed atop a former prison, models the continuities of authoritarianism and neoliberalism; on the other, she contends that the ESMA (Escuela de Suboficiales de Mecánica de la Armada) and Olimpo former detention centers-turned-memory sites in Buenos Aires unleash a more problematized relationship with the past. According to Draper, Punta Carretas subsumes and dissipates uncomfortable questions by interpolating the public as carefree consumers "free" to fall in love via timeless amnesiac consumption—thereby reinforcing the larger "city of impunity" of both market and full step logics. By contrast, ESMA and Olimpo create "critical foldings" in the city, inviting uncomfortable reflection on violent legacies of the authoritarian past. If the former closes the chapter on the dictatorship years, symbolizing the link between forgetting and neoliberalization within "the camouflaged aesthetic of the transition" (129) wherein the past serves merely as ornament, the latter open up unsettling and unreconciled histories insistently again, through these spaces' incomplete, eroding qualities, their lack of make-up. Draper insists that in such spaces "the past slows the present course . . . that defined the transition" (131), opening moments that *exceed* state and market management strategies and "the quantitative logic of sales" (131). Countering the mall's "erasure of temporality" (135) and its utopian illusion of (controlled) freedom—metaphors of the transition itself—ESMA's and Olimpo's disturbing incompleteness "link[s] the genealogical past and present" (147), thereby "interrupting a market driven by the demand to bring closure to the past" (148).

In her analysis of Chilean memorysites, Collins also explores how neoliberal patterns have been partially renegotiated in recent years. Collins argues that the more recent left-leaning social democratic governments of Ricardo Lagos (2000–2006) and Michelle Bachelet (2006–10) have witnessed an *increased* role of the state—counter to the neoliberal norm—in supporting a range of memory initiatives. This support has emerged in the wake of what is arguably *the* upside of globalization for Chile's memory culture: Pinochet's 1998 arrest in London, made possible through transnational application of international human rights law, stimulated a local shift away from pervasive social amnesia toward the increased public support of memory and accountability projects Collins discusses. Yet Collins, like Gates-Madsen, explores the interplay of tensions between the state/governmental sponsors and human rights organizers who find themselves reluctant but necessary partners in the sites' funding and development. A lack of economic resources often forces organizers to seek government support, which has come in a range of forms, each with distinct (procedural and economic) strings attached. An essential tension, notes Gates-Madsen, citing Tappatá de Valdez, surrounds the paradox of the state funding *any* memorial to victims of the state, even if the state is ostensibly reconfigured post-dictatorship. While Collins acknowledges the state's problematic roles in controlling memorysites, in which technocratic frameworks, wittingly or not, may wind up marginalizing the very voices the sites presumably represent, she arrives at an intriguing conclusion about the current "mainstreaming" of memorialization discourse and practice: "As state entities are drawn one by one into the memorialization field . . . a sense of the state's own necessary, and distinct, responsibilities" (257) has developed, including the sense that commemoration of those targeted by state repression is "a legitimate, and/or a necessary, activity for the state to engage in" (250). Perhaps a significant part of what is being remembered through these projects, then, is precisely the role and function of the state as a guarantor of rights (and mitigator of market forces)—functions systematically diminished/forgotten under the neoliberal authoritarian regimes.[36]

Other modes of recollection also have contested predominant patterns. Some commemorations have resisted "fixing" the past aesthetically through the creation of forms that draw attention to their own incompleteness, to their own precarious status as representations, to a need to move viewers/readers dialogically toward tentative interpretations, such as the Memory Spiral in La Plata and other works inspired by the post-Holocaust countermonument tradition.[37] As we have seen, Draper characterizes the ESMA and Olimpo memorysites in this way. Other commemorative works have emerged without planning or state support, such as the graffiti and art that have appeared at the Club Atlético in Buenos Aires—"sprouted from a crack in the sidewalk"[38] in an under-the-freeway excavation site symbolically superimposing modernization's and the dictatorship's costs. Still others resist officially sanctioned circuits, having been produced by non-state

Figure 2. In "30,000," the Argentine sculptor Nicolás Guagnini, himself a family member of several desaparecidos, superimposes the photo of his father used in protests by his grandmother on a fragmentary, prismatic structure, inviting viewer interaction. As one moves around the work, the photograph changes and distorts, bringing some aspects into view as others disappear. The sculpture is displayed at the Parque de la Memoria, Buenos Aires. (Photograph by Laurie Beth Clark and Michael Peterson)

and non-commercial actors for educational or denunciatory purposes, with no aspiration for permanence or institutionality. Kaiser's and Gates-Madsen's discussions of escraches and political performances by the Grupo de Arte Callejero, and Collins's exploration of the Funa's radical approach of direct actions focused on repressors, show that all pose a rejection of, and alternative to, mechanisms for memory/forgetting institutionalized within the hegemonic neoliberal and political paradigms. Although even these works take shape dialogically through and against the dominant narrative, they attempt to resist memory's fixity and commodification through their impermanent (and irreverent) forms and content.

Building on Draper's work, we should also consider the possibility that memorysites may be occupied by both intentional and accidental visitors in ways that counter the overwhelming commodification of *time* under late capitalism. While Diamela Eltit describes the extreme regimentation of bodies under neoliberalism, bodies whose every movement is harnessed in service of production and consumption,[39] Appadurai holds that "there is really little escape from the rhythms of industrial production,"[40] such that even leisure time becomes frenetic, and structuring it becomes work.[41] Perhaps there are ways in which contemplation and reflection themselves, by nature *slow* activities, counter the speed and intensity of the market. These are not *useful* activities from Benjamin Franklin's classic "time is money" perspective; they are not *efficient* in Taylorist terms. They may be *productive,* in terms of potentially fostering collective remembering/forgetting, but not in terms of making an immediately saleable product whose worth is measurable in cash. Appadurai writes that "modern consumption replaces the aesthetics of duration with the aesthetics of ephemerality";[42] by contrast, a photo of the disappeared, the same every time, a portrait that cannot and does not evolve, calls for memory in a "timeless" and "enduring" way that contrasts with the empty "timelessness" of the mall. In this particular sense, then, certain forms of stasis or fixity associated with memorysites and the various ways people engage them might work against hegemonic interests, countering the rapid and the ephemeral, the frenzy of market and work rhythms. In short, slowness, and any non-utilitarian use of time, may be the ultimate anti-neoliberal virtues.[43]

Moreover, as many of the authors in this volume suggest, the history "surrounding" the monuments—including the conflicting social processes preceding and "around" their installation—may reveal more about collective memory and authority than monuments themselves. Keeping *those* stories and dynamics afloat, even in their own precariousness and contradiction, may figure among the most crucial memory work to be done to address the human costs of both authoritarian violence and neoliberalism. Along these lines, the challenging pedagogical modes facilitated by the Comisión Provincial por la Memoria in La Plata (Argentina), in which schoolchildren undertake interactive, dialogic projects geared toward unearthing multiple narratives of the past, offers a powerful example of an ongoing, mobile memory praxis.[44] As Carlos Ossa writes: "In this context, to narrate means to provide a place for what has been scattered, to string together fragile memories using second-hand and stupefied words, to hold onto fragments banished by the language of agreements, to oppose the indolence of a democracy without a sense of tragedy that has made modernization a form of beautified barbarism."[45] Richard explains: "These truncated signs are . . . what should be incorporated into the historical narratives of the Transition, in order to make visible not only the glittering political-administrative and technical-commercial success of democratic modernization within which present-day Chile is clothed, but also what has been overshadowed by it: the fractured and convulsive qualities of shattered biographies, of defenseless subjectivities, of languages and representations replete with scars that the market-oriented frenzy has cruelly dislodged from its consumer shopwindows."[46] In short, such a focus implies a continuous insistence on cultural dialogue and debate, the development of aesthetic practices of memory that reveal its slow, discontinuous, fragmentary, violent, and/or hybrid aspects, and a deep interrogation of past *and present* limitations of neoliberal modernization projects (and their attendant "technologies of dis-remembering").

Like Draper, Ruisánchez Serra addresses a context where the city is rewritten, to both reveal and conceal some of history's contours. Ruisánchez Serra reads the opening of a museum within the former Ministry of Foreign Affairs Chancellery in Mexico City as a "reterritorialization" of the Tlatelolco massacre of 1968 within the current coordinates of globalization and NAFTA. He reveals how this rewriting of urban space, viewed within the broad context of a gentrification of the Centro Histórico that excluded Tlatelolco, effectively sanitizes and distances the violence of the past (and I would add, the present) under a dubious script of successful economic integration, diverting attention from underlying injustices, both past and present. If the memorial largely tames both '68's challenges and Poniatowska's counterhegemonic rendering of them ("What is placed is also placated, placidly brought to peace"), Ruisánchez Serra contends that "in the same sense . . . the streets are rid of those [street vendors] who may pose a danger to the free flow of capital to the Centro Histórico" (187). Disruptive voices and bodies are cast out, banned once again from the (monumental) modernization project and its narratives. And yet the very tensions surfacing around the October 2008 fortieth anniversary of the massacre—including the presence of protesters actively crossing geographic, generational, class, and other boundaries—reveal that this imposition of forgetting has been at best partial and incomplete, leaving a "palimpsest" of memory that refuses total erasure, to invoke Hugo Achugar's take on the Punta Carretas Shopping Center.[47] Ruisánchez Serra's work on polyvocal ("ambiguous," "nomadic," "feminine") readings of the liberties '68 enabled, versus the univocal structurings of the Tlatelolco massacre and memorysite, captures what is most at stake in the struggle for recollection in a context of neoliberal institutionalization and globalization: "the very core of memory before its commodification, and with it, *the possibility of a memory of commodification*" (203) (emphasis in the original). As Ruisánchez Serra powerfully concludes: "To preserve the . . . possibility of that memory process is indeed very well worth marching for, re-reading for, writing for" (203).

In many respects, the phrase "marketing discontent" highlights the paradox facing any alternative discourse produced within the current context of neoliberal capitalist globalization. Challenges to the hegemonic model may be neutralized through deeper insertion into it—that is, through commodification—and as Yúdice, Franco, and Flores write, "The ideological veneer of pluralism admits difference without that difference constituting a threat to state and market systems."[48] There appears to be no "outside" of the market. At the same time, as the cases from Argentina, Uruguay, Chile, Brazil, Peru, and Mexico discussed here show, we must recognize the memories that *do* emerge dialogically from within the interstices and among the residues of the authoritarian/modernization project—voices insistently, if sometimes precariously, interrupting and disrupting the dominant narrative to claim representational power, and to contest (in Anderson's words) *which* "violent deaths must be remembered/forgotten as 'our own.'"[49]

NOTES

Special thanks for Ksenija Bilbija, Cath Collins, Alexandra Huneeus, Nicolás Lynch, Greg Mullins, Leigh A. Payne, Tom Womeldorff, and Tony Zaragoza for their perceptive comments on this chapter.

1. Anderson, *Imagined Communities*, 201.
2. Ibid., 204
3. Ibid., 206.
4. Taylor, *The Archive and the Repertoire*, 21.
5. Most definitions of neoliberalism posit its basic tenets as the promotion of the free market and free trade, deregulation, privatization, the reduction of public spending and the state's role in the economy, and a tacit shift from the concept of "public good" to one of "personal responsibility" (see Elizabeth Martínez and Arnoldo García, "What Is Neoliberalism? A Brief Definition for Activists," www.corpwatch.org/article.php?id=376; Rakocy et al., *Real World Globalization*; and Collins and Lear, *Chile's Free Market Miracle*). However, it may be more precise to note that the state's role has *shifted* rather than *diminished*. Harvey clarifies that the state does intervene to guarantee "the quality and integrity of money," as well as guaranteeing the "military, defense, police and juridical functions required to secure private property rights and to support freely functioning markets" (Harvey, "Neo-

Liberalism as Creative Destruction," 145; see also Harvey, *A Brief History of Neoliberalism*). Klein goes even further: "Far from freeing the market from the state, . . . political and corporate elites have simply merged, trading favors to secure the right to appropriate precious resources previously held in the public domain." She terms this paradigm "corporatist" rather than "neoliberal," and notes that the exclusion of the majority from the benefits of this model results in "aggressive surveillance (once again, with government and large corporations trading favors and contracts), mass incarceration, shrinking civil liberties, and often, though not always, torture" (Klein, *The Shock Doctrine*, 18–19).

6. Sklair, "Social Movements and Global Capitalism," 291, 296–97.
7. The usually cited list includes the governments of Néstor Kirchner and Cristina Fernández de Kirchner (Argentina), Michelle Bachelet (Chile), Tabaré Vásquez (Uruguay), Fernando Lugo (Paraguay), Luiz Inácio Lula da Silva (Brazil), Evo Morales (Bolivia), Rafael Correa (Ecuador), Hugo Chávez (Venezuela), and Daniel Ortega (Nicaragua). In addition, the March 2009 victory of Mauricio Funes of the FMLN in El Salvador marks a significant break from more than a century of conservative rule there. Of these, only the governments of Morales and Chávez have taken a clearly anti-neoliberal stance (in the case of Funes, it is too early to tell).
8. Arguably, then, the so-called "Washington Consensus," as Eric Selbin writes, "was [or, has become] neither, i.e., it had little to do with Washington and far more to do with global capitalist markets, and the 'consensus' was largely [only] among elites" across the Americas (Selbin, "Making the World New," 33).
9. Lynch, "What the 'Left' Means in Latin America Now," 373.
10. Délano and Traslaviña, *La herencia de los Chicago Boys*, 47.
11. Collins and Lear, *Chile's Free Market Miracle*, 3–9.
12. Avelar, *The Untimely Present*, 59.
13. Ibid., 58 (emphasis in the original).
14. Eltit, "La memoria pantalla," 32.
15. Richard, "Presentación," 10 (translations from the original Spanish are my own).
16. See Jameson, *Postmodernism, or, The Cultural Logic of Late Capitalism*, x; Sklair, "Social Movements and Global Capitalism," 291.
17. Verónica Schild, remarks at the plenary session of the "Democracy in Latin America 30 Years after Chile's 9/11" conference, Albany, N.Y., 10–12 October 2003. See also Richard, "Las derrotas son completas sólo cuando los vencidos olvidan las razones por las que lucharon," 10.
18. Yúdice, Franco, and Flores, Introduction to *On Edge*, viii.
19. Ibid.
20. For the term "corporatist," I follow Klein's usage (see Klein, *The Shock Doctrine*, 18).
21. Appadurai, *Modernity at Large*, 3 (emphasis in the original).
22. Ibid., 49.
23. García Canclini, *Consumers and Citizens*, 62.
24. Appadurai's definition: "Mediascapes refer both to the distribution of the electronic capabilities to produce and disseminate information . . . , which are now

available to a growing number of private and public interests throughout the world, and to the images of the world created by these media" (Appadurai, *Modernity at Large*, 35).

25. Per Schudson, *Advertising, the Uneasy Persuasion*, 10.
26. Citing Sarlo, Bilbija notes that such homogenization occurs in tension with heterogenization of cultures under globalization (see Sarlo, *Escenas de la vida posmoderna*, 16). More precisely, we might underscore García Canclini's point that apparent homogenization is actually a (re)iteration of difference: "Globalization [is] a process of fragmentation and recomposition; rather than homogenize the world, globalization reorders differences and inequalities without eliminating them" (García Canclini, *Consumers and Citizens*, 3).
27. I am reminded of Appadurai's take on advertising's role in diffusing social action: "Global advertising is the key technology for the worldwide dissemination of . . . well-chosen ideas of consumer agency. These images of agency are increasingly distortions of a world of merchandising so subtle that the consumer is consistently helped to believe that he or she is an actor, where in fact he or she is at best a chooser" (Appadurai, *Modernity at Large*, 42).
28. Ossa, "El jardín de las máscaras," 73 (my translation).
29. Yúdice, Franco, and Flores, Introduction to *On Edge*, viii.
30. Sklair, "Social Movements and Global Capitalism," 291.
31. Ibid., 305.
32. Marisol LeBrón, "Guatemala's 'Twitter Revolution,'" http://nacla.org/node/5874.
33. Trajković, "Memorabilia and Video Games of the Post-dictatorship Period in Latin America."
34. By contrast to "free trade," I define "fair trade" as a set of practices geared toward favoring commodity producers of the global South, in which the terms of production and profit are determined "fair" by and for producers (and as relevant for a given production process, other pertinent protections are established to protect labor, environment, and human rights) (see chap. 1 in Ransom, *The No-Nonsense Guide to Fair Trade*).
35. Despite the progressive intentions and potential outcomes of human rights work, Greg Mullins argues that "human rights and 'humanitarianism' are extensions of political power within imperial frameworks that claim to critique imperialism, but that may well end up reinforcing it" (Mullins, "Paradoxes of Neoliberalism and Human Rights," unpublished essay, 2).
36. José Ramón Ruisánchez Serra made a similar point in our discussions at the conference "Marketing Memory in Latin America," Madison, Wisc., 11–13 April 2008.
37. Several authors in this volume insightfully build on Young's classic *At Memory's Edge*.
38. Tandeciarz, "Citizens of Memory," 161.
39. Eltit, "La memoria pantalla," 32.
40. Appadurai, *Modernity at Large*, 80.
41. Ibid., 82.
42. Ibid., 85.

43. In pointing this out at the Marketing Memory conference cited previously, Alexandra Huneeus brought to my attention a quote from Milan Kundera's *Slowness*: "There is a secret bond between slowness and memory. . . . In existential mathematics . . . the degree of slowness is directly proportional to the intensity of memory; the degree of speed is directly proportional to the intensity of forgetting" (Kundera, *Slowness*, 39).
44. See Raggio and Salvatori, *La última dictadura militar en Argentina.*
45. Ossa, "El jardín de las mascaras," 73–74.
46. Richard, *Presentación*, 11.
47. See, e.g., Hugo Achugar, "Territorios y memorias versus lógica del mercado (A propósito de cartografías y shopping malls)," www.pacc.ufrj.br/artelatina/hugo.html
48. Yúdice, Franco, and Flores, Introduction to *On Edge*, x.
49. Anderson, *Imagined Communities*, 206.

Bibliography

Achugar, Hugo. *Planetas sin boca: Escritos efímeros sobre arte, cultura y literature.* Montevideo: Trilce, 2004.

Actis, Munú, Christina Aldini, Liliana Gardella, Miriam Lewin, and Elisa Tokar. *Ese infierno: Conversaciones de cinco mujeres sobrevivientes de la* ESMA. Buenos Aires: Altamira, 2006.

Aeberhard, Danny, Lucy Phillips, Andrew Benson, and Rosalba O'Brien. *The Rough Guide to Argentina.* London: Rough Guides, 2008.

Aguayo, Sergio. *1968: Los archivos de la violencia.* Mexico City: Grijalbo, 1998.

Agüero, Ignacio. *Memorial de Paine*, documentary film, 2007.

Alexander, Lawrence A. "Can You Build a Downtown Shopping Center?" In *The Downtown Shopping Center: A New Concept.* New York: The Center, 1975.

Andermann, Jens, Philip Derbyshire, and John Kraniauskas. "No Matarás ('Thou Shalt Not Kill'): An Introduction." *Journal of Latin American Cultural Studies* 16, no. 2 (2007): 111–13.

Anderson, Benedict. *Imagined Communities: Reflections on the Origin and Spread of Nationalism.* London: Verso, 1991.

ANFASEP. *Hasta cuándo tu silencio? Testimonios de dolor y coraje.* Ayacucho: ANFASEP, 2007.

Ang, Ien. *Living Room Wars: Rethinking Audiences for a Postmodern World.* New York: Routledge, 1996.

Angell, Alan. "The Pinochet Factor in Chilean Politics." In *The Pinochet Case: Origins, Progress, and Implications*, edited by Madeleine Davis, 63–84. London: Institute of Latin American Studies, 2003.

Appadurai, Arjun. *Modernity at Large: Cultural Dimensions of Globalization.* Minneapolis: University of Minnesota Press, 1996.

Araújo, Joel Zito. *A negação do Brasil: O negro na telenovela brasileira.* São Paulo: SENAC, 2000.

Arce, Luz. *The Inferno: A Story of Terror and Survival in Chile.* Translated by Stacey Alba D. Skar. Madison: University of Wisconsin Press, 2004.

Archdiocese of São Paulo, Jaime Wright, and Joan Dassin. *Torture in Brazil: A Shocking Report on the Pervasive Use of Torture by Brazilian Military Governments, 1964–1979.* Austin: University of Texas Press, 1998.

Arriagada, Arturo, and Martín Schuster. "Consumo de medios y participación ciudadana de los jóvenes chilenos." *Cuadernos de Información* 22 (2008): 34–41.

Arriagada, Genaro. *La política militar de Pinochet, 1973–1985.* Santiago: Salesianos, 1985.

Ashward, Gregory, and Rudi Hartmann. Introduction to *Horror and Human Tragedy*

Revisited: The Management of Sites of Atrocities for Tourism, edited by Gregory Ashward and Rudi Hartmann, 1–14. New York: Cognizant, 2005.

Avelar, Idelber. *Alegorías de la derrota: La ficción postdictatorial y el trabajo del duelo.* Santiago: Cuarto Propio, 2000.

———. *The Untimely Present: Postdictatorial Latin American Fiction and the Task of Mourning.* Durham, N.C.: Duke University Press, 1999.

Barcellos, Caco. "O *Globo Repórter* sobre a Vala de Perus." In *Mortos e desaparecidos políticos: Reparação ou impunidade?* edited by Janaína Teles, 213–26. São Paulo: Humanitas/FFLCH/USP, 2001.

Barrantes Segura, Rafael, and Jesús Peña Romero. "Narrativas sobre el conflicto armado interno en el Perú: La memoria en el proceso político después de la CVR." In *Transformaciones democráticas y memorias de la violencia en el Perú*, coordinator Félix Reátegui Carrillo, 15–40. Lima: IDEHPUCP, 2006.

Barros, Robert. *Constitutionalism and Dictatorship: Pinochet, the Junta, and the 1980 Constitution.* Cambridge: Cambridge University Press, 2002.

Baudrillard, Jean. *The Illusion of the End.* Stanford, Calif.: Stanford University Press, 1994.

———. *The Intelligence of Evil or the Lucidity Pact.* New York: Berg, 2005.

———. *The System of Objects.* Translated by James Benedict. London: Verso, 1998.

Bellinghausen, Hermann. "Los muchachos de entonces: Entrevista con Elena Poniatowska." In *Pensar el 68*, edited by Luis Franco Ramos, 247–52. Mexico City: Cal y Arena, 1988.

Benedetti, Mario. *El olvido está lleno de memoria.* Buenos Aires: Grupo Editorial Planeta, 1998.

Benhabib, Seyla. "Models of the Public Space: Hannah Arendt, the Liberal Tradition, and J. Habermas." In *Habermas and the Public Sphere,* edited by Craig Calhoun, 73–98. Cambridge: MIT Press, 1992.

Benson, Elizabeth, et al., eds. *Retratos: 2,000 years of Latin American Portraits.* New Haven: Yale University Press, 2004.

Benstock, Shari, and Elizabeth Ferris. *On Fashion.* New Brunswick, N.J.: Rutgers University Press, 1994.

Berliner, David C. "The Abuses of Memory: Reflections on the Memory Boom in Anthropology." *Anthropological Quarterly* 78, no. 1 (2005): 197–211.

Bernhardson, Wayne. *Argentina.* Moon Handbooks. Emeryville, Calif.: Avalon Travel, 2007.

———. *Chile.* Moon Handbooks. Emeryville, Calif.: Avalon Travel, 2007.

Bickford, Louis. "Memoryscapes." In *The Art of Truth-Telling about Authoritarian Rule*, edited by Ksenija Bilbija, Jo Ellen Fair, Cynthia E. Milton, and Leigh A. Payne, 96–102. Madison: University of Wisconsin Press, 2005.

———. "Unofficial Truth Projects." *Human Rights Quarterly* 29, no. 4 (2007): 994–1035.

Bilbija, Ksenija, Jo Ellen Fair, Cynthia E. Milton, and Leigh A. Payne, eds. *The Art of Truth-Telling about Authoritarian Rule.* Madison: University of Wisconsin Press, 2005.

Blondet, Cecilia. *Muchas vidas construyendo una identidad: Las mujeres pobladoras de un barrio limeño.* Lima: Instituto de Estudios Peruanos, 1986.

Bonafini, Hebe de. *Historias de vida, Hebe de Bonafini.* Edited with a preface by Matilde Sanchez. Buenos Aires: Fraterna/del Nuevo Extremo, 1985.

Borea Labarthe, Giuliana. "Yuyanapaq: Activando la memoria en una puesta en escena para recorder." *ILLAPA, Revista del Instituto de Investigaciones Museológicas y Artísticas* 1, no. 1 (2004): 57–68.

Borges, Jorge Luis. *Ficciones.* Translated by Anthony Bonner. New York: Grove Press, 1962.

Boyarin, Jonathan, ed. *Remapping Memory: The Politics of TimeSpace.* Minneapolis: University of Minnesota Press, 1994.

Braxton, Joanne, and Maria I. Diedrich, eds. *Monuments of the Black Atlantic: Slavery and Memory.* New Brunswick, N.J.: Transaction Publishers, 2004.

Britzman, Deborah P. *Lost Subjects, Contested Objects: Toward a Psychoanalytic Inquiry of Learning.* Albany: State University of New York Press, 1998.

Brodsky, Marcelo. *Nexo: Un ensayo fotográfico de Marcelo Brodsky.* Buenos Aires: La Marca, 2001.

Bruner, Edward. "Tourism in Ghana: The Representation of Slavery and the Return of the Black Diaspora." *American Anthropologist* 98, no. 2 (1996): 290–304.

Bucci, Eugênio. *O peixe morre pela boca: Oito artigos sobre cultura e poder.* São Paulo: Scritta, 1993.

Burt, Jo-Marie. "Guilty as Charged: The Trial of Former Peruvian President Alberto Fujimori for Grave Human Rights Violations." *International Journal of Transitional Justice* 3 (2009), 384–405.

———. "La batalla por las barriadas de Lima: El caso de Villa El Salvador." In Comisión de la Verdad y Reconciliación, *Informe Final* (2003), bk. 5, chap. 2.16, 327–50, available at www.cverdad.org.pe.

———. "Sendero Luminoso and the 'Decisive Battle' in Lima's *Barriadas*: The Case of Villa El Salvador." In *Shining and Other Paths: War and Society in Peru, 1980–1995*, edited by Steve J. Stern, 267–306. Durham, N.C.: Duke University Press, 1998.

———. *Silencing Civil Society: Political Violence and the Authoritarian State in Peru.* New York: Palgrave Macmillan Press, 2007.

———. "Los usos y abusos de la memoria de María Elena Moyano." *A Contra Corriente* 7.2 (2010), 165–209.

Cadena, Marisol de la. *Indigenous Mestizos: The Politics of Race and Culture in Cuzco, 1919–1991.* Durham, N.C.: Duke University Press, 2000.

Calveiro, Pilar. *Poder y desaparición: Los campos de concentración en Argentina.* Buenos Aires: Colihue, 1998.

Cárcamo-Huechante, Luis. *Tramas del mercado: Imaginación económica, cultura pública y literatura en el Chile de fines del siglo veinte.* Santiago: Editorial Cuarto Propio, 2007.

Carillet, Jean-Bernard, Charlotte Amelines, Thomas Kohnstamm, and Jolyon Attwooll. *Lonely Planet: Chile and Easter Island.* Footscray, Australia: Lonely Planet Publications, 2006.

Carvalho, Alessandra, and Ludmila da Silva Catela. "31 de marzo de 1964 en Brasil: Memórias deshilachadas." In *Las conmemoraciones: Las disputas en las fechas "infelices,"* edited by Elizabeth Jelin, 195–242. Madrid: Siglo XXI Editores, 2002.

Casado, Matt A. "Peru's Tourism Industry: Growth, Setbacks, Threats." *Cornell Hospitality Quarterly* 39 (February 1998): 68–73.

Casey, Edward. *The Fate of Place: A Philosophical History.* Berkeley: University of California Press, 1997.

Caten, Lara Ten. "1968: O mito que não terminou." *Famecos* 1, no. 2 (1995): 53–63.

Cavallo, Ascanio. *La historia oculta de la transición.* Santiago: Editorial Grijalbo, 1998.

Chandler, Gary, and Paige Penland. *Lonely Planet: Nicaragua and El Salvador.* Footscray, Australia: Lonely Planet Publications, 2006.

Chevigny, Bell Gale. "The Transformation of Privilege in the Work of Elena Poniatowska." *Latin American Literary Review* 13 (July 1985): 49–62.

Chidester, David, and Edward T. Linenthal. Introduction to *American Sacred Space,* edited by David Chidester and Edward T. Linenthal, 1–42. Bloomington: Indiana University Press, 1995.

Clark, Laurie Beth. "Coming to Terms with Trauma Tourism." *Performance Paradigm* 5, no. 2 (October 2009).

Collins, Cath. "Grounding Global Justice: International Networks and Domestic Human Rights Accountability in Chile and El Salvador." *Journal of Latin American Studies* 38, no. 4 (2006): 711–38.

———. "State Terror and the Law: The (Re)Judicialization of Human Rights Accountability in Chile and El Salvador." *Latin American Perspectives* 35, no. 5 (2008): 20–37.

Collins, Joseph, and John Lear. *Chile's Free Market Miracle: A Second Look.* Oakland, Calif.: Institute for Food and Development Policy, 1995.

Conaghan, Catherine. *Fujimori's Peru: Deception in the Public Sphere.* Pittsburgh: University of Pittsburgh Press, 2005.

Contreras Sepúlveda, Manuel. *La verdad histórica: El ejército guerrillero.* Santiago, Chile: Ediciones Encina, 2000.

———. *La verdad histórica II: ¿Desaparecidos?* Santiago, Chile: Ediciones Encina, 2001.

Coral, Isabel. "Las mujeres en la guerra: Impacto y respuestas." In *Los senderos insólitos del Perú,* edited by Steve Stern. Lima: IEP, UNSCH, 1999.

de Certeau, Michel. *Capture of Speech and Other Political Writings.* Translated by Tom Conley. Minneapolis: University of Minnesota Press, 1998.

———. *The Practice of Everyday Life.* Translated by Steven Randall. Berkeley: University of California Press, 1984.

Degregori, Carlos Iván, José Coronel, Ponciano del Pino, and Orin Starn. *Las rondas campesinas y la derrota de Sendero Luminoso.* Lima: Instituto de Estudios Peruanos, 1996.

Délano, Manuel, and Hugo Traslaviña. *La herencia de los Chicago Boys.* Santiago: Ediciones del Ornitorrinco, 1989.

De Lima, Venicio. "Brazilian Television in the 1989 Presidential Election: Constructing a President." In *Television, Politics, and the Transition to Democracy in Latin America*, edited by Thomas E. Skidmore, 97–117. Baltimore: Johns Hopkins University Press, 1993.

———. "The State, Television, and Political Power in Brazil." *Critical Studies in Mass Communications* 5, no. 2 (June 1988): 108–28.

Derrida, Jacques. *On Cosmopolitanism and Forgiveness*. Translated by Mark Dooley and Michael Hughes. London: Routledge, 2001.

Dunn, Christopher. *Brutality Garden: Tropicália and the Emergence of a Brazilian Counterculture*. Chapel Hill: University of North Carolina Press, 2001.

Ejército de Chile. *Historia del Ejército de Chile,* vol. 11, *Nuestros uniformes*. Santiago: Colección Biblioteca Militar, 1985.

Eliade, Mircea. *The Sacred and the Profane: The Nature of Religion*. Translated by Willard R. Trask. San Diego: Harcourt Brace Jovanovich, 1959.

Eltit, Diamela. "La memoria pantalla (acerca de las imágenes públicas como políticas de desmemoria)." *Revista de Crítica Cultural* 32 (November 2005): 26–35.

Escultura y Memoria. Buenos Aires: EUDEBA, 2000.

"Estado de situación," *Reunión constitutiva de la Comisión Pro-Monumento a las Víctimas del Terrorismo de Estado*, Buenos Aires, 18 September 1998.

Estill, Adriana. "The Mexican Telenovela and Its Foundational Fictions." In *Latin American Literature and the Mass Media*, edited by Edmundo Paz-Soldán and Debra A. Castillo, 169–89. New York: Garland, 2001.

Etchecolatz, Miguel O. *La otra campana del Nunca Más*. Buenos Aires: n.p., 1988.

Feitlowitz, Marguerite. *A Lexicon of Terror: Argentina and the Legacies of Terror*. New York: Oxford University Press, 1999.

Feld, Claudia. *Del estrado a la pantalla: Las imagines del juicio a los ex-comandantes en Argentina*. Madrid: Siglo XXI Editores, 2002.

Fentress, James, and Chris Wickham. *Social Memory*. Oxford: Blackwell, 1992.

Finkielkraut, Alain. *In the Name of Humanity: Reflections on the Twentieth Century*. Translated by Judith Friedlander. New York: Columbia University Press, 2000.

Firestone, Matthew D. *Lonely Planet: Panama*. Footscray, Australia: Lonely Planet Publications, 2007.

Fisher, John, Daniel Jacobs, Paul Whitfield, and Zora O'Neill. *The Rough Guide to Mexico*. London: Rough Guides, 2007.

Fodor's Argentina. Edited by Laura Kidder. New York: Random House, 2006.

Fodor's Chile. Edited by Sarah Gold. New York: Random House, 2006.

Frazier, Lessie Jo, and Deborah Cohen. "Mexico '68: Defining the Space of the Movement, Heroic Masculinity in the Prison, and 'Women' in the Streets." *Hispanic American Historical Review* 83, no. 4 (November 2003): 617–60.

Fuguet, Alberto. *Bad Vibes*. Translated by Kristina Cordero. New York: St. Martin's Press, 1997.

———. *Por favor, rebobinar*. Buenos Aires: Alfaguara, 1998.

García Canclini, Néstor. *Consumers and Citizens: Globalization and Multicultural Conflicts*. Translated by George Yúdice. Minneapolis: University of Minnesota Press, 2001.

———. *Consumidores y ciudadanos: Conflictos culturales de la globalización*. Mexico City: Grijalbo, 1995.

Gaskell, George, and Daniel Wright. "Group Differences in Memory for a Political Event." In *Collective Memory of Political Events: Social Psychological Perspectives*, edited by James W. Pennebaker, Darío Páez, and Bernard Rimé, 175–90. Mahwah, N.J.: Lawrence Erlbaum Associates, 1997.

Gaspari, Elio. *A ditadura derrotada*. São Paulo: Companhia das Letras, 2003.

———. *A ditadura encurralada*. São Paulo: Companhia das Letras, 2004.

Gates Madsen, Nancy. "Ruins of the Past." In *The Art of Truth-Telling about Authoritarian Rule*, edited by Ksenija Bilbija, Jo Ellen Fair, Cynthia E. Milton, and Leigh A. Payne, 110–11. Madison: University of Wisconsin Press, 2005.

Giménez, Fabián, and Alejandro Villagrán. *Estética de la oscuridad: Posmodernidad, periferia y mass media en la cultura de los noventa*. Montevideo: Trazas, 1995.

Ginway, Elizabeth. "Literature under the Dictatorship." In *The Brazil Reader: History, Culture, Politics*, edited by Robert M. Levine and John J. Crocitti, 248–53. Durham, N.C.: Duke University Press, 1999.

Gist, Richard, and Bernard Lubin. *Response to Disaster: Psychosocial, Community, and Ecological Approaches*. London: Routledge, 1999.

González, Horacio. "Las sombras del edificio." In *Memoria en construcción: El debate sobre la ESMA*, edited by Marcelo Brodsky, 76. Buenos Aires: La Marca, 2005.

Graham, Melissa, and Andrew Benson. *The Rough Guide to Chile*. London: Rough Guides, 2006.

Grupo de Arte Callejero. "El anti-monumento: Resignación de la memoria histórica." In *Políticas de la memoria: Tensiones en la palabra y la imagen*, edited by Sandra Lorenzano and Ralph Buchenhorst, 211–18. Mexico City: Universidad del Claustro de Sor Juana, 2007.

Guillermoprieto, Alma. *The Heart That Bleeds: Latin America Now*. New York: Alfred A. Knopf, 1994.

Guzmán, Nancy. *Romo: Confesiones de un torturador*. Santiago: Editorial Planeta, 2000.

Guzmán, Patricia. *The Battle of Chile*. Documentary film, 1976.

———. *Obstinate Memory*. Documentary film, 1997.

———. *The Pinochet Case*. Documentary film, 2001.

Hall, Stuart. "Encoding/Decoding." In *Media and Cultural Studies: Key Works*, edited by Gigi Durham and Douglas Kellner, 163–73. Malden, Mass.: Blackwell, 2000.

Harvey, David. *A Brief History of Neoliberalism*. Oxford: Oxford University Press, 2005.

———. "From Space to Place and Back Again: Reflections on the Condition of Postmodernity." In *Mapping the Futures: Local Cultures, Global Change*, edited by Jon Bird, Barry Curtis, Tim Putnam, George Robertson, and Lisa Tickner, 3–29. London: Routledge, 1993.

———. "Neo-Liberalism as Creative Destruction." *Geografiska Annaler: Series B, Human Geography* 88, no. 2 (2006): 145–58.

———. *Spaces of Hope*. Berkeley: University of California Press, 2000.

Henríquez, Narda Z. *Cuestiones de género y poder en el conflicto armado en el Perú*. Lima: CONCYTEC, 2006.
Hilbink, Lisa. *Judges beyond Politics in Democracy and Dictatorship: Lessons from Chile*. Cambridge: Cambridge University Press, 2007.
Hiriart, Hugo. "La revuelta antiautoritaria." In *Pensar el 68*, edited by Hermann Bellinghausen and Hugo Hiriart, 17–21. Mexico City: Cal y Arena, 1988.
Hirsch, Marianne, ed. *The Familial Gaze*. Hanover, N.H.: University Press of New England, 1999.
———. *Family Frames: Photography, Narrative, and Postmemory*. Cambridge, Mass.: Harvard University Press, 1997.
Hite, Katherine. "'The Eye that Cries': The Politics of Representing Victims in Contemporary Peru." *A Contra Corriente* 5, no. 1 (Fall 2007): 108–34.
———. "El monumento a Salvador Allende en el debate político chileno." In *Monumentos memoriales y marcas territoriales*, compiled by Elizabeth Jelín and Victoria Langland, 19–55. Madrid: Siglo XXI Editores, 2003.
Hoheisel, Horst. "Algunas reflexiones acerca del arte de la memoria y de la memoria del arte." In *Políticas de la memoria: Tensiones en la palabra y la imagen*, edited by Sandra Lorenzano and Ralph Buchenhorst, 121–40. Mexico City: Universidad del Claustro de Sor Juana, 2007.
Huneeus, Carlos. *Chile: Un país dividido*. Santiago: Catalonia, 2003.
Huyssen, Andreas. *Present Pasts: Urban Palimpsests and the Politics of Memory*. Stanford, Calif.: Stanford University Press, 2003.
Igartúa, Juanjo, and Dario Páez. "Art and Remembering Traumatic Collective Events: The Case of the Spanish Civil War." In *Collective Memory of Political Events: Social Psychological Perspectives*, edited by James W. Pennebaker, Darío Páez, and Bernard Rimé, 79–102. Mahwah, N.J.: Lawrence Erlbaum Associates, 1997.
Jameson, Fredric. *Postmodernism, or, The Cultural Logic of Late Capitalism*. Durham, N.C.: Duke University Press, 1991.
Jara, Umberto. *Ojo por ojo: La verdadera historia del Grupo Colina*. Lima: Norma Editoriales, 2003.
Jauretche, Ernesto. *Violencia y política en los 70: No déjes que te la cuenten*. Buenos Aires: Colihue, 1997.
Jelin, Elizabeth. , ed. *Las Conmemoraciones: Las disputas en las fechas "in-felices."* Madrid: Siglo XXI, 2002.
———. "The Politics of Memory: The Human Rights Movements and the Construction of Democracy in Argentina." *Latin American Perspectives* 21, no. 2 (1994): 38–58.
———. *State Repression and the Labors of Memory*. Translated by Judy Rein and Marcial Godoy-Anatiria. Minneapolis: University of Minnesota Press, 2003.
———. *Los trabajos de la memoria*. Collección Memorias de la represión, no. 1. Madrid: Siglo XXI Editores, 2002.
Jelin, Elizabeth, and Susan G. Kaufman, eds. *Subjetividad y figuras de la memoria*. Buenos Aires: Siglo XXI Editorial Iberoamericana, 2006.

Jelin, Elizabeth, and Victoria Langland, eds. *Monumentos, memoriales y marcas territoriales.* Madrid: Siglo XXI, 2003.

Jenkins, Henry. *Convergence Culture: Where Old and New Media Collide.* New York: New York University Press, 2006.

Joignant, Alfredo. *Un día distinto*: Memorias festivas y batallas commemorativas en torno al 11 de Septiembre en Chile (1974–2006). Santiago: Editorial Universitario, 2007.

Kaiser, Susana. "*Escraches:* Demonstrations, Communication, and Political Memory in Post-Dictatorial Argentina." *Media, Culture, and Society* 24, no. 4 (2002): 499–516.

———. "The 'Madwomen' Memory Mothers of the Plaza de Mayo; A Case of Counter-hegemonic Communications Developed by a Unique Human Rights Group: Mothers of Disappeared People from Argentina." Master's thesis, Hunter College of the City University of New York, 1993.

———. *Postmemories of Terror: A New Generation Copes with the Legacy of the "Dirty War."* New York: Palgrave Macmillan, 2005.

———. "The Struggle for Urban Territories: Human Rights Activists in Buenos Aires." In *Ordinary Places/Extraordinary Events: Citizenship, Democracy, and Urban Space in Latin America*, edited by Clara Irazábal, 181–208. New York: Routledge, 2008.

Kansteiner, Wulf. "Finding Meaning in Memory: A Methodological Critique of Collective Memory Studies." *History and Theory* 41, no. 2 (2002): 179–97.

Kaplan, Temma. *Taking Back the Streets: Women, Youth, and Direct Democracy.* Berkeley: University of California Press, 2004.

Kehl, Maria Rita. "'Sangue no Araguaia': A fala roubada de *Você Decide.*" In *Mortos e desaparecidos políticos: Reparação ou impunidade?* edited by Janaína Teles, 227–36. São Paulo: Humanitas/FFLCH/USP, 2001.

Klein, Naomi. *The Shock Doctrine: The Rise of Disaster Capitalism.* New York: Picador, 2007.

Kueffner, Stephan, and Kristina Schreck. *Frommer's: Chile and Easter Island.* Hoboken: Wiley Publishing, 2007.

Kundera, Milan. *Slowness.* New York: Harper Perennial, 1997.

Lavine, Steven, and Ivan Karp, eds. *Exhibiting Cultures: The Poetics and Politics of Museum Display.* Washington, D.C.: Smithsonian Institution Press, 1999.

Lazzara, Mauricio. *Chile in Transition: The Poetics and Politics of Memory.* Gainesville: University Press of Florida, 2006.

Lazzara, Michael. "Pinochet's Cadaver as Ruin and Palimpsest." In *Telling Ruins in Latin America*, edited by Michael Lazarra and Vicky Unruh. New York: Palgrave Macmillan, 2009.

Lehrer, Erica, and Cynthia E. Milton. "Introduction: Witnesses to Witnessing." In *Curating Difficult Knowledge: Violent Pasts in Public Places,* edited by Erica Lehrer, Cynthia E. Milton, and Monica Eileen Patterson. New York: Palgrave Macmillan, 2011.

Lennon, John J., and Malcolm Foley. *Dark Tourism: The Attraction of Death and Disaster.* London: Continuum, 2000.

Lerner Febres, Salomón. *La rebelión de la memoria: Selección de discursos 2001–2003*. Lima: IDEHPUCP, CEP, CNDDHH, 2004.

Levine, Robert. *The Power of Persuasion: How We're Bought and Sold*. Hoboken, N.J.: John Wiley and Sons, 2003.

Levinson, Brett. "Dictatorship and Overexposure: Does Latin America Testify to More Than One Market?" *Discourse* 25, no. 1–2 (2003): 98–118

Levinson, Jay Conrad. *Guerrilla Marketing: Secrets for Making Big Profits from Your Small Business*. Boston: Houghton Mifflin, 1984.

Levy, Pierre. *Collective Intelligence: Mankind's Emerging World in Cyberspace*. Cambridge: Perseus, 1997.

Lins da Silva, Carlos Eduardo. "The Brazilian Case: Manipulation by the Media?" In *Television, Politics, and the Transition to Democracy in Latin America*, edited by Thomas E. Skidmore, 137–44. Baltimore: Johns Hopkins University Press, 1993.

Lippard, Lucy. *The Lure of the Local: Senses of Place in a Multicentered Society*. New York: New Press, 1997.

Lira, Elizabeth, and Brian Loveman. *Las ardientes cenizas del olvido: Vía chilena de reconciliación política, 1932–1994*. Santiago: LOM Ediciones, 2000.

Lobo, Narciso Júlio Freire. *Ficção e política: O Brasil nas minisséries*. Manaus: Valer, 2000.

López, Ana M. "Our Welcomed Guests: Telenovelas in Latin America." In *To Be Continued . . . : Soap Operas around the World*, edited by Robert Clyde Allen, 256–75. New York: Routledge, 1995.

Lynch, Nicolás. "What the 'Left' Means in Latin America Now." *Constellations* 14, no. 3 (September 2007): 373–83.

MacCannell, Dean. *The Tourist: A New Theory of the Leisure Class*. Berkeley: University of California Press, 1999.

Machado-Borges, Thaïs. "Brazilian Telenovelas, Fictionalized Politics, and the Merchandising of Social Issues." In *Politicotainment: Television's Take on the Real*, edited by Kristina Riegert, 151–80. New York: Peter Lang, 2007.

Malpas, Jeff. *Heidegger's Topology: Being, Place, World*. Cambridge, Mass.: MIT Press, 2007.

Mariátegui Oliva, Ricardo. *José Gil de Castro "el mulato Gil": Vida y obra del gran pintor peruano de los libertadores: Obras existentes en Argentina y Chile*. Lima, 1981.

Márquez, Alberto, and Antonio Márquez. *Cuatro siglos de uniformes en Chile*. Santiago: Editorial Andrés Bello, 1976.

Martín-Barbero, Jesús. "Memory and Form in the Latin American Soap Opera." In *To Be Continued . . . : Soap Operas around the World*, edited by Robert Clyde Allen, 276–84. New York: Routledge, 1995.

Matta, Pedro Alejandro. *Villa Grimaldi: A Walk Through a 20th-Century Torture Center. A Visitor's Guide*. Santiago, Chile: 2000.

Mattelart, Michèle, and Armand Mattelart. *The Carnival of Images: Brazilian Television Fiction*. Translated by David Buxton. New York: Bergin and Garvey, 1990.

McEvoy, Gabriela. "The Construction of the Heroic Image through Journalistic Discourse: The Case of the Peruvian Activist María Elena Moyano." *Historia Crítica* 35 (January/June 2008): 82–104.

Menchú, Rigoberta. *I, Rigoberta Menchú: An Indian Woman in Guatemala*. New York: Verso, 1984.

Merino, Marcia. *Mi verdad*. Santiago: ATG, 1993.

Miller Klubock, Thomas. "History and Memory in Neoliberal Chile: Patricio Guzmán's Obstinate Memory and the Battle of Chile." *Radical History Review* 85 (Winter 2003): 272–81.

Milton, Cynthia E. "At the Edge of the Peruvian Truth Commission: Alternative Paths to Recounting the Past." *Radical History Review* 98 (Spring 2007): 3–33.

———. "Naming." In *The Art of Truth-Telling about Authoritarian Rule*, edited by Ksenija Bilbija, Jo Ellen Fair, Cynthia E. Milton, and Leigh A. Payne, 104–09. Madison: University of Wisconsin Press, 2005.

———. "Public Spaces for the Discussion of Peru's Recent Past." *Antipoda: Revista de Antropología y Arqueologia* 5 (July–December 2007): 143–68.

Monsiváis, Carlos. *Entrada libre: Crónicas de la sociedad que se organiza*. Mexico City: Era, 1987.

Montalva, Pía. *Morir un poco: Moda y sociedad en Chile, 1960–1976*. Santiago: Editorial Sudamericana, 2004.

Moores, Shaun. *Interpreting Audiences: The Ethnography of Media Consumption*. Thousand Oaks, Calif.: Sage, 1993.

Morand, Paul. *L'allure de Chanel*. Paris: Hermann, 1976.

Moulian, Tomás. *Chile actual: Anatomía de un mito*. Santiago: Arcis, 1997.

Muñoz, Hortencia. "Derechos humanos y construcción de referentes sociales." In *Los senderos insólitos del Perú*, edited by Steve J. Stern. Lima: IEP, UNSCH, 1999.

Navia, Patricio. "Pinochet: The Father of Contemporary Chile." *Latin American Research Review* 43, no. 3 (2008): 250–58.

Noble, John, Andrew D. Nystrom, Morgan Konn, and Michael Grosberg. *Lonely Planet: Mexico*. Footscray, Australia: Lonely Planet Publications, 2007.

Nora, Pierre. "Between Memory and History: *Les lieux de mémoire*." Trans. Marc Roudebush. *Representations* 26 (Spring 1989): 7–24.

———. "Generations." In *Realms of Memory: Rethinking the French Past*, vol. 1, *Conflicts and Divisions*, edited by Pierre Nora, 499–531. New York: Columbia University Press, 1996.

Nunn, Frederick. *Chilean Politics, 1920–1931: The Honorable Mission of the Armed Forces*. Albuquerque: University of New Mexico Press, 1970.

———. *The Military in Chilean History: Essays on Civil-Military Relations, 1810–1973*. Albuquerque: University of New Mexico Press, 1976.

O'Dougherty, Maureen. *Consumption Intensified: The Politics of Middle-Class Daily Life in Brazil*. Durham, N.C.: Duke University Press, 2002.

O'Hare, Greg, and Hazel Barrett. "Regional Inequalities in the Peruvian Tourism Industry." *The Geographical Journal* 165, no. 1 (1999): 47–61.

Oquendo-Villar, Carmen. "Chile 1973: El golpe mediático." Ph.D. diss., Harvard University, 2008.

Ortiz, Renato, Silvia Borelli, and José Ramos. *Telenovela: História e produção.* São Paulo: Brasiliense, 1989.
Ossa, Carlos. "El jardín de las mascaras." In *Políticas y estéticas de la memoria*, edited by Nelly Richard, 71–76. Santiago: Editorial Cuarto Propio, 2000.
Page, Jonathan. *The Brazilians.* Reading, Penn.: Addison-Wesley, 1995.
Palmerlee, Danny, Lucas Vidgen, Sandra Bao, and Andrew Dean Nystrom. *Lonely Planet: Argentina.* Footscray, Australia: Lonely Planet Publications, 2005.
Passerini, Luisa, ed. *Memory and Totalitarianism.* New Brunswick, N.J.: Transaction Publishers, 2005.
Payne, Leigh A. *Unsettling Accounts: Neither Truth nor Reconciliation in Confessions of State Violence.* Durham, N.C.: Duke University Press, 2007.
Pennebaker, James, and Becky Banasik. "On the Creation and Maintenance of Collective Memories: History as Social Psychology." In *Collective Memory of Political Events: Social Psychological Perspectives*, edited by James W. Pennebaker, Darío Páez, and Bernard Rimé, 3–20. Mahwah, N.J.: Lawrence Erlbaum Associates, 1997.
Politzer, Patricia. *Chile: ¿De qué estamos hablando? Retrato de una transformación asombrosa.* Santiago: Editorial Sudamericana, 2005.
Poniatowska, Elena. *Here's to You, Jesusa!* Translated by Deanna Heikkinen. New York: Penguin, 2002.
———. *Massacre in Mexico.* Translated by Helen R. Lane. Columbia: University of Missouri Press, 1991.
Popular Memory Group. "Popular Memory: Theory, Politics, Method." In *Making Histories: Studies in History-Writing and Politics*, edited by Richard Johnson, Gregor McLennan, Bill Schwartz, and David Sutton, 205–52. London: Hutchinson, 1982.
Porto, Mauro P. "Mass Media and Politics in Democratic Brazil." In *Brazil Since 1985*, edited by Maria D'Alva Kinzo and James Dunkerley, 288–313. London: ILAS, 2003.
———. "Political Controversies in Brazilian TV Fiction: Viewers' Interpretations of the Telenovela *Terra Nostra.*" *Television and New Media* 6, no. 4 (2005): 342–59.
———. "Realism and Politics in Brazilian Telenovelas." *Media International Australia* 106 (February 2003): 35–45.
Power, Margaret. *Right-Wing Women in Chile: Feminine Power and the Struggle Against Allende, 1964–1973.* University Park: Pennsylvania State University Press, 2002.
PromPerú. *Manual de importancia e impacto del turismo en el Perú.* Lima: PromPerú, 2000.
———. *Memoria 2001–2006: Comisión de promoción del Perú-PromPerú: Gerencia de planificación, presupuesto y desarrollo.* Lima: PromPerú, 2007.
Quiroga, Patricio, and Carlos Maldonado. *El prusianismo en las fuerzas armadas chilenas: Un estudio histórico, 1885–1945.* Santiago: Ediciones Documenta, 1988.
Raggio, Sandra, and Samanta Salvatori (coordinators); Comisión Provincial por la Memoria. *La última dictadura militar en Argentina: Entre el pasado y el presente. Propuestas para trabajar en el aula.* Rosario: Homo Sapiens Ediciones, 2009.
Rakocy, Betsy, Alejandro Reuss, Chris Sturr, and the Dollars & Sense Collective, eds. *Real World Globalization: A Reader in Economics, Business, and Politics from Dollars & Sense.* 9th ed. Boston: Economic Affairs Bureau, 2007.

Ransom, David. *The No-Nonsense Guide to Fair Trade*. 2nd ed. Toronto: New Internationalist, 2006.
Rêgo, Cacilda. "Novelas, Novelinhas, Novelões: The Evolution of the (Tele)Novela in Brazil." *Global Media Journal* 2, no. 2 (Spring 2003), http://lass.calumet.purdue.edu/cca/gmj/sp03/gmj-sp03-rego.htm.
Reinhardt, Mark. "Picturing Violence: Aesthetics and the Anxiety of Critique." In *Beautiful Suffering: Photography and the Traffic in Pain*, edited by Mark Reinhardt, Holly Edwards, and Erina Duganee, 13–36. Williamstown, Mass.: Williams College Museum of Art; Chicago: In association with the University of Chicago Press, 2007.
Revueltas, José. *El apando*. Mexico City: Era, 1969.
Richard, Nelly. "Las derrotas son completas sólo cuando los vencidos olvidan las razones por las que lucharon (una entrevista con Jorge Arrate)." *Revista de Crítica Cultural* 32 (November 2005): 4–11.
———. Introduction to *Pensar en/la posdictadura*, edited by Nelly Richard and Alberto Moreiras, 73–101. Santiago: Cuarto Propio, 2001.
———. "Presentación." In *Políticas y estéticas de la memoria*, edited by Nelly Richard, 9–14. Santiago: Editorial Cuarto Propio, 2000.
Roht-Arriaza, Naomi. *The Pinochet Effect: Transnational Justice in the Age of Human Rights*. University Park: University of Pennsylvania Press, 2004.
Rojek, Chris. "Fatal Attractions." In *Representing the Nation: A Reader: Histories, Heritage, and Museums*, edited by Jessica Evans and David Boswell, 185–207. London: Routledge, 1999.
Ruisánchez Serra, José Ramón. "Historias que regresan: Topología y renarración en la segunda mitad del siglo XX mexicano." Ph.D. diss., University of Maryland, 2007.
Ruiz Schiavo, Márcio. "Social Merchandising: Using Brazilian Television Miniseries for Drug-Abuse and AIDS Prevention." In *Drug Lessons and Education Programs in Developing Countries*, edited by Henry Kirsch, 255–62. New Brunswick, N.J.: Transaction, 1995.
Salazar, Manuel. *Contreras: Historia de un intocable*. Santiago: Editorial Grijalbo, 1995.
Sapag, Pablo, and Alejandra Sepúlveda. *¡Es la prensa estúpido, la prensa!: Cuando Chile fue noticia . . . Por la razón o la fuerza*. Santiago: Copygraph, 2001.
Sarlo, Beatriz. *Escenas de la vida posmoderna: Intelectuales, arte y videocultura en la Argentina*. Buenos Aires: Ariel, 1994.
———. *Instantáneas: Medios, ciudad y costumbres en el fin de siglo*. Buenos Aires: Ariel, 1996.
———. *Tiempo pasado*. Buenos Aires: Siglo XXI, 2006.
Scarry, Elaine. *On Beauty and Being Just*. Princeton: Princeton University Press, 1999.
———. *The Body in Pain: The Making and Unmaking of the World*. New York: Oxford University Press, 1985.
Scherer, Julio, and Carlos Monsiváis. *Parte de guerra: Tlatelolco 1968: Documentos del*

general Marcelino García Barragán: Los hechos y la historia. Mexico City: Nuevo Siglo/Aguilar, 1999.

Schrift, Melissa, and Keith Pilkey. "Revolution Remembered: Chairman Mao Badges and Chinese Nationalist Ideology." *Journal of Popular Culture* 30, no. 2 (1996): 169–97.

Schudson, Michael. *Advertising, the Uneasy Persuasion: Its Dubious Impact on American Society*. New York: Basic Books, 1984.

Schwenkel, Christina. *The American War in Contemporary Vietnam: Transnational Remembrance and Representation*. Bloomington: Indiana University Press, 2009.

Scott, James C. *The Moral Economy of the Peasant: Rebellion and Subsistence in Southeast Asia*. New Haven, Conn.: Yale University Press, 1976.

Sculpture Prize, "Parque de la Memoria." Buenos Aires: EUDEBA, 1999.

Seaton, A. V. "Guided by the Dark: From Thanatopsis to Thanatourism." *International Journal of Heritage Studies* 2, no. 4 (1996): 234–44.

Selbin, Eric. "Making the World New: Latin American Studies after the Washington Consensus." *Latin American Studies Association FORUM* 38, no. 4 (Fall 2007): 33–35.

Ševenko, Liz. "The Power of Place: How Historic Sites Can Engage Citizens in Human Rights Issues." Minneapolis: Center for Victims of Torture, 2004.

Sheinin, David. *Argentina and the United States*. Athens: University of Georgia Press, 2006.

Shua, Ana María. *La muerte como efecto secundario*. Buenos Aires: Editorial Sudamericana, 1997.

Sikkink, Kathryn, and Carrie Booth Walling. "The Impact of Human Rights Trials in Latin America." *Journal of Peace Research* 44, no. 4 (2007): 427–45.

Silverman, Helaine. "Touring Ancient Times: The Present and Presented Past in Contemporary Peru." *American Anthropologist* 104, no. 3 (2002): 881–902.

Singhal, Arvind, and Everett M. Rogers. *Entertainment Education: A Communication Strategy for Social Change*. Mahwah, N.J.: Lawrence Erlbaum Associates, 1999.

Sirkis, Alfredo. *Os carbonários: Memória da guerrilha perdida*. Rio de Janeiro: Record, 1998.

Sklair, Leslie. "Social Movements and Global Capitalism." In *The Cultures of Globalization*, edited by Fredric Jameson and Masao Miyoshi, 291–311. Durham, N.C.: Duke University Press, 1998.

Sommer, Doris. *Foundational Fictions: The National Romances of Latin America*. Berkeley: University of California Press, 1991.

Sontag, Susan. *On Photography*. New York: Farrar, Straus and Giroux, 1990.

———. *Regarding the Pain of Others*. New York: Farrar, Straus and Giroux, 1990.

Stephens, Beth. "Filártiga v. Peña-Irala: From Family Tragedy to Human Rights Accountability." *Rutgers Law Journal* 37, no. 3 (Spring 2006): 623–34.

Stern, Steve J. *Battling for Hearts and Minds: Memory Struggles in Pinochet's Chile, 1973–1988*. Durham, N.C.: Duke University Press, 2006.

———. *Remembering Pinochet's Chile: On the Eve of London 1998*. Durham, N.C.: Duke University Press, 2004.

Straubhaar, Joseph. "The Reflection of the Brazilian Political Opening in the *Telenovela* [Soap Opera], 1974–1985." *Studies in Latin American Popular Culture* 7 (1988): 59–76.

Straubhaar, Joseph, and Antonio La Pastina. "Television and Hegemony in Brazil." In *The Globalization of Corporate Media Hegemony*, edited by Lee Artz and Yahya R. Kamalipour, 151–68. Albany: SUNY Press, 2003.

Straubhaar, Joseph, Organ Olsen, and Maria Cavaliari Nunes. "The Brazilian Case: Influencing the Voter." In *Television, Politics, and the Transition to Democracy in Latin America*, edited by Thomas E. Skidmore, 118–36. Baltimore: Johns Hopkins University Press, 1993.

Sturken, Marita. *Tangled Memories: The Vietnam War, the AIDS Epidemic, and the Politics of Remembering.* Berkeley: University of California Press, 1997.

Sturken, Marita, and Lisa Cartwright. *Practices of Looking: An Introduction to Visual Culture.* New York: Oxford University Press, 2002.

Taibo, Paco Ignacio, II. *'68.* New York: Seven Stories Press, 1998.

Tamayo, Ana María. "ANFASEP y la lucha por la memoria de sus desaparecidos (1983–2000)." In *Jamás tan cerca arremetió lo lejos*, edited by Carlos Iván Degregori, 95–134. Lima: IEP, 1999.

Tandeciarz, Silvia. "Citizens of Memory: Refiguring the Past in Postdictatorship Argentina." *PMLA* 122, no. 1 (January 2007): 151–69.

Tappatá de Valdez, Patricia. "El Parque de la Memoria en Buenos Aires." In *Monumentos, memorials y marcas territoriales*, compiled by Elizabeth Jelin and Victoria Langland, 97–112. Madrid: Siglo XXI Editores.

Taylor, Diana. *The Archive and the Repertoire: Performing Cultural Memory in the Americas.* Durham, N.C.: Duke University Press, 2003.

———. *Disappearing Acts: Spectacles of Gender and Nationalism in Argentina's "Dirty War."* Durham, N.C.: Duke University Press, 1997.

———. "Trauma as Durational Performance." In *Rites of Return*, edited by Marianne Hirsch and Nancy K. Miller. New York: Columbia University Press, forthcoming.

Tella, Guillermo. *Un crack en la ciudad: Rupturas y continuidades en la trama urbana de Buenos Aires.* Buenos Aires: Nobuko, 2007.

Timerman, Jacobo. *Prisoner without a Name, Cell without a Number.* Translated by Toby Talbot. Madison: University of Wisconsin Press, 2002.

Todorov, Tzvetan. *Les abus de la mémoire.* Paris: Arléa, 1995.

Trajković, Djurdja. "Memorabilia and Video Games of the Post-dictatorship Period in Latin America." Paper presented at the conference on "Marketing Memory in Latin America," Madison, Wisc., 11–13 April 2008.

Tumarkin, Maria. *Traumascapes: The Power and Fate of Places Transformed by Tragedy.* Melbourne: Melbourne University Press, 2005.

Tupac, Diana Miloslavich, ed. *The Autobiography of María Elena Moyano: The Life and Death of a Peruvian Activist.* Gainesville: University Press of Florida, 2000.

Ulfe, María Eugenia. *Itinerarios y ciegos caminantes: El turismo, la memoria y las políticas culturales en Ayacucho.* Lima: IFEA, forthcoming.

———. "Reflexiones sobre los usos del testimonio en la esfera pública peruana." In

Mirando la esfera pública desde la cultura en el Perú, edited by Gisela Cánepa and María Eugenia Ulfe, 203–20. Lima: CONCYTEC, 2006.

Ustra, Carlos Alberto Brilhante. *Rompendo o silencio*. Brasilia: Editora Editorial, 1987.

Ventura, Zuenir. *1968: O ano que não terminou*. Rio de Janeiro: Nova Fronteira, 1988.

Verbitsky, Horacio. *Confessions of an Argentine Dirty Warrior: A Firsthand Account of Atrocity*. Translated by Esther Allen. New York: New Press, 2005.

———. *The Flight: Confessions of an Argentine Dirty Warrior*. Translated by Esther Allen. New York: New Press, 1996.

Vial, Gonzalo. *Pinochet: La biografía*. 2 vols. Santiago: El Mercurio Aguilar, 2002.

Vich, Victor. "Magical, Mystical: The 'Royal Tour' of Alejandro Toledo." *Journal of Latin American Cultural Studies* 16, no. 1 (2007): 1–10.

Vidgen, Lucas. *Lonely Planet: Guatemala*. Footscray, Australia: Lonely Planet Publications, 2007.

Vieira, Patricia. "Torture and the Sublime: The Ethics of Physical Pain in Garaje Olimpo." *Dissidences: Hispanic Journal of Theory and Criticism* 2, no. 1 (2006), www.dissidences.org/GarajeOlimpo.html.

Volpi, Jorge. *La imaginación y el poder: Una historia intelectual de 1968*. Mexico City: Era, 1998.

Warner, Michael. "The Mass Public and the Mass Subject." In *Habermas and the Public Sphere*, edited by Craig Calhoun, 377–401. Cambridge, Mass.: MIT Press, 1992.

Wedeven Segall, Kimberly. "Pursuing Ghosts: The Traumatic Sublime in J. M. Coetzee's Disgrace." *Research in African Literatures* 36, no. 4 (2005): 40–54.

Welch Guerra, Max. *Buenos Aires a la deriva: Transformaciones urbanas recientes*. Buenos Aires: Biblos, 2005.

Weschler, Lawrence. *A Miracle, A Universe: Settling Accounts with Torturers*. Chicago: University of Chicago Press, 1990.

Wilde, Alexander. "Avenues of Memory: Santiago's General Cemetery and Chile's Recent Political History." *A Contra Corriente* 5, no. 3 (Spring 2008): 134–69.

———. "Irruptions of Memory: Expressive Politics in Chile's Transition to Democracy." *Journal of Latin American Studies* 31, no. 2 (1999): 473–500.

Williams, Gareth. *The Other Side of the Popular: Neoliberalism and Subalternity in Latin America*. Durham, N.C.: Duke University Press, 2002.

Williams, Paul. *Memorial Museums: The Global Rush to Commemorate Atrocities*. Oxford: Berg, 2007.

Williamson, John. "What Washington Means by Policy Reform." In *Latin American Adjustment: How Much Has Happened?* edited by John Williamson, 5–20. Washington D.C.: Institute for International Economics, 1990.

Xavier, Ismail. "Lembrar para esquecer." In *Mortos e desaparecidos políticos: Reparação ou impunidade?* edited by Janaína Teles, 247–57. São Paulo: Humanitas/FFLCH/USP, 2001.

———. *O olhar e a cena: Melodrama, Hollywood, Cinema Novo, Nelson Rodrigues*. São Paulo: Cosac and Naify, 2003.

Yoneyama, Lisa. *Hiroshima Traces: Time, Space, and the Dialectics of Memory*. Berkeley: University of California Press, 1999.

Young, James E. *At Memory's Edge: After-Images of the Holocaust in Contemporary Art and Architecture*. New Haven, Conn.: Yale University Press, 2000.

———. *The Texture of Memory: Holocaust Memorial and Meaning*. New Haven, Conn.: Yale University Press, 1993.

Yúdice, George. *The Expediency of Culture*. Durham, N.C.: Duke University Press, 2003.

Yúdice, George, Jean Franco, and Juan Flores. Introduction to *On Edge: The Crisis of Contemporary Latin American Culture*, edited by George Yúdice, Jean Franco, and Juan Flores. Minneapolis: University of Minnesota Press, 1992.

Yuill, Stephanie Marie. "Dark Tourism: Understanding Visitor Motivation at Sites of Death and Disaster." Master's thesis, Texas A&M University, 2003.

Zapata, Antonio. *Sociedad y poder local: La comunidad de Villa El Salvador, 1971–1996*. Lima: DESCO, 1996.

Contributors

REBECCA J. ATENCIO is an assistant professor of Luso-Brazilian Literary and Cultural Studies at Tulane University. Her main area of research is the intersection of human rights activism and cultural production in contemporary Brazil.

KSENIJA BILBIJA is a professor of Spanish and the director of the Latin American, Caribbean, and Iberian Studies Program at the University of Wisconsin, Madison. She is the author of *Yo soy trampa: Ensayos sobre la obra de Luisa Valenzuela* (2003); *Cuerpos textuales: Metáforas del génesis narrativo en la literatura latinoamericana del siglo XX* (2001). Bilbija is also a volume editor of *The Art of Truth-Telling about Authoritarian Rule* (2005) and *Akademia Cartonera: A Primer of Latin American Cartonera Publishers* (2009).

JO-MARIE BURT is an associate professor of Political Science at George Mason University, and she has been a visiting researcher at the Pontific Catholic University of Peru. She is author of *Political Violence and the Authoritarian State in Peru: Silencing Civil Society* (Palgrave Macmillan, 2007).

LAURIE BETH CLARK is a professor in the Art Department at the University of Wisconsin, Madison, where she teaches courses in video, performance, installations, and visual culture. Since 2001, she has been studying trauma tourism from a comparative international perspective. Some of this work can be downloaded at www.traumatourism.net.

CATH COLLINS is a professor of Politics at the Universidad Diego Portales, Santiago, Chile. She works on human rights prosecutions and related processes in the Southern Cone, and is the author of *Post-transitional Justice: Human Rights Trials in Chile and El Salvador* (Penn State University Press, 2010).

SUSANA DRAPER is an assistant professor at the Department of Comparative Literature at Princeton University. She is currently working on *The Prison, the Mall, and the Museum: Afterlives of Confinement in Postdictatorship Latin American Society)*, a book-length project on the reconfiguration of spaces and temporalities in post-dictatorship culture.

NANCY GATES-MADSEN is an assistant professor of Spanish at Luther College. Her current research explores the legacies of authoritarianism in the Southern Cone, and her work has appeared in the journals *Letras Femeninas* and *Latin American Theatre Review*, and in the collection *The Art of Truth-Telling about Authoritarian Rule*.

SUSANA KAISER is associate professor of Media Studies and chair of Latin American Studies at the University of San Francisco. Her research focuses on communication, cultural/political memory, and human rights. Her book *Postmemories of Terror: A New Generation Copes with the Legacy of the "Dirty War"* (2005) explores young Argentineans' memories of the last dictatorship.

CYNTHIA E. MILTON is Canada Research Chair in Latin American History and an associate professor in the History Department at the Université de Montréal, Canada. She is the author of *The Many Meanings of Poverty: Colonialism, Social Compacts, and Assistance in Eighteenth-Century Ecuador* (Stanford University Press, 2007) and a volume editor of *The Art of Truth-Telling about Authoritarian Rule* (2005) and *Curating Difficult Knowledge* (2011).

ALICE A. NELSON is a member of the faculty in Latin American Cultural Studies at Evergreen State College. She is the author of *Political Bodies: Gender, History, and the Struggle for Narrative Power in Recent Chilean Literature*, and the translator, with Silvia Tandeciarz, of Nelly Richard's *Masculine/Feminine* and *The Insubordination of Signs*.

CARMEN OQUENDO-VILLAR is a Jacob Javits Fellow at New York University's Kanbar Institute of Film and Television in the Tisch School of the Arts, where she is continuing her filmmaking training, and a researcher and film curator at the Hemispheric Institute of Performance and Politics.

LEIGH A. PAYNE is a professor of Sociology and Latin America at the University of Oxford and a visiting professor of Political Science and Global Studies at the University of Minnesota. In addition to book chapters and journal articles, she is author of *Unsettling Accounts: Neither Truth nor Reconciliation in Confessions of State Violence* (1998); *Uncivil Movements: The Armed Right Wing and Democracy in Latin America* (2000); and *Brazilian Industrialists and Democratic Change* (1994). She co-authored the book *Transitional Justice in Balance: Comparing Processes, Weighing Efficacy* (2010).

JOSÉ RAMÓN RUISÁNCHEZ SERRA is an assistant professor in the Department of Hispanic Studies at the University of Houston. He is the co-editor of *Materias dispuestas: Juan Villoro ante la crítica* (Candaya, 2009), and the editor of *Libro mercado: Literatura e intervenciones en el mercado* (forthcoming). His fifth book of fiction, *Nada cruel*, was published in 2008 by ERA. He conducts a weekly book show: Letrero.

MARÍA EUGENIA ULFE is a Peruvian anthropologist working on memory, performance, and political violence in the Andes. She is an assistant professor in the Department of Social Sciences (Anthropology) and academic coordinator at the Graduate School of the Pontificia Universidad Católica del Perú.

Index

KSENIJA BILBIJA is a professor of Spanish and the director of the Latin American, Caribbean, and Iberian Studies Program at the University of Wisconsin, Madison.

LEIGH A. PAYNE is a professor of Sociology and Latin America at the University of Oxford and a visiting professor of Political Science and Global Studies at the University of Minnesota.

Library of Congress Cataloging-in-Publication Data
Accounting for violence : marketing memory in Latin America /
Ksenija Bilbija and Leigh A. Payne, eds.
p. cm.—(The cultures and practice of violence series)
Includes bibliographical references and index.
ISBN 978-0-8223-5025-5 (cloth : alk. paper)
ISBN 978-0-8223-5042-2 (pbk. : alk. paper)
1. Violence—Social aspects—Latin America. 2. Memory—Social aspects—Latin America. 3. Memorials—Latin America.
4. Collective memory—Latin America. I. Bilbija, Ksenija.
II. Payne, Leigh A. III. Series: Cultures and practice of violence series.
HN110.5.Z9V514 2011
303.6098—dc22 2010054446